THE POLITICS OF RIGHTS AND
THE 1911 REVOLUTION IN CHINA

The Politics of Rights and the 1911 Revolution in China

Xiaowei Zheng

STANFORD UNIVERSITY PRESS
STANFORD, CALIFORNIA

Stanford University Press
Stanford, California

© 2018 by Xiaowei Zheng. All rights reserved.

No part of this book may be reproduced or transmitted in any form or by any means, electronic or mechanical, including photocopying and recording, or in any information storage or retrieval system without the prior written permission of Stanford University Press.

Printed in the United States of America on acid-free, archival-quality paper

Library of Congress Cataloging-in-Publication Data

Names: Zheng, Xiaowei, author.
Title: The politics of rights and the 1911 Revolution in China / Xiaowei Zheng.
Description: Stanford, California : Stanford University Press, 2018. | Includes bibliographical references and index.
Identifiers: LCCN 2017046983 (print) | LCCN 2017048479 (e-book) | ISBN 9781503601093 (e-book) | ISBN 9780804796675 (cloth : alk. paper) | ISBN 9781503601086 (pbk. : alk. paper)
Subjects: LCSH: China—History—Revolution, 1911–1912. | Sichuan Sheng (China)—Politics and government—20th century. | Civil rights—China—Sichuan Sheng—History—20th century. | Political culture—China—Sichuan Sheng—History—20th century. | Constitutional history—China—Sichuan Sheng.
Classification: LCC DS773.55.S54 (e-book) | LCC DS773.55.S54 Z47 2017 (print) | DDC 951/.036—dc23
LC record available at https://lccn.loc.gov/2017046983

Cover design: Rob Ehle

Typeset by Newgen in 10.5/12 Sabon

To my grandparents, Zheng Tianxiang (1914–2013) and
Song Ting (1918–2013)

Contents

Acknowledgments	ix
Introduction: The Political Transformation of 1911	1
1. Sichuan and the Old Regime	15
2. The Ideas of Revolution: Equality, the People's Rights, and Popular Sovereignty	47
3. The Project: The Chuan-Han Railway Company and the New Policies Reform	83
4. Can Two Sides Walk Together Without Agreeing to Meet? Constitutionalists and Officials in the Late Qing Constitutional Reform	109
5. The Rhetoric of Revolution: The Rights of the Nation, Constitutionalism, and the Rights of the People	139
6. The Practice of Revolution: Organization, Mobilization, and Radicalization	167
7. The Expansion and Division of Revolution: Democratic Political Culture in Action	197
8. The End of Revolution: The Rise of Republicanism and the Failure of Constitutionalism	227
Conclusion: The Legacy of the 1911 Revolution	249
Appendix: The Pu Family of Guang'an County	259
Notes	265
Bibliography	327
Index	341

Acknowledgments

This is a joyful moment for which I have been waiting for a long time. Over the many years since I began this project, I have benefited from the advice, wisdom, and encouragement of many people, and it is now my great pleasure to acknowledge them. First of all, Joseph Esherick was the best mentor a student could possibly hope for. He was generous, sharp, strict, and always there when I needed him. Joe also taught me how to do social history and structural analysis. Paul Pickowicz was the mentor who taught me how to humanize history, how to tell an engaging story, and how to write well. They have remained a constant source of love and inspiration. I also thank Richard Madsen, Takashi Fujitani, John Marino, Cynthia Truant, Weijing Lu, Suzanne Cahill, Marta Hanson, Stephan Tanaka, and Kuiyi Shen. Throughout, Mary Rankin, Frederick Wakeman Jr., Elizabeth Perry, Wen-Hsih Yeh, Matthew Sommer, Edward McCord, Joshua Fogel, Joan Judge, Kenneth Pomeranz, Bin Wong, Jeffery Wasserstrom, Wang Di, Luo Zhitian, Zhang Kaiyuan, Zhang Haipeng, Cui Zhihai, Li Xizhu, Wang Min, Hazama Naoki, Murata Yūjirō, Ogata Yasushi, Sang Bing, and Xu Jilin have all given me encouragement to take on the project presented here.

Several other people have my deep appreciation. At Peking University, Deng Xiaonan, Yan Buke, and Mao Hanjian stimulated my fascination with political and institutional history. Their influence will be obvious to any informed reader of this book. Niu Dayong and Zhu Xiaoyuan deserve special credit for getting me thinking about being a professional historian. Their faith in me played an important role in whatever success I may have enjoyed. At Yale University, Jonathan Spence, Valerie Hansen, Beatrice Bartlett, Annping Chin, and James Scott gave me confidence and encouraged me to pursue my research and study. To these teachers, I am forever grateful.

This book would not have not been possible without the support of my colleagues and friends at University of California at Santa Barbara. Mhoze Chikowero, Anthony Barbieri-Low, Sabine Frühstück, John Nathan, Xiaorong Li, Xiao-bin Ji, Kate McDonald, Sherene Seikaly, Cecilia Méndez, and Veronica Castillo-Munoz have all engaged with this manuscript. They offered me love, feedback, and key intellectual support. In addition, Sharon Farmer, Sears McGee, Luke Roberts, Elizabeth Depalma Digeser,

Terence Keel, John Majewski, Lisa Jacobson, Erika Rappaport, Shu-Chuan Bella Chen, Katherine Saltzman-Li, and Mayfair Yang have made Santa Barbara my second home. I wish to express my gratitude to all my colleagues for creating such a welcoming place to teach and research. Special thanks also to Gao Song for his assistance with mapmaking, to Cathy Chiu for locating important primary sources for me, and to Q. Z. Lau for help with the bibliography.

A number of other scholars, editors, and friends provided valuable criticism as I prepared the present book. The following people did me the honor of commenting on all or part of the manuscript: David Strand, Li Huaiyin, Henrietta Harrison, Wang Di, Yiching Wu, and Prasenjit Duara. The two readers for Stanford University Press have my most sincere thanks for their insightful and detailed comments, and for the exceptional speed with which they reviewed my manuscript. My friends Jenwa Hsung, Sandra Ward, and Nathaniel Rich have spared me from grammatical mistakes and made my language more powerful. Last but not least, my editor, Jenny Gavacs, expertly guided me through the editorial and publication process. My deepest thanks go to the entire team at Stanford University Press: Alan Harvey, Jenny Gavacs, Richard Gunde, James Holt, Kate Wahl, and their colleagues, for steering my book into print with great efficiency, quality, and competence. Stanford University Press is the best academic publisher a first-time author could possibly have. Without their faith and understanding, publishing this book would not have been a possibility.

In the Sichuan Provincial Archives, Xinjin County Archives, the First Historical Archives, Hōsei University Library, and the Sanetō Keishū collection at Tokyo Municipal Library, I received nothing but kind assistance. My hosts at Sichuan University provided both support and friendship. I want to thank Chen Xiang, Gou Deyi, Li Deying, Liu Yi, Wang Dongjie, Yang Xingmei, and Zhou Ding for their care. The renowned expert on the 1911 Revolution in Sichuan, Professor Wei Yingtao, gave me much-needed encouragement when I first embarked on rewriting the revolution. Most important, Professor Dai Zhili, whose lifelong work was distilled in the multivolume *Collection of Historical Materials on the Sichuan Railway Protection Movement*, also generously shared with me his original materials, including a complete set of the *Newsletter of the Sichuan Railway Protection Association*. I will be forever indebted to him.

My research received generous funding from a variety of sources. An SSRC International Dissertation Field Research Fellowship and a Pacific Rim Dissertation Research Fellowship supported my archival research in China. A UCSD Humanities Center Writing Fellowship, a UCSB Hellman Research Fellowship, a UCSB Faculty Career Development Fellowship, and a UCSB Regents Junior Faculty Fellowship supported the writing of the dissertation and the book. Portions of the book were published first elsewhere and are reprinted here by permission: part of Chapter 4 from "Configuring a Constitutional State: Officials and Assemblymen at the 1909 Sichuan Provincial Assembly Meeting," *Twentieth-Century China* 38, no. 3 (October 2013): 230–53; and part of Chapter 5 from "The Railway Movement in Chengdu: Sovereignty of the Nation and Rights of the People," in Ogata Yasushi, ed., *The 1911 Revolution in Global History* (Tokyo: Kyūko Shoin, 2013), 196–222.

This book would not have been possible without my family and friends. My parents, Zheng Yisheng and Zhao Jieping, have given their unflagging support and love. I am thankful to them for instilling in me a lifelong desire to learn and to explore the world. Inspiration and intellectual exchanges also came from my best friends: Wang Jinping, Ouyang Mijian, Wang Li, Li Zhipan, Zhao Hui, Jeremy Brown, Matthew Johnson, Dryden Hull, Liu Yue, Zhang Hui, Liu Kuan-yen, Liu Qing, Li Wenjie, Zhou Zhan'an, and Gao Bo. This book is dedicated to my grandparents, Zheng Tianxiang (1914–2013) and Song Ting (1918–2013), who were revolutionaries throughout their entire lives. They raised me, gave me a sense of meaning in life, and made me an idealist. Even though they were not able see the book before it was finished, their spirit is present in this book. And that spirit will stay with me for the rest of my life.

THE POLITICS OF RIGHTS AND THE 1911 REVOLUTION IN CHINA

Introduction

THE POLITICAL TRANSFORMATION OF 1911

China today declares itself a republic. From 1912 onward, notwithstanding political turmoil, assassinations, factionalism, civil wars, invasions, and revolutions, the polity of China has remained, in name, republican. Whether it was the Beiyang warlords, the Nationalists, or the Communists in power, the selection of the head of state has invariably been "by the people," and the "popular will" of the nation has steadfastly remained the basis of state sovereignty. Nevertheless, despite the succession of eleven central government constitutions and constitutional drafts written between 1908 and 1982, China has yet to attain constitutionalism. Since 1908, when the Qing government promulgated the Principles of the Constitution, four different regimes—one monarchical and three republican—have each regarded a constitution as the preeminent foundation of political life. Nonetheless, Chinese constitutions have not carried actual authority, the rule of law has yet to gain real purchase in the political system, and officials exercising governmental powers have not been amply bound to observe the limitations on power that are set out in the ostensibly supreme, constitutional law.

Indeed, the perseverance of republican rhetoric and the failure of constitutional practice seem to be the very hallmark of modern Chinese politics. Looking back at the first years of the republic, one can see these defining features already in place. As we will see, the rise of republicanism and the failure of constitutionalism in early Republican China had much to do with the way the 1911 Revolution took shape. This book tells the story of the political transformation that created modern Chinese politics: how did the old, imperial order collapse and the new, modern politics, with the distinctive characteristics described already, come into being? In answering this question, this book offers a reinterpretation of the 1911 Revolution that emphasizes the significance of a new political culture of "rights" (*quan, quanli, minquan,* and *guoquan*), "equality" (*pingdeng*), and "popular sovereignty" (*minzhu, guomin zhi zhuquan, zhuquan zai guomin,* and *minquan*).¹

Rereading the Events of 1911

In the summer of 1911, an unprecedented popular movement suddenly sprang to life, shaking the status quo in Chengdu, the capital of Sichuan province. The Qing court's announcement of its intent to nationalize the privately owned Chuan-Han (Chengdu-Hankow) Railway Company and take out foreign loans to pay for it agitated the entire city. For the first time, commoners and elites joined together in a single, unified political organization—the Sichuan Railway Protection Association (Sichuan baolu tongzhihui)—in opposition to the court. A proliferation of branches of the association organized by neighborhood, occupation, gender, and social group mushroomed at an astonishing rate. The Children's Street Branch, the Women's Branch, the Students' Branch, the Mechanical Workers and Printers' Branch, the Silk Guild Branch, and even the Beggars' Branch were set up in less than a month's time. Chengdu residents eagerly joined the branches, attended their public meetings, listened to speeches, read newsletters, and contributed money. Painters, schoolchildren, sedan-chair carriers, rickshaw pullers, policemen, artisans, blind performers, and prostitutes donated their savings. Buddhist and Daoist monks, Christians, Muslims, chieftains of the Qiang ethnic group, and even Manchus, the ruling ethnic elite of the Qing, all participated with zeal.²

The gentry-led Railway Protection Association stepped up to provide direction, setting the common objective for all participants expressed in the rallying cry, "To protect the railway and break the [foreign-loan] treaty" (*baolu poyue*). Its official publication, *Newsletter of the Sichuan Railway Protection Association*, was printed daily. Sold at the price of one cent and often given away for free, it achieved a circulation of nearly fifteen thousand copies.³ The newsletter's rhetoric was driven by three novel political concepts: the rights of the nation (*guoquan*), constitutionalism (*lixian*), and the rights of the people (*minquan*), all of which together served as the key ideological justification for the movement's anti-Qing stance. Using new political repertoires such as newspapers, pictorials, vernacular poems, and public speeches, movement leaders instilled new political ideas in their followers and assembled a broad coalition of supporters. Even some local officials sympathized with the movement and offered their support. A sedan-chair carrier donated his hard-earned money to the Railway

Protection Association, proudly proclaiming that "coolies are citizens too" (*lifu yi xi guomin fenzi*).[4]

Remarkable for the times, and no doubt from the perspective of the court, the masterminds of the movement were not among the usual troublemakers for the dynasty. The movement leaders in 1911 Sichuan were no common rioters (*luanmin*), rebel bandits (*panzei*), or revolutionary gangsters (*gefei*). They were instead, by and large, renowned members of the gentry (*shi*), who, created by the state through the civil service examination system as qualified candidates for officialdom (*guan*), had been willing to partner with the state for centuries in Chinese history (see Chapter 1). The backbone of the movement leaders was a group of Sichuan constitutionalists who secured powerful political standing with their provincial assembly activities, controlled the cities' lucrative and respectable businesses, and enjoyed exalted status stemming from both their imperial examination degrees and their knowledge of "new learning" (see Chapter 2). Many of them had studied in Japan and upon their return held official posts in the government.[5] However, rather than conforming to the conventional role of Confucian scholar-officials (*shidafu*)—that is, helping the monarchy solve problems and maintain the imperial order—they took a confrontational stand. By mobilizing a novel political discourse, they forged a broad, new political community of supporters and mounted a serious challenge to the authority of the Qing. It was here, in Sichuan, that the 1911 Revolution began.

The betrayal by the gentry and the uniting of gentry, officials, and commoners against the Qing under a shared new agenda was, however, not unique to Sichuan. In fact, in all fourteen provinces that declared independence from the Qing in 1911, the gentry and officials—the key constituents of the infrastructure of imperial rule—turned their backs on the monarchy. With their defection, the fall of the dynasty became inevitable. Consider, for instance, the fast-moving chain of events that occurred across all fourteen provinces in the critical months of October and November, beginning with the province of Hubei.

On October 10, junior officers in the Hubei New Army rose up in a mutiny. Encountering little resistance, these anti-Manchu revolutionaries occupied the administrative office of the governor-general in Wuchang, besieged the city, and declared the province independent.[6] Senior New Army officers sided with the rebels, and the leading constitutionalist and chairman of the Hubei Provincial Assembly, Tang Hualong, joined the new government and appealed to other provinces to support the revolution.[7]

By October 22, the revolutionary fire had spread to Hunan province. The anti-Manchu New Army officers rioted. The Qing governor hastily abandoned his post, and Tan Yankai, chairman of the Hunan Provincial

Assembly, emerged as a key supporter of the revolution. After the original rebel leader was killed in a factional conflict, Tan took over the governorship. On the same day, the New Army officers in Shaanxi province also rose up. With backing from the Elder Brothers Society (Gelaohui), the rebelling officers quickly took over the Manchu garrison and occupied the provincial capital. The new revolutionary government meanwhile relied upon local gentry and students who had studied in Japan to maintain order.[8]

The next day, on October 23, in Jiujiang city in Jiangxi province, New Army officers with anti-Manchu sentiment rose up against the court; a week later, the constitutionalists in the provincial capital, Nanchang, followed suit, conceiving a plan for independence.[9] In Shanxi province, on October 29, a group of junior officers in the New Army revolted. They killed the Qing governor and turned to their Japan-trained commander, Yan Xishan, for help. Working closely with the chairman of the Shanxi Provincial Assembly, Yan secured his post as the new governor, from which he supported the revolutionary cause.[10] On October 30, in Yunnan, the anti-Manchu revolutionary officers in the New Army struck a swift blow against the Qing. Though not as deeply involved as their counterparts in other provinces, Yunnan provincial assemblymen offered indispensable administrative help to the new regime after independence was declared.[11] Thus, in the first six provinces to revolt against the Qing, the initial actors were anti-Manchu revolutionaries in the New Army. Revolutionaries activated the uprisings, but the spark ignited by their mutiny would not have developed into a full-scale prairie fire had it not attracted support from other important elite players such as senior army officers and provincial assemblymen, both belonging to the political elite class.

The subversion by the gentry—the assemblymen being the most active among them—and the acquiescence of officials were all the more obvious in the following three provinces. In Guizhou, provincial assemblymen almost single-handedly established a democratic republic.[12] In Zhejiang and Fujian, assemblymen and anti-Manchu revolutionaries jointly led the revolt. On November 4, the vice-chairman of the Zhejiang Provincial Assembly, Shen Junru, appealed to the Qing governor for independence. Meanwhile, revolutionaries in the Zhejiang New Army mutinied. One day later, provincial assemblymen, together with the revolutionaries, declared Zhejiang independent from the Qing.[13] Likewise, on November 8, Fujian provincial assemblymen passed a motion calling for "peaceful independence" from the Qing.[14] Under the joint leadership of the assemblymen and the revolutionaries, Fujian became independent and republican on November 9.[15]

Most curious of all are the cases of Jiangsu, Guangxi, Anhui, Guangdong, and Sichuan, where independence was achieved entirely by gentry and officials, with little or no help from the anti-Manchu revolutionaries. On November 4, in Suzhou, Jiangsu province, gentry and merchants (*shenshang*) petitioned the Qing governor of Jiangsu, Cheng Dequan, to declare independence. One day later, Cheng openly defected, and he subsequently played a crucial role in the nationwide 1911 Revolution.[16] On November 7, provincial assemblymen in Guangxi decided to sever their ties with the Qing.[17] On November 8, Anhui, after painstaking deliberation by the provincial assembly leaders, declared independence from the Qing.[18] On November 9, Guangdong's gentry and merchants gathered at the provincial assembly hall and declared independence. After numerous meetings following the Wuchang uprising, they agreed that "autocracy has lost influence and republicanism is the trend of the future," and they aimed to build a regime in which "all people" would "enjoy the happiness of equality and republicanism."[19] Finally, Sichuan declared independence on November 22. On November 14, the acting governor-general Zhao Erfeng had released the railway movement leaders whom he had earlier arrested. Persuaded by pro-gentry officials, Zhao turned his power over to Pu Dianjun, the Sichuan Provincial Assembly chairman.[20]

By the latter half of November 1911, China's most powerful political elites had defected from the Qing. One leading group of them, the dominant constitutionalists from Jiangsu and Zhejiang provinces, had proposed a plan for uniting all of the southern forces into one polity under the principle of republicanism. Believing that "republicanism had been accepted by the public opinion (*yulun*) in China," they took the federalist system of the United States of America as their model, vowing to "immediately emulate the United States of America in calling upon a national convention, regarding it as our temporary authoritative legislature."[21] It was this group of elites, Zhao Fengchang, Zhang Jian, and Zhuang Yunkuan in particular, who initiated the truce between the Qing Beiyang army and the revolutionary armies in Wuchang, elected the southern delegates to negotiate with the northern leader Yuan Shikai, supported Sun Yat-sen to be the first provisional president of the republic, and penned the abdication edict for the Manchu Qing court.[22] The edict, claiming that "the power to govern is now transferred to all in the country" (*tongzhiquan gongzhu quanguo*) and that "a constitutional republic is now the state system of our country" (*gonghe lixian guoti*), signaled the end of the monarchy and the birth of the Chinese republic.

A contemporary observer, contrasting the loyalty of officials and gentry during the Taiping Rebellion (1850–1864) with their complete lack of loyalty in 1911, offered this insight:

When Wuchang was lost, from the provincial governor, treasurer, and surveillance commissioner, to the prefect and the magistrate, all officials in the city committed suicide. Countless gentry and commoners followed suit. This signified merely that the officials knew the meaning of a righteous death, and the gentry and commoners repaid the officials with gratitude. Because so many people had died for justice, order was easily restored after the Taiping Rebellion. Today, however, we have heard too many stories of officials and gentry running away and too few stories of them dying for justice. This is an immeasurable disgrace to the dynasty.[23]

Indeed, Sun Yat-sen's Revolutionary Alliance (Tongmenghui) and other anti-Manchu revolutionary groups had been laboring for years to bring down the Qing. But a critical question remains: why did the Qing collapse so utterly in a mere four months' time after an impressive 267 years of rule? As the eminent late Qing scholar Zhang Jian lamented, "Not from ancient times until the present day has a dynasty ever been so easily lost."[24] The complete betrayal by the political elite explains the speed and ease with which the dynasty fell, and also reveals the extent to which the old forms of legitimacy had lost their power.

Clearly, 1911 was a major rupture in Chinese politics. The end of the Qing signaled not just the end of a dynasty, but also the collapse of the old political system and the emergence of new ways of thinking about the nature of government. As noted by the previously mentioned observer, it was because so many people were willing to die for the old order that it was quickly restored after the Taiping Rebellion. In 1911, by contrast, faith in the old regime, which had so powerfully motivated officials, gentry, and commoners, was nowhere to be found. Between 1860 and 1911, something fundamental had changed in the minds of the Chinese people. This book explores that fundamental change in political ideas and culture, and in particular, how that change informs the question of how and why the revolution took place.

Engaging the 1911 Revolution Historiography

More than a hundred years have passed since the 1911 Revolution first broke out in China. In that time, China scholars have produced numerous works on the subject and offered various explanations of the event. Having focused on the anti-Manchu revolutionaries, the urban elite, modern state builders, or luminary thinkers, these previous studies form a foundation for the analysis presented here. However, key features concerning the revolutionary politics and culture still require serious study.

Early interpretations that appeared shortly after the revolution attributed the revolution to the radicals in the New Army, as well as to the

Beiyang Army's Commander Yuan Shikai.²⁵ Beginning in the 1920s, explanations offered by the Nationalist supporters of Sun Yat-sen stressing the leading role of the Tongmenghui, and in particular of Sun Yat-sen, eventually became orthodox.²⁶ The Communists inherited the Nationalist interpretation of the revolution and also emphasized Sun's importance. In the past one hundred years, official writings have persistently foregrounded the role of Sun even though he and his organizations primarily limited their activities to overseas Chinese and had only partial infiltration into China.²⁷ In more recent years, scholars have challenged this Sun-centric argument, and studies of revolutionary groups other than the Tongmenghui have also appeared.²⁸ However, confining the focus of their inquiry to the beliefs and behavior of anti-Manchu revolutionary leaders eclipses the more broadly shared and longer-lasting experience of the revolution itself.

A second and also pervasive approach to the study of the revolution is social interpretation, including both Marxist and non-Marxist analyses. In Marxist accounts, the 1911 Revolution is described as a class struggle in which the bourgeoisie led the masses to topple the Qing ruling house, with both the Tongmenghui and the constitutionalists regarded as political representatives of the growing bourgeoisie.²⁹ As the most influential defender of the Marxist account, Zhang Kaiyuan, historian and chair of the 1911 Revolution Research Group, regularly maintains that the revolution was "a revolution of the bourgeois class." Led by Zhang's superb research team in Wuhan, a series of empirical studies has emerged regarding the role of industrialists, merchants, and other urban elites in the revolutionary era.³⁰

The non-Marxist social interpretations come mainly from non-Chinese scholars, who argue that the revolution was rooted in long-term changes in society, and in particular, in the expanded functions of the local elite after the Taiping Rebellion.³¹ Synthesizing various analyses that focus on the local elite, Mary Rankin gives arguably the most complete social interpretation.³² Deploying a state-society dichotomy as the main analytical framework, Rankin summarizes the history of the late Qing as "a revolutionary movement of society out from under the old state control, the emergence of new social classes, the redefinition of political relationship, and the creation of a new state structure and ideology."³³ The non-Marxist position challenges the Marxist focus on the bourgeois class but for the most part implicitly accepts the central premise of the Marxist argument, that is, that an interpretation of the revolution consists of an account of social origins and outcomes. Taking the two together, we see that by focusing on prior economic and social factors, social interpretations tend to overlook the realm of ideas and downplay the innovative revolutionary process itself, wherein a new political consciousness and new political identities took shape.

A third and increasingly influential position is that of modernization theory, in which scholars revive Alexis de Tocqueville's theme of the aggrandizement of state power.[34] The focus here is no longer on a specific social group that led the revolution, but rather on the modernization of the state. Philip Kuhn, for example, traces the origins of the revolution to the practice of the absolute monarchy and emphasizes the role of the "established literati," that is, those who held a provincial-level degree and, by virtue of their regular gatherings in Beijing, could be considered a "national out-of-office elite."[35] The standard modernization account argues that the reluctance of the Qing to expand in size and function to anywhere near modern standards of government—measured, for example, by the ratio of the number of officials to the overall population—created enormous pressure for a statist solution and serious conflicts between the central officials and the "established literati."[36] This account considers the revolution a brief interruption of the more fundamental process of modern state building. This approach has been extremely valuable in helping us understand the pressure the state faced before the revolution. It is less successful, however, as an explanation of why the revolution broke out in the way it did and how it developed as it did, once it had begun.

Last, on the margins of the debate stands the intellectual and cultural history of the revolution. Beginning with Joseph Levenson's *Confucian China and Its Modern Fate* in 1958, intellectual historians have explored the changes that occurred in the late Qing and have argued that there was a deep-seated shift in Chinese thinking.[37] A key proponent of the intellectual interpretation is Zhang Pengyuan, who convincingly points out the critical role played in the revolution by the constitutionalists and, above all, Liang Qichao.[38] In recent years, there has been a cultural turn in the study of late Qing history, and a key emphasis has been on the emergence of the new-style intellectuals in the last decades of the Qing. We now understand a lot more about what educated Chinese were reading and learning, and the environment of their study.[39] To further demonstrate the changes in political culture that followed the revolution, Henrietta Harrison and David Strand have vividly exhibited the emergence of a new, republican political life in early twentieth-century China through meetings, speeches, rituals, customs, and symbols.[40] While this intellectual and cultural history has greatly enhanced our understanding of the values and sentiments in the years immediately surrounding the revolution and has directly inspired the present work, it does not engage with the revolutionary process itself. There is a disconnect between intellectual concepts and how they were implemented in actual revolutionary actions. How and in what concrete ways ideas contributed to the process of revolution remain to be explained.

Each of these interpretations has made a crucial contribution to elucidating the nature of the 1911 Revolution. However, important aspects of the revolutionary process, that is, how and why the revolution happened in the ways that it did, are still unclear. There has been insufficient discussion of revolutionary ideologies, their origins and development, as well as the overlapping interests, the rhetoric, the common purpose, and the political values and repertoires created and utilized in mobilizing supporters from the masses. The transformation in political legitimacy, the broader participation and shared cultural experience, the building of solidarity between the elite and the commoners, and the explanation for why such collective action endured in the revolution—all of these topics deserve further study.

Reinterpreting the Revolution

This book aims to rehabilitate the political and cultural experience of the 1911 Revolution. It conceptualizes the character of the revolutionary process, explains how and why the revolution happened in the ways that it did, and evaluates the legacy of the revolution beyond a reductive focus on immediate outcomes. In this book, I argue that the 1911 Revolution was not just an important political event in Chinese history but also heralded the very birth of modern Chinese political culture. The revolution was a political transformation spearheaded by new ideas, in particular, the notions of rights, equality, and popular sovereignty, which stimulated the Chinese elite into changing the old political order. The major force behind that intellectual change was the late Qing gentry-turned-constitutionalists. Together with the officials they influenced and the masses they encouraged, they brought down the old regime and ended the Manchu dynasty. The revolutionary process they helped set in motion created a republican political culture that enshrined popular sovereignty as the fundamental principle. However, key modern constitutional concepts, for example, the separation of powers and limited government, were by no means implemented in any serious fashion. Impassioned public opinion via mass propaganda—newspapers, pamphlets, public speeches, demonstrations, and meetings—rather than careful institutional design became the main mechanism for realizing political change, a key feature that impacted Chinese politics throughout the entire twentieth century.

To determine the nature of the revolutionary process, I have clarified my focus and sharpened my methodologies. First, this book persistently situates ideas and culture in concrete events and social context. Revolutionary politics was the dialectic interaction between structure and ideas within the revolutionary process. At heart, my analysis is an untangling of this multiplicity of forces that eventuated in the revolution.[41] In doing so, Joseph Esherick's *Reform and Revolution*, though published forty years ago, still influences my study of the revolution. Like Esherick, my approach is multidimensional. My difference from him lies in the fact that his lens "has scanned the realm of social structure and has focused on the social content of political movements and the social consequences of articulated politics," while mine has focused on determining the discursive and practical unity in the revolutionary process and on theorizing the nature of the long-lasting political culture that was invented in the revolution.[42] While Esherick stresses the alienation of the elite from the masses, I see the solidarity and shared cultural practices between them. In my study, it was the elite who created the constitutional-turned-revolutionary movement by mobilizing the masses with a new political rhetoric and repertoire, whose impact and legacy were much greater than we have previously known.

It is important to recognize that political culture was not just a matter of slogans or abstract theorizing. The emergent political culture was made possible by the leaders, but it took definitive shape only in the midst of revolution, when it was given voice and form by a larger political alliance, which itself was molded by its responses to the new rhetoric and ideas. Drawing on Lynn Hunt's formulation of "political culture," namely, "the values, expectations, and implicit rules that expressed and shaped collective intentions and actions," this book calls attention to the general principles of revolutionary language, the common political impulse of movement leaders, and the dominant attitudes in society at large.[43] This book also emphasizes the new forms of subjectivities engendered by the revolution. As Michel Foucault notes, "It matters little if [the revolutionary upheaval] succeeds or fails."[44] What is significant is the manner in which the revolution turns into a "spectacle" and "the way in which it is received all around by spectators" who let themselves "be dragged along by it."[45] The larger masses in the 1911 Revolution were often, and more importantly, not mere spectators but also participants and dreamers. Even though the result of the movement, the founding of a republic, was not what the constitutionalists originally had in mind—rather, they had desired a constitutional monarchy that honored popular sovereignty—the democratic political culture they disseminated, which was then shaped by the larger masses in the process of the revolution, was conducive to the birth of the republic.

Methodologically, my investigation concentrates on one province to showcase the interplay between structure and ideas in the revolutionary event. On the one hand, China had a unique elite class, the "established literati," who, by studying the same curriculum and passing the same examinations, shared similar political aspirations. The protagonists of my story—the Sichuan constitutionalists—belonged to this group. In the late Qing, they were also influenced by Western political concepts. Through studying in Japan and through reading modern periodical presses, they, whether in Tokyo, Chengdu, other counties in Sichuan, or elsewhere in China, became both fervent students and key disseminators of these ideas. On the other hand, each province had its particular socioeconomic structure. Many provinces were building railways, but in no province was railway construction as urgent as in Sichuan. In 1911, four provinces were affected by the nationalization policy, but only in Sichuan did a revolution break out. This had much to do with Sichuan's geographical isolation, its relative wealth and high level of urbanization, the strong presence of its secret sworn brotherhood, the Gowned Brothers (*Paoge*) (see Chapter 1), and the specific ways in which the New Policies reform (1901–1911) was carried out in the province (see Chapters 3 and 4). In this sense, although the focus of this book is on Sichuan, it is not a history of the 1911 Revolution of Sichuan per se. The struggles in Sichuan were emblematic of wider conflicts despite their local uniqueness. By focusing on Sichuan, I am able to look at all of the relevant factors—cultural, socioeconomic, and political—and pay careful attention to their interactions.

The Choice of Sichuan and the Narrative Framework

The choice of Sichuan as the focus of my case study is a conscious one. As the first province to seriously challenge the Qing regime in 1911, Sichuan set in motion the nationwide revolution. On September 14, 1911, the important Tongmenghui leader Song Jiaoren praised the fortitude and solidarity demonstrated by Sichuan: "Ever since [the Railway Protection movement] began, the Sichuan people have persisted. They have been opposing the government for over two months. The strength of their will and the power of their determination are extraordinary. The people in Hunan, Hubei, and Guangdong have showed us nothing comparable." Song then encouraged revolutionaries in these provinces to take up arms and join the people of Sichuan "to overturn the evils of despotism and build a republic."[46] The impact of Sichuan was widely noted and well documented in sources on revolutionary movements in neighboring provinces such as Yunnan, Shaanxi, Hubei, and Hunan.

Equally important, primary sources on the revolution in Sichuan are both rich and colorful, opening a window on the changes in political culture and structure as they occurred. The Sichuan Provincial Archive, the Sichuan Provincial Library, and more than a dozen county archives have preserved a large number of documents covering various aspects of the movement. In particular, Dai Zhili's three-volume *Collection of Historical Materials on the Sichuan Railway Protection Movement (Sichuan baolu yundong shiliao huizuan)*, which contains 1,910 documents collected from 750 monographs, pamphlets, and posters, serves as a solid foundation for reconstructing the 1911 Revolution to the fullest extent possible. The abundance of Sichuan republican gazetteers has vividly demonstrated the fundamental change of political culture and structure that the 1911 Revolution brought to the local people. In Da county in eastern Sichuan, for example, 1911 led to "much talk about freedom (*ziyou*) and a fashion of advocating equal rights (*pingquan*)."[47] In Luzhou prefecture in southern Sichuan, the Republican era ushered in a new society: "Since the establishment of the republic, people of the traditional four classes [gentry, peasants, artisans, and merchants] have come to be equal to one another (*simin pingdeng*); society has been fundamentally transformed."[48] The relationship between the ruler and the ruled was also altered. "Nowadays, as county chief executives try a case, people stand rather than kneel. The executives thus have no authority that keeps the ruled in awe (*wuwei kewei*)."[49] Gazetteers reveal that a significant number of people in Sichuan embraced the new political values of republicanism. When President Yuan Shikai tried to make himself emperor in 1915, "Sichuanese eagerly joined the Anti-Yuan Army to defend republicanism. They contributed decidedly to bringing down the monarchy of Yuan, just as the soldiers from Yunnan did."[50] Indeed, Sichuan is an excellent locale for examining how politics changed in 1911, in ways that were irrevocable.

My narrative structure has a close relationship to my methodology, which is examining the interaction between structure and ideas in the process of revolutionary events. Chapter 1 articulates the nature of the old regime and its collaborative model of relations between the elite and the state in Sichuan. A rich and self-sufficient region, Sichuan was fully incorporated into the Qing empire only in the 1850s. Soon after that, the collaborative model was called into question as population growth, rebellions, and foreign invasion eroded the established power structure and destabilized the old regime.

Chapter 2 examines the most formative intellectual influences on the Sichuan constitutionalists, and Chapters 3 and 4 explore their economic and political activities before the 1911 Revolution. Like their cohorts from other provinces, the Sichuan constitutionalists took Liang Qichao as their spiritual leader. Most of them had studied at Hōsei University in Japan, where they were also heavily influenced by the French legal tradition, especially its key concepts of rights, equality, and popular sovereignty. Their exposure to radical political thought while studying in Japan, in addition to reinforcing a tradition of elite activism, created a Chinese constitutionalism that was full of contradictions: while claiming to represent the people, these constitutionalists were at the same time the most aggressive agents in imposing state-building projects on local communities. Missing from their thinking was an emphasis on the virtues of limited government (Chapter 2). Acting on the discourse of rights, the constitutionalists of Sichuan took over the Chuan-Han Railway Company but ended up exacting even more taxes from the common people (Chapter 3). Legitimized by the late Qing constitutional reform and using the same discourse of rights, they strove to be the real power holders in the newly enhanced state. Via provincial assembly debates, they obtained both a solid organizational foundation and a political reputation that was unmatched by any other group (Chapter 4).

Chapters 5, 6, and 7 investigate the experience of the 1911 Revolution in Sichuan. Chapter 5 scrutinizes the rhetoric created by the Sichuan constitutionalists as they took their struggle to the streets. By deploying political concepts like the rights of the nation, constitutionalism, and the rights of the people, and by creating a common purpose "to protect the railway and break the treaty," the movement leaders drew ordinary people into collective action. Combining a new political repertoire with old cultural symbols, they effectively mobilized people from different walks of life against powerful opponents. Chapter 6 analyzes the mechanisms by which the movement spread beyond the provincial capital and throughout the entire province. Chapter 7 chronicles the expansion and division of the revolution. During the revolution, the newly crafted political culture with rights at its core was practiced by a large group of activists; this lent the revolution strength and legitimacy.

Chapter 8 explores the end of the revolution. In Sichuan, the emergence of the discourse of popular sovereignty as a new source of power created opportunities for nonactivists to join the revolution and control its politics. This chapter suggests that the valorization of claims of the "people" and the "public opinion" also worked to prevent the creation of a stable constitutional order. The conclusion evaluates the long-term impact of the revolution. Marking the rise of a new political consciousness, thousands of men and women gained firsthand experience in the public arena: they talked, read, and listened in new ways; they voted, protested, and joined political parties. After 1911, the old, imperial political culture was abandoned in favor of a popular republicanism in which elected assemblymen, students, intellectuals, and other members of society collaborated and competed in creating a new Chinese nation. The 1911 Revolution inaugurated China's modern era: it was through this revolution that modern Chinese politics came into being.

1   Sichuan and the Old Regime

In historian S. A. M. Adshead's view, until the twentieth century Sichuan was "the best province of a traditional empire."[1] A territory the size of France, Sichuan was rich in resources, boasting superb premodern agriculture, an excellent intraprovincial communications network, a high level of urbanization, and abundant energy sources. Long a part of China proper, Sichuan had been depopulated during the late Ming rebellions but was quickly resettled by a vigorous group of people. By the end of the Qing, Sichuan had a population of forty-five million.[2]

Despite its prosperity, however, the province was isolated from the rest of the empire, and from a modern development perspective, Sichuan was considered backward. A Sichuanese student overseas wrote in 1901: "The land, climate, history, society, literature, and arts of Sichuan clearly differ from those in the Yellow River basin, the Pearl River region, and the lower Yangzi delta. It is a place of its own . . . almost an independent country."[3] At the turn of the twentieth century, few people would have imagined Sichuan becoming a pioneer of radical political movements; however, just a decade later, it was in Sichuan—rather than in the more economically advanced and politically central parts of the country—that the first, most dramatic, and most far-reaching provincewide revolution involving the modern politics of rights, citizenship, and nationalism broke out.

The task of this chapter is to introduce Sichuan as the place it was before the New Policies reform (1901–1911), in order to set the stage for the revolution that followed. In addition to discussing Sichuan's unique geographical and socioeconomic structures and its imbalance in internal and external communications, the chapter also pays close attention to the functioning of the Chinese imperial system—the old regime—in Sichuan, which shared much with the rest of the empire. Like other parts of the empire, beginning in the mid-nineteenth century Sichuan struggled to survive the pressures and changes brought about by domestic rebellion and foreign intervention. An imperial mobilization in the aftermath of the Taiping Rebellion (1850–1864) fully integrated Sichuan into the Qing empire. However, the defensive posture of the old regime in the face of rebellions in the mid-nineteenth century destabilized the old power balance among the imperial center, the provincial leaders, the local elite, and the common people. Not long after, the so-called missionary cases (*jiao'an*), that is, confrontations between Christians and non-Christians ranging from harassment to deadly riots, added another dimension to the tension. Increasingly unequal to its tasks, the traditional polity found its legitimacy severely questioned, in both Sichuan and elsewhere.

Sichuan: A "Heavenly Land" in Isolation

Before the twentieth century, Sichuan drew nothing but unanimous praise (see Map 1.1). The official geography described it as "a land rich and fair, with an abundance of rivers and streams, fertile lands, forests and bamboo

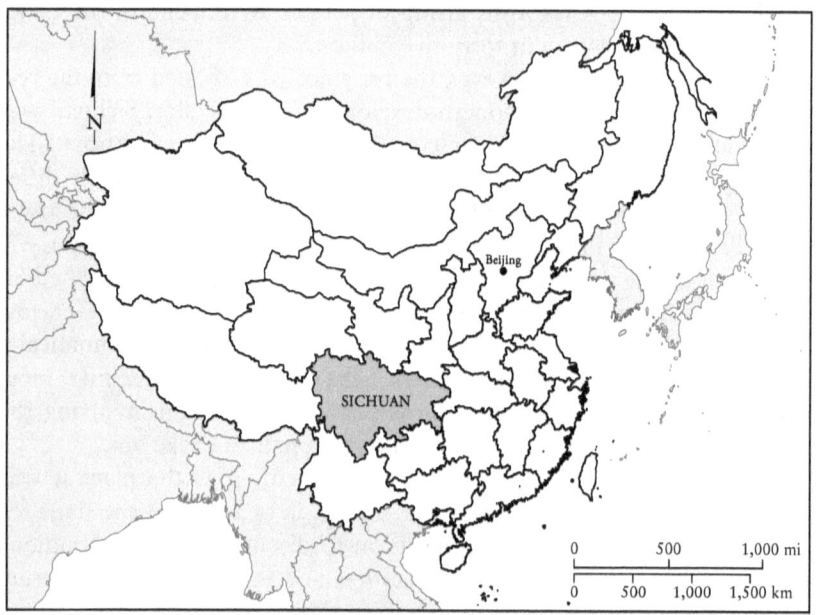

MAP 1.1. Sichuan in the Qing empire.

groves, vegetables and fruit."⁴ Early in his tenure, Xiliang, the Sichuan governor-general from 1903 to 1907, noted that "its products are abundantly rich" and that "the land is spacious and the people numerous."⁵ Europeans were equally enthusiastic. German geographer Ferdinand von Richthofen observed that Sichuan had "a degree of ease and well-being as regards the sustenance of life, not common in other provinces of China."⁶ And the British Blackburn mission of 1896–1897 reported, "Rich in everything which goes to support trade, agriculture, mineral wealth, products of skilled labor and the comparative wealth of its people, this province is par excellence the market, of all others, it should be our endeavor to gain."⁷

Located at the southwestern corner of the Qing empire, Sichuan was poorly linked to the rest of the empire. It is surrounded by mountains and plateaus, all at least 3,300 feet high. A Chinese proverb says, "It is more difficult to ascend to Sichuan than to ascend to heaven." In the same vein, Richthofen marveled that "this population is connected with the rest of the civilized world by one inconvenient mountain-road . . . and one large river."⁸ In the face of this geographical isolation, Sichuan managed to maintain its rugged self-sufficiency.

Traditional agriculture flourished in Sichuan. The province not only produced more grain than any other province in China but also ranked among the highest in terms of both output per capita and yield per cultivated acre.⁹ Protected by the northern rampart of the Daba Mountains from the dry, cold winds of Central Asia, yet open to the warm, wet winds from the South China Sea, Sichuan enjoyed an exceptional climate that was generally humid in both summer and winter, thus supporting many varieties of grain and allowing for double-cropping. In addition, thanks to a fiftyfold population increase over the course of the Qing, a ready supply of labor was available for terracing hillsides: "Where the angle of a slope is 30 degrees, the whole hillside is usually covered with fields from the bottom to the top."¹⁰ As a result, Sichuan had a greater percentage of cultivated land than other southern provinces. Blessed with a favorable climate and an industrious population making optimal use of its land, Sichuan was among the most productive agricultural areas in the empire.

Observers also noted that wealth from Sichuan's agriculture was more equitably distributed than in other parts of the empire. Richthofen wrote: "The inhabitants are evidently in a state of general prosperity. In the cities and in the country there is a certain luxury in dress and habitations in Sz'-chwan as compared with other provinces." Wealth appeared to be "more evenly distributed and therefore, more conspicuous."¹¹ The reason for this was migration. Sichuan was colonized not by clans as in south

China, but by nuclear families and individuals, providing an infrastructure of independent family enterprise that underlay the achievements of Sichuanese agriculture.[12]

Sichuan also enjoyed better intraprovincial communications, both by water and by land, than most other regions of China. Although Sichuan was admittedly disadvantaged in its communication with other provinces of the empire, its excellent internal communications made its external isolation trivial at a time when interregional exchanges amounted to only a low percentage of the gross national product. The province had a superb network of navigable water routes. According to historian Wang Di, there were 540 rivers in the province, more than ninety of them navigable.[13] Sichuan's major axis was the Yangzi River, to which all of Sichuan's secondary rivers were linked, forming a complete network of navigable water routes. Twenty-nine navigable river lines linked directly to the Yangzi, constituting 2,234 navigable kilometers (see Map 1.2). Six secondary river axes ran through the province: the Min, Tuo, Jialing, Fu, Qu, and Qian rivers (see Map 1.3). In view of all this, transportation by water in Sichuan, though inferior to the superb water route system of the lower Yangzi delta, was impressive. There were about two million Sichuan men working as boat trackers during the Xuantong reign (1909–1911). These

MAP 1.2. The Yangzi River in Sichuan.

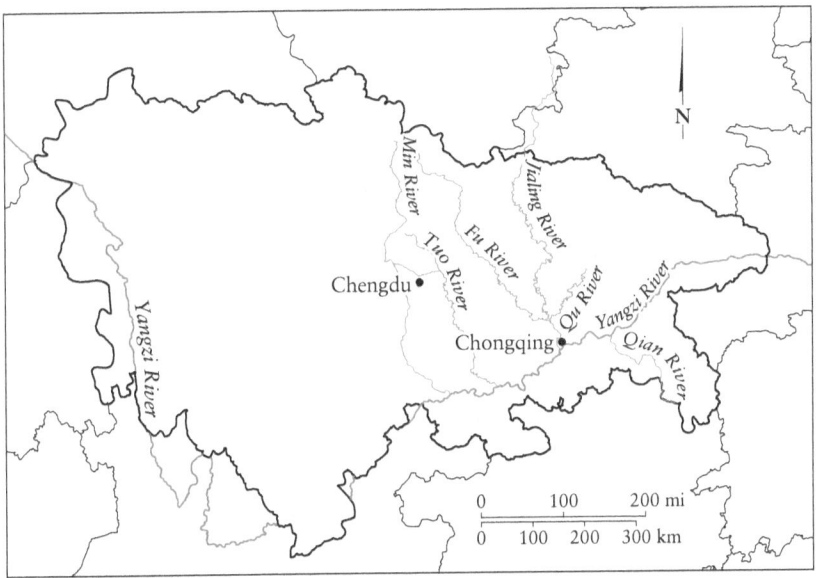

MAP 1.3. The six secondary rivers of Sichuan.

boats, traveling up and down the rivers of Sichuan, connected residents and goods within this vast province.[14]

Land transportation in Sichuan was another matter. High mountains and rugged terrain in the upper Yangzi River region made travel by land difficult. Even so, Sichuan had a comprehensive overland transportation structure made up of two kinds of roads: provincial highroads and local footpaths.[15] The provincial highroads, built and maintained with state revenue, were twenty-one feet wide and "well paved with flagstones, wide enough for the pack-trains to pass each other, and kept in excellent repair."[16] They were used principally for military and political purposes. The fastest service, 345 kilometers per day, was reserved for urgent matters such as the announcement of the death of a governor-general or the loss of a key battle. The 230-kilometer-per-day service was for transmitting notices of impeachment of officials or reports on sentences of death every fall. The 115-kilometer-per-day service was for transferring regular memorials and reports by provincial officials; at the beginning of every month, provincial documents were collected and dispatched to Beijing. Because Chengdu was 2,735 kilometers away, it took eight, twelve, and twenty-four days, respectively, for Sichuan documents to reach the capital.[17] Along the routes that connected post stations, four major highroads were constructed, all converging on the political hub, Chengdu (see Map 1.4).

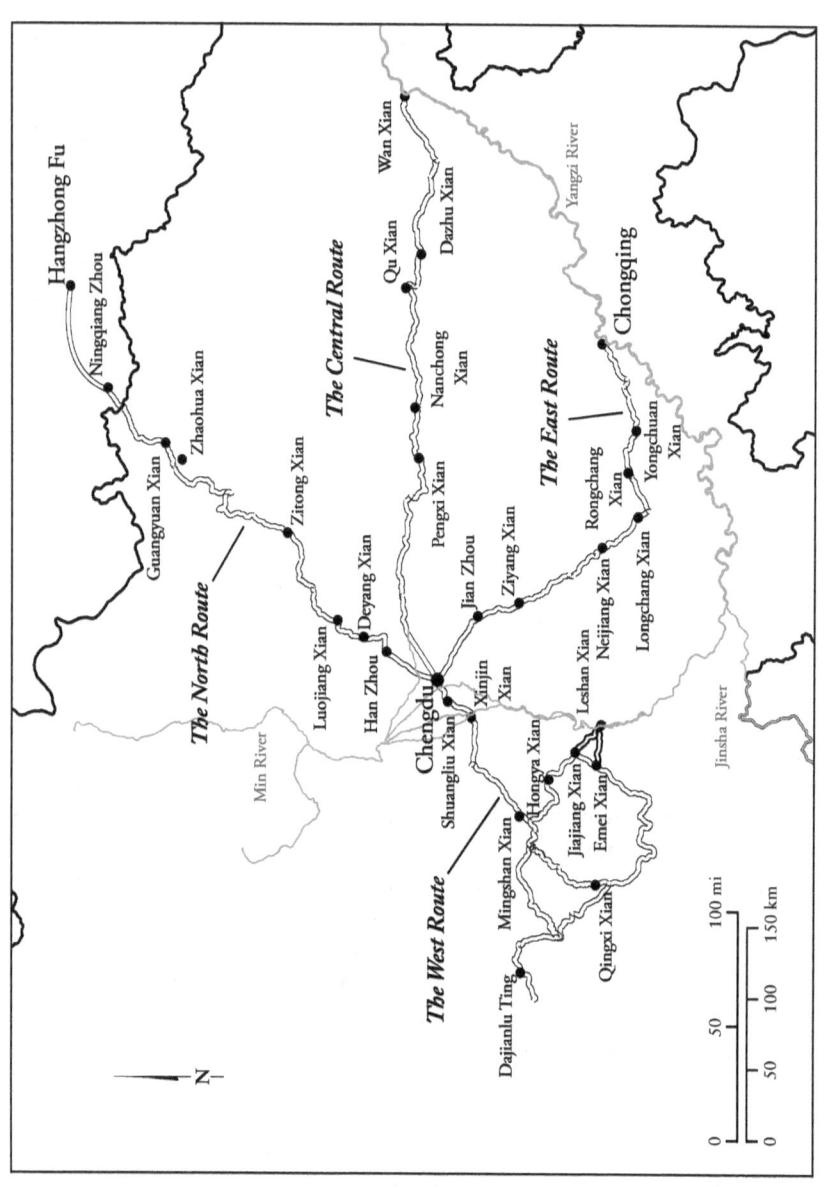

MAP 1.4. The four main routes in Sichuan (1644–1911).

In addition to the official highroads, there were roads paved by each county, town, and village. County roads were about ten feet wide; county footpaths varied from six feet to less than 1.6 feet in width, and most were paved with flagstones. According to Richthofen, Sichuan had "an infinite number of footpaths [that] permeate the country; and there is probably no hilly region in China so well provided with them."[18] The highroads and the footpaths connected Sichuanese from all over the province. To a large degree, Sichuan's affluence was attributable to its intraprovincial communications and transport system, which made commerce a thriving and essential part of Sichuanese daily life.

With both water and overland networks of communication, Sichuan possessed an impressive urban structure. The British consul-general in Chengdu, Alexander Hosie, estimated in 1904 that 30 percent of the province's population was urban.[19] Contemporary economist Dwight Perkins confirms the view that Sichuan had a high level of urbanization. Perkins's map of Chinese cities shows that in 1900, seven of the forty-six cities with a population of ten thousand or more were in Sichuan, a number not exceeded by any other province. In addition to the three main centers, Chengdu, Chongqing, and Ziliujing, there were numerous smaller cities, usually at intersections of the communications grid. The wealth of Sichuan's cities, large and small, depended on the wealth of the province's villages.[20]

A comprehensive explanation for the prosperity that made such an impression on outsiders must include the relative richness of energy resources. Sichuan had an abundance of human muscle, animals, water, and wood. There was no shortage of labor in the province, particularly as the population rose from twenty million in 1800 to more than forty million in 1900.[21] As for livestock, Adshead, for example, estimates that there were ten thousand water buffalo in Ziliujing alone.[22] Canals on the Chengdu Plain boasted tens of thousands of water wheels used to grind rice and power spinning wheels and looms.[23] The province also demonstrated considerable ingenuity in the use of coal and natural gas. For example, natural gas has been used since the third century to boil brine for salt, and according to archaeologist Lothar von Falkenhausen, the region's subterraneous salt deposits have been, and remain today, an important element in the long-lasting economic prosperity of the Sichuan region.[24]

All of these factors—flourishing premodern agriculture, an elaborate intraprovincial communications network, a high level of urbanization, and abundant sources of energy—formed the basis of Sichuan's reputation for affluence in the nineteenth century. But while everyone agreed that Sichuan was a "heavenly land" (*tianfu zhi guo*), this wealth was confined within the province. The danger of travel on the rapidly flowing Yangzi River and the discomfort of the journey via horse or sedan chair on the "one inconvenient mountain-road" made it exceedingly difficult for the Sichuanese to connect to the outside world. This isolation severely restricted the further development of the province's economy, which remained mainly agricultural and traditional.

The imbalance between the internal and external communications of Sichuan greatly influenced its historical trajectory. Sichuan was full of potential but underdeveloped; its commercial economy was lively but isolated; the province was rich but its fortunes limited and restrained within its borders. As wealth and power became the most urgent goals for the Chinese political elite at the beginning of the twentieth century, Sichuan's demand for an end to its isolation also became more forceful. As a result, there arose an urgent call for modern transportation—railways and steamships—to connect the province to the outside world.[25] In particular, almost all of Sichuan's elites and officials favored the development of a provincial railway. For them, a railway would finally liberate the massive province from its seclusion and enable it to fully realize its boundless potential.

The Old Regime: The Chinese Imperial System

If topography, modes of production, and commerce all had a fundamental influence on the lives of the Sichuanese, the political system was no less of a formative factor. In 1646, following the victory of Prince Aisin Gioro Hooge's banner troops, the Manchus subjugated Sichuan. The conquerors inherited, and continued, the old regime—the Chinese imperial system—for the ruling of provinces in China proper. Founded on the philosophical traditions of Confucianism and Legalism, the Chinese imperial system depended on both formal and informal governments to fulfill the daunting task of governing this expansive territory.[26] Having survived numerous rebellions and much chaos, the core of the imperial system remained, demonstrating its flexibility and potential for adaptation. Before turning to the changes that would ultimately topple the imperial regime, let us first explore its workings.

THE OLD REGIME AND ITS POLITICAL CULTURE

The advent of the Chinese imperial system, which originated in the Qin dynasty and matured in the Han dynasty, followed an age of social and metaphysical crisis (500–200 BC). The Zhou state of the "Golden Age" had disintegrated socially, the enfeoffment system had collapsed, and "barbarians" posed a constant threat. With the breakdown of the Zhou political order, which claimed its authority from Heaven, came an end to the metaphysical belief that government is by nature authoritarian. This separation of Heaven and humankind was in need of repair as the political milieu changed.[27]

The unification of China under the Qin in 221 BC and the more stable unification under the Han after 206 BC required a bridging of the gulf between Heaven and man. The solution was a syncretized Confucianism. This new imperial political ideology drew inspiration from various philosophical schools. From Confucianism it acquired an ethical base and an emphasis on hierarchical relations and structures; from Legalism it borrowed rational statecraft; from yin-yang theory it adapted models of the cosmos; and from Daoism it embraced the vital link between the cosmos and individual human beings. Confucianism was no doubt at the forefront, but also indispensable were elements from Legalism such as a rationalized bureaucracy, detailed written laws with harsh punishments, layers of bureaucratic oversight and inspection, and centralized political rule under one autocrat.[28]

In the making of this ideology, Dong Zhongshu (179–104 BC) was arguably the most influential of all the early Han thinkers.[29] Sociologist Zhao Dingxin has summarized Dong's synthesis, which was gradually exalted to orthodoxy, as, first—following Warring States cosmologists—affirming that humans are an integral part of Heaven. Heaven expresses its displeasure through unusual weather or natural disasters, and grants the right to rule—the so-called Mandate of Heaven—only to good and virtuous rulers. Second, the social order must be regulated by three cardinal principles: the ruler directs the ministers; the father directs the son; and the husband directs the wife. Third, the most important duties of the ruler are to promote moral behavior by supporting Confucian education and to maintain social order by establishing good laws. Law and punishment must be exercised in ways that reinforce the Confucian social order centered on the three cardinal principles.[30]

The legitimacy of the imperial system lay in the cosmology of this state ideology. According to S. N. Eisenstadt, "Conceptions of the tension between the transcendental and the mundane order . . . were couched in relatively secular terms of a metaphysical or ethical, rather than religious distinction between these two orders."[31] This secular expression of the tension between the heavenly world and the human one entailed a specific approach to structuring the latter through the cultivation of a social, political, and cultural order to maintain cosmic harmony. This involved viewing the "secular as sacred" and "the human community as a holy rite."[32] Accordingly, as Eisenstadt puts it, to maintain cosmic harmony, "there developed in China a very strong emphasis on civility as the central legitimating criterion of the sociopolitical order."[33] This civility (*li*) tended to be formulated as a mixture of the sacral and the legal, centered mostly on the emperor and manifested in both the patterns of political struggle and the system of law that characterized imperial China.

Chinese sociopolitical institutions echoed this pattern of legitimation. To fully understand the Chinese imperial system, it is necessary to look closely at the modes of control employed by the rulers and, in particular, at the distinctive role of the scholar-officials (*shidafu*).[34] In the full-fledged Chinese imperial system, literati were not merely scholars, but rather, they served as the most important reservoir for recruitment to the bureaucracy and thus were called "scholar-officials."[35] Together with the emperor and his entourage, scholar-officials constituted the principal partners of the ruling coalition, to the near-total exclusion of other social elements. At the same time, scholar-officials were not simply bureaucratic functionaries either. Originating from the aristocratic class in the feudal era—the Zhou dynasty (1046–256 BC)—they had long been considered embodiments of culture and moral exemplars. Because of these cultural and moral roles, scholar-officials enjoyed a certain independence from the imperial court, which helped balance the center's imperial power. They were, in short, a stabilizing mechanism that undergirded the Chinese imperial system.[36]

Ideally, scholar-officials occupied the space between the emperor and the common people as gentlemen who practiced civility and, by doing so, helped the emperor rule his country, as well as gained authority and legitimacy for themselves in society. However, in reality, for two millennia the imperially organized Chinese system constantly interacted with and battled against nomadic empires formed and reformed in the steppes. The imperial order as a political, social, economic, and cultural system was often at stake and had to always adjust itself.[37] Notably, and particularly relevant to the story presented here, in the Southern Song period (1127–1279), Neo-Confucianism as a learning and social practice emerged as an alternative solution to the breakdown of the early imperial order. The leading Neo-Confucian intellect and organizer, Zhu Xi, formulated a theory that placed the grounds of moral authority and responsibility in the individual. Thus, it was not the prerogative of the court and the government to tell people how to behave. Rather, literati cultivated themselves and put their learning into practice by taking responsibility in local society.[38]

By the end of the twelfth century, a coherent Neo-Confucian program for literati learning and social transformation under literati leadership was in place.[39] The Mongol Yuan dynasty (1271–1368) instituted Neo-Confucianism as the new state ideology, which lasted through the Ming dynasty (1368–1644) until the Qing dynasty (1644–1911).[40] The Qing imperial policy retained the Four Books (*Great Learning*, *Doctrine of the Mean*, *Analects*, and *Mencius*, the authoritative Confucian classics written before

300 BC) and Zhu Xi's commentaries on them as important subjects tested in the examination system, and thus ensured that the empire's educated elite would continue to be conversant with Zhu Xi, even when literati intellectual culture was moving away from philosophy.[41] Meanwhile, the Confucian interest in how the social system, government, economy, and culture can be made to further human community and welfare spoke to the Qing scholar-officials.[42] Like their predecessors, they were a primary carrier of the Confucian-Legalist order and its political, moral, and cultural orientations. Their influence on all levels of Chinese society led to an all-encompassing control by the imperial hegemonic ideology that severely limited people's ability to imagine a different order.[43]

Thus, although all institutional spheres in China underwent far-reaching changes—not only dynastic changes and divisions of the empire, but also developments in the structure of the economy and the polity—in comparison with other axial-age civilizations, the institutional effects of these changes were limited. The numerous new ideological developments that emerged in imperial China most often yielded only secondary interpretations of the values that were already dominant. Even the ones that came close to breaking the existing mold—Neo-Confucianism, for example—tended to accept the ideology and symbolism of the Mandate of Heaven and did not give birth to radically new orientations or new institutional patterns, particularly with respect to the accountability of rulers and the system of prestige based around the center.[44] In spite of the clear interventions of nomadic rulers and non-Chinese political regimes, there were continuities that cut across the long historical time frame.[45]

For this reason, the Chinese imperial system is "perhaps the best illustration of Gramscian hegemony," as its cultural institutions reinforced its political ones, and vice versa.[46] Ideology was of critical importance to the Chinese imperial system. The Confucian state ideology was the philosophical foundation of the system, and the distinct assemblage of social and political forces that shaped the key bearers of this ideology—the scholar-officials—constituted the sociopolitical power of the old regime. This hegemonic political culture and the Chinese elite's identification with this culture were the "secret" to the tenacity of the old regime.

FORMAL GOVERNMENT

Authority in the Central Government

With this understanding of the ideology of the Chinese imperial system, attention can now be turned to the concrete modes of control employed by the Manchu Qing rulers as they governed the majority population in China proper, the Han Chinese, who made up over 90 percent of the population. On the one hand, there was an alien side to Qing rule. In state appointments, Manchus had an advantage over Han. In the metropolitan administration, the Qing instituted a dyarchy, allocating half the positions to imperial clansmen, Manchu bannermen, Mongol bannermen, Chinese bannermen, and bond servants of the Upper Three banners (Bordered Yellow, Plain Yellow, and Plain White), and the other half to the Han.[47] At the provincial level, bannermen overwhelmingly outnumbered Han Chinese as governors of provinces. Garrisons at various viceregal seats were further evidence of alien rule: conquerors not only lived separately from the rest of the population, but also enjoyed special allowances from the state and married only among themselves.[48] On the other hand, the Qing rulers adopted the Chinese-style administrative system from the Ming. They inherited the Ming's method of dividing its Chinese territory into the same hierarchy of provinces, prefectures, and counties and they also retained the Ming's provincial, prefectural, and county seats.[49]

The central government interacted with the people of Sichuan according to the Confucian-Legalist model. The emperor, for Sichuanese, was the Son of Heaven. Since his legitimacy came from Heaven and he possessed the Mandate of Heaven, the emperor occupied the pinnacle of authority. Even though the political system revolved around the emperor, discourse about the people (*min*) was by no means unimportant. In Mencius's concept of *minben* (the people as the base), for example, the happiness of the people was a test of whether the will of Heaven had been fulfilled. Confucianism believed that *tianzi* (the Son of Heaven) held *tianming* (the Mandate of Heaven) as long as he expressed *tianyi* (the will of Heaven). However, this did not leave the people any real mechanism to be effective power players, because "Heaven's hands could not be forced."[50] In historian Joseph Levenson's words, "Popular discontent was a portent, as a flood might be a portent, of the loss of the mandate; it was a sign, perhaps, of the loss of imperial virtue. But a flood was not to be greeted with fatalistic acceptance."[51] Popular approval operated only as a sign of some higher ratification of the emperor's legitimacy.

Provincial Government

The Manchu rulers began building civil and military bureaucracies soon after the Qing established its power in Sichuan in 1646. These hierarchies were staffed by men from outside the province, appointed directly or indirectly by Beijing. The highest official in Sichuan was the governor-general (*zongdu*). Under him were three other provincial civil officials—the treasurer (*buzhengshi*), the surveillance commissioner (*an'chashi*), and the commissioner of education (*xuezheng*)—and the top military official, the

Green Standard commander (*tidu*). There was also the Chengdu commandant (*Chengdu jiangjun*), equal in rank to the governor-general, who was in charge of the banner soldiers in the Manchu garrison.[52]

Where civil affairs were concerned, the Sichuan governor-general often had absolute authority even though the original purpose of having provincial treasurers and surveillance commissioners was to prevent him from amassing excessive power. Most of the memorials written by provincial officials, for example, were forwarded to Beijing by the governor-general, a gesture demonstrating that provincial officials showed "respect and harmony."[53] In Sichuan, because of the great distance to Beijing, the governor-general was sometimes called the "Son of Heaven Overseas" (*haiwai tianzi*), a clear indication of the authority of the post.

The provincial treasurer was in charge of personnel affairs and taxation. As the provincial civil official second only to the governor-general, the treasurer managed three key subordinates: one in charge of promotions, transfers, and demotions of Sichuan officials; a second in charge of collecting taxes and funds for the provincial treasury, which held about three million taels of silver; and a third in charge of drafting documents.[54] The surveillance commissioner administered legal matters for the province and reviewed trials and lawsuits submitted by local offices, which he retried and judged in the eighth month of each year. The governor-general would then report the verdicts to the Board of Punishment in Beijing.[55] The Sichuan commissioner for education was a part-time post that managed the civil service examinations. After the examination system was done away with in 1905, the office was given the responsibility of setting up modern, or "new-style," schools, producing new textbooks, and selecting local educational officials.[56]

The governor-general was also the commander in chief of the military. The main military force in Sichuan, the Green Standard Army (also called the Governing Battalions, or *zhiying*), was led and managed by the Green Standard commander, who was under the governor-general's command.[57] At the beginning of the dynasty, there were eighty Green Standard battalions in Sichuan, divided into four garrisons: the East Sichuan garrison, in Chongqing; the North Sichuan garrison, in Baoning; the Jianchang garrison, in Ningyuan, near the border with Yunnan; and the Songpan garrison, in Songpan, on the Sichuan-Tibetan border (see Map 1.5). The Green Standard's fighting capacity was low. Zhou Xun, an assistant in the Sichuan provincial government and an acute observer of the late Qing administration, wrote that "even after China was opened and foreign threats had become frequent, the Green Standard did nothing to toughen itself. Every year, the same old maneuvers were practiced and no change took place."[58]

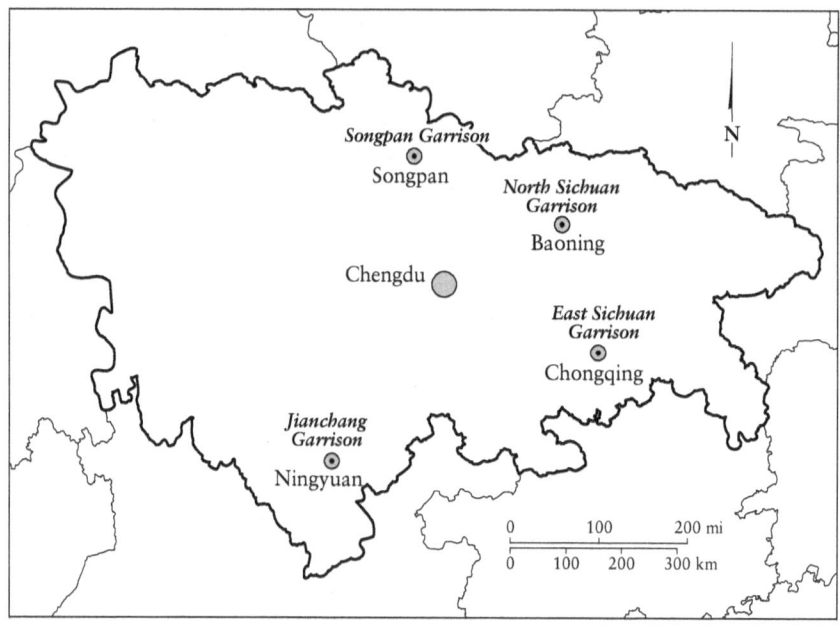

MAP 1.5. The four military districts in Sichuan (1644–1911).

By the time of the Taiping Rebellion, the Green Standard Army in Sichuan had become so feeble that midway through the rebellion, Governor-General Luo Bingzhang established an entirely new force, the Defense Army (*fangjun*).[59] The Defense Army, commanded by the governor-general with the Green Standard commander and modeled after the Hunan Army—a regional army that helped defeat the Taipings—soon became the principal suppressor of riots and rebellions in Sichuan. After the court initiated the New Policies reform, 80 percent of the Green Standard soldiers were dismissed, and the Songpan and Jianchang garrisons, which remained, were reformed according to the Defense Army model.[60] The Defense Army was again reorganized by Governor-General Zhao Erxun, who expanded its twenty-nine battalions to thirty-six, divided them into six routes, and stationed them along the provincial border.[61] In particular, the battalions assigned to border affairs under Zhao Erxun's brother, Zhao Erfeng, were regrouped into the Patrol and Defense Forces (*xunfang*), which became the most effective of all the old-style armies in Sichuan.

In addition to the Green Standard Army and the Defense Army, Sichuan also had bannermen stationed in Chengdu headed by the Chengdu commandant, a post established in 1776 after the Qianlong emperor led troops to pacify the Sichuan-Tibetan border. The Chengdu commandant historically enjoyed close relations with the Songpan and Jianchang garrisons. Gradually, as the banner troops became ineffective, most military matters in the province came to be managed by the governor-general, leaving the commandant mainly to serve as the leader of the banner population of ten thousand living in the Manchu quarter of the city of Chengdu.[62]

Relative to the size of the province—the annexing of the Sichuan-Tibetan border region in 1906 had made Sichuan the largest of all the provinces in China proper—the provincial government until the late nineteenth century was small, comprising a handful of civil and military officials taxed with managing a territory of over forty million people. Small as it was, it rose to the challenge of handling the problems arising in the old regime.[63]

Local Government

Immediately below the provincial government was the circuit (*dao*), led by a circuit intendant (*daotai*),[64] and below the circuit was the prefectural tier, consisting of prefectures (*fu*), independent subprefectures (*zhilizhou*), and independent departments (*zhiliting*).[65] Next came the county-level echelon, which included subprefectures (*zhou*) and departments (*ting*) as well as counties (*xian*). During the Xuantong reign (1909–1911), there were seven circuits, twenty-eight prefectural-level administrations, and 140 county-level administrations.[66] It was these county-level governments that the Qing state relied upon for daily governance.

Ch'ü T'ung-tsu's authoritative *Local Government in China Under the Ch'ing* and Wang Di's comprehensive *Striding out of a Closed World* illuminate the details of the structure and function of the local government in Sichuan. The 140 county-level governments were divided into four categories depending on how easy or difficult it was considered to rule them. All local governments centered on a district seat, which was a walled city surrounded by towns and villages. In each county-level government, control from Beijing was enforced by the magistrate, who was an agent of the state, abiding by the state's code of administrative regulations and operating under the direct supervision of the prefects.[67]

The most important person in a local government was the magistrate. He was responsible for maintaining order, collecting taxes, and trying legal cases. In Qing China before the 1906 constitutional reform, no legislative branch existed, and administrative and judicial functions were combined in the magistrate's office.[68] In ruling the county, the magistrate relied on clerks, runners, servants, and secretaries. Clerks prepared and processed documents for the local government. The endemic corruption of clerks would contribute to unrest over taxation in the final decades of the Qing rule.⁶⁹ Runners served the government as messengers, guards, and police. Like clerks, runners were natives of the province and held onto their positions as long as they could.⁷⁰ The magistrate tended to be closer to his servants and secretaries than to the clerks and runners, the latter being local while the former were usually nonnative to the county like the magistrate himself. Although not officially employed by the government, servants were customarily involved in the flow of documents, court dealings, and taxation. Secretaries constituted a brain trust that helped magistrates operate the government. All secretaries, also hired by the magistrate himself, were literati: typically they held the *juren* degree, usually the lowest degree that qualified one for an official appointment.⁷¹

With help from clerks, runners, servants, and secretaries, magistrates assumed a wide range of administrative duties. County governments were the lowest official tribunals of the Qing state. A magistrate's duties combined those of judge, prosecutor, police chief, and coroner. Every month, about six to nine days were reserved for accepting civil complaints. Ordinary people could appeal to a higher yamen only on the grounds that a magistrate had failed to accept the complaint or had judged it unfairly.

Magistrates were also in charge of collecting the land tax (*tianfu*). In the Qing, the land tax, also called the "standard tax" (*zhengliang*), was a landowner's basic tax responsibility. To make tax collection more efficient, a reform to "merge the poll tax with the land tax" (*tanding rumu*) was implemented in the 1720s. The land tax was paid in money and levied according to the fertility of the soil; the poll tax (*dingyin*), which was in principle levied on all males between sixteen and sixty years of age, was no longer collected as an independent item. Together they were designated *didingyin* or *zhengliang*. People who had no land were thus exempted from the poll tax. The reform was applied throughout Sichuan by 1763.⁷² Thereafter, the job of the magistrates was to prepare the land tax records, calculate the tax rates on various kinds and grades of land, send tax notices to taxpayers, and display the information on a stone tablet in front of the county yamen.

Last, magistrates were responsible for maintaining order, and they did so via the *baojia* system. The *baojia* was a neighborhood police network for detecting lawbreakers, and it was used by the local government to control the local people, for an individual's activity was unlikely to escape the neighbors' notice. The magistrate was in charge of organizing households into *pai* (ten households), *jia* (a hundred households), and *bao* (a thousand households) as security units. In theory, the magistrate appointed the heads of *bao* and *jia*, using them as his agents. In reality, the *baojia* was often managed by local notables, with the magistrate supervising them from above.⁷³

Sichuan and the Old Regime 31

Local government in the Qing was thus comprehensive in its functions. Even at this lowest echelon of the bureaucracy, power was clearly directed toward the center. For example, all cases involving death sentences were reviewed by the governor-general, and the final approval of all penalties more serious than beating had to come from the Board of Punishment in Beijing.[74] All of this was to ensure that the Qing state at the central level maintained control over its local administrations.[75]

THE INFORMAL MODE OF CONTROL:
GENTRY AND LANDOWNERS

The formal Qing government was effective overall. However, relative to the huge population of China, the formal bureaucracy was tiny, obliging the Qing state to mobilize the local elite to facilitate its rule. To understand how this informal mode of control in Sichuan worked, one must first understand the local power structure below the county level. In 1890, a Sichuan local gazetteer succinctly summarized local power dynamics: "First in power come the gentry (*shen*, or *shenshi*); next, the landowners (*liang*, or *lianghu*); third, the Gowned Brothers (*Paoge*)."[76] Sichuan's Qing sources corroborate this view, repeatedly using the term *shenliang* ("gentry and landowners") when describing local power dynamics. The *shen* and *liang* together controlled local society, and it was with them that the Qing rulers collaborated in consolidating their control at the local level.

Gentry were the most important leaders in Qing local society. Generally speaking, *shen* were former officials and *shi* were holders of degrees and academic titles, or, more freely, people who read books.[77] In the Qing dynasty, *shenshi* referred to men who held a degree or an official appointment. Included were officials, active and retired, and holders of degrees, civil and military. The majority of *shenshi* obtained their status through the civil service examinations and played an important role in establishing the authority of the emperor and in educating the people to respect that authority. Their function as moral exemplars was recorded by the local gazetteers of Sichuan:

In the Qing dynasty, when the civil service examination was functioning properly, those with moral integrity were deeply respected. Those who had passed the examinations served with principle, and many were promoted into officialdom. Even those who were not so lucky in obtaining official posts wrote essays and taught students. These people, if they were fathers, taught their children to behave correctly; as brothers, they encouraged their siblings to act well. They were good teachers and good friends.[78]

Historian Chang Chung-li, in his classic work *Chinese Gentry*, describes in detail the position and function of *shenshi*. *Shenshi* were the social equals of officials. In contrast to commoners, *shenshi* were exempt from the submissive etiquette that commoners had to observe. The prestige of the *shenshi* was also reflected in the Qing legal code. They were protected by law against commoners, and if a member of the *shenshi* was insulted or injured, the offender was punished more severely than if he had wronged a common subject.[79] *Shenshi* were also granted economic privileges and an exemption from the corvée. They were exempted from the corvée because their cultural refinement did not permit them to engage in manual labor. This exemption then relieved them from the corresponding converted corvée tax, which was a considerable portion of the tax burden. Accordingly, the position of *shenshi* was both desired and respected.[80]

In administering local society, the Qing state relied heavily on the *shenshi*. A handbook for magistrates declared:

The high families (*shen*) are not to be disturbed. They should be met in a virtuous manner and received courteously and are not to be repressed with power and prestige. Also scholars (*shi*) are at the head of the people, and since the laws and discipline of the court cannot be exhaustively explained to the people, and since scholars are close to the people and can easily gain their confidence, learned and virtuous scholars are exactly the ones to rely upon in persuading the people to follow the instructions of the officials.[81]

Influential as the *shenshi* were, other social groups also helped the Qing state manage public affairs. The second most powerful group in Sichuan was the landowners (*lianghu*). The *lianghu* were a major source of land tax revenue, which lent them considerable economic power in local society. While the gentry tended to be esteemed, *lianghu* were less generously portrayed. Not infrequently they were referred to as "rustic landowners" (*tu lianghu*) or "uncultured landlords" (*tu dizhu*), derogatory terms construing them as ignorant and illiterate. The populace may not have entirely respected them, but the landowners were nonetheless members of the Sichuan elite and were energetically involved in the daily management of their local society. Together, the gentry and the landowners took responsibility for keeping order and levying taxes. In general, the gentry set the rules and provided advice, while the actual execution and enforcement of taxation was the work of the more down-to-earth landowners.

The principal duty of the gentry and the landowners (*shenliang*) was assisting the magistrate in collecting taxes. In Sichuan, the land tax was not levied directly by the magistrate; the *shenliang* served as a key intermediary. In Yunyang county, for example, "every autumn, the magistrate would invite the urban and rural *shenliang*—those who wore special hats and sashes were the *shenshi* and those who rented out their land were called *lianghu*—to his residence to discuss appropriate taxes and the conversion rate between copper and silver. This event is known as 'discussing the tax rate' (*yiliang*)."[82] Once the tax rate and the conversion rate had been established, the procedure was that the land tax would first be advanced by the *shenliang*, who would then be reimbursed by the local peasants. This was known as "monopolizing the collection of taxes" (*baolan*). Wang Di notes that Sichuan's *shenliang* did this willingly. On the one hand, it showed that the *shenliang* were "loyal" to the regime, in return for which they were "awarded or appointed to government positions."[83] On the other hand, they also profited from lending money to ordinary taxpayers. For example, in Nanchuan county, "the magistrate invited the powerful gentry to discuss the tax levy. On this occasion, the market price for one tael of silver was about one thousand copper coins. However, after consultation with the gentry, the value of one tael of silver was raised to seven thousand coins. This resulted in a considerable profit for the magistrate and the gentry."[84]

Preserving order was the second main function of the *shenliang*. As stated earlier, order was enforced below the county level by the neighborhood police network, the *baojia*. In Ba county in 1810, for example, the magistrate ordered *baojia* leaders to weed out thieves and other suspicious individuals in their locales: "All leaders of *bao*, *jia*, and *pai* should constantly check on local residents. Whoever looks unfamiliar should be driven out. Those who have moved outside their *jia* should be listed and recorded, and those who have moved in only recently should be listed carefully so as to preserve law and order."[85] Most of these leaders—*baozheng* or *baozhang*, *jiazheng* or *jiazhang*, and *paitou*—were members of the *shenliang* and had a certain social status. In Ba county, for example, *paitou* had to be "capable" and "respected by the local residents."[86] In Da county, "*baozheng* had to be degree holders or elders, invited by county magistrates or recommended by local gentry. They were confirmed for their posts by the yamen with a certificate but were not paid salaries."[87] The tasks of these local leaders were not easy; however, these positions ensured protection and conferred a certain status in local society. Thus, many local elites opted to take the job.[88]

Beyond taxation and policing, there were a number of other tasks—welfare, arbitration, and public works, among others—that were performed by the *shenliang* and given certificates by officials.[89] In theory, the *shenliang* could have become a force challenging the state; however, that generally did not occur in China. The *shenliang* were not participants in self-government; rather, their prestige and status were conferred by the state. The *shenshi* received either an official title or a degree from the state; the *lianghu* enhanced their status in their locale by taking on public jobs that helped with the administration of the state. In other words, the key qualifications for membership in China's local elite were based in the current political order.

In Sichuan author Li Jieren's words, the powerful men in the Qing were those who had "some sort of connection with officials."[90] Even the external style of officials became an object of imitation for common Sichuanese. The people of Chengdu at the end of the nineteenth century were mocked by social critic Fu Chongju as "shamelessly ingratiating themselves in front of officials" and "arrogantly imitating officials' manners," that is, officials' ways of talking and dressing.[91] Officials, gentry, and landowners constituted the political elite in Sichuan. All three depended on the authority of the state for status and prestige and in exchange offered their loyalty and service to the state. This was the old regime in Sichuan.

Actual Governance of Sichuan and the Effect of the Taiping Rebellion

With this understanding of the ideology and structures of the old regime, the question then becomes, How, in actuality, was Sichuan governed? Was it taxed heavily? Was order enforced? What was the relationship between Sichuan and the court in Beijing, which had to rule from a distance of over a thousand miles?

THE GOVERNANCE OF SICHUAN: MONEY

In S. A. M. Adshead's view, up until the Taiping Rebellion, Sichuan remained "an interior off-shore island in relation to the main body of the Chinese empire . . . a continental Taiwan or Hainan." In his words, "Although the formal government in Sichuan was rationally and effectively organized, as well or better one may think than government in the outer provinces of Spain under the Habsburgs or the Ottoman Empire, the prevailing impression it conveys is one of lightness and limitation."[92] Perhaps the most striking indication of the "lightness" was the small sums of taxes levied in Sichuan. The tax revenue of Sichuan in 1850, according to Adshead, was only 1.3 million taels of silver. Raised under five items of taxation, this was approximately 0.5 percent of an estimated gross provincial product of 252 million taels, assuming a population of thirty-five million and a per capita annual income of 7.5 taels.[93]

The land tax, or standard tax, was the most important levy in the traditional economy. Sichuan enjoyed an extremely low land tax rate. Ever since the Ming dynasty, Sichuan's land tax had been light, owing to its small population and the small amount of land registered in the official tax records. On this, the Sichuan provincial gazetteer during the Kangxi reign noted, "The amount of land tax for all of Sichuan was that of a [single] prefecture in Jiangsu or Zhejiang."[94] The lightness of Sichuan's land tax was also a matter of early Qing economic policy. At the beginning of the Qing, because of the devastating Zhang Xianzhong Rebellion, the state virtually stopped levying land tax in Sichuan. In 1661, for example, Sichuan was taxed only twenty-seven thousand taels of silver and 928 *dan* (about fifty-five tons) of grain, which together constituted only 6.6 percent of the land tax levied in 1578 in the Ming.[95] The lightness of taxation in Sichuan remained unchanged throughout the Kangxi reign (1661–1721). The Qing's policy of "increasing the population without adding tax" (*zisheng rending, yongbu jiafu*) was a boon to the economic growth of Sichuan. The Kangxi emperor declared: "The wastelands in Sichuan have now been developed. If we begin levying land tax according to the actual amount of arable land, every year we would raise almost 300,000 taels of silver from Sichuan. However, I think our treasury is sufficient, and there should be no need to add to the burden to the Sichuan people."[96]

If "light corvée and low taxation" (*qingyao bofu*) was the state policy distinguishing the early Qing period, the reign of the Yongzheng emperor (1722–1735) that followed was marked by rigorous state building and ambitious reforms. However, taxation in Sichuan remained light. In 1728, for example, Sichuan's land tax was only 40 percent that of the Wanli reign (1573–1620) in the Ming dynasty, even though the total amount of taxable land in Sichuan was 3.4 times that in the Wanli era.[97] Thanks to these lenient policies, Sichuan's population grew quickly. By 1850, Sichuan had been transformed from a depopulated province to the most populous province in the Qing empire.[98]

Population growth continued in Sichuan throughout the eighteenth and nineteenth centuries. But the arrival of migrants from central and south China and the extensive population growth led to new problems. As Robert Entenmann observes, "By the late eighteenth century, Sichuan itself was overpopulated and the province lacked a safety valve of its own."[99] To make things worse, the rising price of silver in the nineteenth century also led to hardship for peasants. Because of the large amount of opium imported into China and the corresponding outflow of silver, the price of silver rose dramatically—between 1836 and 1860, for example, it rose from seven hundred to two thousand copper coins per tael.[100] Since all taxes in the Qing were paid in silver, the increased price of silver was the equivalent of increasing taxation.

After the 1850s, Sichuan became a hotbed of tax resistance. The privatization of tax collection by the *shenliang* produced numerous opportunities for them to exploit small farmers. In some localities, *shenliang* went so far as to monopolize the entire tax collection. In Sichuan, riots frequently broke out in protest of the *shenliang* charging exorbitant fees. For example, in 1875 in Dongxiang county, local commoner Yuan Tingjiao led three thousand followers against the tax-collecting gentry, who charged excessive interest on their tax-related loans to the farmers and set extreme copper-to-silver conversion rates.[101] And in 1884 in Dayi, Gowned Brothers leader Yang Hongzhong took up arms against the overt extortion by the county magistrate and clerks.[102]

By the late nineteenth century, these issues of institutionalized corruption, overpopulation, and the rising price of silver had grown worse and were compounded by an insufficient supply of land. The numbers of dissatisfied migrants and natives continued to increase, swelling the ranks of bandits and threatening local order.[103] In 1883, Governor-General Ding Baozhen reported, "Sichuan has become a land where bandits are as ubiquitous as grass. The *guolu* bandits, the secret brotherhoods, the religious sects, and the salt bandits are everywhere."[104] To make things worse, after China's defeat in the Sino-Japanese War (1894–1895), the Qing state began levying more taxes on Sichuan to help pay an indemnity to Japan. In 1900, the total tax levy from Sichuan was 8.7 million taels raised under fourteen items of taxation—a sharp increase from half a century before, when the tax levy had been only 1.3 million taels of silver raised under five items of taxation. In other words, taxation was 6.7 times heavier in 1900 than in 1850.[105]

An analysis of how Sichuan's tax revenue was allocated between 1850 and 1900 shows Sichuan's contribution to the empire. In 1850, revenue from Sichuan was 1.3 million taels. Of this, 0.7 million, that is, more than half, remained in the province, while 0.6 million was sent to Beijing. The situation did not change radically during the Xianfeng reign (1850–1861). By the beginning of the Guangxu reign in 1875, however, Sichuan was spending more of its revenue in assignments to the capital and to other provinces than within its own borders. In 1886, Sichuan's revenue was 5.9 million taels: 2.5 remained in the province, 1.3 was sent to Beijing, and 2.1 was assigned to other provinces. The balance came back right before the twentieth century. In 1900, the revenue was 8.7 million taels, of which 4.2 was retained in Sichuan, while the rest was spent outside the province.[106] In short, Beijing was able to extract a great deal of revenue from Sichuan. Despite a growing number of tax riots between 1850 and 1900, the old regime in Sichuan remained in place.

THE GOVERNANCE OF SICHUAN: ORDER

In the old regime, another indication of the limited power of the formal bureaucracy at the local level was the small number of people it employed.

In 1900, there were only 168 civil officials in all of Sichuan. The military in Sichuan consisted of a banner garrison of 2,500 men and the combined Green Standard and Defense Army of 24,900 men.[107]

The Qing rulers relied on other forces to maintain order. Among these, the local militia (*tuanlian*) was the most prominent. *Tuan* referred to the militias organized by the local *shenliang* to "keep local order and to watch out for each other." *Lian* referred to select militia members who were chosen to be sent to the county seats, where they were put under the command of the county magistrate. The members of *lian* were responsible for suppressing bandits and thieves, quelling riots, and guarding the city gates.[108]

At the beginning of the Qing dynasty, the Manchu rulers were suspicious of any organized force among the Han Chinese, but the White Lotus Rebellion (1794–1804), which grew out of a tax protest by a secret religious society, changed that.[109] Because Sichuan was one of the three provinces (with Hubei and Shaanxi) involved in the White Lotus Rebellion, militia had been organized there in response. In Sichuan, large households were ordered to provide three to four militia members; middle-sized households, two to three; and small households, one. During peaceful times, the militia was charged with ensuring public security. During chaotic times, it was deployed to suppress rebels and cut off their food supplies.[110]

The militia was invigorated during the Taiping Rebellion. In February 1853, the Qing court ordered every province to organize militias. Sichuan responded by expanding its militia. While militias helped the Qing state survive the Taiping Rebellion, the consequences of developing them were also disturbing: the militarization of the local elite created a power base that could compete with the state, and the previously loosely linked *shenliang* became organized and strengthened.

THE GOWNED BROTHERS AFTER THE TAIPING REBELLION

In Sichuan, the Gowned Brothers—the secret sworn brotherhood of the province—as a social force gathered increasing power after the Taiping Rebellion. There is no doubt that the *shenliang* ruled local society; however, the influence of the Gowned Brothers grew as the Qing state became ever more ineffective at governing an alarmingly increasing population. For those who lacked the power to seek redress of grievances on their own, the protection offered by the Gowned Brothers was attractive.[111] Historian Fu Chongju provides this definition: "Gowned Brothers was the association of members who were linked by sworn brotherhood in ceremonies of mixing blood and lighting incense. If mingled with bandits, they were called 'secret societies' or 'secret bandits.' Those who had not been involved in criminal activities were simply called 'Gowned Brothers.'"[112]

Unlike the *shenliang*, the power of the Gowned Brothers derived from the strict discipline and connectedness of their organization. Any Gowned Brother lodge would help members of other lodges as they would help their own, providing them money and lodging, and protection for those wanted by the authorities. In this way, the Gowned Brothers established a close-knit self-protection network. According to an account from the end of the Qing, whenever the Gowned Brothers came to a place, the local lodge would prepare a banquet, and the local lodge leader would give money to the leader of the visitors, which would then be distributed to each member of the visiting group.[113]

For years, scholars have debated the origin of the Gowned Brothers.[114] The Gowned Brothers began as bandit bands originated from the native bandits of Sichuan, guolu, who had existed in Sichuan from the very beginning of the Qing dynasty. Starting in the 1850s, they grew in power and became organized.[115] During the 1850s and 1860s, the Gowned Brothers developed more sophisticated rituals and ceremonies.[116] By the 1870s, as the land-to-labor ratio decreased intensely, the Gowned Brothers had become increasingly appealing and had emerged as a powerful social force in Sichuan, attracting soldiers, sailors, miners, laborers, salt smugglers, unemployed vagrants, actors, yamen runners, artisans, small shopkeepers, pawnbrokers, water carriers, and sedan-chair carriers.[117] These men, who ran protection rackets, gambling houses, and opium dens for a living, as the next section shows, would become a leading force in the anti-Qing and antiforeign resistance to come. Gradually, in the 1880s, even militiamen joined the Gowned Brothers, both for self-protection and for access to its network of power.

In the last two decades of the Qing, the Gowned Brothers had transformed from a group of social outcasts into a powerful organization that officials and elites had to tolerate. As one report noted, the Gowned Brothers "at the beginning, were those unlawful bandits who came together to bully other people. Later, the gentry and the wealthy people followed suit. *Shenliang* also formed Gowned Brothers associations to protect themselves."[118] In a similar vein, the *Sichuan Gazette* (*Sichuan guanbao*) reported, "*Shenliang* used this act [of affiliating themselves with sworn brotherhoods] to protect themselves and to form a wide alliance so as to strengthen their dominance and build their prestige locally."[119]

As the Gowned Brothers became increasingly important in the late nineteenth century, they also began assuming public responsibilities, particularly for local police and defense. For instance, the renowned Gowned Brother and a commander of the Railway Protection Army during

Sichuan's 1911 Revolution, Hou Baozhai, had served as the head of the swift-hand runners (*kuaiban*) and the police runners (*buban*) of Xinjin county and later acted as the chief training officer of the militia bureau.[120] Nonetheless, in spite of their growing prowess, the Gowned Brothers before the twentieth century did not confront the old regime face-to-face but rather collaborated with the regime for survival and expansion. A Sichuan prefect commented on this occurrence and wrote, "Once [the secret societies bandits] were charged with crimes, they would seek protection and help from their public-office-holding secret society brothers."[121] Overall, the midcentury rebellions did not bring down the old form of dominance, but forced it to adjust. However, this adjusted equilibrium was precarious. Any rise in the level of tension in one direction or another—imperial, provincial, or international—could upset this tenuous balance.

Crisis in the Old Regime: The Missionary Cases in Sichuan

As the old regime struggled to sustain the alliance of the court, the provincial leaders, and the local *shenliang*, the arrival of foreign powers added a new dimension of tension. By the end of the nineteenth century, China had become a client state of the Western powers. Only by accepting their demands for commercial, diplomatic, and missionary privileges could the Qing obtain some respite. In Sichuan, the threat of foreign powers was embodied in the handling of an increasing number of missionary cases. Though the Taiping Rebellion did not overthrow the old regime, the missionary cases severely threatened its legitimacy.

DEVELOPMENT OF CHRISTIANITY IN SICHUAN

Sichuan had been a key target for the Catholic Church. Adshead notes that it was members of the Société des Missions Étrangères in the eighteenth century, in particular Jean-Martin Moye (1730–1793), who created what Richthofen described as "a far more numerous community of Catholic Christians than in any other province."[122] The Tianjin Treaty of 1858 and the Beijing Treaty of 1860 had given foreign missionaries the right to enter inland China and to acquire property. In Sichuan in particular, after the Yantai Treaty of 1874, which made Chongqing a treaty port, Catholicism expanded, as did the amount of land and other property obtained by the Catholic Church. By 1904, there were 379 French missionaries in Sichuan, ministering to a large Catholic community. Protestantism came later.[123] It was not until 1877 that the first permanent Protestant mission station was established by the China Inland Mission, but growth thereafter was rapid.[124]

Taking Catholicism and Protestantism together, the Sichuan Foreign Affairs Bureau recorded a total of 514 foreign clergymen in the province in 1909. Chinese Catholic converts numbered 141,135, and Protestants 36,823.[125] In Chengdu, about 0.6 percent of the people were Christians, and in Chongqing about 0.2 percent. In total, of the entire Sichuanese population of forty-five million at the end of the Qing dynasty, Christian converts accounted for about 178,000, or 0.4 percent. Although Christians accounted for a relatively low percentage of the population, Christianity had a disproportionately large effect on political and cultural life in late Qing Sichuan.[126]

The new privileges exacted in the post–Opium War treaties—the 1874 Yantai Treaty for Sichuan in particular—led to a sharp increase in missionary power in Sichuan.[127] As Judith Wyman and Wang Di have both explicated, the expansion of Christianity was related to the deterioration of Sichuan's economy in the second half of the nineteenth century. Peasants often converted to Christianity to avoid increased oppression from officials and the *shenliang*. In some Sichuan counties, "commoners, virtuous or evil, converted to Christianity. . . . They all used [being Christian] for protection."[128] Additionally, it was noted that "when Chinese Christians had a legal case, the runners and clerks dared not extort extra fees. Even officials changed their attitude."[129] In many places in Sichuan, churches became deeply involved in local economic disputes. When local non-Christians and Christians got into an argument, the latter often sought help from the churches, which usually sided with their converts and defended them. It was precisely under these conditions that the missionary cases grew into a serious problem in Sichuan.[130]

MISSIONARY CASES AND THEIR IMPACT

Missionary cases began occurring in big numbers in the 1860s. According to Wang Di, from 1861 to 1910 there were as many as 127 large-scale cases in Sichuan.[131] These cases can be divided into three stages. Among the large cases in the 1860s and 1870s were the Youyang riot, the Qianjiang robbery, and the Jiangbei dispute, all initiated by the *shenliang* with the goal of minimizing missionary influences. In the 1880s, power wielded by foreigners had extended, and the incident involving the Chongqing Christian merchant, Luo Yuanyi, eventually resulted in the demotion of the magistrate of Ba county and brought a handsome indemnity to foreign missionaries. In the 1890s, missionary powers grew even further. In 1895 there was a riot in Chengdu, which resulted in China paying an indemnity of 750,000 taels of silver. Following that was the legendary anti-Christian riot, the Yu Dongchen Rebellion, which cost Sichuan over a million taels of silver.

Most of the missionary cases of the 1860s and 1870s came about because of the *shenliang*'s anxiety about churches. In the old regime, Christianity was considered heterodox, a cult.[132] The anxiety was worsened as churches began intervening in the local economic order. In 1846, the central government announced that all the Catholic Church properties that had been confiscated during its proscription of the church in the Yongzheng reign should be returned. After this edict, Catholic priests in Sichuan successfully claimed ownership of a number of offices, homes of the gentry, and other properties.[133] In addition, missionaries also enjoyed extraterritoriality, a privilege that inevitably threatened the domination of the *shenliang* in local society.

In the 1860s and 1870s, the presence of Catholicism was clearly felt by the Sichuan *shenliang*. Documents from Ba county detailed the *shenliang*'s responses to this situation and showed that all three major missionary cases of this period—the Youyang, Qianjiang, and Jiangbei cases—were initiated by the *shenliang* out of fear of losing control. In all three cases, the local government sided with the *shenliang* and together they struggled to preserve their dominance. Nonetheless, these men had to listen to their superiors in Beijing, whose policies were at odds with theirs. In the 1870s, for example, the French missionaries involved in the Jiangbei case, after having complained numerous times to the prefectural and provincial authorities in Sichuan but been given no answer, sought help from Beijing.[134] The intervention of the Office for the Management of Affairs of All Foreign Countries, known as the Zongli Yamen, supported the missionaries. This initiated a new power dynamic: Chinese Christians saw that the missionaries had support from the court, while local officials understood they had to be more careful when dealing with Christians. By the end of the 1870s missionaries had become an increasingly significant power base that had begun to affect the old pattern of local dominance.[135]

During the 1880s more people with wealth and prestige were becoming Christians, and a new term, "religious gentry" (*jiaoshen*), frequently appeared in local documents. It was within this milieu that the 1885 Chongqing anti-Christian riot took place. It involved Luo Yuanyi, a fifty-four-year-old salt magnate from Chongqing whose family had belonged to the Catholic Church for generations.[136] The riot began with attacks on the homes, churches, and offices of Western missionaries in Chongqing on July 1, 1885. According to top provincial officials, "the origin of the problem was the French and the British occupying strategic spots in Chongqing city, which raised commoners' worries and fears."[137] By the second day, the focus of hostility had turned toward Chinese Christians, with Luo's house becoming a primary target. In preparation, Luo had hired more than a hundred men to protect his home.[138] When his men were injured,

Luo ordered the rest—armed with guns, knives, swords, and clubs—to use force. Three people were killed by Luo's men and twenty-two were wounded.[139] While Luo and the missionaries saw this as a clear-cut case of self-defense, local officials judged otherwise. Luo was arrested and charged with murder. Several months later, he was accused of provoking the entire incident.[140]

The most telling part of this case was the defendant's attempt to enlist the central government against the local authorities who were prosecuting him. Luo, well aware of the problem he had brought upon himself, engaged in a metropolitan accusation (*jingkong*)—a direct appeal involving going to the capital to make a complaint—against the local officials who had arrested him. He was fully aware of the people and the institutions he could enlist in his defense, especially the Zongli Yamen.[141] The Luo Yuanyi case became so serious that it involved an edict issued directly by the Guangxu emperor. Citing precedents to bolster his decision, the emperor convicted Luo as the primary provocateur, and on January 30, 1887, Luo was executed in Chengdu.[142] However, the case lingered on and the ultimate result of the case was hardly a victory of the Sichuan officials. Although Luo failed to save himself, the magistrate of Ba county was also demoted.[143] Sichuan was ordered to pay 220,000 taels of silver to the French missionaries, twenty-three thousand to the Americans, and eighteen thousand to the British.[144]

In fact, over the course of the 1880s, the continual indemnities and demotions from cases like this one reflected both the ongoing expansion of the power of missionaries and the conflict local officials experienced between sympathy for the local gentry and loyalty to their superiors. The result was that the authority of the Qing central state continued to decline.

In the 1890s, missionary power expanded even further. The Qing's defeat in the Sino-Japanese War of 1894–1895 left it with even less bargaining power. Western ambassadors constantly intervened. Under these circumstances, requiring local governments to "protect the churches" became an empirewide policy of the Qing government.[145] The Chengdu riot of 1895 was a typical example of missionary cases in this era. The triggering incident was a minor burglary, which led to a riot involving a small number of people agitated by a rumor of foreigners eating children, initiated by a shout of "Attack the foreigners!" According to an American clergyman, the riot was a result of deep distrust of foreigners among the Sichuanese, which "became all the more acute after China's defeat in the Sino-Japanese War."[146] As a result, this burglary-turned-riot caused an indemnity of 750,000 taels of silver and further local alienation from Beijing.

Notably, Gowned Brothers played a prominent role in the missionary cases of the 1890s. From the 1870s on, with obvious acquiescence from gentry and officials, the Sichuan Gowned Brothers had already initiated a series of attacks against missionaries and Chinese Christians. It was also in this environment that the Yu Dongchen Rebellion (1897–1899) occurred. The rebellion took place in the town of Longshui in Dazu county, near Chongqing. In Longshui, Christianity had a strong presence, and local Christians competed with the gentry, landowners, and the Gowned Brothers for influence and power. In fact, the aforementioned gazetteer who ranked gentry, landowners, and Gowned Brothers as first, second, and third continued by saying, "in addition, we also have to count those Christians in."[147] In Dazu, there had been resistance to Catholicism as early as 1861, and Yu Dongchen had twice led local people to attack churches in 1886 and 1887; in addition, local officials shared the *shenliang*'s and the Gowned Brothers' repugnance for Christians and missionaries. It was against this background of Dazu that Yu Dongchen rose up for the third time in 1897:

> We, humble subjects, have been living under [the Qing] dynasty for two hundred years. We have been gratefully living on the ruler's land and eating the grain grown on that land. We are always loyal and practice filial piety. We have learned from [the sage kings] Yao and Shun, studied the classics, and obtained methods for dealing with outsiders. However, as foreigners came via steamship and commerce developed, missionaries also expanded their power. Foreigners took over our lands and businesses and used opium to poison our bodies and our hearts. Since the Daoguang reign, they have become ever more menacing. They raped our women and antagonized our people. They controlled our yamen and humiliated our court. They occupied our capital, Beijing, and took our treasures. They took our children as food and they made our debts enormous. They burned down our palace and invaded our tributary states. They occupied Shanghai and took over Taiwan. They forced us to open ports in Jiaozhou and partitioned our territory. There was never before a point in our history when we were humiliated like this!
>
> Even though I, Yu Dongchen, have not really read much, I still understand the great principle (*dayi*). Faced with the increasingly overbearing Christian converts who had bullied my friend Jiang Zanchen, I could not bear it any longer. I also blame the officials (*guanfu*). They did not do a good job in judging the matter. They encouraged the foreign tigers and wolves and wronged the good people of our dynasty!
>
> I have decided to attack foreign churches. Even though this is doing wrong, by doing wrong things against bad people, I am doing good deeds for my friends. I have decided to rise up to clear away all the humiliations of our country. I declare that we only exterminate the foreigners and do not rebel against the dynasty. Whoever treats us like enemies, we shall treat them like foreigners and like those who are not subjects of our dynasty. We will kill them as if they had violated the law and had violated the principles of us righteous people.[148]

Placing blame not only on missionaries and converts but also on government officials for supporting them, Yu argued that by attacking churches he was promoting "the great principle." Also in his announcement, Yu called upon the *shenliang* to join him and back him with money and grain, which many did. It was the protection offered by the local elite that had enabled Yu to rebel several times and avoid punishment for eleven years. Local officials had also been sympathetic. Yet despite the sympathy they had for the Gowned Brothers, imperial edicts put them in a quandary. They had to obey orders to keep their jobs, but in doing so they alienated the *shenliang*. No matter what the actual views of local officials might have been, the result of the Yu Dongchen Rebellion was a one-sided loss for the Sichuanese. Because of the rebellion, Sichuan had to pay one million taels of silver to the missionaries as indemnities.[149]

The consequences of the missionary cases were far-reaching. They were, for one thing, costly. For example, France obtained 943,597 taels for the Chengdu riot, while 1,186,100 taels (including interest) were paid as indemnities for the Yu Dongchen Rebellion alone, significant sums considering that provincial revenue was less than nine million taels that year. In 1900, indemnity payments related to missionary cases were equivalent to 13 percent of Sichuan's annual tax revenue.[150] It was obvious to the Sichuan elite that the Qing state could no longer protect them. The alliance between the elite and the state found itself on shaky ground. And a new affinity—one between the elite and the Gowned Brothers—was in the making.

Conclusion

Before the 1850s, the old regime functioned fairly well in Sichuan. The province thrived economically; the imperial administration was limited but effective, and with the help of the *shenliang*—the dominating elite in local society—it engaged in an easy relation with the loosely structured Sichuan society. In the mid-nineteenth century, especially during the Taiping Rebellion, the central government relied upon Sichuan for money, which elevated the province's importance within the empire. By relying heavily on the provinces, Sichuan included, the Qing succeeded in suppressing the Taipings.

The midcentury rebellions had been suppressed, but at a high cost: the dilution of the center's authority. At the top was an uneasy alliance between the court and powerful provincial leaders. Below that, control over tax collection had been lost to the elite; the privatization of public resources was rampant in every level of society. Still, despite their increased power, provincial officials and the local elite did not challenge the legitimacy of the old regime. Collaboration between officials and the elite continued, though an important new social force, the Gowned Brothers, had become powerful.

The missionary cases diminished the legitimacy of the center and changed the Sichuan elite's attitude toward the court. The push from the foreigners for more political and economic rights aggravated the already strained relationship between the central government and the Sichuan people, as provincial frustration and xenophobia produced confrontations undesired by Beijing, and large indemnities for foreign missionaries made it difficult for the province to pay imperial subsidies without yet more tax increases. Elites came to the realization that they could no longer rely upon the state for protection and the foundation of the old regime—the alliance between the state and the local elite—began to crumble. As the presence of foreign powers became ever more evident in the 1890s, the Gowned Brothers joined forces and challenged the Qing rulers. Throughout the 1890s, the old regime was increasingly unequal to its tasks. Although a drastic rethinking of the ideology of the old regime and an overhaul of its structure had not yet come about, it was only a matter of time. A new kind of transformation was on the horizon.

2 The Ideas of Revolution

EQUALITY, THE PEOPLE'S RIGHTS,
AND POPULAR SOVEREIGNTY

At the most turbulent moment of the 1911 Revolution, Acting Governor-General Zhao Erfeng of Sichuan expressed his astonishment and disbelief that the leaders who were rebelling against the Qing state were neither common rioters (*luanmin*) nor rebel bandits (*panzei*), but renowned members of the gentry (*shi*).[1] All were classically trained degree holders who had gained prestige and status from the Qing, and most had studied in Japan with the support of government funding. Rather than conforming to the conventional notion of a Confucian gentleman's role, that is, helping solve problems for the emperor, these gentry from Sichuan took a confrontational stand. Championing a new political discourse, they successfully instigated the revolution by arguing against the policy of nationalizing the Chuan-Han Railway Company and effectively mobilizing a large number of supporters.

One of these men, Deng Xiaoke, came from an influential industrialist family in Chongqing and was part of the first cohort of Sichuanese who had studied in Japan. In Tokyo, Deng became a disciple of Liang Qichao and a strong advocate of constitutionalism. After receiving his law degree from Hōsei University, Deng was appointed a secretary of the Ministry of Finance (Duzhibu zhushi).[2] Luo Lun, meanwhile, was a vice-chairman of the Sichuan Provincial Assembly and a leading figure in the Sichuan learned circles (*xuejie*). Born into a rich landowning family in Xichong county, Luo was respected for his knowledge of the Confucian classics and for earning his *juren* degree at a young age. A follower of Kang Youwei and Liang Qichao, Luo became a radical teacher in several new-style schools in Sichuan, where he introduced students to the anti-Manchu revolutionary newspaper *Minbao*, which openly promoted the idea of popular sovereignty.[3] No doubt even more upsetting to Zhao was Yan Kai, the son of longtime Zhao family friend Yan Jigu, who at age sixteen had attended the aristocratic South School (Nanxue)—affiliated with the Imperial Academy in Beijing—and at twenty-seven obtained his *jinshi* degree. After completing his studies at Tokyo Imperial University, Yan was given the privileged title of Hanlin academician and appointed the chief manager of the Chengdu branch of the Chuan-Han Railway Company, enjoying both political and economic prestige.[4] Zhang Lan from Nanchong county was a *xiucai* degree holder who received government sponsorship to study in Japan, where he became an admirer of Kang Youwei and Liang Qichao and petitioned for the drafting of a constitution in China.[5] Finally, there was Pu Dianjun, born into an esteemed family of Guang'an county that had produced degree holders for ten consecutive generations (see the Appendix).[6] A *xiucai* at twenty and a *juren* at twenty-nine, Pu was Sichuan's top-ranked scholar in the provincial exam (Figure 2.1). In 1905, Pu was sent by the court to study at Hōsei University after earning his *jinshi* degree. Upon returning, he was appointed a secretary of the Ministry of Law (Fabu zhushi) and an adjunct at the Institute for Constitution Compilation (Xianzheng bianchaguan xingzou). Highly regarded by his fellows, Pu was elected chairman of the Sichuan Provincial Assembly in 1909, at the age of thirty-four (Figure 2.2).[7]

Most of the aforementioned gentlemen belonged to families that had "received the kindness of the emperor for generations" (*shishou huang'en*). But by the end of the nineteenth century, the inadequacy of the old regime was felt by these "established literati."[8] They reflected deeply on the constitutional crisis in the old regime and explored new ways to tackle it. It was their ideological departure from the old, entrenched thinking and

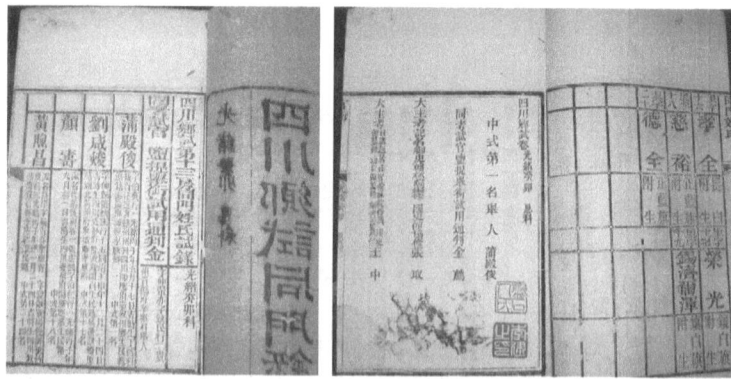

FIGURE 2.1. Pu Dianjun earning first place in the *juren* examination in Sichuan. *Guangxu Guimao enke Sichuan xiangshi tongmenlu* (List of *juren* degree holders from the 1903 provincial-level exam) (1903): 1.

FIGURE 2.2. Sichuan gentleman Pu Dianjun. *Wikipedia*.

their foregrounding of the new discourse of equality (*pingdeng*), rights (*quan, quanli, minquan,* and *guoquan*), and popular sovereignty (*minzhu, zhuquan zai guomin, guomin zhi zhuquan,* and *minquan*) that paved the way for the revolution to come.⁹

Constitutional Crisis in the Old Regime: Reflections of Wei Yuan and Feng Guifen

The old regime, as seen in Chapter 1, was an imperial system of government. At the top ruled the emperor, surrounded by relatives and councilors, and enjoying incomparable supremacy as the Son of Heaven. Despite the persistence of the Mencian "the people as the base" (*minben*) argument—meaning that the Son of Heaven must express the will of Heaven by preserving the material basis of the people's subsistence—an emperor's claims to power were neither invalidated by popular discontent nor legitimized by popular approbation. In the Chinese imperial system, the gentry were the ruling class, having always played the role of moral exemplars in a political culture that valorized hierarchical obedience. Alexander Williamson, an evangelist of the London Missionary Society, observed that gentry were the "soul and real rulers" of the Qing empire and "the key to influencing China and changing the discourse and action of the Chinese in general."[10] Naturally, it was also in their abandonment of the traditional mode of thinking that the old regime lost its most solid social foundation.

Philip Kuhn demonstrates how, before the arrival of Westerners in China, Chinese political activists of the nineteenth century were already dealing with questions of participation, competition, and control in the context of conditions inherited from the eighteenth century. A culmination of trends of crisis in the 1790s led the Qing empire toward disaster, with leadership at the center the weakest it had ever been and factionalism prevailing at the court. Corruption in county governments was rampant and "the misdeeds of county magistrates [were] a hundred times worse than ten or twenty years ago."[11] Despite migration and land clearance, the land-to-population ratio had sunk precariously low, and with overcrowding came environmental troubles. Compounding the miseries of land shortage was mismanagement by money-hungry officials. Together, these trends constituted a long-term change that led some elites to recognize that "constitutional" issues were at stake.

Imperial power in Qing China, as Benjamin Elman observes, was rarely "naked"—that is, political power in the empire was filtered through Confucian moral and political philosophy into institutional and symbolic systems, and political language drawn from the classics represented the ideological voice of the late imperial state. Elman reveals in his study of Changzhou New Text Confucianism that when the normative institutions of late imperial Chinese political culture failed to communicate morally compelling ideals, alternative expressions emerged to challenge the public legitimacy of the Qing state. By 1800, institutions of the past, whether defending Han or Song learning, were undergoing a crisis of confidence, and a pivotal event was the turn to Gongyang Confucianism, which emphasized an esoteric reading of the classics as an implicit guide for reform. Beginning with Zhuang Cunyu and Liu Fenglu, New Text Confucians appealed to a reformist reconstruction of the past to authorize the present and to prepare for the future, and Confucius reemerged as a voice for voluntarism and statecraft. Even though these Changzhou scholars had not yet formulated a concept of political revolution or developed a full understanding of social progress, their notions of historical change and their advocacy of practical institutional reform were important stepping-stones to the later reformers' New Text vision of political transformation.[12]

Wei Yuan (1794–1856), a New Text scholar and student of Liu Fenglu, and arguably the most talented thinker of his time, believed that the best means of tackling the political crisis of the old regime—that is, the decline of a polity that was increasingly unequal to its tasks—lay in literati activism. His commentary on the classic *Book of Odes* proposed moving literati from apathy to public commitment and from silence to expression of opinion.[13] Yet, at the same time, Wei wanted a more powerful and dynamic central state, one that could deal more effectively with domestic and foreign troubles. For Wei, it was the time not for weakening authoritarian rule, but for strengthening it.[14]

By the time Wei Yuan was five years in his grave, China had become a client state of the Western powers. Of the generation of 1860s political activists, Feng Guifen (1809–1874) was the most influential. Feng not only gave concrete form to what Wei discussed only in theoretical terms, but also adapted Western political ideas to the issues of the old agenda.[15] Kuhn's analyses of two essays from *Essays of Protest* by Feng Guifen— one advocating broadening political participation and the other proposing better and denser political control in the villages—yield insights into how political activists in the 1860s tackled the constitutional problems of the old regime. In the first essay analyzed by Kuhn, "Making the Evaluation of Officials a Public Process" (Gong chuzhi yi), Feng criticized the existing practice of selecting officials, which relied on the judgment of a small body of high officials who made their selections from among those who had qualified through written exams. He proposed instead that high posts be subject to nomination by the bureaucracy at large and that the group with the power to nominate local officials be expanded to include first-degree holders and village elders.[16] In the second essay, "On Restoring the System of Local Headmen" (Fu xiangzhi yi), Feng proposed a new kind of middleman chosen by villagers through paper ballots by groups of one hundred and one thousand households.[17] He believed that the pressures of China's overcrowded village society required something better than the existing system of informal delegation of power to local bosses, and his solution was to use local men whom the populace would trust because they had chosen them.[18]

At heart, Feng's proposals aimed at making central officials responsible to the bureaucracy at large and local officials responsible to the elite of their communities. As Kuhn puts it, Feng "was no liberal," nor "do his writings reveal any intimation of popular sovereignty or popular rights"; his position was close to that of his intellectual forebear Wei Yuan, who believed that the public interest was more widely internalized among the elite than conventional wisdom assumed.[19] Meanwhile, although Feng acknowledged no foreign source for his proposals, they bore the influence of Western ideas: no idea was less congenial to the Chinese system than that of "equally weighing votes," and it was precisely this notion that spawned the privileged Chinese bureaucrats' great antagonism toward Feng's proposals.[20]

During the Hundred Days' Reform in 1898, a quarter century after Feng's death, the reformist Guangxu emperor circulated the *Essays of Protest* to government officials in Beijing and demanded comments. The responses revolved around two points: first, the necessity for a rigid demarcation between officials and nonofficials, and second, the fear that a quasi-official elite would arrogate power to themselves and neglect the public interest.[21] Kuhn believes that these responses reveal the inner core of Chinese authoritarianism. These officials, who thought public virtues were not adequately internalized to permit people to pursue their private interests unchecked, believed that "only regular bureaucracy can prevent the elite from pursuing their private interests," "only the upper layers of the ruling group can attain the kind of objectivity needed to keep the bureaucracy as a whole from pursuing private interests," and "only the emperor can ensure that the system as a whole is directed toward the public interest." There was no faith in the commoners: "The disposition of the people is not that of antiquity."[22]

Presenting a contrast is James Madison's far more optimistic assessment of commoners' civic nature from the early years of America.[23] The essential question addressed by the *Federalist Papers*, as Kuhn states, is how to reconcile the public interest with a multiplicity of private interests. Madison's answer was to resort to men who were better suited than their compatriots to discern the public interest, and who, by virtue of their election as representatives, "may best discern the true interest of their country," and whose "patriotism and love of justice will be least likely to sacrifice it to temporary or partial considerations." Importantly, Madison's representative principle rested on the premise that civic virtue, though specifically concentrated in men of character and wisdom, was widespread among the populace, though in a less-refined form. Republicanism depended on it: without virtue in the people, good government is inconceivable. In Madison's eyes, the disposition of the people was, in its civic sense, equal to "that of antiquity."[24]

Madison's sense of the public interest differed from the mandarin one. The pessimism of Feng's critics was such that, in their minds, the inability of commoners to choose the right leaders precluded the possibility of effective representation. Without civic virtue, villagers and low-level bureaucrats alike would easily be deceived by the wiles of ambitious villains. Lacking alternatives, authoritarian leadership by regular bureaucrats seemed to be the only reasonable solution.[25] Thus, it was not until the next generation that Chinese thinkers openly embraced the prospect of representative government.

Western Influences and Kang Youwei: "The Axiom of Humanity" Is Equality

As Chinese literati combed the Confucian classics for a solution to the contemporary political crisis, Western ideas also came to China and helped shape the ways people thought and made sense of their world. How did the Chinese, who had long regarded their culture as superior, come to terms with the reality of a world dominated by Western powers? The crisis of confidence extended from imperial institutions to the very Confucian values that scholars and their ancestors had served, and out of this crisis came the most influential thinker of the 1890s, Kang Youwei. In the early 1890s, Kang, who had already attracted some attention for his interest in reform, burst upon the intellectual scene in China with a call for radical institutional transformation and dominated the attention of Chinese literati for the whole decade.

Broadly speaking, Western ideas came to China through three channels: missionary publications, translated books published in Shanghai, and writings of Chinese who had been to the West. Kang Youwei himself had been immersed in Western thinking through exposure to all of these channels. In his writings, Kang left numerous traces of how Western concepts shaped his reform agenda.[26] Missionary newspapers played an essential role in the introduction of certain key political concepts to the Chinese. Ever since the first Chinese-language missionary press, *China Monthly Magazine* (*Cha shisu meiyue tongji zhuan*), published from 1815 to 1821, missionaries had regarded Chinese literati as their chief potential readers. Managed by Robert Morrison and William Miline of the London Missionary Society and printed in Malacca, this newspaper was sent to Guangdong province and distributed free of charge to examinees at the county, prefectural, and provincial examinations.[27] In 1846, following the defeat of the Qing in the Opium War, the Daoguang emperor lifted the sanction against Catholicism in China, and the sanction against Protestantism was lifted too. Following this policy change, a great number of missionaries came to China. The newly arrived missionaries quickly realized they had to rely upon written media to overcome the language (dialect) barriers to proselytizing in China. To attract more readers, they downplayed the importance of Christian teachings in their publications and included more information on Western science and politics. From 1850 to 1890, there were approximately seventy-six newspapers in China, of which 60 percent were missionary newspapers.[28]

Among them, the *Globe Magazine* (*Wanguo gongbao*), published from 1868 to 1907, was the longest lasting and arguably the most influential Chinese missionary journal of the nineteenth century. Having evolved from a Christian newspaper, in 1874 *Wanguo gongbao* was transformed by its creator, John Young Allen, into a general journal that aimed to "expand information on geography, history, civilization, politics, religion, science, art, industry, and other advanced knowledge of Western nations."[29] In 1875, Allen authored an influential article in *Wanguo gongbao*, introducing the ideas of natural rights, equality, democracy, and constitutionalism to his Chinese readers:

> Of all the organizing political principles in the Western nations, the most important of all is that the power to govern (*zhiguo zhiquan*) is of the people (*shu zhi yu min*), by the people (*chu zhi yu min*), and for the people (*wei minjian suo she ye*). The rationale for such a political principle is that [the rulers and the ruled] are equal to one another as they are both human beings. If we look at Heaven and Earth, we see all people receive warmth from the same sun, breeze from the same wind, and moisture from the same rain. All people need clothes when they feel cold and food when they feel hungry. Their desires for warmth and sustenance are the same, despite their social status, high or low. If we look at their ears, eyes, hands, and feet, we see that monarchs and ministers have the same number as humble people. Thus, we realize that the law of a state (*zhiguo zhi fa*) should come from the people and not from one ruler. Even though we sometimes need to concentrate the people's power (*quan*) in one person and make him the ruler, this ruler must be publicly elected, and so must officials assisting him. The way to assure that this one ruler, who has gathered all the people's power to govern, will be beneficial to commoners rather than detrimental, is to have a constitution (*zhangcheng*).[30]

These ideas, based on the principle of equality, were fundamentally at odds with existing Chinese values. By pointing to democracy as the most important political principle of the Western nations and laying out the moral underpinning of that principle, namely, the equality of all human beings, Allen noted that the power of the people to rule is a right, self-evident and inalienable. Furthermore, Allen argued, the equality of all should serve as the guiding principle for determining how a polity is constituted. The right to govern lies with and is conferred by the people. In this article, Allen also introduced the concrete form of a democratic governmental system to the Chinese. He elucidated the function of the constitution, explained the workings of the three separate branches of government—the executive (*xingquan*), the judicial (*zhanglü*), and the legislative (*yifa*)—and emphasized the supremacy of the legislative branch, noting that in the U.S. Congress, "all representatives [in the house] must be both directly and publicly elected by the common people."[31]

Wanguo gongbao was filled with articles like this. Meanwhile, in 1887, Alexander Williamson established the Chinese Book and Tract Society (Tongwen shuhui) in Shanghai, which later became the prominent Society for the Diffusion of Christian and General Knowledge among the Chinese (Guangxuehui). The energetic Timothy Richard soon took charge of Tongwen shuhui. To better understand his potential audience, he conducted a survey and published the following results:

The population of chief civic officials above the county level is 2,289, of military officers above the battalion level is 1,987, of academic officials above the prefectural level is 1,760, of teachers at various academies is 2,000, and of high-level adjuncts in provincial capitals is 2,000. If we add to this the 5 percent of all 600,000 literati above the *xiucai* level, which comes to 30,000 and the 4,000 family members of all the above elite households, we have our target audience of 44,036 men and women, readers we should work hard to influence.[32]

Richard then declared that he would focus on transforming the hearts of these 44,036 Chinese first, as they would then transform all of China. In 1889, Tongwen shuhui took over *Wanguo gongbao* and expanded the writing team from John Young Allen alone to include Richard and other talents, such as Alexander Williamson, Gilbert Reid, and W. A. P. Martin.[33]

The newly energized *Wanguo gongbao* continued spreading Western knowledge to Chinese, and it was via *Wanguo gongbao* that many members of the Chinese literati learned about the structure and mechanism of a representative government and the notions of democracy, egalitarianism, and constitutionalism. *Wanguo gongbao* also offered specific analyses and suggestions for solving China's political problems. Another article by Allen, for example, pointed out the two major dilemmas of the old regime: first, China's provinces were huge centrifugal forces despite their seeming obedience to the court in Beijing; and second, commoners in China had no power, whereas officials were all-powerful and overbearing. To solve these dilemmas, Allen proposed to establish a system of "the rule of law," that is, a government of constitutionalism: "From the king and the queen to all the commoners, everyone should be under the law and obey the law. The life and property of the common people are to be preserved by the law. All people under the law should be equal."[34]

Wanguo gongbao soon became a favorite paper of progressive-minded Chinese literati. In addition to sending the journal to examinees at various levels of the civil service examination, the editors also launched essay competitions with prizes to attract readers. In 1894, for example, an essay competition with five given subjects was launched simultaneously in Zhili, Guangdong, Zhejiang, Jiangsu, and Fujian provinces. Six classes of awards were set up, and 172 people participated. Kang Youwei, a longtime and fervent reader of *Wanguo gongbao*, took part in the essay competition and won a class-six award. By the end of 1896, circulation of the journal had grown from one thousand to four thousand copies a month, with the majority of readers being "famous officials, esteemed gentry, and important merchants."[35]

Wanguo gongbao was also a major catalyst for the development of Chinese constitutionalist thinking. In Kang's second memorial to the Guangxu emperor, known as the "ten-thousand-word letter" and published in Shanghai by the literatus Shen Shandeng (1830–1902) in the summer of 1895, the proposals—to "reform the currency system, build railways, manufacture machines and steamships, open mines, stabilize silver prices, and build a postal system" in order to enrich the state (*fuguo*); to "reform agriculture, develop industry, offer better conditions for commerce, and develop a welfare system for the poor" in order to nurture the people (*yangmin*); and to "establish schools and newspapers" in order to educate the people (*jiaomin*)—were taken almost directly from *Wanguo gongbao*.[36] After reading it, Richard was shocked; he wrote, "I am completely surprised. The memorial has summarized all my arguments. It is like a small compass to my political theories!"[37] In 1894, Tan Sitong, another famous reformer, had explicitly quoted Richard's political ideas as a means of changing China.[38] And Liang Qichao, in his influential essay "General Arguments for Reform," took Allen's exact wording when emphasizing the importance of education in his reform. In 1896, when compiling a reading list for Chinese students, Liang listed *Wanguo gongbao* as one of the "best Western books."[39]

Besides missionary newspapers, the second kind of influential publications consisted of books published by the translation office of the Jiangnan Arsenal. For example, *Compilations of Recent Developments in the West* (*Xiguo jinshi huibian*), a quarterly translation of excerpts from major European, American, and Japanese newspapers, which collated accounts of major events in the West, was published by the translation office between 1873 and 1899. The *Compilations* deeply influenced the thinking of Kang Youwei and was regarded by Liang Qichao as a "must-read" for people interested in current affairs.[40] Another key book produced by the office was the Chinese edition of William Chamber's *Homely Words to Aid Governance* (*Zuozhi chuyan*), translated by John Fryer in 1885. This book systematically introduced Western concepts of liberty, equality, and democracy to its Chinese readers, leaving a deep impression on Chinese intellectuals, including Kang, Liang, and Zhang Taiyan.[41] Consistently over a period of forty years (1868–1909), the translation office published 196 books, systematically introducing and spreading to the Chinese knowledge about Western science, technology, history, and legal and political systems.[42]

A third major source of inspiration for Kang and other political activists was the writing of Chinese who had been to the West. Wang Tao, one of the most important among them, launched the influential Chinese-owned newspaper *The Globe* (*Xunhuan ribao*) in Hong Kong in 1874. Drawing on firsthand knowledge of the West from his stay in Britain from 1867 to 1870, Wang attributed the wealth and power of the European nations not to their advanced weapons but to their political systems. Between 1874 and 1884, upon his return to Hong Kong, Wang published a large number of political commentaries urging the court to reform its political system. Notably, Wang departed from the earlier reform thinkers (Feng Guifen, for example) in his explicit criticism of the autocratic monarchy:

Before the Three Dynasties [Xia, Shang, and Zhou, in ancient times], the monarch and the people were close to each other and the state ran well. After the Three Dynasties, the monarch and the people separated from each other and politics became worse every day. After the Qin dynasty, the monarch was exalted and the people were ever more debased. The monarch became aloof and unreachable, and the opinions of the people were cut off from the ruler. Being so far away from the monarch, how could the people express their grievances to him? Even if the people were leading miserable lives, the monarch would not know a thing about it. Even if the people shouted aloud, the monarch would not hear a sound from them.[43]

Wang argued that the real source of China's weakness was its political system—the autocratic monarchy. The end result of continuing autocracy would be the loss of the people's hearts, in which case no one would contribute to the country and there would be no wealth or power. Wang advocated the abandonment of autocratic monarchy and the promotion of democracy as the means for China to achieve wealth and power. Besides Wang Tao, Guo Songtao, the first Chinese diplomat to live in Europe for an extended period of time, wrote *London and Paris Diaries* (*Lundun yu Bali riji*), which had a lasting impact on the political debate among Chinese intellectuals after being published in 1879. Guo described the democratic systems of government and the various forms of elections in the West, using the term "the rule of the people" (*minzhu*) in opposition to "the rule of the monarch" (*junzhu*), and the term "the power of the people" (*minquan*) in opposition to "the power of the monarch" (*junquan*).[44]

It was under these Western influences that Kang began to formulate his reform ideas. Having read about equality, the people's right to rule, and democracy, and having learned the critique of autocratic monarchy, he was ready to depart from the old mode of thinking—authoritarianism and the disbelief in ordinary men's public virtues—that had precluded democratic government as a political option for China. Kang reflected in his autobiography:

Since that time [meeting with the erudite scholar Zhang Dinghua in 1879], I abandoned the study of textual criticism and study for the examinations; I focused on nurturing the heart.... I considered saving the world as my calling. I obtained and studied the *Compilations of Recent Developments in the West*, the *New Records of Traveling the Globe*, and other Western books.... I also went to Hong Kong that year and was impressed by the orderliness of the city..., which made me see that Westerners had effective laws to rule their countries. All of these inspired my pursuit of Western knowledge.⁴⁵

Kang had come from a Neo-Confucian family background, and both his great-grandfather and his grandfather were students of the Cheng-Zhu School. In his youth, Kang had been influenced by his teacher Zhu Ziqi, a leading figure in late Qing eclectic studies that advocated the merger of Han and Song learnings with an emphasis on moral cultivation and practical statecraft. However, Kang quickly became attracted to Lu-Wang Confucianism, which freed him from feeling overburdened by traditional textual study, and to Buddhism, which enabled him to find an acceptance of this world and awakened him to the realization that his life's purpose was "to set in order all under Heaven."⁴⁶

Throughout the 1880s, Kang systematically studied Western ideas. He traveled to Shanghai several times and bought books on Western learning, "devoting himself to studying Western books" (*dagong xishu*). After several years of study, in 1884 Kang arrived at the idea that "all things in the world are equal" (*daxiao qitong*) and then in 1885 went on to write the *Axioms of Humanity* (*Renlei gongli*).⁴⁷ Though this book has been lost, it is possible to reconstruct Kang's early ideas from other works he wrote around this time. In his *Complete Book of True Principles and Public Laws* (*Shili gongfa quanshu*), he characterized equality as the "most beneficial public law" for humanity. "Equality among humanity" (*renlei pingdeng*), argued Kang, was the axiom.⁴⁸ Judging both from this work and another, *Esoteric and Exoteric Essays of Master Kang* (*Kangzi neiwai pian*), it is evident that equality was a central idea for Kang at this stage.

The organizing principle of the Chinese monarchy, however, was the opposite of this axiom. The practice of the Chinese imperial system was, according to Kang, "to exalt the emperor and dishonor the minister, to elevate the men and debase the women, and to uplift the masters and degrade the slaves." He viewed the result as disastrous, noting that the ministers, frightened by the hegemony of the monarch, dared not speak, and that women were held back from studying and were consequently foolish. Yet all of these manifest inequalities were considered "the norm." Such a phenomenon was "not a result of following the axiom but of allowing things to happen by default."⁴⁹ Kang strove to live in a world of equality, "where men and women are equal to each other, the monarch is not autocratic, the minister is not debased, and the emperor and the minister weigh the same," a natural corollary being that the current Chinese political system should be overturned, with equality as the basis for establishing political institutions and drafting laws.

Kang's rare talent as a constitutional thinker lay in his ability to discern the social, cultural, and historical contexts in which political systems existed. Comparing China and the West, he noted that the differences between them lay both in historical context and in political values. For example, because China was "a unified country with a vast territory," to ensure that one emperor could control and maintain order in this huge domain, the cardinal principle (*yili*) for Chinese rulers was to establish the hierarchical three cardinal guides (*gang*, ruler guides subject, father guides son, and husband guides wife). In contrast, European countries had small domains and constantly competed with one another; therefore, to ensure that they would not lose in these competitions, the principle there was for European monarchs to treat their people as equals so that the energy of the people would be directed at helping their country outcompete others. In this way, Kang demonstrated that the differences between China and the West were not simply the result of different political cultures but also the result of different underlying social and historical realities.[50]

If throughout the 1880s Kang had been much preoccupied by the concept of equality, which built on an abstract "axiom of humanity," by the late 1890s he had produced a synthesis of his political and philosophical position and was able to enrich the concept of equality with Confucian conceptual resources. For example, appropriating Confucian elements to express his reformist ideas, the term "great unity" (*datong*) came to be used. For Kang, the concept of great unity, which appears in the classic *Book of Rites,* came to mean a new egalitarian utopia in which all social divisions and hierarchies would be erased.

In 1891, drawing upon Liao Ping's *On the New Text and Ancient Text Learning* (*Jin gu xue kao*), Kang Youwei published *An Inquiry into the Classics Forged During the Xin Period* (*Xinxue weijing kao*), which argued that the Old Text classics were forged by Liu Xin, who lived toward the end of the Former Han dynasty and provided the ideological underpinnings for Wang Mang's usurpation of the Han throne. The authentic Han learning, Kang asserted, should be sought in the New Text school that had prevailed in the Former Han dynasty. With these arguments, Kang attempted to pull the rug out from under the Old Text versions of the classics and thereby establish the New Text versions as the genuine repository of Confucius's teachings.[51]

In 1897, Kang took the next step, showing that the central ideal of the New Text school was practical statecraft and that Confucianism was oriented toward institutional reform rather than toward the preservation of ancient doctrines and institutions. Once again drawing on the work of Liao, Kang published *Confucius as Reformer* (*Kongzi gaizhi kao*), which held that Confucius composed the Six Classics with the purpose of setting forth for posterity his ideas on institutional reform. In Kang's view, Confucius was an "uncrowned king," who had designed a set of new institutions in the Six Classics as directions for the future. To portray Confucius as a forward-looking king who viewed history as linear progress toward an ideal future, Kang drew upon another ideal of the Gongyang tradition, the doctrine of three ages, which contained an embryonic concept of historical progress. Human history, Kang believed, passes from the Age of Disorder (*juluan shi*), through the Age of Approaching Peace (*shengping shi*), toward the final Age of Universal Peace (*taiping shi*). Each of the three ages has its appropriate political system: the rule of multiple kings (*duojun wei zheng*) for the Age of Disorder; monarchy (*yijun wei zheng*) for the Age of Approaching Peace; and democracy (*min wei zheng*) for the Age of Universal Peace. Through this reading of the Gongyang doctrine, Kang claimed that the ideal of practical statesmanship lay at the core of Confucianism and required institutional reform for its realization.[52]

Provocatively, *Confucius as Reformer* presented readers with a fresh approach to reading the classics. Kang encouraged them to be innovative and to "reveal the profound principles" that were *not* explicit in the text. The classics thus became a guide for reform: the goal was not preserving the Confucian system but political action.[53] It was also in this sense that the thought of Kang (*Kangxue*) most effectively undermined Confucianism, as it did so from within. Kang Youwei clearly had liberated many young Chinese intellectuals by setting them free from a dogmatic reading of the classics. In 1897, Liang Qichao replicated Kang's teaching style at the Shiwu Academy in Hunan province, where he successfully molded the minds of many future political activists.[54]

For many young Chinese students at the time, it was Kang's idea of *datong*—which was now imbued with a new sense of *pingdeng*—that was the most refreshing and groundbreaking. Kang's *Complete Book of True Principles and Public Laws* was written around 1891, when Liang Qichao first began studying with him. Liang described the "ecstasy" he felt when he first learned about the idea of *datong*: "I was intensely determined to disseminate this idea broadly. Even though Kang Youwei felt that the moment had not yet arrived, I could not help it."[55] Throughout Liang's career, he often favorably mentioned the idea of *datong* and considered it Kang's most important contribution to the Chinese intellectual world.

From Monarch's Power to People's Power, from Rule of the Monarch to Rule of the People (1895–1898)

The year 1895 was a turning point in Chinese constitutional history. In the spring of 1895, Chinese literati gave voice to their fury over the humiliating peace treaty just signed with Japan following China's defeat in the Sino-Japanese War, in the form of a "petition" submitted to the Censorate (Duchayuan) by candidates for the metropolitan examination. The famous Republican-era scholar Chen Yinke, grandson of the late Qing reformist official Chen Baozhen, offered an insightful observation of the different elite actors who precipitated the Hundred Days' Reform in 1898: there were reform-minded officials like Guo Songtao and Chen Baozhen, who aimed to borrow Western law to change the Chinese institutions, and there was Kang Youwei, who used the Gongyang interpretation of Confucianism to bring about political change. Historian Mao Haijian meticulously calculates that in 1895, organized by high-level officials, as many as thirty-one petitions protesting the peace treaty signed by 1,555 candidates had been sent to (and reached) the emperor. Kang Youwei's own petition, which claimed to be signed by 1,200 *juren* candidates from eighteen provinces, was in fact never submitted.[56]

Yet still, in this petition, the so-called ten-thousand-word letter that was later published in Shanghai, Kang argued that the solution to changing China's situation was to make systematic reforms (*bianfa*). Among the reforms he suggested, the most radical was to let the gentry and the general populace elect representatives (*shimin gongju*) to serve in Beijing as "court gentlemen for consultation" (*yilang*, a Han-dynasty term), who would offer criticism of imperial commands and serve as spokesmen for the people:[57]

> Above, they are to broaden His Majesty's sage-like understanding, so that he can sit in one hall and know the four seas. Below, they are to bring together the minds and wills of the empire, so that all can share cares and pleasures, forgetting the distinction between public and private. . . . Sovereign and people will be of one body, and China will be as one family. . . . With 400 million minds as one mind, how could the empire not be stronger?[58]

Here, Kang proposed that all the people of the nation should come together in force. Philip Kuhn reads Kang's vision of the nation as possessing a radical leveling effect, making nationhood the common property of all Chinese, of high station or low.[59] Furthermore, Kang proposed that the way to energize the people to strengthen the nation was to have a constitution: "A constitution, once enacted, binds the rulers and all others alike. The ruler's person is inviolable, as administrative responsibilities are shouldered by the government. In this way the sovereign and the people are welded together into one body politic. How can the nation not be strong?"⁶⁰

The government had its source of power in the people. This idea, after the war with Japan, became increasingly popular. In March 1895, for example, the great translator and scholar Yan Fu published his most scathing article, "In Refutation of Han Yu" (Pi han). Vehemently attacking the system of monarchy, Yan quoted Western political philosophers and wrote that in those powerful nations the people are "the true masters of the state," the state is "the public property of the people," and the monarchs and ministers are simply "the servants of the state." In China, however, the power of the state had long been "stolen" by the emperors, beginning in the Qin dynasty. Autocracy had "destroyed the talents of the people, dispersed their power, and diluted their virtue." Thus, to restore to the people, the true masters of the state, "their naturally conferred freedom," the rule of the absolute monarch had to be overthrown.⁶¹

Developed by the *Kangxue* scholars such as Kang Youwei and Liang Qichao and other reformist thinkers influenced by Western learning (*Xixue*), such as Guo Songtao and Yan Fu, the "new learning" (*xinxue*), which focused on political change, thrived between 1895 and 1898.⁶² China's reform activists began propagating their ideas about the rule of the people (*minzhu*) and the power of the people (*minquan*) through the press, urging other educated elite to join their cause of restructuring the political system. The most influential among these reform newspapers was *Chinese Progress* (*Shiwu bao*), led by the exceptionally talented writer Liang Qichao. In 1896, with much emotion and power, Liang wrote his famous "General Arguments for Reform" (Bianfa tongyi) for *Chinese Progress*: "We now have a huge mansion that has existed for over a thousand years. Its tiles have been ruined; its pillars have collapsed. It is not that the mansion is not big enough. Yet, if a thunderstorm comes suddenly, the mansion will surely be totaled and break down."⁶³ After thirty years of the Self-Strengthening movement, which aimed at saving China via military and industrial modernization, Chinese intellectuals finally believed that it was the political system that made the most significant difference between defeat and victory.

It was Liang Qichao who most eloquently expressed the idea of *minquan*—which most often meant "the power of the people" at this stage of development but occasionally meant "the people's rights"—as necessary to the strengthening of the nation. Liang blamed monarchical despotism for China's peril:

Ever since the Three Dynasties, the power of the monarch (*junquan*) has been exalted and the power of the people (*minquan*) increasingly reduced. This was the origin of China's weakness. The people who committed the biggest crimes were the first emperor of the Qin dynasty, the first emperor of the Yuan dynasty, and the first emperor of the Ming dynasty.[64]

Just like in this article, Liang also juxtaposed the people (*min*) to the emperor (*jun*) in his other articles, as in this comment: "There are histories of monarchs, histories of countries, and histories of the people. Histories of the people flourished only in the West, while in the Middle Kingdom, such history hardly existed at all."[65] And, a more direct critique of Chinese imperial ideology is his lament that, in Chinese history, all institutions existed "to preserve the one household of the monarch, rather than to preserve the people under Heaven."[66]

Following Kang's strategy of treating Confucius as a reformer, Liang's early *minquan* discourse (from 1895 to June 1898) often employed Confucian tropes with frequent allusions to the classics. For example, Liang wrote, "Studies of the great unity in the Spring and Autumn Period were all about the people's power (*minquan*)," and "The rule of benevolence was to serve the people. The political practice of Western nations of today is similar [to benevolent rule]."[67] However, Liang's idea of *minquan* was innovative.[68] When Liang Qichao, Ou Qujia, Tang Caichang, and other radical reformers were hired as teachers at the Shiwu Academy (Shiwu xuetang, or Academy of Current Affairs), established in October 1897 in Changsha, the capital of Hunan province, they ever more aggressively disseminated the idea of *minquan*. In Changsha, where new journals (*Xiangxuebao* and *Xiangbao*) and an influential new study society (Nanxue hui) were established, in addition to the increasingly popular idea of people's power (*minquan*), the idea of equality (*pingdeng*) also loomed large. In journal articles, classrooms, and meetings of the study society, Liang and his colleagues relentlessly propagated *minquan* and *pingdeng*. Fan Zhui advocated that for China to survive, the ruler had to "abandon his private interest" and implement the principle that "all people are equal" (*renren pingdeng*) and "all powers are equal" (*quanquan pingdeng*).[69] Setting forth a primitive sense of the concept of natural rights, He Laibao asserted that "the rights of the people" (*minquan*) were self-evident and inalienable, for "they do not require others to give them to me, to supervise me or urge me."[70] Bi Yongnian believed that all people were created equal (*pingdeng*), because "all people are receiving the same energy from Heaven and Earth" and "all people have their self-determining right to exist in this world." For Bi, the right to self-determination belonged to commoners and to kings, royalty, and ministers alike, and the state was owned by commoners and kings, royalty, and ministers alike.[71]

Conservatives condemned the ideas of Liang and his comrades as "an equalization of power between the emperor and the people." In a letter campaigning for the closing of the Shiwu Academy, Bao Fengyang and seven other Hunan conservatives wrote:

Nowadays, Kang Youwei and Liang Qichao confuse the world by promoting the ideas of the people's power (*minquan*) and equality (*pingdeng*). Our question is: If power were channeled downward, then who would rule the state? If the people are all self-determining (*zizhu*), then what should the monarch do? In that sense, the earth under Heaven would be in great chaos. These teachings about equality (*pingdeng zhishuo*) are an abandonment of the principles of ethics (*mieqi renlun*) and are most abhorrent.[72]

The letter argued for closing the Shiwu Academy because while it had been "originally established [to prepare quality candidates] to help with the urgent situation," it had become a place for "teaching people about equality and giving the people political power."[73] Even more subversively, it had become a force advocating "collective rule by the monarch and the people together" (*junmin gongzhu*).[74] The teaching of *minquan* had promoted a sense of equality that deeply threatened those hoping to reinforce monarchical rule and traditional social hierarchies.

Mighty official and scholar Zhang Zhidong shared a similar antagonism toward *minquan*. Zhang was recorded as saying in 1897: "Kang and his like talk about Confucius being a reformer. Though claiming to revere Confucius, what they really are doing is defaming the saint. Equality (*pingdeng*) and equal power for all (*pingquan*), these two cannot be allowed even in ten thousand years!"[75] Even if Zhang supported the acquisition of Western knowledge—study abroad by Chinese students, translation of Western and Japanese books, and acquisition of information from foreign newspapers—in *Exhortation to Learning* (*Quanxuepian*) he harshly criticized the teaching about *minquan*, claiming that it was directly opposed to the cardinal guide between the ruler and the subject.[76]

In June 1898, the Guangxu emperor launched the Hundred Days' Reform and announced decrees enacting many of Kang's reform proposals. The conservatives at court quickly staged a coup. Although Kang and Liang were exiled to Japan in September 1898, equality and the people's power as concepts were spreading among the literati elite in China. Perhaps because their teachings "were easy, and graduation [from the Shiwu Academy] not difficult," or because "they used the façade of great unity to capture people's attention," the influence of Kang and Liang was such that "at the top, they had supporters, and from the bottom, they had followers."[77] The legacy of the Hundred Days' Reform was momentous.[78] The suppression of the reform shook China's educated class and set a large number of them against the Qing.[79] But more important, *minquan* emerged in the political discourse of China. Even though at that moment the idea of "rights" had not yet been articulated, *minquan*—as well as its implication that the people should have some participatory role in the polity—became a motto in Chinese politics. More members of the elite began to agree that broader political participation was vital to save China from foreign imperialists, and they aspired to voice their opinions on politics.

The Coming of the Discourse: Minquan *as the People's Rights and the Advent of Constitutionalism*

SETTING UP THE PRINCIPLES: RIGHTS, LIBERTY,
POPULAR SOVEREIGNTY, AND THE RELATIONSHIP
BETWEEN THE NATION AND ITS PEOPLE
(OCTOBER 1898–FEBRUARY 1903)

In 1898 the exiled Liang Qichao settled in Japan, where he revived his career as a political theorist. The intellectual environment in Japan was extremely exciting. A wider range of books, journals, and pamphlets propagating Western political theories and the Japanese concepts of freedom (*jiyū*) and the people's rights (*minken*) were published among Chinese student circles, with the number peaking in 1903.[80] Some of Liang's most emotion-laden and influential essays were produced during the period 1898–1903, before the debate between reformers and revolutionaries that began in 1905. In fact, conventional historiography's portrayal of the intellectual scene in Tokyo as a competition between reform and revolution—represented by the extended antagonistic debate between constitutionalists and revolutionaries—does not do justice to the complex intellectual environment there before that debate. It was during the period from 1898 to 1903 that key concepts such as liberty, rights, nation, and popular sovereignty were widely debated, generating new ideas about how public affairs should be managed.

Discussions during this period focused not on the means of political transformation (the chief divergence between reformers and revolutionaries), but on the organizing principles of a new national entity called "China." Not surprisingly, Liang Qichao was the intellectual center of the movement in Tokyo, where he systematically read Western political theory that had been translated into Japanese. From 1898 to 1903, he wrote some of his most radical essays, most of which were published in the newspaper *China Discussion* (*Qingyibao*) (1898–1901) and in the *New People's Journal* (*Xinmin congbao*) (1902–1907). Essays in these early years defined key terms such as nation (*guo*), state (*guojia*), and citizens (*min*), and elaborated the relationship among them. Rather than indiscriminately introducing new ideas to his Chinese readers, Liang persistently focused on a single imperative as his guide when choosing theories and authors to study and write about, that is, the need to save China. Moreover, Liang did not simply copy Western and Japanese concepts; he redefined and creatively applied them in building his own theoretical framework. Even though Liang would in later years change his mind multiple times, there was still a remarkable consistency in his thinking. At the core of his early writings was a discourse about rights (*quan, quanli*)—national rights (*guoquan*) and citizens' rights (*minquan*)—and a debate about where sovereignty (*zhuquan*) should be located. These early writings had long-lasting effects, inspiring future leaders in the 1911 Revolution to formulate their political vision and leaving a significant political and cultural legacy that has lasted through the entirety of the modern period in China.

China Discussion was the first major journalistic platform for Liang Qichao after he arrived in Japan. As he later recalled in 1901, the primary focus of *China Discussion* was the promotion of the people's rights (*minquan*).[81] Liang's writing for the journal reflected the most radical phase of his thinking, as he had just escaped China after the traumatic aftermath of his failed reform. It was also then that Liang extensively talked about revolution and proposed collaborating with the famed anti-Manchu revolutionary leader, Sun Yat-sen. Liang's ideas were also shaped by his immediate intellectual environment, Japan. At this time in Japan, freedom (*jiyū*) and the people's rights (*minken*) came to be central to the political demands made by Japanese intellectuals, who molded Liang's definition of *minquan*.[82] In 1899, Liang published "An Outsider's Words of Warning" (Caomao weiyan) for a collection of essays entitled *Treatise on Liberty* (*Ziyou shu*) and serialized in *China Discussion*, in which he copied Miyama Toratarō's definition of *minken* word for word: "*Minquan* was Heaven endowed. The rights of the ruled cannot be snatched by their rulers, the rights of sons cannot be taken away by their fathers, and the rights of younger brothers cannot be snatched by their older brothers."[83] Liang held that *minquan*, just like *minken*, is innate: it is neither provided by the ruler nor dependent on the ruler's endorsement.

Besides being influenced by the Japanese *minken* thinkers, Liang also ferociously read about and warmly embraced Western political theories through Japanese translations; Darwin, Montesquieu, Hobbes, Rousseau, John Stuart Mill, and Adam Smith all became Liang's inspiring intellectual mentors. Among them, Rousseau fully captured the attention of Liang. Wang Yao, in her brilliant dissertation "Rousseau and the Intellectual World in China (1882–1911)," chronicles Liang's every encounter with the French philosopher and demonstrates that Liang was the most important introducer of Rousseau to Chinese readers: of the 142 articles in Chinese devoted to Rousseau between 1882 and 1911, which Wang has painstakingly collected from all major newspapers, journals, books, and pamphlets, Liang wrote thirty-six in total, that is, 26 percent, which put Liang in a position far surpassing Yan Fu and all other anti-Manchu revolutionary intellectuals such as Zhang Taiyan and Wang Jingwei.[84]

The first mention of Rousseau appeared in 1899 in the twenty-seventh issue of *China Discussion*. In the article "The Demarcation Between the Civilized and Uncivilized People" (Wenye sanjie zhibie) for the *Treatise on Liberty*, Liang introduced Rousseau's social contract (*minyue*) theory and described it as the key to the success of the French Revolution.[85] Immediately following that article, in 1900 Liang published another, "Destructivism" (Pohuai zhuyi), for the *Treatise on Liberty*, in which he most enthusiastically praised Rousseau and called for the introduction of Rousseau to China, praising the truths discovered by him, that is, liberty and the social contract, as the most "suitable theories for today's China."[86]

For Liang, Rousseau embodied both passion and truth, and the passion displayed in Rousseau's writings would lift the Chinese people beyond their slavish mentality and set them free. By promoting him, Liang was hoping to enlighten the Chinese people, making sure that "the country stands as a self-determining nation" (*guoguo zizhu*) with "the people being independent citizens" (*renren duli*).[87] For example, in his 1901 *China Discussion* article, "The Similarities and Differences in the Changing Ideas of the State" (Guojia sixiang bianqian yitong lun), Liang compared and contrasted differing ideas of the state (*guojia*). In old Europe, "the state (*guojia*), the monarch (*junzhu*), and the people (*renmin*) all existed for God. God was the governing body (*zhuti*) of the country." In old China, "the state (*guojia*) and the people (*renmin*) all existed for the monarch (*junzhu*). The monarch was the governing body of the state." In Europe in the nineteenth century, "the state was established for the people. The monarch was only a small branch of the state and he existed for the people. The people were the governing body of the state."[88] For Liang, only this third kind of state could be called a "complete nation-state" (*wanquan guojia*), for its people have a real stake in the polity and can fully exercise their political rights.[89]

Acknowledging the theoretical origin of the complete nation-state in Rousseau's concept of equal rights (*pingquan*), Liang declared, "The rights of the people are naturally given; every person has the right to be self-determining, and they are all equal to each other. The state is founded under a contract by the people; thus the people have unlimited power and the government must listen to the opinions of the people."[90] This was also the origin of modern nationalism, "the brightest, the grandest, the most just '-ism' in the world," which "guaranteed the preservation of freedom for the people in their own nation, yet also made sure that one nation's people did not impair the freedom of other people."[91] Liang did note the rapid expansion of imperialism in the 1900s and recognized that imperialism was in vogue in the world, along with statism, which "gave the state precedence over its people, and emphasized the government over the people." However, even though he saw the valuable practicality in statism, Liang maintained that one should not argue for statism in China, for without going through the phase of nationalism, "China would never become a complete nation!"[92]

In November and December 1901, Liang published his most comprehensive essay on Rousseau, "Notes on Rousseau" (Lusuo xue'an) in *China Discussion*, thoroughly introducing the French philosopher's ideas to Chinese readers. Considering this article together with what we have learned thus far, we can say with confidence that the two most important concepts Liang adopted from Rousseau were his concept of freedom and his theory on the legitimacy of the state. First, for Liang, all citizens without exception have the right to be free. At the same time, freedom has a limit—not infringing upon others' freedom—that ought to be guaranteed by the law. Second, Rousseau's theory provided Liang with a standard for judging the legitimacy of a state. As quoted earlier: "The state is founded under a contract by the people; thus the people have power and the government must listen to the opinions of the people." It was indeed Rousseau's theory that enabled Liang to assert that popular sovereignty was the fundamental trait of a legitimate, modern state.[93]

Unlike his writings before the exile, by 1902 Liang had shed the classical Confucian overtones and left the Mencian notion of *minben* behind him. Via introducing ideas that deeply differed from the *minben* tradition—freedom, human rights, popular sovereignty, and the social contract—Liang's writings promoted concepts for modern politics and ushered in a new stage of political discourse for the Chinese people. In his 1902 article "On the Boundaries Between the Government and the People" (Lun zhengfu yu renmin zhi quanxian), Liang differentiated *minben* from *minquan*—the former referred to the preservation of the material basis of the people by the ruler, and the latter referred to the people's naturally given and inalienable rights.[94] Liang made it clear that it was the people's inalienable rights that guaranteed them an independent political stake, and he wrote:

The sages in China talked about benevolent rule, while scholars in the West promoted the idea of liberty (*ziyou*). . . . Benevolent rule talks about protecting the people and ruling them (*biyan baomin, biyan mumin*). . . . Even though Confucius and Mencius and all those great sages persistently propagated [the idea of benevolent rule], they still could not prevent tyrannical and despotic kings from constantly coming and exploiting our people. All this was because only the rulers had rights and the ruled did not have any.[95]

By now Liang had clearly understood the potential conflict between the ruler and the people, and contrary to Kang's idea that "the sovereign and the people are welded together into one body politic," he believed that having sage kings govern was not enough. The solution he proposed was to demarcate the limit of power and to recognize the people's innate status as equal to that of the rulers:

> People who rule must have their power restrained. . . . This is what we mean by demarcating the boundary of power between the government and the people, and what we mean by granting the people equal status when they face the government. The government and the people . . . negotiate and decide the boundary between them. It is not the government that grants people their rights. . . . If the government can give people their rights, it can easily take them back. This is the key difference between Western government and Confucian-Mencian benevolent rule.[96]

Also in this article, as historian Tsuchiya Hideo articulates so well, traces of the concept of the state as an organic entity, from Swiss legal scholar Johann Kaspar Bluntschli (1808–1881), appear. Liang would later become more influenced by Bluntschli, pushing for the sovereignty of the state rather than the sovereignty of the people.[97] Yet, as Tsuchiya states, Rousseau's influence never disappeared. In this article, for example, Liang modified Rousseau's original idea of the social contract—which defines the relationship between the state and the people and claims that state sovereignty lies with the people—and replaced "state" with "government," thus partially keeping Rousseau's idea of popular sovereignty as he addressed the relationship between the government and the people, even though he advocated for the sovereignty of the state.[98]

By 1902, Liang's anti-despotic, naturally given, pro-equality account of *minquan* was being propagated effectively. Analogizing the state to a company, and the monarch and the ministers to managers, rather than owners, of the company, Liang wrote in 1902 in "On the New People" (Xinmin shuo):

> The state is like a company. The court is like an office for the company. Those who are in charge of the court are like the ones who manage the office. The state is like a village. The court is like a guesthouse for this village. Those who are in charge of the court are like the ones who manage the guesthouse. Does this mean that the company was established for the office? Does this mean that the village was set up for the guesthouse? The answers are too obvious to be debated.[99]

Liang's genius with analogies like this helps explain why he was so successful as a propagandist as well as a theorist. It is through these rustic analogies that Liang was able to convey his points to the population beyond the elite: it is the regular citizens who should be in charge of the state, just like the shareholders in the company and villagers in the village. This particular analogy, ingenious and entirely homely, appeared repeatedly in the later political discourse of the Chinese elite as they struggled against the court. During the 1911 Revolution in Sichuan, similar analogies served as a powerful rallying cry for movement leaders to mobilize commoners to fight against the usurper of power, the Qing court.

Also published in 1902, *The Chinese Soul* (*Zhongguohun*), one of the most influential pamphlets of the 1900s, crystallized this radical view. First published in 1902, it contained a number of radical articles that Liang and his colleague Meng Maihuai had written for *China Discussion* from 1899 to 1901, along with articles Liang had written for the *New People's Journal* in 1902.[100] For example, in his impassioned essay called "Chastising Onlookers" (He pangguanzhe wen), Liang asked, "Who are the masters (*zhuren*) of the nation?" And he answered: "They should be the people in the nation. The reason Western nations are so powerful is nothing other than that the people in their nations fulfill their duty as masters." Maintaining that officials should not be the masters of a nation, since they only "went for the jobs to show off their status and gain economic advantages, leaving the country of China feeble and weak," Liang argued that China could be saved only by transforming ordinary people into "masters."[101]

Liang endeavored to explain the relationship between the nation and the people. In his "On Young China" (Shaonian zhongguo shuo), Liang ardently invoked the national consciousness of Chinese youth and urged them to establish China as "a complete nation-state," as had never before existed. Lamenting that China was repeatedly called "an ancient big empire" by both Westerners and the Japanese, Liang believed that there existed a young China that was "full of hope," "exuberant in spirit," "forward-looking," "fearless," "progressive," "risk-taking," and, ultimately, "fresh and young."[102] He urged Chinese youth to take up the responsibility of building a complete nation-state, a real "entity where there is land and people, and the people on the land determine political affairs, drafting laws and preserving them."[103] In another essay, "On Recent Trends in the Competition Between National Citizens and the Future of China" (Lun jinshi guomin jingzheng zhi dashi ji zhongguo qiantu), Liang further elaborated: "The nation (*guo*) belongs to the people (*min*); this is why we say the nation is 'a public asset of the people.'" A nation comes into existence only when the people come together to compose it.[104] Notably, *The Chinese Soul* also included Liang's "The Similarities and Differences in the Changing Ideas of the State," which was discussed earlier as clearly promoting popular sovereignty.

The circulation of *The Chinese Soul* was extensive: at least two editions were published during the Qing dynasty, in 1902 and 1903. The original 1902 edition, published in two volumes by the famous Guangzhi Publishing House of Shanghai, was sold "at big bookstores in all provinces" at the price of three *jiao* (thirty cents).[105] In addition to at least five reprints of this pamphlet, there were several pirated versions that circulated in a number of provinces.[106] *The Chinese Soul*'s impact ought not to be underestimated. Many intellectuals vividly remembered reading this pamphlet as students at the end of the Qing. The famous historian Xiao Yishan (1902–1978) of Jiangsu province wrote: "As soon as I started to read books, I read out loud the extremely widely known *Chinese Soul*. At that time, I had not yet heard about *Minbao* or *Revolutionary Army* [*Geming jun*, the influential revolutionary pamphlet by Zou Rong]."[107] According to Xiao, Liang Qichao's essays were "well organized" and "very clear"; they "had a captivating power in evoking the reader's emotions." Xiao claimed that no other book had influenced him more.[108] New Culture movement's leader Gao Yihan (1885–1968), of Anhui province, remembered the exciting experience of reading *The Chinese Soul* and the *New People's Journal* and realizing that China was weak not because "its people are evil and backward," but because "its government is evil and backward."[109] It was then, for the first time in his life, that Gao thought of overthrowing the Qing and establishing a new government.

In Sichuan, *The Chinese Soul*'s impact was both enduring and profound. Huang Jiqing (1904–1995), later a geologist, remembered that *The Chinese Soul* filled him with love and a sense of responsibility for his country. It also seems that the impact of this pamphlet went beyond elite circles and major cities. A Gowned Brother leader from Pi county in Chengdu prefecture, Zhang Dasan, read it and was stirred by its ideas. Upon hearing of this, members of the Chengdu branch of the Revolutionary Alliance contacted Zhang and convinced him to join them.[110] Written with Liang's magical pen that enlivened and evoked great emotion, *The Chinese Soul* became one of the most exciting reading experiences for an entire generation of Chinese.

Likewise, Liang Qichao's *New People's Journal* was equally impressive. The early articles of the journal represented its radical phase—"On Revolution" (Shi ge) and "On the New People" (Xinmin shuo), for example—and the journal continued to develop Liang's ideas about limiting the power of the government and expanding the power of the people. Despite being published in Yokohama, Japan, its circulation in China was extensive, with four circulation stations even in the inland province of Sichuan, and ninety-seven stations in forty-nine cities throughout the rest of China.[111] With such popularity, the concepts of self-determination (*zizhu*), the people's rights, and equality, along with the conviction that "sovereignty lies with the people," permeated the minds of students throughout China.

Even though Liang became more conservative after his return from the United States in November 1903, it was his earlier, radical line of thought—namely, that the nation belongs to the people, the nation's sovereignty is derived from the people, and the people are the true masters of the nation—that circulated most widely and became his most influential legacy. It is true that in October 1903 Liang published "The Theory of Political Expert Bluntschli" (Zhengzhixue dajia bolunzhili zhi xueshuo), in which he pointed out the impracticality and idealism of Rousseau's theory concerning the origin of the state; yet, as Hazama Naoki compellingly argues, this later focus of Liang on state sovereignty did not take away his commitment to the people's rights. The rights of the nation (*guoquan*) and the rights of the people (*minquan*) had always coexisted in Liang's mind, like "the dual focuses of an oval."[112] In Tsuchiya Hideo's words, Liang was "not talking about individualism but citizens being independent; not about statism but about saving the nation."[113] Through Liang's writings between 1898 and 1902, the two key concepts of *minquan* and *guoquan* gained tremendous popularity among the reading public in China. *Minquan* and *guoquan* would live in the hearts of the educated elite, who would then bring them to bear on their everyday political practice and power struggles, thereby spreading them to the general population in China.

MAPPING OUT THE MEANS: THE ADVENT OF CONSTITUTIONALISM

On June 7, 1901, Liang Qichao published his thesis "On Establishing a Constitution" (Li xianfa yi). In this article, Liang drew the important link between a constitution and popular sovereignty and maintained that the only way to preserve the rights of the people (*minquan*) was to promulgate a constitution: "The constitution and the rights of the people, these two things are indispensable to each other. This is both an unchanging truth and an experience learned from various countries in the world."[114]

Dividing political systems into two kinds—constitutional and autocratic—Liang defined the state as "an entity that contains territory and people" and classified states as either headed by a monarch or by the people. Writing that a "political system (*zhengti*) is the system in which a certain politics operates to govern the people in a country," Liang identified three kinds of political systems in the world—the autocratic political system headed by a monarch, the constitutional political system headed by a monarch, and the constitutional political system headed by the people.[115] The decisive ingredient in a political system, for Liang, was the constitution—not whether the head of the state was the people or a monarch—because a constitution determines how power operates; how the monarch, the officials, and the people should act; and how their relations should be governed.[116]

In particular, even though Liang understood that "a constitutional system (*lixian zhengti*) is a system of limited powers" (*xianquan zhi zhengti*), he especially emphasized that *minquan* was integral to making a constitutional system work: "If there is no *minquan*, even if there is a constitution, it can only be a piece of paper and will not help at all."[117] Later, in his article "On Legislative Power" (Lun lifa quan), Liang insisted in the same vein that legislative power must belong to the nation's citizens. When interpreting the French political philosopher Montesquieu's theory of the division of power, Liang again insisted that the "sovereignty of a state lies with the people" and argued that such a principle should be exemplified by the people's legislative power.[118]

Liang believed that the Qing could survive only by adopting a constitution. Beginning his line of argument from a theoretical perspective, Liang contended that an autocratic state would be governed well under a good ruler, but would decline under a mediocre ruler and be trapped in chaos under a tyrant; however, a constitutional state provides protections that prevent such negative outcomes. First, a constitution protects the people from evil and incompetent rulers: "The hereditary rule of the monarch and the sovereignty of the state have their respective territories," and thus "there is no way that evil-minded monarchs could seize the opportunity to do evil." Second, a constitution protects the populace against evil ministers: "Ministers are elected by a majority in the parliament and the monarch would rely on the will of the people to appoint ministers; then there would be no wicked ministers amassing power." Third, a constitution guarantees that it is the people who decide policies: "The imperial edicts will follow what national citizens want and what the parliament approves. . . . Only those policies sanctioned by the parliamentary majority are implemented." Fourth, the ruler is shielded from popular complaints: "Commoners can petition parliament about their grievances for change and improvement; thus, how would there be any grievances directly against the ruler?"[119] Thus, in theory, a constitutional system would prevent opposition to the ruling house.

Having offered a more theoretical argument for a constitutional system, Liang then called for it from a practical perspective. Using the histories of various European nations, he demonstrated the necessity of such a system, warning that "resisting it would lead to a serious delay of progress for a nation-state."[120] *New People's Journal* systematically published articles on the theories and history of constitutions. In its sixth issue, Liang wrote: "All great civilized nations in the world today have constitutions. The constitution is the basic energy (*yuanqi*) of a nation. [Acquiring a] constitution is the most urgent problem that China has to solve today."[121]

Liang was once again leading the intellectual tide as he established the intimate relationship between the people's rights and constitutionalism. For Liang, constitutionalism was the path to realizing both the people's rights and popular sovereignty. Specifically, Liang's remedy for transforming China into a constitutional state did not include abandoning the monarchy; instead, China should opt for constitutional monarchy. A constitutional republic was too radical, as it required changing the head of state; in addition, "the competition of presidential elections would be too cutthroat and that would do no good for the state." Though not overthrowing the monarchy, Liang considered his program a "political revolution," in contrast to Sun Yat-sen's revolution targeting the ethnically Manchu ruling house of the Qing. Other Chinese political theorists agreed. Yang Du, for example, who contributed a great deal to the introduction of constitutionalism at this time, wrote: "Let us first put aside the issue of whether China should be a republic or not. We see that . . . [in a constitutional monarchy,] the people and the monarch negotiate to form a contract that limits the power of the monarch so that it does not harm the power and rights of us masters (*zhuren*)."[122] Indeed, from 1898 to 1903, constitutional monarchy was one of the best-developed political theories among those that were debated by Chinese students in Japan.

While Chinese intellectuals in Japan laid out both the principles of what the ideal Chinese polity should be and a plan for bringing it into being, support for constitutionalism was also growing in China.[123] On June 16, 1902, the *Chinese and Foreign Daily* (*Zhongwai ribao*) published an editorial asserting that the most effective way of strengthening a country was to "establish a constitution." It urged the Qing court to "pick the good constitutions of various Eastern and Western countries, compile them into a book, and carry [the constitutional principle] out."[124] In the same year, the *Bulletin of Politics and Arts* (*Zhengyi tongbao*), a journal owned by reformers in the Jiangsu-Zhejiang region, argued that a constitutional monarchy would "limit the power of the ruler and protect the rights of the ruled," "solidify national security and enhance the happiness of the ordinary people," and "eliminate public danger and achieve public wealth." The article concurred with Liang Qichao on the purpose of a constitution: "A constitution would determine the boundaries of the three branches of political power. It would establish the people's rights and duties."[125] Furthermore, *L'Impartial* (*Dagongbao*), another newspaper that robustly argued for constitutionalism, used the occasion of the Guangxu emperor's birthday on August 18, 1903, to publish a special birthday greeting in an enormous font: "One person is having his birthday and we hope that our emperor can live forever; if we establish a constitution soon, then our dynasty will live on and on."[126] An editorial in the same issue declared that for politics to work, it was necessary to "first establish a constitution and offer people their political rights," and only by doing so "could China be saved."[127] As historian Hou Yijie concludes, "The reformers had now changed their name to 'constitutionalists.'"[128]

The Enlightenment in Sichuan

PU DIANJUN AND HŌSEI UNIVERSITY

This description of the background of the general development of reformist thought in China sets the stage for a close look at the ideas and aspirations of the Sichuan constitutionalists, among whom Pu Dianjun was unquestionably the leader. As a later *Shibao* article described it, Pu's reputation reached such a level in Sichuan that "people would erect a shrine for him."[129] In a 1920s retrospective, the famous socialist writer Guo Moruo—who was a student in Chengdu in the 1900s—compared Pu's influence on Sichuan to that of Lenin and Trotsky on Soviet Russia.[130]

After passing the *xiucai* examination at age twenty, Pu went to Beijing to take his *juren* examination three years later, in January 1898; it was there that he first encountered constitutionalist ideas. On April 12, 1898, Pu attended a meeting of Kang Youwei and Liang Qichao's Society for National Preservation (Baoguohui), where he found Kang's call for reform compelling.[131] At the end of September 1898, Pu witnessed the execution of the six leading reformers, including his friends from Sichuan, Yang Rui and Liu Guangdi. Instead of making a *juren* of Pu, the experience in Beijing made him a committed Kang-Liang follower.[132] Back in his hometown of Guang'an, Pu launched his campaign for a new education system, merging three old Confucian academies into one new-style institute, the Zijin School, where he taught current political events along with Confucian classics and invited scholars of "new learning" to be the instructors. It was at Zijin that Pu first became friends with Luo Lun and Zhang Lan, two other important future constitutionalists of Sichuan. After passing the *jinshi* examination in 1904, Pu was sent to Japan in 1905 to study constitutional matters.[133]

During his three years in Japan (1905–1908), Pu developed his knowledge of constitutionalism. Pu's thinking was profoundly shaped by Liang Qichao, as is evident from a comparison of their writings. For example, Liang's metaphor of the state as a business, which analogized the court and the people to the managers and the owners, was used repeatedly by Pu during the Railway Protection movement in 1911 (see Chapter 5). Pu accepted Liang's concepts of the people's rights and popular sovereignty, inherited Liang's understanding of the relationship between the people's rights and constitutionalism, and adopted Liang's proposed remedy for transforming China—a constitutional monarchy.

Pu and his generation of Chinese constitutionalists were not only inspired by Liang Qichao but also shaped by their shared experience of studying in Japan.[134] Between 1898 and 1911, more than forty-five thousand Chinese students studied in Japan, the majority focusing on law and politics.[135] Hōsei University, known in English as the University of Law and Politics, played a particularly crucial role in educating Chinese students about constitutionalism. Song Jiaoren, Wang Jingwei, Ju Zheng, Tang Hualong, Pu Dianjun, Shen Junru, Lei Fen, Luo Jie, and Yi Zongkui, to name just a few, were all trained at Hōsei. They came from diverse geographic locations in China—Hunan, Hubei, Jiangsu, Zhejiang, Sichuan, and Guangdong—and differed in their political affiliations. The first three—Song Jiaoren, Wang Jingwei, and Ju Zheng—belonged to the Tongmenghui, the leading radical revolutionary group, while the latter six were constitutionalists. Tang Hualong, Pu Dianjun, and Shen Junru were leading members of the end-of-Qing provincial assemblies, serving as chairs or vice-chairs of the assemblies. Lei Fen, Luo Jie, and Yi Zongkui were the "three heroes" (sanjie) at the National Assembly, vehemently attacking the autocracy of the Qing state and promoting the notion of minquan. Despite their divergent political affiliations, all were trained at Hōsei and were exposed to the same political concepts there.[136]

The prominence of Hōsei University in the history of Chinese constitutionalism should be ascribed to the Hōsei Short-Term Program for Qing Overseas Students (Qingguo liuxuesheng fazheng sucheng ke), which was founded owing to the efforts of Fan Yuanlian, a Shiwu Academy graduate who was studying at Hōsei. Deeply concerned about the Qing's lack of constitutional experts, Fan urged the Qing ambassador to Japan, Yang Shu, and the president of Hōsei University, Ume Kenjirō (1860–1910), to establish a special program for quickly educating Chinese students about constitutionalism. After much discussion, Ume, also an eminent civil legalist, designed the program. Textbooks for the program, compiled by Ume and other reputable Japanese scholars, were written in Chinese so that students could study without having to acquire proficiency in Japanese. The program used Hōsei University faculty and also invited eminent scholars from Tokyo Imperial University, including the renowned constitutional scholar Minobe Tatsukichi (1873–1948), to teach. All classes were taught in Japanese with simultaneous translation by Chinese students.[137]

Unlike many Japanese universities whose legal courses were based on the German model, Hōsei's Law Department, which had been set up by French legal scholar Gustave Émile Boissonade de Fontarable (1825–1910), followed the French model. Originally a school of law called the Tokyo Company of Law (Tokyo Hōgakusha) established in 1880, it was renamed the Tokyo School of Law (Tokyo Hōgakkō) in 1881. From 1883 onward, the school was headed by Boissonade and run according to the French legal tradition. In 1889, the Tokyo School of Law was combined with a school of French studies, the Tokyo French School (Tokyo Futsugakkō), and in 1903 it adopted the final version of its name, Hōsei University (Hōsei Daigaku). As law professor Ding Xiangshun argues, Boissonade established a tradition of liberalism at Hōsei, notwithstanding that the Meiji constitution (1889), patterned after the German constitution, stressed authoritarianism with its claim that "sovereignty lies with the emperor." Even if French liberalism did not figure in mainstream Japanese legal discourse, Boissonade replicated curricula he had taught at the University of Paris and above all emphasized the importance of rights and popular sovereignty in his teaching.[138] Boissonade's legacy was carried on by other notable figures who helped to lay the foundation of Hōsei University, including Mitsukuri Rinshō and Ume Kenjirō. Mitsukuri translated several French liberal classics, and Ume, the "father of the Japanese civil code," continued the liberal tradition. Qing students entering Hōsei were exposed to the spirit of French liberalism, with an emphasis on republicanism and human rights.[139]

In May 1904, the Hōsei Short-Term Program for Qing Overseas Students welcomed its first group of students, ninety-four in number. The curriculum for the one-year course of study (later extended to one and a half years) included a general introduction to law (*faxue tonglun*), civil law (*minfa*), commercial law (*shangfa*), state law (*guofaxue*), administrative law (*xingzhengfa*), codes of punishment (*xingfa*), international law (*guoji gongfa* and *guoji sifa*), regulations of the local court system (*caipansuo goucheng fa*), civil and criminal procedure law (*minxing susong fa*), and introductory studies in economics, finance, and penology.[140] Instructors included Ume, who taught civil law and the general introduction to law, and Minobe, who taught constitutional law.[141]

In particular, Minobe's understanding of constitutionalism heavily influenced Chinese students. A liberal thinker, Minobe believed that "the fundamental spirit of constitutionalism is liberty and self-governance."[142] The purpose of constitutionalism, he insisted, was to realize "freedom" and "equality," and thus "sovereignty must reside with the people."[143] As a corollary, Minobe emphasized the role of parliament in the polity and at times equated "constitutionalism" with "a political system that has a parliament." In a constitutional state, "first, parliament should be the representative organ of national citizens" and second, "should supervise the administrative organ."[144] Constitutionalism, he argued, "is also the politics of public opinion," and the right of national citizens to freely criticize politics is fundamental.[145] While Minobe had yet to finalize his emperor organ theory—which claims that the emperor is an "organ of the state" as defined by the constitutional structure, rather than a sacred power beyond the state itself—while teaching at Hōsei, he had long incubated the idea.[146]

From 1904 to 1908, five cohorts of students were trained in the Hōsei Short-Term Program. Of the more than two thousand Chinese students in these five cohorts, 1,215 graduated.[147] The graduates included many future Chinese political leaders who would go on to play key roles in modernizing the legal system in late Qing and early Republican China.[148] Although obviously not able to produce comprehensively trained legal experts, the intensive program did provide China with a large group of legal scholars possessing a useful base of general knowledge. Many who entered the program had *juren* or *jinshi* degrees or had served in public office, which gave them the resources to carry out what they had learned at Hōsei in the constitutional reform that came after. Of the core group of Chinese constitutionalists in the late Qing—the chairs, vice-chairs, and resident representatives of the provincial assemblies—forty-eight had studied at Hōsei. Moreover, twenty-one members of the National Assembly had been trained at Hōsei.[149]

It is no exaggeration to say that Hōsei University provided them their constitutional knowledge and shaped their understanding of rights and sovereignty.[150] Furthermore, after the Qing launched the constitutional reform in 1906, many of the textbooks used in the provincial law schools also came from Hōsei. Among Hōsei graduates who used their textbooks from the program to teach their own students back home were Zhang Zhiben (Hubei), Chen Shutong (Zhejiang), and Shao Cong'en and Chen Chongji (both Sichuanese who played major roles in facilitating Sichuan's independence from the Qing), thereby disseminating concepts such as popular sovereignty and the people's rights to the rest of the educated elite in China.[151]

One concrete example of the influence of Hōsei on Chinese constitutionalism was the Ezhou Provisional Constitution (Zhonghua minguo Ezhou linshi yuefa), "the first republican constitution in China" and "the precursor of all Chinese republican constitutions."[152] Song Jiaoren and Tang Hualong jointly drafted the constitution after the Wuchang uprising, with help from Zhang Zhiben, Ju Zheng, Zhang Guorong, and Huang Zhongkai, all of whom had been trained at Hōsei. The liberal influence is unmistakable in the text of the Ezhou Provisional Constitution's declaration that "sovereignty lies with the people" (*zhuquan zaimin*). Tang Hualong wrote while drafting it that he intended the new constitution to establish republicanism (*gonghe guoti*), democracy (*minzhu zhengti*), constitutionalism (*lixian zhengzhi*), responsible government (*zeren neige*), party members as representatives (*zhengdang yiyuan*), and the rights and responsibilities of the citizens (*renmin zhi quanli yiwu*). All these ideas could be traced to Boissonade's French tradition of liberalism.[153]

Trained at Hōsei, Pu Dianjun and other Sichuan constitutionalists—Deng Xiaoke, Xiao Xiang, Chen Chongji, and Shao Cong'en—naturally grew close to ideas such as rights, popular sovereignty, equality, freedom, and republicanism. In particular, their sense of the people's rights at that time applied specifically to the rights of Sichuan taxpayers regarding the Chuan-Han Railway Company. To truly protect the rights of the Sichuanese, they demanded that the railway company be privately managed on a permanent basis (see Chapter 3). In addition, the people's rights were explicitly asserted at the 1909 Sichuan Provincial Assembly meeting, at which Pu and his colleagues clashed with the Sichuan governor-general in their insistence on no taxation without supervision (see Chapter 4).

THE ENLIGHTENMENT IN SICHUAN

The passionate writings of Liang Qichao and other reformers also circulated widely among the educated elite in Sichuan. Liang's *New People's Journal*, produced in Yokohama, had three circulation stations in Chengdu and one in Luzhou.[154] In addition to imparting to Chinese youth ideas of equality, rights, and popular sovereignty, the *New People's Journal* was significant in a practical way. Many students believed it would help them succeed in the civil service examination after the Qing launched an examination reform in 1902, changing from "eight legged essays" (*bagu*) to "policy questions" (*cewen*).[155] Hubei student Zhu Zhisan wrote in his diary in 1903 that Liang's essays had inspired and shaped the way people wrote in the policy questions part of the new examination.[156] Zhejiang intellectual Wang Lifu recalled that many examinees brought the *New People's Journal* with them as "materials" to prepare for the reorganized civil service examination: "Among those who performed outstandingly in the examinations, a great number of them benefited from this journal."[157] Similarly, local Sichuan students called Liang Qichao "Mr. New People" (Mr. Xinmin) and talked among themselves about the fact that the best way to advance in school was to emulate Mr. New People's ideas and style. After new-style schools mushroomed around the country following the New Policies reform, Liang's impact was even greater.[158]

According to the late Qing cultural critic Fu Chongju, of Chengdu, constitutionalist and reformist newspapers like *Eastern Times* (*Shibao*), *Chinese and Foreign Daily*, *China Daily* (*Shenzhou ribao*), *Shuntian Times* (*Shuntian shibao*), and *Shanghai News* (*Shenbao*) were officially circulating in Chengdu in the late Qing period, with *Shibao* being a favorite among local elites in Sichuan.[159] Occasionally, there were also anti-Manchu revolutionary newspapers circulating in Sichuan. According to Huang Shou, a student in Sichuan in the 1900s, issues of *People's News* (*Minbao*) were smuggled into the province from Japan. And Luo Lun, a leader of the Railway Protection movement in 1911, was precisely identified as the key person to have exposed students in Chengdu to ideas from *Minbao*.[160]

Novelist Li Jieren, a student in Chengdu in the 1900s, also vividly described the impact of newspapers on the Sichuan elite. Through these newspapers and through study groups formed by the elite, the discourse about rights spread through Sichuan's cities and towns. With their exposure to newly introduced concepts such as the nation (*guo*), the people (*min*), and the people's rights (*minquan*), the Sichuan elite underwent their own enlightenment.[161] Li Jieren's detailed depictions of people's lives in Chengdu from 1901 to 1910 convey a sense of how these new ideas moved the local Chengdu elite to see the world in a different way. After the humiliating debacle of the Boxer Uprising, the great fear of China being carved up by foreign invaders, the strong yearning for national salvation, and the consensus favoring serious political reform all prompted China's educated elite to take even more radical political steps. From the Qing court at the top to the common gentry at the bottom, there was widespread enthusiasm for reform. A Sichuan literatus stated: "Since the allied troops of eight nations invaded China, the court has been in a disadvantaged position. . . . Officials, educated elite, and even commoners all realize that things cannot continue in the old way. . . . All who have any knowledge about the world tend to accept the new teachings. Everyone who knows anything about the global situation knows it is necessary to reform (*weixin*)."[162]

Beginning in 1903, after the New Policies reform in education, new-style schools proliferated in Sichuan's big cities such as Chengdu, Chongqing, and Luzhou. In Chengdu, for example, students in these schools began obtaining Liang Qichao's writings from the Eryoushan Bookstore and the Huayang Book Market. Some of them went on to open their own private new-style elementary schools—in Li Jieren's words, "hoping to enlighten the children of ordinary Chengdu families."[163] These students, having accepted many of Liang's ideas and having been influenced by his radical thinking, then encouraged their pupils to "be masters themselves."[164] This is one way in which the notion that "we, the people, are the masters of the state" became increasingly popular. Li Jieren wrote that in a new-style school in Chengdu, when facing the portrait of the Guangxu emperor, one student refused to kneel, asserting that "the emperor does not deserve [the kneeling ritual]."[165]

The authority of the monarchy was diminishing. The imperial state, the gentry, and Confucian ideology had evolved so closely in tandem that they were virtually inseparable. When one fell, they all fell together. A new way of conducting politics was imagined, and the educated elite were equipped with the concepts and the language to carry it out. The discourse about rights provided Chinese literati with both a fresh understanding of their relationship with the Qing rulers and a new set of alternative rules to use in reconstituting the Chinese polity. In particular, upon their return from Japan, the Sichuan constitutionalists invigorated the political enlightenment; they introduced more books and published more papers to convey the idea of rights so as to kindle a new sense of community.[166]

Conclusion

Equality, the people's rights, popular sovereignty, and constitutionalism were key ideas promulgated in the writings of Liang Qichao that were widely disseminated in pamphlets and newspapers. As his followers grew in number, these ideas became a force unto themselves. In the 1911 Revolution in Sichuan, these terms were to become vital rallying cries that enabled movement leaders to mobilize thousands of followers. In Western political science, the concepts of limited government and separation of powers are usually seen as the touchstone of modern constitutionalism, as in Charles McIlwain's influential definition: "All constitutional government is by definition limited government. . . . 'Constitutional limitations,' if not the most important part of our constitutionalism, are beyond doubt the most ancient."[167] In contrast, Chinese constitutionalism was regarded as a means for the common people to obtain power, rights, and sovereignty in the state, as seen both in the writings of Liang Qichao and in the training Chinese students received at Hōsei University.

Liang's proclamation that everything depends fundamentally on the people was a provocative statement. He viewed the rights of the people as the foundation of a new political life. But who were the people? And how could a government or a political movement establish the space in which those rights are exercised? The Sichuan constitutionalists, also referred to in this book as the Sichuan elite and the Sichuan overseas students, took Liang Qichao as their spiritual leader, but Liang was absent at precisely the point where they faced the most momentous decision—namely, how such a future could be realized in a pragmatic manner. The Sichuan elite's activism was further shaped by participation in the experimental New Policies reform. During the reform, they brought to the discourse about rights a certain realism, combining political principles with political practice. This is the subject of the next chapter.

3 The Project

THE CHUAN-HAN RAILWAY COMPANY AND
THE NEW POLICIES REFORM

In 1906, when Sir John Jordan returned to China after an eight-year absence to serve as the British ambassador in Beijing, he found that a "new generation" of elites had emerged. These elites, having realized that "a new arena outside the traditional dynastic order had opened," energetically participated in public affairs that concerned both national and provincial interests.[1] As part of this generation, the overseas students of Sichuan province joined the New Policies reform, tasted real political struggle, and became part of the rapidly changing late Qing political scene.

The Qing government's last-gasp reform provided an opportunity for the new-style elites to acquire power, leading to an expansion of the political system. Under intense pressure to implement a deluge of edicts from the center in the New Policies reform, provincial government officials such as Sichuan governor-general Xiliang needed new talent to grind out plans for executing the constant directives from Beijing. Seizing this opportunity, the overseas students of Sichuan created effective political networks as they engaged with the provincial government in an intricate dynamic of challenge and collaboration.

This chapter relates the story of the Sichuan overseas students and their interactions with the Qing state—specifically with provincial officials as representatives of the state—regarding the Chuan-Han Railway Company. After collaborating closely with provincial officials to set up the railway company, driven by their concept of rights (*quan* or *quanli*) and, particularly in this case, shareholders' rights (*gudong quanli*), they eventually locked horns with those same officials over the ownership of the company and ultimately challenged the very legitimacy of the state.

The New Policies Reform: First Stage (1901–1905)

The allied sacking of Beijing in 1900 shook the Qing court. The Boxers had been provoked by the conservative Manchu princes at court; in contrast, south China, ruled by reform-minded Han officials, was relatively peaceful. After the humiliating ending of the allied expedition—with the court having to flee as far as to the inland province of Shaanxi—the conservative faction and the anti-foreign group at the court was discredited and crushed. After the Boxers, even at the Qing court there was talk about the need for a reorganized state. The Boxer Uprising also demonstrated the power of mass movements: the widespread anti-foreign resistance in its wake forced foreigners to realize the folly of any ambitions for partitioning China.

On January 29, 1901, while on her way back to Beijing after having fled the allied expedition, Empress Dowager Cixi issued an edict in the name of Emperor Guangxu, declaring: "There are everlasting canons, yet there are no permanent laws. . . . In the past ten years, wrongs had accumulated, yet officials had followed the old rut. . . . Now that negotiations for peace are ongoing, all political affairs should be reorganized so that our country can become wealthy and powerful in time."[2] She then called for high-level Qing officials to submit detailed plans for reforming the institutions of government.

This edict marked the beginning of the New Policies reform. On April 21, 1901, the bureau to lead the reform, the Office of Governmental Affairs (Zhengwuchu), was established, with key Manchu and Han ministers serving as its members. On October 2, Cixi issued another edict, this time in her own name (*yizhi*), reasserting her determination to "reform for self-strengthening." With the Empress Dowager clearly signaling the seriousness of her intent, reform soon became the keynote of politics. Still, Cixi made a distinction between her reform and the reform of Kang Youwei: "The so-called new laws pronounced by the treasonous Kang Youwei were to create chaos in our institutions (*luanfa*), not to reform them (*bianfa*)."[3]

The 1901 edict's solicitation of suggestions for reform resulted in a flood of memorials by officials from all over China. Historian Hou Yijie identifies three types of suggestions. The first type was a continuation of the policies of the Self-Strengtheners, which aimed at leading the Qing to wealth and power through modernization. The most important of these were from Governors-General Zhang Zhidong and Liu Kunyi of Huguang and Liangjiang, who in three jointly written memorials suggested four policies for constructing a new education system, twelve for adjusting the old methods of governing, and eleven for learning from the West. They championed new regulations, promoted new transportation systems, and recommended abandoning the civil service examination system. They proposed the manufacture of more copper coins (to curb the crisis caused by the shortage of silver), the training of the New Armies, the establishment of new-style schools, and the development of commerce and industries. These three memorials in effect became the blueprint for the New Policies reform in its first stage (1901–1905).[4]

Memorials of the second type promoted constitutional monarchy, with Li Shengduo, ambassador to Japan, leading the charge on that front. In June 1901, Li wrote:

The key to a successful reform is to have a principle. Without a principle, the concrete regulations will lead only to disaster. Recently, successful reforms in various countries have taken the constitution as the foundation for building a strong state. . . . I have looked around the world, and have not seen a country that is strong and wealthy that lacks a constitution.[5]

In the same vein, in early February 1902, Minister Sheng Xuanhuai hinted at initiating a political reform to emulate the legal codes of Germany and Japan. In August 1902, Censor Zhao Binglin proposed that constructing a constitution would be the best way to prevent revolutions: "With a constitution, all military, legal, and financial matters will be carried out according to the public will. The emperor and the commoners share the same concerns, and the talk about revolutions will not confuse people or shake their hearts any more."[6]

The third category of proposals, a middle ground between the first and the second, suggested establishing assemblies (*yihui*) as a means of initiating political reform. A proposal by Governor-General Tao Mo of Liangguang, which blamed the failure of politics on the lack of communication between the government and the common people, epitomized this position. Tao wrote: "The assembly is the place where politics are discussed. . . . Via the assemblymen, the government will thus come to understand the likes and dislikes of the people, eliminating the barriers to communication between the two."[7]

Heeding the advice of the first group, Cixi rejected any move toward representative government. From 1901 to 1905, the New Policies reform followed the advice of officials advocating modern state building, with prominent provincial governors-general like Zhang Zhidong, Liu Kunyi, and Yuan Shikai being its key advocates. In line with their recommendations, three influential new policies were implemented between 1901 and 1905. The first was to promote privately owned companies and industries. In September 1903, the Ministry of Commerce was established. All of the commercial railways and industries came under the purview of this new office. Importantly, a freshly drafted Commercial Code (Shanglü) explicitly preserved the property rights of industrialists and merchants.[8] The second policy was to create an educational system that was new in both form and substance. In 1902, with Zhang Baixi taking the lead, the court issued the Imperially Endorsed Statutes of Public Schools (Qinding xuetang zhangcheng), ordering the transformation of old-style private academies (*sishu*) into new-style schools (*xuetang*). In 1904, with Zhang Zhidong taking the lead, a revised Statutes of Public Schools (Zouding xuetang zhangcheng) was issued, and it formally laid the foundation for a modern education system, dividing schools into elementary, intermediate, and higher levels. Marking the radicalism of the educational reform, the civil service examination was abolished on September 2, 1905.[9] Last, the third implemented policy established a new security system, including both military and police forces. In December 1903, the Qing established a new center in Zhili for training soldiers, setting out to build so-called New Armies and drawing up the blueprint for a reformed military system.[10]

In Sichuan, provincial officials were also following these imperial edicts to modernize their province. Although its reform efforts lagged behind those of such places as Liangjiang, Huguang, and Zhili, Sichuan was deeply affected by the New Policies. Crucial changes took place in the functioning of the state in the last years of the Qing, as provincial governments assumed an aggressive role in managing the political and public lives of the people in response to edicts from the center.

The establishment of a new police system in 1901 was the first reform undertaken by Sichuan. Under the effective leadership of Japan-trained official Zhou Shanpei, a new police system was set up, first in Chengdu and then gradually in Sichuan's outlying counties. As an agency of the modern state, the police system clashed with existing local practices such as the local *baojia* system, and the police system became a key impetus for people's aversion to the reform.[11] In 1903, Governor-General Cen Chunxuan initiated a campaign to modernize the military, reforming Sichuan's armed forces as another project for strengthening the state. By 1911, a new regiment (*zhen*), the Seventeenth Regiment, had been established. It was in this regiment that ambitious men like Yin Changheng, a Sichuanese officer who eventually took over the revolutionary regime via a coup in December 1911, would flourish and amass power for their own purposes (see Chapter 8).[12]

Education was the second principal emphasis of the Sichuan New Policies reform. In June 1902, the first higher-education academy in the province was established in Chengdu, and thereafter "new learning" was introduced systematically. By October 1905, according to a memorial by Governor-General Xiliang, various counties in Sichuan had also established new-style schools: "There are two teachers' normal colleges, one in Chengdu and the other in Luzhou, and 110 preparatory teachers' normal schools. High schools number eight, higher elementary schools eighteen, first-level elementary schools 4,017, combined elementary schools thirty-eight, and part-time elementary schools thirty-four."[13] In 1909, Sichuan—together with Zhili—was one of the two provinces where the number of new-style schools surpassed ten thousand, with an estimated student body of between two hundred thousand and three hundred thousand. These schools—some publicly established, but most privately endowed—became places where young intellectuals could absorb new knowledge.[14] In addition, in 1903, Governor-General Xiliang began sending Sichuan students to study in Japan. The majority—more than four hundred—returned to Sichuan to establish their own schools, including "medical schools, military schools, schools of commerce, political and law schools, railway schools, mining schools, and also specialized schools for planting mulberry trees [for the silk industry]."[15] As a result, a wide range of Sichuanese youth were exposed to new ideas, paving the way for the 1911 Revolution.

The third emphasis of the Sichuan reform in this stage, and the one most relevant to our story, was the building of new industries and transportation systems, the key focus being the establishment of the Chuan-Han Railway Company. The provincial government created an environment that benefited the economy, giving rise to a new type of industrial elite derived mainly from the powerful gentry and merchant classes.[16] The Commercial Bureau, the Mineral Bureau, the Lottery Bureau, and the Bureau for Encouraging Industry were quickly established by the provincial government, all of them aiming to facilitate the growth of the modern industrial sector of the provincial economy.[17]

Indeed, the main emphasis in this first stage of the New Policies reform was on increasing the effectiveness of the state. The Qing rulers expected to combat the anti-Manchu element in society by demonstrating that they could provide the ideas, plans, and leadership needed to save the country from imperialism. The reform proposals were instituted to secure national integrity against the encroaching European and Japanese powers; their objectives were to usher in a strong, centralized state capable of organizing and funding a modern army and to secure the compliance of a large proportion of the people. Although most proposals had been raised by the Self-Strengtheners of an earlier generation, it was the New Policies reform that put the proposals into effect.

The Creation of the Chuan-Han Railway Company

In Sichuan, the key project that emerged was the Chuan-Han Railway Company, which was initiated by the state and then gained a great deal of attention and support from the elite. In the nineteenth century, railroads were the most important land-based link between countries and the most potent new technology that promised substantial economic development in its wake. Railroad building was a key element in the development of modern industry, a national market system, and a modern state. China's first great period of railroad development, from 1895 to 1911, witnessed the rapid expansion of the country's rail network from 410 to 9,300 kilometers of track. Historian Ralph Huenemann notes the predominance of foreign influence at this stage of railway development, with foreign investors building 90 percent of the lines, and state-owned and privately owned "self-reliant" (*ziban*) railways each financing 5 percent.[18]

Foreign powers quickly resumed constructing railroads in their colonial spheres of influence after the 1901 Boxer Protocol. The Qing court's welcoming attitude toward foreign investment was evident: "Whether they are Chinese or foreign, officials or private merchants, all are allowed to build railways," and the Concise Regulation on Railways stated, "Whether a Chinese company or a foreign company, they are all protected by the government."[19] In Shandong, the German railroad line from Jiaozhou to Ji'nan was opened to traffic in 1904, and in Yunnan, the French continued their railroad development linking southwest China to their colonies in Indochina. The British, recovering from the impact of the Boer War, suspended major projects in the years immediately after 1900, with the exception of the line from Beijing to Shanhaiguan. Meanwhile, the Americans resumed building the strategic Canton-Hankow line, and construction of the Belgian-owned Beijing-Hankow line was moving forward rapidly. During this period, foreign powers used railroads as a principal means to exert control over China, and the Chinese viewed them as the most visible manifestation of imperialism in the Middle Kingdom. As Huguang's governor-general Zhang Zhidong commented, "Railways are like a pair of scissors; wherever they arrive, territory will be lost [to the foreigners]."[20]

In this context, Sichuan, whose abundance of mineral and natural resources had long attracted foreign investors, became a focal point of competition among various imperialist powers. The British and the French were the main competitors over railway building in Sichuan. In 1853, the British proposed a rail network that would link Sichuan southward to the Yunnan-Burma region and northward to Hankow in central China.[21] A railway concession along the Yunnan-Burma line granted to the British in 1897 was only the beginning: a British officer afterward wrote explicitly of their goal to link this railway to Sichuan and eventually to the rest of China. Behind this plan was Britain's determination to prevent the French from interfering with commerce and trade in western Yunnan and its desire to ensure completion of the trunk line between India and Shanghai, via Sichuan and Hankow.[22] To this end, the British established a company called Yunnan in 1899 and dispatched separate investigative teams to survey the routes for three planned railway lines: Burma to Yunnan, Yunnan to Sichuan, and Chongqing to Chengdu.[23] Equally aggressive in pursuit of their interests in Sichuan, the French tried their best to "make sure that the British attempt at colonizing Burma would fail," and determined that "before [the British] get their way in Yunnan and establish their influence there, [we] must extend our power into all of those provinces."[24] In 1898, after France gained the concession to build railway lines from Vietnam to Yunnan, a Japanese diplomat commented, "The true intention of the French is not confined within Yunnan, but is to gain Sichuan."[25]

In the ensuing competition between the British and the French at the turn of the twentieth century, the French, whose investors got an earlier start in building the Yunnan-Vietnam railway, seemed to be winning. Under this pressure, British investors wrote to Sichuan governor-general Cen Chunxuan with great persistence, requesting permission to build railways in Chengdu, Guan county, Ziyang county, and Jiangkou district in Chongqing. They also proposed building railways linking Sichuan to Tibet. To realize these ambitions, the British sent delegates to pressure the provincial government.

These demands put Qing officials on the alert. The Ministry of Foreign Affairs wrote in a memorandum to the court: "Sichuan is full of resources. Just by linking Sichuan to Hankow, goods from Sichuan can be sold to other provinces and Sichuan will profit from it. . . . Nowadays, the ministers of Britain and the United States keep asking for permission to build railways in Sichuan!"[26] In 1903, a series of successful bids for control over railway construction by foreign powers in China prompted the Qing state to take a stronger stand on preserving national sovereignty, with railways as a central focus. Phrases like "to recover sovereign rights," "to protect railways," and "to have self-built railways" echoed throughout the country.[27]

On July 11, 1903, while on his way to assume his post as Sichuan governor-general, Xiliang wrote to the court, petitioning for permission to institute a Chuan-Han Railway Company to "utilize resources and preserve national sovereignty." Xiliang enumerated his reasons:

Of all competitions among strong nations, the influence and power [of a nation] always follow its railways. I have never heard of any strong nation allowing others to build its own railways, which would lead to losing benefits, power, and sovereignty. Right now, at a time of reform and self-strengthening, China has many pressing things to achieve, but it cannot slow down in building railways. . . . Foreigners have "drooled with envy" for a long time over Sichuan and have been conniving to appropriate railway building in Sichuan for themselves. Meanwhile, some Chinese have also secretly colluded with foreigners. . . . Unless we have an officially established provincial railway company and draw upon all-Chinese capital to build the railroad and to preserve sovereignty, the situation will indeed be perilous.[28]

The soon-to-be governor-general went on to describe Sichuan's strategic location: "On the west, Sichuan is adjacent to Tibet; on the south, Sichuan is linked to Guizhou and Yunnan. And Sichuan is on the upper reaches of the Yangzi River." Sichuan's railways were relevant to the geopolitics of the entire Qing empire: "If the railway concession in Sichuan is lost to foreign investors, then all provinces along the Yangzi River will lose their safeguard!"[29]

Xiliang's proposal met with strong support from the Ministry of Foreign Affairs, yet the ministry suggested that concrete regulations should wait for the Ministry of Commerce to be established and given time to deliberate.[30] In September 1903, soon after the formation of the Ministry of Commerce, Xiliang wrote a second memorial to the court:

After I entered Sichuan and observed the Sichuan people, I realized that Sichuanese are easily agitated and that even the Sichuan gentry are impetuous. Even if the Boxers in Sichuan have been quenched, bandits are widespread and may rise up readily. Thus, establishing a reliable railway is also important to keeping the local order.[31]

Xiliang tirelessly pressed the court to approve his proposal. Regarding the financing of the company, Xiliang optimistically believed that "everyone will know that the railway will be successful" and that "no one will hesitate to back up their support with donations."[32]

Xiliang's efforts finally paid off. In January 1904 the Chuan-Han Railway Company was established in Chengdu, with decisive power over it in the hands of the provincial government. The railway company became the first provincially owned railway company in China. In a surge of nationalistic sentiment, similar ventures were organized in other provinces, and by the end of 1907 at least nineteen of these provincial railroads had been chartered.[33] Established as an anti-imperialist endeavor to fend off foreign investors, the Chuan-Han Railway Company was from the very beginning closely associated with the issues of the recovery of national rights and national sovereignty. This strong connection between nationalism and the railway would later make the Sichuan Railway Protection movement an important center of revolutionary activities.

A Railway Company of the Sichuanese: The Role of the Sichuan Overseas Students

With the Chuan-Han Railway Company established in Chengdu, however, Governor-General Xiliang had great difficulty attracting sufficient Chinese investment. The company's need for capital—fifty million taels of silver—was massive, and Xiliang had overestimated the Sichuanese people's willingness to invest their own money in railways. Months after he established the company, Xiliang wrote, "The Sichuan people have limited vision," and, "In the past, Sichuanese donated money to support their neighbors in building industries but did not benefit from it. After these bad experiences, Sichuanese became wary."[34] Finding it "impossible to raise" the millions of taels the Chuan-Han Railway Company needed for the projected 1,980-kilometer railway that would pass through some of the most rugged terrain in all of China, Xiliang was unable to get the company up and running during the first nine months after its establishment.[35] It was under these circumstances that Sichuan overseas students stepped in.

In October 1904, three hundred Sichuan students studying in Tokyo held a meeting. Collectively, they issued a statement: "The railway matter is truly urgent now. To alleviate the danger of this railway being owned by foreign powers, the company has to have real influence. Real influence comes from strong financial support. . . . If this railway were lost to the foreigners, then all of China would be in trouble."[36] Aware that if they could not raise enough funds for the Chuan-Han Railway Company, it would surely be lost to foreign bankers—and even though "half of the Sichuan students were poor" and they all "remained abroad"—the students vowed to "be the first group of Sichuanese who will not only talk but also take action."[37] The Sichuan Overseas Students Association (Sichuan tongxianghui) gathered sixty thousand taels of silver and pledged to collect another three hundred thousand.[38]

The students also wrote to Governor-General Xiliang with proposals for raising the capital for the railway. First, they argued that the government should tax the sale of opium, salt, tea, and liquor. Second, it should gather funds from the copper coin bureaus and from local governments throughout Sichuan. Third, and most important, a surcharge on the tax on the grain produced by Sichuan's landowners and peasants should be imposed. This was, in fact, the *first* proposal for levying a compulsory land-tax-based surcharge for building the railway.[39]

It was the intensified international competition over Sichuan's railroads that induced the overseas students to take action. Cheng Changqi, an overseas student originally from Qianjiang county in Sichuan, chronicled in his diary the actions of the Sichuan students from September 24, 1904, to January 22, 1905. The first record in his diary reads:

September 24. Wu Daquan received a letter from his friend in Chengdu, who wrote, "The British have sent people to investigate and survey the roads in Sichuan, and the French have seized permission to excavate coal and *tung* oil in Ba and Wan counties." . . . If our railways are lost to them, then our Sichuan will follow the path of Manchuria and all of Sichuan's people will become slaves! One of our fellow students suggested that we students from Sichuan should gather to discuss how to deal with this issue. Mr. Zhou [Zhou Ziting, a Qing academic officer, the supervisor of Sichuan students in Japan] said that to make this happen we must first collect fifty thousand in silver in Japan, buy machines, and hire engineers and send them back to start building the railroads; meanwhile, we should urge Governor-General Xiliang to resolutely resist the foreigners.

September 25. At noon, we went to Kinki Hall [a popular meeting place for Chinese students in Tokyo] to discuss railway issues. Altogether more than a hundred students came. We all agreed to donate money and urge General Xiliang to decisively resist [the foreign demands].[40]

To amass sufficient funding for the Chuan-Han Railway Company, the overseas students took a proactive step:

October 2. Raining. At seven in the morning, I went to Kinki Hall. Around nine, people gradually began to gather. Altogether 230 people came. We elected an executive committee of the Sichuan Overseas Students Association. After that, we discussed the railway issue. Deng Xiaoke showed us the draft of the telegram that was about to be sent to Governor-General Xiliang: "Having heard that the British and the French are being aggressive in demanding railway concessions, we Sichuan students will do all that we can, donate our money, and gather more funds for this public work in our province. We swear to sacrifice our own interests, hoping that we can meet your expectations. We suggest you do the following: First, honor the Japanese Railway's guarantee of a 4 percent dividend to investors. Second, utilize all the public funds (*gongfei*) in the province to build the railway. Third, send people to investigate, evaluate, and map out the railroad line to better persuade the gentry and the merchants to invest." After we agreed on the telegram draft, we all donated. In the end, 20,000 taels of silver were collected. . . . Altogether we swore to take up the task of gathering more than 320,000 taels of silver for the railway company.

October 5. Raining. At nine, Deng Xiaoke sent a brief letter saying that "Shanghai's *Shibao* today reported that the Ministry of Foreign Affairs ordered the Sichuan governor-general to proceed quickly in building the railway in order to impede foreign demands. Our action was timed perfectly. How great!"[41]

The 320,000 taels of silver were far less than the amount needed, prompting the Sichuan students to devise other fund-raising approaches, which they proposed in a petition to Xiliang:

October 8. Sunny. Thirty-one people [the executive committee of the Sichuan Overseas Students Association] discussed the railway matter once again. Deng Xiaoke said that when Japan was trying to build its railways it utilized two methods: one was stocks; the other was bonds. We should use the method of "voluntary surcharge taxes" (*juanshu*) to issue railway bonds.[42] We agreed. Soon, some proposed the idea of taxing opium planters, and some proposed the idea of using extra public funds to buy bonds. We decided to base our advice on these ideas and wrote a petition to Governor-General Xiliang. We all agree that railway bonds (*zhaipiao*) are the best idea, so that the ownership rights to the railways will belong to the commoners (*min*) and the government's power will be limited to offering protection only.

October 22. Light rain. I went to the meeting of the executive committee, which was held at the Qing Students Guesthouse. Deng Xiaoke and Gu Bie came first, and brought the "Letter to General Xiliang" and their petition to Xiliang on building railways. Both were written passionately, with genuine feeling, and included a broad view of the global situation. Deng said that the letter was actually penned by Zheng and Jiang from other provinces.[43]

It should be noted that this idea of issuing railway bonds to be financed via a universal surcharge met with opposition from "80 to 90 percent of the entire student body," who "argued that commoners in China were already poor and distressed."[44] Despite sharp divisions among the students that even led to physical confrontations, the executive committee rejected the opinions of the dissenters and went ahead with their proposal for railway bonds.[45]

The year 1904 would prove a critical one for the Sichuan overseas students. It was their fund-raising in support of the Sichuan railway that initiated their active role in provincial affairs, leading to a new type of collaboration with the government.[46] The overseas students of Sichuan who stepped up to help the government solve its financial difficulties with the railway-building project gradually expanded their influence and began negotiating with the government for more power. Having gained widespread recognition for and influence from their fund-raising for the railway, these students emerged as leaders of "the Sichuan people" and later became leaders in the late Qing constitutional reform and the Sichuan Provincial Assembly. Drawing on the strong following they had attracted by the spring of 1911, in the summer they effectively orchestrated the Railway Protection movement.

Upon hearing that the British had entered Sichuan's rivers, some of the students requested permission from the supervisor of the overseas students, Zhou Ziting, to return to Sichuan.[47] Continuing to treat the railway matter as their top priority and constantly discussing possible solutions,[48] these students kept a close eye on the railway issue unfolding in Chengdu.[49] They were well connected through personal correspondence with important Chengdu elites such as Hu Jun (1869–1909), who regularly sought the students' ideas for implementing the railway project.[50]

Finally, on October 22, 1904, the students found a way to resolve the difficulty of collecting capital for the railway company. In their petition to Xiliang, "Our Opinions on the Chuan-Han Railway Company," they wrote, "Procrastination can never lead to any accomplishments. . . . To make sure that this huge enterprise succeeds, we must devise other means to collect capital rather than relying solely upon private stock."[51] Specifically, the students proposed three sources of railway capital. The first was private capital (*minkuan*), stock willingly bought by the Sichuan people; the second was official capital (*guankuan*), from the provincial revenues in the provincial treasury; and the third, and most crucial, was public capital (*gongkuan*), which in reality referred to the surcharges levied by various local governments—surcharges that the majority of people would be obligated to pay. The petition proposed: "We should divide all prefectures and counties into three levels: rich, intermediate, and poor. Then, according to the quality of the land and the grain production of each taxpayer, we should add a surcharge to the land tax, starting with those whose land tax is higher than one tael of silver, so that no small farmers are charged."[52]

The *gongkuan* surcharge was considered "stock collectively bought by various prefectures and counties." The dividends based on the *gongkuan* would not be returned to taxpayers, but were to be used "for public ends in counties and prefectures."[53] Despite the increased burden this surcharge would place on Sichuan's land-tax payers (*lianghu*), the overseas students insisted that it be levied because of the urgent need, claiming that Sichuanese had become more "open-minded" and arguing that since "all fathers and elders must know the important relation between the railway rights and national sovereignty . . . [they] should feel grateful about the tax, rather than resisting it!"[54] The *gongkuan*, later renamed *zugu* (railway tax), became the key means of solving the railway company's financial problems.[55]

Xiliang accepted the students' recommendations. In his memorandum "Regulations on the Recruitment of Capital for the Chuan-Han Railway Company," Xiliang wrote that "all qualified farmers who produce a grain output over ten *dan* [592 kilograms] of grain have to turn in an extra amount of three percent of that output of grain for railway stock, on top of the standard tax."[56] Reporting to the court in January 1905, Xiliang specified:

If the landowner produces more than ten *dan* of grain, he has to turn in an extra amount of three *dou* [that is, 3 percent] of his grain in exchange for railway stock. Those who produce more shall be levied more accordingly. No matter whether the land is public property or temple property, both should turn in the *zugu*. Only those who produce less than ten *dan* of grain will be exempted.[57]

The standard tax under the Qing was a land tax; therefore, all landlords, independent peasants, and whoever was regarded as a land-tax payer had to pay the *zugu*. Immediately after the publication of Xiliang's first *zugu* regulation, the issuance of another regulation, "Detailed Plans on Levying the Zugu According to Grain Output," significantly expanded the category of *zugu* payers. This second regulation decreed that the railway tax be collected not only from standard-tax payers but also from tenants "when their deposit may be heavy but rent is light," and from debtors, stating that "when [debtors] use rent to pay for their debt," if they "produce more than ten *dan* of grain on their rented land, [they] must pay *zugu* as well."[58] As a result, from 1905 on, a great number of Sichuanese were subject to the *zugu* and by default became shareholders of the railway company.[59]

To be sure, *zugu* payers would earn a 4 percent dividend, which was to be paid in the twelfth month of each year. Compared to the students' original proposal, under which no dividends were to have been given to *zugu* payers, Xiliang's final implementation was a better deal for taxpayers. From 1905 on, the *zugu* was levied together with the land tax in all 140 counties in Sichuan (except for Ebian, Maogong, Dajianlu, and Lifan, which were classified as poor counties). Aside from the *zugu*, the other sources of the railway company's capital included private stock, official stock, public stock (which after 1905 referred only to revenue received from local governments), and surcharges on the sale of opium, salt, tea, and liquor.

The *zugu* tax was compulsory: all taxpayers were subject to the rules and required to pay the tax, regardless of whether they wanted to be a company stockholder or whether they wished to own stock. To implement this mandatory taxation, Xiliang ordered the establishment of *zugu* bureaus in prefectures and counties across Sichuan: "All prefectures and counties need to establish a *zugu* bureau. The government shall select two or three members of the gentry to manage the levying of the *zugu*. These people shall be paid a salary." Since the *zugu* was levied on the basis of the amount of grain that each household produced, it was therefore important that production be "investigated by the local *baojia* leaders, who, under the management of the gentry, shall calculate and turn in the amount."[60] This process created a new special interest group of local gentry overseeing the operation of *zugu* taxation, and the *zugu* bureaus would come to exert great power over the subsequent Railway Protection movement.

In general, the levying of the *zugu* was successful, as it accounted for the largest percentage of the Chuan-Han Railway Company's capital. Unlike in Guangdong and Hubei provinces, where the stockholders of the railways were rich merchants who purchased the stock voluntarily, in Sichuan, the shareholders of the Chuan-Han Railway Company included a large number of peasants. According to historian Nishikawa Masao, in a typical county of southern Sichuan, 16.3 percent of the land-tax payers had to hand in the *zugu*.⁶¹ The amount of *zugu* far exceeded the land tax.⁶² As of 1910, peasants and tenants, together with landlords, had contributed to the company a capital investment of as much as 9,280,000 taels of silver, amounting to almost 80 percent of its total capital.⁶³ In addition, most of the bureaucrats from Sichuan, whether high or low ranking, were also landlords and paid the *zugu* tax (Figure 3.1).

Interestingly, although it placed a huge burden on Sichuan's peasants, the *zugu* did not turn out to be the most "hated" tax, possibly because of the extravagant propaganda by the Sichuan overseas students, who portrayed the *zugu* as a wise investment. Coming from members of wealthy and influential Sichuan families, this view carried considerable weight. A prime example of such propaganda was a letter dated November 27, 1904, titled "An Open Letter to All Sichuan Fathers and Elders on the Chuan-Han Railway Matter by Sichuan Students Studying in Japan." The letter read, "Among all devices used to carve up China, the cruelest and the most effective is the railways."⁶⁴ Korea, India, and Manchuria were used as examples of the inevitability that a loss of railway rights would en-

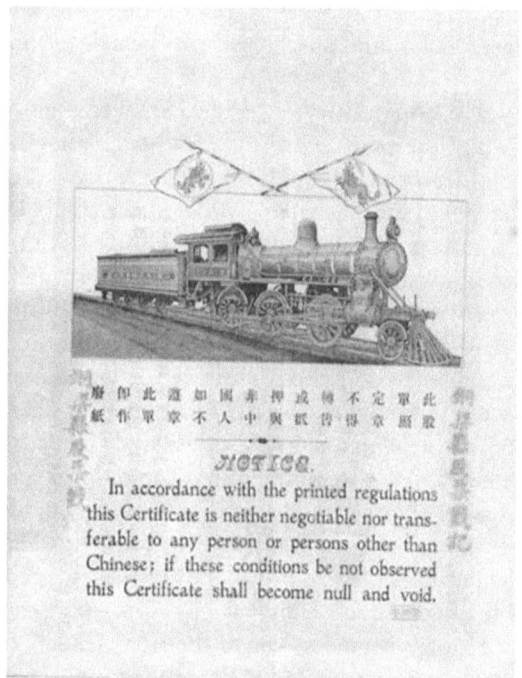

FIGURE 3.1. Chuan-Han Railway Company stock certificate. *Zhongguo touzi zixun wang* (Information for Chinese investors), http://www.xx007.com/show.aspx?id=198532&cid=8.

tail a subsequent loss of national sovereignty, and a warning was sounded that "the day when the railways of Sichuan are lost to other nations will mark the beginning of the subjugation of all land and people in Sichuan by other countries!" This emotional letter crafted by the Sichuan Overseas Students Association attempted to rally provincial pride to prompt people to pay the railway tax: "The people of Sichuan are the most righteous and responsible people among the Chinese. . . . A sage once said, "If only the Sichuanese were left, then even if all of China were devastated, there would still be hope for redemption."[65] Therefore, "fathers and elders of Sichuan" should never think of the railroad as only "a matter for the government or a problem for the state," nor should they think that "the railroad had nothing to do with our humble livings and lives." Rather, every Sichuanese should contribute money to the railway company. All "should consider the big picture" and "not run away from the call."[66]

The letter then attributed Western nations' power to their economic institutions: "They combine their capital and organize large corporations so that small businesses with limited capital cannot compete. . . . If we Sichuanese do not combine our capital in a large enterprise, then the Western monopolistic capitalists will come in and seize all of our assets."[67] The situation was serious: "With half of our mineral rights owned by foreign investors already, if we also lose the railway to them, then the 'blood vessels' of our nation will be controlled by others, and there will be no way for us to escape the control of foreigners and be self-reliant again!"[68] Furthermore, the Sichuan overseas students assured their fellow Sichuanese that railways generated significant profits: "All railway companies in the world today are making profits that are ten times or even hundreds of times the original investment."[69] They used Japan as an example, noting that "Japan Railway stock, first priced at fifty yen per share, has now risen to 750 yen per share; Sanyō Railway stock, first priced at fifty yen, has now risen to 600 yen per share." Railroads in Britain and in the United States "were all making money." They explained that railways are profitable because they "increase the circulation of goods . . . and if the circulation of goods is accelerated, then the country will be rich and powerful." Finally, students claimed to know of "no case in which building railways has not been profitable!"[70]

This lengthy letter ended with a call to the Sichuanese to "combine their wealth" and "invest in the railways." To further assuage commoners' doubts about investing in the company, the students promised to "learn good management practices from foreign companies and run the company according to the new Commercial Code so that no officials would extort its capital, and to ensure that its investors would have company oversight,"[71] urging "all people, from rich landowners, to local bankers, to small shop owners, to workers, to people in temples, to women, to children, to sojourning merchants in Sichuan, to buy railway stock!"[72]

In addition to petition letters like this one, which targeted the educated elite, students also published advertisements in the vernacular aimed at mobilizing the wider populace. One such advertisement declared: "This is a matter of life and death. Rich and poor, old and young, male and female, upper class and lower class, smart and dull, strong and weak, we Sichuanese, all 79,493,058 of us, must wake up! Wake up!"[73] The writer then encouraged all those who wished to reprint the pamphlet to do so freely, hoping that more pamphlets would be sent to more counties throughout Sichuan.[74]

Some patriotic "righteous men" did in fact reprint and circulate these pamphlets. Among them was Zhao Xi'en, a minor official at the Xuzhou prefecture post office, who reprinted this pamphlet and another surviving example of these pamphlets related to railway matters, *Detailed Explanation by Sichuan Overseas Students of the Importance of Railways*. Zhao Xi'en wrote in the preface of his reprint:

This matter [referring to the content of the pamphlets, the railway issue] is directly related to the life and death of the Sichuanese. Thus, I, who work in a southern Sichuan post office and have the job of transferring information promptly, am afraid that those who live far away are unable to learn about this. Therefore, I gathered some capital, made this reprint, and mailed it around, hoping that more people will understand [the importance of the railway matter].[75]

An important patriotic discourse surrounding the railway was taking shape in Sichuan. However, despite the extravagant propaganda, the burden the *zugu* placed on the Sichuanese was difficult to conceal, as verified in a memorial sent by a Sichuan metropolitan official in November 1910, which stated: "The capital of the railway is gathered from the people of Sichuan. That money is the sweat and blood of the little peasants.... This is a huge burden for peasants: for a small household, it takes them more than ten years to get one share. The profit is hard to see, while the burden is hard to get rid of, and they suffer from this exploitation."[76]

The collaboration between Governor-General Xiliang and the Sichuan overseas students in Japan who offered their thoughts on solving the financial crisis of the railway company was integral to making the Chuan-Han Railway Company functional. The managerial and organizational power of the government facilitated the levying of the *zugu* tax, and the Sichuan overseas students orchestrated an elaborate patriotic propaganda campaign that, from the very beginning, connected the *zugu* to provincial and national loyalty. The involvement of the Sichuan overseas students in the Chuan-Han Railway Company began with their support of provincial officials; however, as time passed, their disagreement with the government about how the railway company should be managed became increasingly obvious. They wanted more.

Commercialization of the Chuan-Han Railway Company: "Rights" of the Shareholders

A SHARED OWNERSHIP

Collaborators in levying the *zugu* for the Chuan-Han Railway Company, the Sichuan overseas students and the provincial officials soon became competitors for the leadership of the company. This, nonetheless, was more than simply a power struggle among Sichuan elites, who linked their fight with the discourse on "rights," asserting that those who contributed financially to the railway company deserved the right to manage it. If taxpayers were not given the rights they deserved, then there was no reason they should continue paying taxes: a simple step toward the insistence on "no taxation without representation."

In fact, hints of problems with the railway company began to appear as early as 1904. "An Open Letter to All Sichuan Fathers and Elders on the Chuan-Han Railway Matter by Sichuan Students Studying in Japan," for example, attributed the Sichuanese people's lack of enthusiasm for building railways to the management by "old-style bureaucrats, who ... were not trustworthy."[77] Students also raised concerns about the supervision (*jiandu*) of managers, cautioning that "if the company continued to be controlled by officials," then gentry and merchants "will not dare to trust [management] and will fear that the officials in charge might engage in corrupt activities."[78] This position stood in serious contrast to that of the old-style Chinese merchants, who had often relied upon and sought help from officials. The students then argued that the only way to resolve the crisis of trust in the management of the company was to run it according to the Commercial Code, which would necessitate overhauling the management of the railway company:

All the capital for the railway company came from the people, so all regulations of the railway company should be collectively decided by the people. All those who have invested in the company should obtain their rights in drafting the charter of the company and in supervising its affairs. If we could make the company entirely supported by private capital, then we would not have to rely upon governmental officials, which would be the best for all concerned.[79]

The overseas students were not the only ones actively promoting the commercialization of the company; most of the bureaucrats from Sichuan were *zugu*-paying landlords, and in Beijing some of the metropolitan officials were taking the same stance as the overseas students. Following the lead of those powerful Sichuan-born bureaucrats in the capital, other shareholders with large stakes also demanded control over the company. A literatus named Zhang Luocheng, for example, proposed transforming the Chuan-Han Railway Company into a business that was entirely owned by the shareholders (*minyou*).[80]

In an attempt to appease the discontented Sichuan-born metropolitan officials, Governor-General Xiliang adopted a formula of "shared management by the government and merchants (*guanshang heban*)." On July 25, 1905, he proposed to offer more posts in the railway company to Sichuan gentry and also claimed that the company would do its best "to rid itself of its bureaucratic style of management," "to combine the investment of officials with that of the people," and to "make sure that the company is managed by officials and gentry together."[81] Xiliang then added more posts for Sichuan gentry at various branches of the Chuan-Han Railway Company. Under the chief supervisor (*duban*), who was officially appointed by the Qing government, Xiliang added one manager from the gentry on top of the one official manager to each branch of the company. Important figures like Shen Bingkun, an official manager, Qiao Shunan, a manager from the gentry, and Shi Dianzhang, the chief auditor, were appointed to their posts in 1905.

FROM CO-OWNERSHIP TO COMPLETE OWNERSHIP BY THE SHAREHOLDERS

Concurrent with the efforts of the Sichuan merchants and elites to take control over the railway project from the provincial bureaucracy, the wide-ranging Rights Recovery movement was active throughout the Qing empire. Movements in Hunan, Hubei, and Guangdong to recover railway rights from foreign investors (1904–1905) and the Suzhou-Hangzhou-Ningbo Railway movement in Jiangsu and Zhejiang provinces (1905–1907) appealed to a broad constituency, lending further encouragement to the Sichuan students in their struggle. In 1906, Sichuan overseas students Pu Dianjun, Hu Jun,[82] Xiao Xiang, Deng Rong, Zhang Zhiyuan, and Li Dajun, together with another three hundred people, formed the Chuan-Han Railway Improvement Society (Chuan-Han tielu gaijinhui). Pu and his colleagues suggested that the railway company be completely privately managed so as to protect the economic rights of the people of Sichuan and avoid the theft of railway funds by the government. To make their voice heard, the Improvement Society published a monthly journal, *Report on Improving the Chuan-Han Railway Company*, using firsthand evidence to carefully document its case for commercializing the railway.⁸³ Every month, the *Report* was mailed to the central government in Beijing, as well as to the county governments and various professional associations in Sichuan.

The *Report* cited Qing law to support the argument that the company had to be a private enterprise. These overseas students' struggle for control of the railway was a contest between old and new ways of looking at the issue of "self-interest" (*li*). Traditionally, "self-interest" was to be sacrificed when it conflicted with "righteousness" (*yi*). Gentlemen should not talk about interest; the notion of interest was associated only with lowly people. Instead, the gentry should all be thinking about the public will. Here, however, the students were overtly promoting the self-interest of the railway investors, which they argued was protected by Qing law. Students quoted the Commercial Code to explicitly promote the notion of private interests, arguably a subversive position in light of the traditional Confucian mode of thinking, which tended to deny the legitimacy of self-interest.

In one of Pu's influential polemics, the pamphlet *On Improving the Chuan-Han Railway Company*, he quoted the newly approved Commercial Code and attacked the government for ignoring its own decrees.⁸⁴ Demanding that the company be managed according to the Commercial Code because "all those who have invested are shareholders of the company, who have rights," the *Report* urged that the company be placed under private management, and then that shareholder meetings be held according to the Company Code (Gongsilü), that a board of directors be elected, and that auditors and managers be selected at all levels.⁸⁵ In this document that was signed by more than forty students, Pu Dianjun elaborated on their stand in promoting the legality of the shareholders' rights:

> The establishment of the company was not by the people; rather, the people were forced to comply with the company's orders. In this way, the company has lost its status as the legal representative of the people. Two years after the opening of the railway company, there were still only provincial commissioners serving as managers, but no board of directors and no auditors. None of the rights of the shareholders were guaranteed.⁸⁶

The pamphlet continued, "Now the main source of capital of the railway company is the *zugu*, which comes from the people and not officials. Thus, in principle, the company should belong to the people, not to officials. It is not right that the railway is controlled by officials."⁸⁷ Shrewdly, the students counted the exact number of taels of silver contributed to the railway company by officials: altogether the government contributed only 280,000 taels. In the author's mind, this number, compared to the five million total taels of *zugu*, was so insignificant that "to call the company even co-managed by merchants and officials is not right!"⁸⁸

In his conclusion, Pu maintained that inequitable ownership led to four practical problems for the company: stagnation in railway stock sales, unlimited embezzlement of the *zugu* by officials, misuse of the *zugu*, and an unclear boundary of power between officials and gentry merchants, all of which had to be addressed.[89] He then proposed several ways of improving the situation. First, because all of the capital of the railway company came from the people, the company's name should be changed accordingly to the Private Chuan-Han Railway Company (Shangban Chuan-Han tielu gongsi). Then, the total amount of money needed to build the railways of Sichuan should be announced to the public as soon as possible. Last, the means of levying the *zugu* needed to be improved, and the starting point for levying the *zugu* should be fifty *dan* (2,960 kilograms) of grain so that the *zugu* would not unfairly burden poor peasants.[90]

If the tone of *On Improving the Chuan-Han Railway Company* was mild, a simultaneous 1906 poster was a vituperative rendering of the same message. The poster, "Proposing a Private Chuan-Han Railway Company," excoriated the bureaucrats in the company:

The Chuan-Han Railway Company of today benefits only a small number of tiger- and wolf-like officials. It also benefits only a few gentlemen—the oxen and horses. It is the common people who suffer most from the company. This means that the principal goal of the current Chuan-Han Railway Company is to drain the blood of seventy million people to satisfy the desires of a few wolves, oxen, and horses. There is no other purpose![91]

This heated message appears to have been written by the same person who penned the milder *On Improving the Chuan-Han Railway Company* or someone connected to him, because the two documents shared a number of the same metaphors. Evidently possessing insider information about the railway company, the anonymous author of the poster went on to reveal that "even before the construction of the railways began, the abuse of the railway company's capital was apparent: six-sevenths of the investment had been wasted already."[92] The author pointed out that the Chuan-Han Railway Company, though controlled as it was in 1906 by both the government and the Sichuan elite, was still enormously corrupt. Via their positions in the company, Sichuan governmental officials and the Sichuan bureaucratic elite brazenly embezzled the railway capital for their own use:

In the fifth month of the thirty-second year of Guangxu, the capital collected amounted to almost 5,000,000 taels of silver; however, at the end of that month the account balance became only 1,430,000 taels. Aside from money taken by the government for military usage, most of the missing 4,000,000 taels of silver were appropriated and wasted by the officials and the elite in the Chuan-Han Railway Company. For example, more than 3,000 taels were used for just one banquet.[93]

The key problem, as the poster pointed out, was the lack of a supervision system within the company to ensure that money coming from the Sichuan people was actually used for railway construction. In addition, there was a dearth of professionalism in the company: "The company is controlled by laymen who have no expert knowledge about railways. . . . They apply methods used by magistrates to govern—namely, beating people up and slapping them with a bamboo stick—as their approach to managing the company. Those who are in charge are the governor-general and the provincial commissioners, and those who carry out the work are literati and *jinshi* degree holders."[94] Therefore, the only way to fix the problems in the railway company, the poster declared, was to "destroy the savage official (*yeman guanban*) company and construct a civilized private (*wenming shangban*) company!"[95] An astonishing mockery of the authority of the bureaucracy, this message equated official management of a modern enterprise to barbarism and private management to being civilized. Even more radically, the poster proposed that all Sichuanese should declare: "No private railway, no buying railway stock or paying the railway tax!" If only everyone in Sichuan firmly believed this, "then the railway company would be left with no capital, the barbarian official company would collapse, and the civilized private company would rise!"[96]

In sum, using the Commercial Code as a weapon, Pu Dianjun and his comrades made the case for the legitimacy of the *zugu* payers' right to be in charge of the management of the railway company. This argument would surface repeatedly in the Sichuan people's struggles against the court, as seen in later chapters. Commoners in Sichuan who paid the railway tax, repeatedly told by the agitated students that they had both the rights and the power to determine things, were for the first time taught to embrace the notion that they were true public stakeholders. Furthermore, acutely conscious of the urgent national crisis that Sichuan and the Qing empire faced while also hammering home the concept of taxpayers' rights, Sichuan students in Japan linked the issue of privatizing the railway company to the larger issue of popular sovereignty and saving China in general. The argument went as follows: Since the government had no major source of savings for building the railway, if the railways were not privately owned, there would be a serious lack of capital because no one would want to invest in the company. The construction of the railway would be severely delayed, which would in turn endanger the attempt to fend off foreign imperialism. If the ownership of the railway company were not privatized, the Sichuanese people would feel so "oppressed and exploited" that they would become bandits and thieves, upsetting the stability and order of society.

If urging the government to give the Sichuan railway taxpayers their rights was the "soft way" to make the provincial government hand over control of the company to the shareholders, the harsher tactic was exposing the corruption of officials' handling of railway issues. In the first issue of the *Report on Improving the Chuan-Han Railway Company*, Pu Dianjun published a disturbing account on the amount of money appropriated by the current management of the railway company, "Report on the Copper Bureau Appropriating the Railway Capital of the Chuan-Han Railway Company." The Copper Bureau was the agency of the provincial government responsible for producing copper coins, and Sichuan officials appropriated some railway capital and diverted it into a start-up fund for the bureau.

Pu Dianjun had informants in Chengdu who were insiders in the company. The transformation into a company co-managed by officials and gentry enabled more gentry to see, from the inside, how the company worked. Liu Yiming, the first to bring this issue into question, "saw caskets of taels of silver being carried out of the company," and after asking around was told that "the Copper Bureau needed money and so it utilized the capital of the Chuan-Han Railway Company." This was how the Sichuan people initially found out about the misappropriation of the railway capital. Pu issued a stinging indictment: "The Copper Bureau has not been established yet, the copper is only on its way, and the startup of copper production will take forever. Already, the capital of the railway has been usurped!" Although a number of gentlemen of Sichuan sent a petition to the provincial officials demanding that the Copper Bureau return the appropriated capital to the railway company, they received no reply from the governor-general. Rumor had it that Governor-General Xiliang was "furious" and "put it aside."[97] In frustration, the gentry managers in the railway company went public with the story of the Copper Bureau incident.[98] From the beginning of the *zugu* levy to 1906, Pu Dianjun's investigation found that the Copper Bureau had usurped more than 2.1 million taels of silver of capital from the company, a huge loss given that only five million taels of capital were levied in total. Angrily accusing provincial officials of breaking the law, Pu suggested that the Sichuan governor-general was "impairing the authority of the central government."[99] By circulating this report widely, he put immense pressure on Sichuan's provincial officials.

In the fight against the Sichuan officials, overseas students also united with Sichuan-born metropolitan officials in Beijing. Pu and his comrades constantly cited provincial officials' misdeeds in handling railway issues in their letters and petitions, which put pressure on Governor-General Xiliang.[100] Moreover, Pu Dianjun dispatched more investigators to uncover problems in every branch of the railway company; investigative reports about the Chengdu, Beijing, and Yichang branches poured in, charging that the company was corrupt, slow-moving, and too bureaucratic.[101] These reports, citing legal codes of the Qing and declaring that the railways had to be privately managed according to the law, were mailed each month to the central government in Beijing, the county governments, and the railway shareholder associations in Sichuan.[102]

On February 20, 1907, Governor-General Xiliang announced, under pressure, that the company was to be transformed from a co-ownership company to one that was supervised by officials and managed by merchants (*guandu shangban*). The radical Sichuan students could not accept this arrangement. As Pu and his comrades reported, although a research bureau (Chuan-Han tielu yanjiu suo) was established so that gentry would be consulted, the main decisions were still made by Xiliang and the official managers.[103] Therefore, until 1907, even though the Chuan-Han Railway Company was formally co-managed by merchants and officials, power still lay in the hands of officials, and the Commercial Code of the Qing, which enumerated the rights that all shareholders deserved, was not applied. Pu Dianjun and his like did not give up and refused to accept this arrangement.[104]

On March 4, 1907, Governor-General Xiliang reported to the court that the Chuan-Han Railway Company would be transformed into a privately owned company, with Sichuan natives Qiao Shunan and Hu Jun as the chief manager and vice-manager, respectively. After a long and protracted struggle, Sichuan students' efforts finally paid off and the railway company became completely privately managed, with the Sichuan shareholders in control. Shortly after the big change in management in March 1907, a newly adopted company charter was issued. The new charter explicitly protected the rights of shareholders. The railway company set up shareholder associations: there were three auditors and a board of thirteen directors, who were to be in charge but also required to discuss railway issues regularly with the company's managers. As for the shareholder associations, only people with stock worth at least fifty taels of silver were given the right to participate. A shareholder had to have more than five thousand taels of stock to be elected as a board member and more than 2,500 taels of stock to be elected as an auditor. These regulations demonstrated that the Chuan-Han Railway Company was a private company, over which the providers of its capital held authority. Furthermore, a *zugu* bureau to which people with *zugu* worth more than three *dan* (178 kilograms) could be elected was established in every county. This regulation prevented the arbitrary appointment of *zugu* bureau personnel and improved the conditions of levying the *zugu*.[105]

While these changes represented a considerable improvement, overseas students were still unsatisfied and continued their criticism of Sichuan officials. For one thing, the lingering power of the provincial government remained strong in the newly privatized company. No branch managers of the company could be appointed without governmental approval, and local governments still had supervisory power in the levying of the *zugu*. In addition, the shareholder associations, though provided for in the charter, had yet to be fully established.

Continuing their campaign, in the fifth issue of the *Report on Improving the Chuan-Han Railway Company* published in late 1907, the overseas students again proposed to establish shareholder branches in all Sichuan counties so as to create supervision over the management company and ensure that shareholders had their voices heard in company meetings.[106] As a result, shareholder associations were systematically set up after 1907, and the gentry who worked in these bureaus would become another strong force in the Sichuan Railway Protection movement in 1911. In 1908, the railway company finally made its last personnel changes: Hu Jun, a Chengdu gentleman who had greatly accelerated the commercialization process and had been in contact with the Sichuanese students since 1904, was appointed chief manager of the railway company in Chengdu; Qiao Shu'nan, a Sichuan-born metropolitan official, became the Beijing manager; and Fei Daochun, another Sichuan gentleman, became the manager in Yichang.

Following the change in leadership, the new private company began issuing the *Newsletter of the Private Sichuan Chuan-Han Railway Company*, a newspaper registered under the Qing Ministry of Posts and Communications that was publicly circulated so that a wider range of people could track the development of the railway company. The monthly newsletters publicized laws related to railway issues and exposed misconduct and corruption within the company. Their purpose was clear: all shareholders would now be able to supervise the operation of the company. Even so, the levying of the *zugu* tax remained a problem. Not surprisingly, this time it was the gentry in the *zugu* bureaus who used their power to embezzle revenue from the *zugu* tax. But this newly developed gentry corruption could no longer be concealed, as branches of the shareholder associations were by then in operation, investigating and monitoring the *zugu* bureaus and enabling taxpayers to recognize and complain about the problem and to feel that they had some say in railway matters.[107]

Importantly, the leaders who actively led the Chuan-Han Railway Improvement Society were Pu Dianjun, Xiao Xiang, Chen Chongji, Shao Cong'en, and Deng Rong, all overseas Sichuan students who had close ties to the Sichuan gentry back home. In their struggle to establish control over the railway company, they leveraged the new conception of law and the discourse about rights, and in the process became well known among a great number of Sichuan gentry, gathered a substantial following, and developed excellent reputations. Thanks to their efforts, the notion that taxpayers deserve rights—in essence, no taxation without representation—first entered public discourse in Sichuan. This powerful idea would soon be extended to other spheres of struggle. Furthermore, their methods of petitioning, publishing, holding meetings, persuading, and distributing pamphlets and posters also became useful in campaigning and communication, and would be used more extensively in Sichuan's later political struggles. Even before the local-level constitutional reform and provincial assembly elections began in 1908, progressive Sichuanese had employed a new discourse about rights in order to contend with the state, and in the process, through numerous reports and pamphlets, conveyed this notion to a wider sphere of people.

Conclusion

The story of the last ten years of the Qing has been told in many different ways. It was a complicated time: a time of reform, of revolution, of collapse, of regeneration. Change was the order of the day. Until the 1970s, in Taiwan, mainland China, and the United States, Sun Yat-sen's credentials as the "revolutionary" father of modern China were unquestioned. As a consequence, scholarship that privileged Sun's role in creating "modern China" dismissed as false and futile the Qing government's last-gasp reform efforts to build a modern nation on the foundation of an empire. These earlier narratives portrayed the New Policies as empty gestures on the part of a Qing court desperate to stave off the attacks of its critics but determined not to submit to anything more than superficial change.

Recent scholarship has taken a much more favorable view of the reform. This writer is among those who argue for recognizing the profound impact of the late Qing reform on local society. Late Qing state building affected the Chinese polity in important and wide-ranging ways. As Prasenjit Duara points out, this top-down state effort at modernization had significant social implications. The implementation of the New Policies changed Chinese community dynamics in fundamental ways, creating immense tensions in rural society, where the tax increases and incomplete bureaucratization of the New Policies era led to "state involution" and the disintegration of long-standing community institutions.[108] Mary Rankin and William Rowe, from a different angle, stress the societal power that arose in the late Qing.[109] Rankin describes local elite activism in the wake of the Taiping Rebellion and the effective managerial power that local community leaders obtained. She argues that the post-rebellion reconstruction fostered an expansion of elite-managed local activity. As their dissatisfaction with the state surged during the era of the 1911 Revolution, the elites were able to use the associations they had developed as a solid organizational base to overthrow the Qing.[110] In a similar vein, in Hankow, Rowe found a rapidly expanding elite public sphere, the key element of which was not rational discussion, but management by elites in an extrabureaucratic domain.[111]

Both portrayals capture essential features of this perplexing period. The Sichuan story demonstrates that the New Policies reform provided the chance for a new group of political elites to develop and deploy their power. Rather than representing a "society" that was always in opposition to the "state," this elite was at first in close collaboration with the state and initially gained its new authority and power through such collaboration. In particular, elite Sichuan students, most of whom had studied law and politics, and the leaders among them—Pu Dianjun, Xiao Xiang, and Deng Xiaoke—all being followers of Liang Qichao and graduates of Hōsei University, were ardent believers in constitutionalism and strong advocates of the rights of the people. It was during the building of the Chuan-Han Railway Company that they began to practice their new repertoire of struggle—holding meetings, filing petitions, and propagandizing their ideas in widely circulated publications. They secured a stronghold in the economic sphere, gained a political reputation, and attracted a large number of followers. All of this paved the way for the confrontations at the Sichuan Provincial Assembly and culminated in the later Railway Protection movement.

4 Can Two Sides Walk Together Without Agreeing to Meet?

CONSTITUTIONALISTS AND OFFICIALS IN THE LATE QING CONSTITUTIONAL REFORM

On October 14, 1909, the Sichuan Provincial Assembly held its first meeting in the newly constructed assembly hall in Chengdu. Like all constitutionalists across the Qing empire, the assemblymen had awaited this moment with much anticipation since the launch of the constitutional reform in 1906. The opening ceremony was an event of great significance, with all high-level provincial officials—the governor-general, the treasurer, the commissioner of education, the surveillance commissioner, the head of the provincial police, the commissioner of commerce, the tea and salt circuit head, the Chengdu prefect, the Chengdu magistrate, and the Huayang county magistrate—present at the meeting hall by eight in the morning.[1] With all but one of the 105 Sichuan assemblymen in attendance, starting at ten that morning the assembly held a formal election to choose its leaders. Pu Dianjun, the much-respected *jinshi* degree holder, graduate of Hōsei University in law and politics, former secretary of the Ministry of Law, and adjunct of the Institute for Constitution Compilation, was elected chairman of the assembly.[2] Xiao Xiang, former secretary of the Ministry of Punishment, also a *jinshi* degree holder and graduate of Hōsei University, was voted vice-chairman. Luo Lun, a *juren* degree holder and an influential figure in the literary circles in Chengdu, became the second vice-chairman.[3]

After the election, Governor-General Zhao Erxun gave his opening remarks, voicing enthusiasm for constitutionalism:

Fortunately, today our state policy (*guoce*) has been established; all people have their hearts set on one road—constitutionalism. . . . All of those new things like self-government, police, new education, industry, etc., have been included in a nine-year plan for constitutional preparation. We, officials and gentry, should all follow a proper sequence and achieve them step by step. I, your governor, will carefully examine and investigate the special circumstances of Sichuan.[4]

Zhao's eagerness to build constitutionalism was shared by the assemblymen. Expressing his gratitude toward the court for launching this political reform, Chairman Pu Dianjun said:

> Sichuan is geographically far away from the center, and communications are inconvenient. . . . In political thinking and ability, compared to the capital and the southeastern provinces, Sichuan is backward. Nevertheless, today we Sichuanese receive the same treatment as other provinces: we Sichuanese can also talk about our provincial politics as much as is needed. This is all because of the kindness and generosity of the court. All we Sichuan gentry, fathers and sons, elders and youngsters, should show our gratitude by advocating [constitutional politics] and trying our best to help our province progress.[5]

Representing all assemblymen and the people of Sichuan, Pu thanked Governor-General Zhao Erxun, saying that they cherished his input. Speaking for all officials, Zhao offered his recognition of the contribution and dedication of the gentry-scholars: "Always, I see outstanding people from within China struggling to strengthen the country. Day and night, they submit proposals in the hopes of leading our country to acquire wealth and power. Are they not sincere in their hearts to do so?" Zhao assured the assemblymen that things would be different from then on because "our state policy"—constitutionalism—was "solidly established."[6]

The seeming concord on the general principle of establishing constitutionalism came to an abrupt end with the start of discussion on the concrete issue of how taxes should be levied and distributed and who had the authority to decide these matters. It soon became obvious that beneath the façade of agreeing to build a constitutional state for China, assemblymen and officials disagreed on almost every aspect of how to construct such a state. What was the legitimacy of such a state? How should it be structured and its power distributed? In building constitutionalism, what exactly were elected members of the provincial assembly supposed to do, and what were officials supposed to do? These questions pervaded the entire Chinese experiment with constitutionalism in the late Qing.

Using Sichuan as an example, this chapter examines the two divergent configurations of constitutionalism at the time of the constitutional reform, one coming from officials such as Governor-General Zhao Erxun, who claimed that "all political power belongs to the state," and the other from constitutionalists such as the Sichuan assemblymen who, though inarticulate at first, firmly announced when the meeting closed a month and a half later that there would be "no taxation without supervision." Both views surfaced during the 1909 Provincial Assembly meeting, and the differences between them emerged as a clash of divergent political principles in the course of debates over forty-two bills before the assembly. Participants quickly learned to use the new political institution—the assembly—to debate, legislate, and represent "the people" as a rival to officialdom.

The Coming of the Constitutional Reform

The initial programs of the New Policies reform, which focused on increasing the effectiveness of the state, did not satisfy radical reformers like Liang Qichao, who criticized the government's methods as insubstantial.[7] As an alternative, they wanted a fundamental political reform buttressed by new political principles such as the people's rights and constitutionalism. For them, the foundation of reform *was* constitutional reform.[8]

This constitutional cause was advanced by international crises that generated a strong sense of urgency. In the aftermath of the signing of the Boxer Protocol between the Qing and the Eight-Nation Expeditionary Force, an emboldened imperialist presence exerted itself more aggressively than before. By the summer of 1905, the Qing had lost complete sovereignty over Manchuria. The British advance in Lhasa, the German progress at Boyang Lake in Jiangxi province, the assertive Russian moves along the northwestern border, and the expansion of British and French spheres of influence all prompted demands for radical change in China. Liang and his comrades, though agreeing with the revolutionaries that the country needed an overhaul, worried that revolutionary activities would wreck the country in the face of dangerous enemies from abroad.[9]

In addition to Liang and his comrades, another group of political elites was also converted to the constitutional cause. One in particular, Zhang Jian, holder of the first place (*zhuangyuan*) in the metropolitan-level civil service examination and a much-respected adviser to various Qing governors-general, carried enormous weight. In 1903, Zhang visited Japan for the first time and was deeply impressed by the energy displayed by the Japanese people. While visiting Hokkaido, Zhang wrote in his journal that the reasons for China's failure to achieve wealth and power lay in the fact that "the power holders in China are both foolish and indolent."[10] The only way for the country to achieve wealth and power, Zhang argued, was by making a "fundamental change in its political system" via constitutional reform.[11] Zhang was soon joined by Tang Shouqian and Zheng Xiaoxu, both renowned gentry with countrywide reputations.[12] Their status and connections afforded them political influence over the power politics of the late Qing. Before long, Zhang's group, primarily made up of gentry from Jiangsu and Zhejiang provinces, grew into a powerful political force that could sway both public opinion and the attitudes of officials.

It was the Russo-Japanese War (1904–1905) that transformed constitutionalism into a nationwide movement. The war began on February 8,

1904, and an editorial published in the *China and Foreign Affairs Daily* (*Zhongwai ribao*) five days later urged readers to pay particular attention to the war between Japan, a constitutional monarchy, and Russia, an imperial autocracy, as a proving ground for political systems. It stated, "The strength of a nation does not come from the race of its people but from its political institutions."[13] Another article declared, "From this war onward, the ideals of our countrymen will be greatly changed."[14] To conservative officials' contentions that "the Japanese soldiers, having been given power, will think only about themselves," the constitutionalists offered this rejoinder: Because the people's rights are endowed by Heaven and "citizens of a constitutional state fight for their Heaven-endowed rights (*tianquan*), the Japanese will throw themselves into battle fearlessly."[15] The hope of the constitutionalists was that Japan would win the war, thereby validating their assertion that only constitutionalism could save the country.

No sooner had the war broken out than constitutionalists in Jiangsu and Zhejiang began liaising with Qing officials to advance their cause. They proposed sending important ministers abroad "to learn from the new politics of various nations . . . and assert national sovereignty (*zhuquan*)."[16] The first memorial sent to the court to promote constitutionalism was composed by Sun Baoqi, the ambassador to France. In April 1904, influenced by his younger brother Sun Baoxuan, a key constitutional advocate of Zhejiang, Sun Baoqi wrote:

The reason that the New Policies reform is not having an effect is that there is no central principle to the reform. . . . One way to eradicate the obstacles to reform and to push the reform forward is to emulate the constitutional systems of various other countries. We should learn from British, German, and Japanese political institutions and transform ourselves into a constitutional country.[17]

In great detail, Sun Baoqi advocated re-creating the Japanese Diet (parliamentary) system in China. To add weight to his opinion, Sun sent a private letter to Hunan governor Duanfang urging him and the governor-general of Huguang, Zhang Zhidong, to write a joint memorial to help convince the court.

Other Jiang-Zhe constitutionalists were also actively making connections with Qing officials with the aim of fashioning a political force to launch constitutional reform. In May 1904, Zhang Jian initiated correspondence with the governor of Jiangsu, Wei Guangtao, and the governor-general of Huguang, Zhang Zhidong, to advocate constitutionalism. In June, Zhang Jian contacted the governor-general of Zhili, Yuan Shikai, in an attempt to gain his support. That same month, Zhang and Tang Shouqian made similar overtures in attempting to influence metropolitan officials, in particular Grand Councilor Qu Hongji.[18]

The Russo-Japanese War proceeded as the constitutionalists expected. In May 1905, Russia's entire Baltic fleet was sunk in the Tsushima Strait, leading to total victory for the Japanese. To the overjoyed constitutionalists, the implication was clear: Russia's defeat would make it more difficult for the court to hold up the example of that country's political system as justification for their refusal to grant the Chinese people their political rights. By 1905, in the face of unflagging attempts at persuasion and the unmistakable result of the Russo-Japanese War, many prominent Qing officials, especially the powerful governors and governors-general—Yuan Shikai, Zhang Zhidong, Duanfang, Cen Chunxuan, and Zhou Fu—had showed sympathy for the constitutional cause. After Zhang Jian's persistent urging, Yuan Shikai decided to throw his support behind constitutional reform. In July, Zhou Fu further proposed setting up a system of checks and balances and establishing the separation of the three branches of government. In August, Cen Chunxuan announced his approval for setting up a constitutional system. Furthermore, the influential grand councilor Qu Hongji suggested sending high officials to European nations and to America to study their political systems. By this time, five of the eight governors-general of the Qing—the governors-general of Yungui, Liangguang, Liangjiang, Huguang, and Zhili—had suggested establishing a constitutional system, and Sichuan governor-general Xiliang had advised sending a mission to foreign nations to study their political systems.[19]

The constitutionalists in Jiangsu and Zhejiang clearly played a key role in pushing the Qing government toward constitutional reform. Sichuan's constitutional elite, though not as influential as their Jiang-Zhe counterparts, also contributed to the constitutional cause. Sichuan overseas students were arguably among the most radical overseas constitutionalist groups. In January 1905, Deng Xiaoke of Sichuan drafted an open letter, "Our Opinions on Returning the Power," demanding that Empress Dowager Cixi return power to the Guangxu emperor and that the court transform the Qing into a constitutional government. And another Sichuan student, Zhang Lan, volunteered to travel to Beijing, plead with the court, and articulate the students' constitutional hopes and aspirations.[20] Taken together, these constitutionalists, presenting themselves as the representatives of the people, declared that "the grand hope of constructing a constitution is the dominant principle in Western political theory, and it is also the greatest joy of the people."[21]

In July 1905, the late Qing reform entered a new stage, as working toward constitutional reform finally became a state policy. Following a decision on July 9 to send officials to study foreign legal and political systems, the court issued an edict on July 16 appointing five leading officials to travel abroad to investigate all aspects of governmental administration, with the intention of adopting the best among them. The New Policies, initially hardly more than an extension of the reforms associated with the Self-Strengthening movement, had now become a far-reaching transformation of the polity.

After some twists and turns, the constitutional mission set out in December 1905. The final appointees—Imperial Prince Zaize, Hunan governor Duanfang, Shuntian prefect Li Shengduo, junior vice president of the Board of Revenue Dai Hongci, and Shandong treasurer Shang Qiheng—were divided into two groups, one led by Dai Hongci and the other by Zaize. On December 7, the first group—Dai Hongci and Duanfang—left Beijing for Shanghai, and from there they made stops in Japan and the United States before traveling to Britain, France, Germany, Austria, Russia, Italy, Denmark, Sweden, Norway, Holland, Switzerland, and Belgium. On December 11, the second group—Zaize, Shang Qiheng, and Li Shengduo—departed from Beijing, also making Japan their first stop, followed by the United States, Britain, France, and Belgium. The two groups of investigators met in Brussels in June 1906 and then left Europe for China on July 12. After returning to Shanghai on July 21, Dai Hongci and Duanfang met with the Jiang-Zhe constitutionalists as many as four times to discuss issues of constitutionalism. And while passing through Tianjin on August 6, Dai Hongci and Duanfang met with Yuan Shikai to discuss both constitutional reform and administrative reform.[22]

Most members of the mission had no experience traveling abroad, and their trip was both quick and cursory. Yet, however superficial their contact may have been, they were deeply impressed by what they saw, and when after eight months they returned to China, these imperial delegates all became firm supporters of constitutionalism. It is worth noting that they recommended to the court that it mirror the constitutional system of Meiji Japan, which they argued would strengthen rather than weaken the authority of the emperor by deflecting to the cabinet and its prime minister political criticism that would otherwise be directed at the emperor himself. Upon returning from abroad, Zaize was resolute in advocating constitutionalism. On July 24 and 25, 1906, he was received by Empress Dowager Cixi. In a memorial following the meeting, Zaize attributed the wealth and power of strong foreign countries to the fact that every one of them had a constitution. Zaize also tried to ease Cixi's concern about losing power. Far from "strengthening the people and weakening the court," he wrote, "the constitution of Japan directs power toward the center" and thus should be the model for China. Dai Hongci and Duanfang were equally firm in their positions. Received by Cixi after their return to Beijing, they too assured her that constitutionalism would only strengthen the country and not erode the power of the emperor.[23]

Two important documents were produced after the trip, both of which set out principles and plans for conducting constitutional reform in China: "Memorial to Set Up the Principle of the Country," submitted by Duanfang, and "Memorial to Reorganize the System of Administration," jointly submitted by Duanfang and Dai Hongci. In particular, the first memorial laid out the key principles for constitutional reform:

First, all in the country are equal [citizens] before the law; all distinctions [between people] should be eradicated. Second, national affairs should be decided by public opinion. Third, all the advantages of the Chinese and Western nations should be adopted to attain the security and growth of both the state and the people. Fourth, the organs of the imperial palace and the government should be divided and clarified. Fifth, the boundary between central and local government should be clarified and self-governance should be practiced. Sixth, a fiscal system should be established that sets clear budgets and expenditures.

The memorial then requested that the above principles be "introduced to all people under Heaven as the fundamental principle of the country" and gave a schedule for implementing them: "Within fifteen to twenty years, a constitution should be established, parliamentary representatives elected, a parliament opened, and all practices in politics should follow the constitutional model."[24]

Ironically, both this memorial and the other one, "Memorial to Reorganize the System of Administration," were written by Liang Qichao, who was at the time a fugitive from the Qing government, with a price of a hundred thousand taels on his head. The discovery in 2008 of Liang Qichao's draft by Peking University researcher Xia Xiaohong finally unlocked the mystery of the authorship of these two essays.[25] In terms of the content, "Memorial to Set Up the Principle of the Country" systematically reflected on the failure of the previous Self-Strengthening movement, and its underlying logic replicates Liang Qichao's 1901 article "On Constitutionalism" (Li xianfa yi), which ascribed China's weakness and poverty to its autocratic political system and argued that only through transformation into a constitutional monarchy could the country attain wealth and power. Furthermore, the six proposals in this memorial, explicitly asking for political equality, represented a radical departure from traditional political morality, which was based on political hierarchicalism. They expressed, in Liang Qichao's language, a strong anti-autocratic spirit.

Close scrutiny of the contents of the two memorials leads one to wonder whether Duanfang, Dai Hongci, or the three other imperial delegates truly regarded constitutionalism in the same way as Liang Qichao. All five delegates became strong advocates of constitutionalism following their mission abroad, and there is little reason to doubt that the moves toward constitutional government were in substantial measure a response to the various challenges to Manchu legitimacy at the time.[26] However, there is no indication that these officials were planning on transferring power to a parliament and allowing the legislative branch to lead the government, and there is no indication that they truly wanted to grant political power to "the people." On the contrary, as in the case of Zaize, the intent of these delegates was to use constitutionalism to "strengthen power at the center."[27] Thus, even though officials had to rely on Liang Qichao's talent to fulfill their obligation to write reports on constitutionalism, they did not share with Liang a commitment to the deeper principles underlying his advocacy of constitutionalism. For these officials, constitutionalism was a way to achieve national wealth and power. But for Liang and other constitutionalists, constitutionalism was also an institution to guarantee popular sovereignty and the rights of the people.

Despite the deeply entrenched ideological differences between officials and constitutionalists, their collaboration continued. While reform-minded officials tried to persuade the court to accept constitutionalism, constitutionalists worked hard at shaping public opinion and persuading more political elite to join their cause. Finally, on September 1, 1906, the court announced the launch of constitutional reform: "At this moment in time, the only way for [the empire] to survive is to emulate and carry out constitutional reform. Sovereignty resides with the emperor, but various matters should be determined by public opinion. To eradicate the old evils and to clarify officials' responsibility, we must begin with reform in administration."[28] This edict marked the beginning of a new era in Chinese politics and offered great hope to many Chinese people. Thrilled by the expectation that they were to become stakeholding citizens, they responded to the announcement of the edict with celebrations far and wide throughout the Qing empire.[29]

The Practice of Constitutional Reform

STATE POLICIES

The first step toward constitutionalism was a reorganization of the administrative system, another idea from Liang Qichao, who first presented it in the memorial he wrote for Dai Hongci and Duanfang, "Memorial to Reorganize the System of Administration." On September 2, 1906, the Qing court appointed fourteen officials to draw up plans for the reorganization and another three to review those plans. Five guidelines for overhauling administration were defined, of which three were most important:

to "emulate the administration of the constitutional nations," to "make sure that all officials perform their responsibilities and that no sinecures be allowed," and "to uphold the idea that the responsibilities of the three branches—executive, legislative, and judicial—should be clarified and separated."[30]

Administrative reform, which began at the central level, encountered major obstacles from the beginning.[31] Two issues in particular were the main sources of contention, one being whether to abolish and replace the Grand Secretariat (Neige) and the Grand Council (Junjichu) with a "responsible cabinet" (zeren neige), and the other being whether to roll back the independent authority of provincial officials in an attempt to recentralize authority in Beijing. The impact of these reforms, as summarized by historian Hou Yijie, was real. As Hou states, while a new cabinet was not established at this stage of the reform, the central administration did undergo several important changes: one was a decrease in the number of grand councilors; a second was a decrease in the number of officials in each ministry and the abandonment of the Manchu-Han dyarchy and ethnic slots in the core agencies of the metropolitan government; a third was the establishment of the principle of the separation of the judicial and executive branches; and a fourth was the specialization of ministers for their particular posts. Finally, preparations were made to establish a National Assembly (Zizhengyuan), a national audit office, a new navy, and a military advisory department, and to divide up the navy and the army and separate the military orders from the administration of the military.[32]

The failure to establish a cabinet was a disappointment to some constitutionalists. The founder of L'Impartial, a famous Kang-Liang follower and Manchu constitutionalist, Ying Lianzhi, for example, regarded the reform as superficial, lacking the essence of a true reform. But an argument can be made that constitutionalists like Ying may have been too cynical. The central-level administrative reform enacted the principle of separating the executive and judicial branches of government and prepared for the building of a National Assembly, both of which were unprecedented in Chinese history.[33]

Having completed the reshuffling of the central government, the court shifted focus to the reform of provincial and local administrations. On July 7, 1907, after numerous debates and a test run in Manchuria, Prince Yi-kuang and Grand Councilor Sun Jia'nai issued "Proposal for the Reform of Local Administration," which included several key changes.[34] First was the establishment of a provincial-level council in which provincial officials would meet regularly to decide important matters; this would help curb the autocratic power of the governors and governors-general. Second was the abolition of the posts of all yamen runners and clerks, to be replaced by professional positions filled via examination. These new positions were to be specialized according to the matters under their charge: police, education, agriculture, industry, commerce, communications, prisons, and of course, taxation. Third, all provinces would now have a new provincial judicial commissioner, called supervisor of the law (*tifasi*), who would manage the administration of the judicial system and supervise judicial proceedings in courts at all levels. Finally, the proposal requested that provincial officials set up local administrative councils (*dongshihui*), as well as local and county-level councils for discussing local affairs (*yishihui*); these formal organizations would enable local elites to participate in local governance and assist local officials.[35] The "Proposal for the Reform of Local Administration," as we will see in the case of Sichuan, would greatly disturb local society.

The preparation for constitutionalism from 1906 to 1907 had been mainly focused on administrative changes; the assassination of Anhui governor Enming on July 6, 1907, by a revolutionary named Xu Xilin, however, dramatically accelerated the reform. Reacting promptly, the court issued a decree on July 8, two days after the assassination, stating that all officials and commoners (*renmin*), not just those who were originally allowed to submit palace memorials, could send proposals on issues of constitutionalism.[36] This edict permitted a much broader group of junior officials and scholar commoners to have their ideas forwarded to the center by either the Censorate or provincial officials. Never before in Chinese history had a government formally recognized the right of the common people to participate in and discuss political affairs. From that point on, constitutionalism became the new rallying cry among the educated elite in China, and officials, including Manchus, expressed their determination to endorse the reform.[37]

Beginning in the second half of 1907, preparations for constitutionalism were enacted at dizzying speed. Officials at all levels were required to establish "study groups on constitutionalism" (*xianzheng yanjiu hui*) and "schools of law and politics" (*fazheng xuetang*) to cultivate talent for the constitutional reform.[38] Then, in an unmistakable signal that constitutional reform was being taken to a new level, an edict was issued on August 13 to establish a special political organization for constitutional change—the Institute for Constitutional Compilation.[39] On August 24, Prince Yikuang detailed the specific regulations that would govern this new agency, including that its primary responsibilities would be to "discuss all matters related to constitutional reform, conduct related investigations, and study constitutions of other nations in order to draw up a constitution and related regulations."[40] On October 26, the *Political Gazette* (*Zhengzhi guanbao*) was launched as the official publication of the Institute for Constitutional

Compilation to introduce edicts concerning domestic politics to a wide-ranging group of readers. Many radical-minded intellectuals who had studied abroad were installed in this institute, and they took a leading role in propelling true reform from the top.[41]

The wave continued to build: On September 20, in response to growing demands for the opening of a parliament, Cixi issued an edict in her own name (*yizhi*) that clarified the vague promise she had made a year earlier about parliament, declaring that her ultimate intention was to establish "a bicameral deliberative body." As a preparatory step, she ordered the immediate creation of a National Assembly, appointing Prince Pulun and Grand Secretary Sun Jia'nan as its co-presidents and charging them with the task of drawing up a detailed plan together with the Grand Council. In addition, the court decided to send more ministers abroad to study constitutions and tried hard to eliminate sources of friction between the Manchus and the Han so as to reduce the mounting ethnic antagonism between them.[42]

Needless to say, the court relied on the constitutionalists to conduct these reforms. In March 1907, for example, Minister of Justice Dai Hongci wrote to Liang Qichao asking for ideas on how to set boundaries between the Ministry of Justice (Fabu) and the Office of Central Judicial Affairs (Daliyuan).[43] Meanwhile, the Institute for Constitutional Compilation gathered a group of highly capable legal professionals, most of whom had been trained overseas. In his meticulous study of the institute personnel's backgrounds, historian Peng Jian notes that law school graduates of Japanese, British, American, and German universities made up the majority of the institute's staff. Some, like Yan Fu, Zhang Zongxiang, Lu Zongyu, and Cao Rulin, had served the Qing state for a time. Others, such as Sichuan's Pu Dianjun, Zeng Jian, and Li Jixun, had just graduated and returned from overseas.[44]

ENLIGHTENING THE PEOPLE, GETTING ORGANIZED,
AND PETITIONING TO OPEN A PARLIAMENT

As the court rapidly promulgated edicts for the constitutional reform, constitutionalists around the Qing empire were busy enlightening people about constitutionalism. Merchants were an important audience. A coalescence of Chinese merchant groups had commenced in January 1904. The Regulation on Chambers of Commerce ordered merchants in the Qing empire to establish associations at all levels of towns and cities. All provincial capitals were expected to establish a general chamber of commerce (*shangwu zonghui*), small cities were expected to establish a branch of the chamber of commerce (*shangwu fenhui*), and county townships were expected to set up commercial offices (*shangwu gongsuo*). By 1911 there were 669 chambers of commerce in China, with 12.4 percent of those in Sichuan alone.[45] Merchants, many educated in new-style schools and capable of reading newspapers, began to see themselves as active citizens. Many participated in the Rights Recovery movement to regain railway rights from foreign investors, a movement that the constitutionalists played an essential role in organizing.[46]

Another important audience for the constitutionalists was students in modern-style schools. These schools not only taught students to read newspapers but also instilled in them a strong sense of nationalism and political responsibility. Also, from 1901 onward, an increasing number of Chinese students headed abroad to study. Whereas only a thousand Chinese students were studying in Japan in 1903, the number had increased to eight thousand by 1905.[47] Many of these students brought new political ideas home with them. Furthermore, students within China had easy access to *Xinmin congbao*, *Zhongguohun*, and other reformist publications that propagated the ideas of rights of the people, popular sovereignty, and constitutionalism.[48] After 1906, the number of students sympathetic to constitutionalism grew rapidly, and study groups mushroomed all over the country. In Shanghai, Jilin, Guangdong, Hunan, and Guizhou, constitutional associations, which had the basic features of a political party, were developing apace.[49] These constitutional associations published newspapers and textbooks, set up schools of self-governance, proposed new regulations, and helped pave the way for planning the provincial assemblies, in the process becoming increasingly influential throughout China.

The constitutionalists were also mobilizing themselves. In the winter of 1906, after the Qing court declared the launch of constitutional reform, Liang Qichao was eager to get back to politics. From then until the summer of 1907, Liang was in frequent correspondence with constitutionalists Yang Du, Jiang Guanyun, Xu Fosu, and Xiong Xiling, discussing the possibility of establishing a formal political party.[50] Liang's initial plan to unite all the constitutionalists—both the overseas student constitutionalists and the Jiang-Zhe constitutionalists—did not work out. After Yang organized his own political party, the Association for Constitutional Government (Xianzheng gonghui), in the fall of 1907, Liang also organized his first formal political party, the Political Information Institute (Zhengwenshe).[51]

Among the efforts of these constitutionalists, it was Yang Du's call for opening a parliament that launched an important political trend. From January 1907 on, using the *New China Newspaper* (*Zhonghua xin bao*) as his base, Yang wrote numerous editorials urging the creation of a parliament, maintaining that "having a parliament is the only way to fight against the government and transform it from an irresponsible one into a responsible one." Beginning on September 25, 1907, Yang organized delegates to go to Beijing, sending petitions to the Censorate and then to the court.[52] Yang's focus on building a parliament was endorsed by Liang Qichao, who believed that by simplifying constitutionalism to concentrate on the idea of establishing a parliament, the constitutionalists had finally found a tool that was direct enough to mobilize the masses.[53] Together, through important newspapers such as *Shibao* and *Xinmin congbao*, Liang and Yang shaped public opinion.[54] As a *Shibao* article put it in early 1908, "'Parliament, parliament,' this is the rallying cry!"[55] Soon the Jiang-Zhe constitutionalists also turned their attention to the issue of establishing a parliament, and, influenced by them, many members of China's educated elite began to consider a parliament the key to constitutional reform and the foundation for solving all of China's other problems. A participant in the Zhejiang Railway Rights Recovery movement, for example, wrote, "We should first set up a parliament; then the rights over mines and railways can be preserved."[56]

By December 1907 several constitutionalist groups—such as the Association for Constitutional Government led by Yang Du, the Political Information Institute led by Liang Qichao, and the Association for Constitutional Preparations (Yubei lixian gonghui) headed by Zhang Jian, Zheng Xiaoxu, and Tang Shouqian—had all initiated parliamentary petitions. These groups, first separately and then together, launched a serious lobbying effort, soon followed by local self-government organs with petitions of their own. The result was a torrent of similarly worded petitions from various political groups flooding the court in Beijing. Constitutional elites from Henan, Anhui, Jiangsu, Jilin, Hunan, Zhili, Shandong, Beijing, Guangdong, Shanxi, and Zhejiang all sent in petitions demanding the establishment of a parliament.[57]

With Chinese constitutionalists united, the petitions to open a parliament created great pressure on the court, forcing it to recognize the demand and deal with it. On June 8, 1908, Grand Councilors Zhang Zhidong and Yuan Shikai invited officials of the Institute for Constitutional Compilation to discuss the matter. While central officials were debating how many years it would take to open a parliament, petitions continued to arrive from Guangdong, Guizhou, Fujian, Fengtian, Jiangxi, Sichuan, and elsewhere. At the same time, reform-minded provincial officials responded to the petitions in their memorials, likewise requesting the establishment of a parliament. More officials in the system began taking the constitutionalists' side.

As a result, Cixi finally announced a timetable for establishing constitutionalism and gave her approval to a series of documents drawn up by the Institute for Constitutional Compilation and submitted on August 27,

1908: the "Constitutional Outline" (Xianfa dagang), the "Outline of Parliamentary Regulations" (Yiyuanfa yaoling), the "Outline of Election Regulations" (Xuanjufa yaoling), and the "Items of Preparation" (Zhunian choubei shiyi qingdan). These documents emphasized the separation of powers of the three branches of government as a key principle and claimed that a constitution was to be regarded as the ultimate authority that even the emperor had to obey. While the nine-year timetable did not satisfy everyone, reform was nonetheless accelerated at all levels of government.[58]

The Constitutional Reform in Sichuan

STATE REORGANIZATION UNDER ZHAO ERXUN

Important changes had been taking place in the functioning of Sichuan provincial and local governments in the later years of the Qing (see Chapter 3).[59] Nevertheless, the "Proposal for the Reform of Local Administration" announced on July 7, 1907, made things more complicated and contentious. On the one hand, the proposal gave the green light for the expansion of provincial government, which would threaten the power of local elites and alienate them from the state. On the other hand, the proposal also presented an opportunity for self-governance, which led to an emboldened, empowered, and increasingly politically proactive group of provincial and local elites.

It should be recalled here that in Sichuan there was robust elite activism and provincial officials had shown considerable tolerance for the management of county affairs by the local gentry.[60] Consider the example of the Three-Fees Bureau (Sanfeiju), which drew its name from the three most onerous fees collected in serious criminal cases. First established as a managerial body to oversee the payment of the three fees to protect people from extortion, the bureau had been proposed by twenty-five Ba county gentry in 1859. The Ba county magistrate agreed to the proposal and gave the power of levying the three fees to the gentry, a format later extended to the entire province.[61] Gradually, the bureau's influence was extended to other types of cases. By the early Guangxu reign, the bureau had expanded its role to include civil disputes, and as the magistrates were in need of gentry assistance in collecting new taxes in the late Qing era, the Three-Fees Bureau was involved in that process as well.[62] This power of the gentry, however, was put to a stop when Zhao Erxun assumed the post of governor-general in 1908. Upon his arrival, Zhao accused the bureau of having become a haven for corruption and claimed that outlandish deficits were being incurred as managers made payments in areas well beyond the bureau's purview. To fix the problem, Zhao issued a new set of regulations regarding the bureau activities, with the specific aim of tightly controlling it under the provincial government.⁶³

Zhao's action was, in fact, part of a grander reform plan. The Qing court's first step toward constitutionalism, as noted earlier, was the reorganization of its administrative system, and it was precisely in the name of "constitutional reform" that Zhao Erxun launched his state-building projects.⁶⁴ Among the five governors-general Sichuan had during the New Policies reform era, Zhao was the most ambitious. According to Zhou Xun, who served as a secretary in the provincial government in Sichuan, the two most burdensome new bureaus added under the New Policies were the New Tax Bureau (Jingzhengju) and the Police Bureau (Jingchaju). The first was established by Zhao Erxun himself, and the second took full shape during his term, although it was established earlier.

Zhao set up the New Tax Bureau as soon as he became the governor-general of Sichuan.⁶⁵ The bureau rapidly established branches in all of the prefectures and counties of the province. The traditional way of levying taxes had been via local leaders (*lizheng* or *jiazheng*) who, recommended by powerful local elites, were supposed to protect local interests and negotiate with officials. A magistrate would come to a locality, tell the local gentry the number of taels of silver he proposed to collect in tax, and then discuss with them the feasibility of collecting that amount. The gentry would negotiate the number with the official, and after a deal was struck the local gentry would treat the official to an elaborate banquet, with both sides satisfied (see Chapter 1). The establishment of the New Tax Bureau, however, changed everything. The magistrate and the local gentry ceded their power over taxation to the commissioner of the New Tax Bureau. The commissioner came to the locality and asked the magistrate for the predetermined amount; if there were people who resisted paying or if the magistrates were unable to fulfill the levy, the commissioner would report the delinquency of the county magistrates to the provincial capital. As part of the process of modern state building, the New Tax Bureau had its own personnel and even its own office space in local counties, independent of county officials. It was the New Tax Bureau that put the wealth of the Sichuan people into the hands of the governor-general and the central government he served.⁶⁶

The New Tax Bureau also took over a great number of taxes, including those on liquor, oil, property, and pigs.⁶⁷ Because every prefecture and every county now had a local branch, the bureau became a key facilitator of the state's expansion of power into local society. The amount levied by the New Tax Bureau comprised the majority of the tax burden on the Sichuan people, greater than all other kinds of tax, including the railway tax (*zugu*). In Dingyuan county, for example, the level of taxation by the

New Tax Bureau was thirty times that of the land tax (*diding*) and several times the amount of other surcharges.⁶⁸ As confirmed by archival evidence, Zhou Xun, who systematically reviewed the history of taxation in Sichuan, noted that the surcharges on land tax—including extra charges (*jintie*), voluntary surcharge taxes (*juanshu*), and new voluntary surcharge taxes (*xin juanshu*)—were not, in fact, the greatest burden. Rather, it was the New Tax Bureau that made the biggest difference: the largest amount came from taxation on pigs, liquor, oil, sugar, and property, and the bureau made sure that much of the tax was levied effectively. All of this generated great resentment of Zhao Erxun and the New Tax Bureau.

The other provincial administrative reform that greatly influenced the lives of the Sichuanese was the establishment of the new police system, which was first set up in September 1902. The mastermind behind the Police Bureau was the Japan-trained official Zhou Shanpei, who drafted its rules and regulations. Under his able leadership, the new police system was established in Chengdu and gradually elsewhere—by April 1906, it had spread to more than seventy counties and prefectures. In 1907, Zhou was appointed by the provincial governor to head a new office in charge of all police matters. After Zhao Erxun became the governor-general in 1908, he gave Zhou unwavering support.

The amount of money levied to support the police system was exorbitant. Former governor-general Xiliang noted that the police were in principle funded by taxes used for the local militia, but whenever that amount was insufficient, new taxes were created and then made permanent.⁶⁹ Before the New Tax Bureau was officially established and became the chief provider of police funding, the revenue came from a variety of sources, including taxes on shops (*dianpu juan*), attending performances (*xi juan*), opium gum (*yan juan*), and teahouse tables (*zhuomian juan*), as well as the tax levied to pay for government-operated scales to ensure accurate measurement of the *dou* (*dou juan*). After the New Tax Bureau's establishment, most of its revenue went toward expansion of the police system.⁷⁰ And as the Fushun county gazetteer recorded, charges for the police were some of the heaviest of all those imposed to fund local public services.⁷¹

The police were a disruptive presence within the populace. Even the Qing court in Beijing noted the abusiveness and lawlessness of the police in most of the provinces and how much they disturbed the local people.⁷² Sichuan's police system might have been even worse than most. The *Sichuan Gazette* reported that "once the police system came to Sichuan, its evil became uncontrollable."⁷³ In part, the extremely negative reaction toward the police in Sichuan was generated by the power struggle between the old-style neighborhood administrative system (*baojia*), which was controlled by the local gentry, and the new police system, which was installed by the provincial authorities. As governor-general, Zhao Erxun extended the reach of the local police system to nearly all of Sichuan, including the countryside. The constant conflicts between the *baojia* and the police escalated contention in local society to new levels.

By reorganizing the provincial administration, Zhao's "constitutional reform" changed the balance of power between the state and the elite in Sichuan and disrupted local society. During the constitutional reform, modern state building was taking off in Sichuan. The expansion of new provincial bureaucratic organs gave provincial officials more venues for directing and controlling local affairs. In Sichuan in particular, under the strong management of Zhao Erxun, the new provincially directed organizations were expanding, and some, including the police and taxation bureaus, became vertical structures able to reach below the county level. While these organizations guaranteed that the needs of the provincial government would be efficiently met, such state building angered local gentry whose former power of negotiating and collecting taxes had been taken over. These circumstances laid a foundation for the 1909 Sichuan Provincial Assembly debates and the later Railway Protection movement, in which the local people were ready to be mobilized to fight against the power of the state.[74]

THE BUILDING OF THE PROVINCIAL ASSEMBLY

At the same time that Zhao Erxun was reorganizing and expanding the state in the name of constitutional reform, the Sichuan elite were legalizing and accumulating their own power. The most crucial event for the Sichuan elite and the most relevant to this story was the establishment of the provincial assemblies. The official origin of the provincial assemblies was the court's promulgation of the sixty-two-clause Regulations for Provincial Assemblies and the 115-clause Regulations for Provincial Assembly Elections issued on July 22, 1908.[75] The court gave further instructions to provincial governors, stipulating a one-year deadline for the establishment of the assemblies. Provincial officials were required to set up preparatory bureaus, which were to be jointly run by officials and members of the local elite. These bureaus would oversee two rounds of elections: in the first round, eligible voters would choose electors, who in the second round would elect the actual provincial assemblymen (Figure 4.1).

On October 14, 1909, the Provincial Assembly in Sichuan was established. As described by historian Zhang Pengyuan, the average age of the assemblymen was thirty, most held official degrees, and with the exception of a few large merchants, all were respected gentry.[76] Among the 105 assemblymen, former students who had studied in Japan wielded the

FIGURE 4.1. Campaigning for the election of the Provincial Assembly. *Shibao*, March 31, 1909.

greatest influence. These students, who regarded themselves as Sichuanese (*Sichuanren*) and considered their views representative of "the views of the public" (*gongyi*), came to have a weighty impact on public opinion. Having already established their influence over the Chuan-Han Railway Company, these students-turned-assemblymen found that the opening of the 1909 Provincial Assembly finally provided them with an organizational base in the political arena.

Constitutionalism was the talk of the day. In Sichuan, both constitutionalists and officials agreed that political reform was the only way to save China. Whether or not the two sides were committed to the same philosophical understanding of constitutionalism, both held that a constitutional monarchy would make China stronger, as it undeniably had for Japan. The two sides cooperated closely and, in fact, Sichuan was considered a model for implementing the constitutional reform and Zhao Erxun a progressive official well versed in the "new learning."[77] However, as both elites and statesmen acquired significantly more power through the new institutions created in the constitutional reform, conflicts developed between them. While the new provincial bureaucratic organs were expanding, new self-government organizations also emerged as a social base for the Sichuan elite and constitutionalists to wield power. Soon, as will be seen in the Provincial Assembly debates, the collaboration between the constitutionalists and the officials disintegrated, and the differences in political ideologies between the two sides became more distinct than ever.

The 1909 Sichuan Provincial Assembly

"ALL POLITICAL POWER BELONGS TO THE STATE"

At the opening ceremony of the first Sichuan Provincial Assembly meeting on October 14, 1909, Governor-General Zhao Erxun was invited to give the first speech. Zhao appealed to the assemblymen to act properly. First, assemblymen were to "eliminate the barrier" (*rong zhenyu*) between themselves and officials. Second, assemblymen had to "understand the boundaries of their power" (*ming quanxian*). Third, they needed to "aim at achieving public welfare" (*tu gongyi*) rather than pursue personal interest. Fourth, they were to "think broadly" (*mou yuanda*) and make the entire state (*guojia*) their first priority. Fifth, assemblymen needed to "deal with practical matters" (*wu shiji*) instead of speaking empty words. Finally, they needed to "achieve their plans in an orderly and gradual manner" (*xun cixu*).[78]

Zhao Erxun stressed and spoke at length on the rationale behind the first two of the six guidelines. He explained that his first request of "eliminating the barrier" between officials and gentry was the only way for the two sides to achieve solidarity and jointly save the country (*guo*). Only by doing so could officials and gentry "develop an intimate relationship" with each other, such that the gentry could better appreciate the difficulties of officials and officials more effectively protect the rights and interests of the gentry.[79]

In laying out the rationale behind his second request, that assemblymen should "understand the boundaries of their power," Zhao revealed much about his understanding of the power of the state. While praising assemblymen as "the leading scholars in the literary circles" and "the moral exemplars of all Sichuan gentry," Zhao had little sympathy for their ambition to exercise real power, asserting that "all political power belongs to the state" (*yiqie quanli jie shuzhiyu guojia*):

We should certainly make sure that [you know] the boundaries of [your] power. Today is a time when statism (*guojia zhuyi*) is in vogue; all political power belongs to the state. Officials are the operational body (*jiguan*) of the state. Officials do not have power; all their power is held by the state. Assemblymen are representatives of the people. The people do not have power; all their political rights—to talk about politics—are also endowed by the state. Even though today we often talk about the power of the officials and the power of the people, they are either exercising the state's power or are recognized by the state; neither officials nor the people have any power of their own.[80]

Rather than believing that the rights of the people were self-evident, naturally given, and inalienable, as many Chinese constitutionalists had argued,[81] Zhao believed that the state endowed the people with their political rights. It was the abstract entity, "the state" (*guojia*), that had self-evident authority and held ultimate power.[82] Zhao Erxun's reading was apparently enough for him to tap into an influential German political theory of the late nineteenth century—statism—to further strengthen his arguments. But what kind of state was this? Who represented the state in actuality?

When Zhao quoted the late Guangxu emperor as saying that "ultimate power belongs to the imperial court (*daquan tongyu chaoting*), and various political affairs are up for public opinion (*shuzheng gongzhu yulun*)," he seemed to be equating the court (*chaoting*) with the state (*guojia*).[83] But Zhao stopped there and did not pursue this point further; the rest of his speech made little mention of the court and never again associated court with state. He seemed to be doing his best to keep the state as a faceless entity.

In the same vein, Zhao also did not equate the state with officialdom. On the contrary, he made it clear that the state was above officials and, by nature, was a collectivity (*gong*). In a nice parallel, Zhao made it sound as if officials and the people were equal counterparts under the supreme state:

Because officials receive their operative power from the state, they should preserve that power and not disturb the people's rights of political discussion. And because the people obtain from the state the rights that allow them to discuss politics, they should limit themselves to the terrain of political discussion and not infringe upon the rights of officials to exercise the state's power.[84]

Zhao here once again clarified the boundary of power between the people and officials. Summing up this point, he quoted the late Guangxu emperor: "The right of making suggestions belongs to the people, and the right of administering belongs to the government."[85]

Upon hearing what Zhao Erxun had to say, Provincial Assembly Chairman Pu Dianjun ventured a response. Pu, who desired more flexibility for the assemblymen, found the repeated call that they "should stay within the terrain of political discussion and not infringe upon the rights of officials to exercise the state's power" discomfiting: "In terms of the boundary of power between the gentry and officials, it will only become clear when concrete matters concerning gentry and officials arise."⁸⁶ But aside from this vaguely articulated complaint, Chairman Pu had little to say. Summing up his rejoinder to Zhao, he said:

> The purpose of setting up the Provincial Assembly is for all people to help revive state affairs (*guoshi*). All people, both from above and from below, should consider state affairs as their top priority and should not impose a barrier between officials and gentry. Gentry and officials are both fellow countrymen (*benguoren*), and are all helping to manage our state affairs. . . . We should work together to achieve mutual understanding and mutual trust.⁸⁷

At that moment, despite being imbued with ideas about the power and rights of the people, Sichuan assemblymen were incapable of convincingly articulating their principles and challenging the authority of provincial officials. In contrast, Governor-General Zhao conveyed a vision of the state that was much more sophisticated and developed. Although for him the state in essence meant the court, by making it faceless—something unrelated to the court and distinct from officials—Zhao set up the state as something both omnipotent and collective in nature, with officials and the people seemingly equal counterparts under it, presenting a conception of the state that sounded much grander than just the court in Beijing.

DEBATES IN THE SICHUAN PROVINCIAL ASSEMBLY

Nonetheless, the subsequent course of events soon shifted the power dynamic between the Sichuan elite and the governor-general. At the opening ceremony, the assemblymen had not yet developed the cogent and compelling political arguments that would later help them assert their influence and power, but they would very quickly learn to deploy them.

The Sichuan assemblymen set to work as soon as the opening ceremony ended. From the second day, October 15, 1909, the chairman and the two vice-chairmen commenced with the daily business of the provincial assembly. Four secretaries were selected to take charge of making regulations, transcribing meeting records, accounting, and attending to other miscellaneous matters. Detailed and elaborate regulations were drafted: fifty-two regulations on discussions in meetings, thirteen on maintaining security, eight rules on proposing bills, and twenty-eight codes of conduct for the secretaries. All regulations were passed with majority votes from the assemblymen and gained approval from the governor-general. To maintain order during assembly meetings, assemblymen were assigned, by lot, into three different sections (*bu*), each of which elected a section leader via secret ballot.⁸⁸

After the allocation of seats, four key committees were set up to deal with the following areas of responsibility: the first committee dealt with bills proposed by the governor-general and assumed the responsibility of drafting initial responses to those bills; the second committee dealt with proposals coming from assemblymen and assumed the responsibility of developing those proposals into formal bills; the third committee dealt with proposals from the common people and from local self-government organizations; and the fourth committee dealt with punishing the misdoings of provincial assemblymen. The assemblymen themselves elected the chairs of the four committees, and the committee members were chosen by lot. In addition, a special committee of exceptionally capable people recommended by the other four committees was set up to handle particularly important matters. In total, it took the Sichuan assemblymen fifteen days to finish organizing their committees.[89]

The actual discussion began on October 28. According to the summary given by Pu Dianjun at the assembly's closing ceremony, during the monthlong period from October 28 to November 29, forty-two bills were formally discussed. Of those bills, five came from Governor-General Zhao and thirty-seven from assemblymen. By the end of the monthlong period, the assembly had addressed twenty-four bills (by either passing them or defeating them), while discussion of another eighteen bills was still ongoing.[90] Before delving into a case study of one particular debate, it is essential to have a general idea of the bills proposed by the governor-general and the assemblymen.

Zhao Erxun proposed five bills, and their tenets were consistent and unmistakable. Zhao's continual emphasis on the interest of the central and provincial governments reflected his clear desire for a provincial government with the strength to extract more resources from the locale. A typical bill of this sort was one concerning the police budget. In order to obtain enough revenue to establish a provincewide police force so as to fulfill the New Policies reform obligation, Zhao proposed to appropriate the budget formerly designated for the militia (*lianfei*) for police use instead. In addition, he asked for the assembly's permission to add two new taxes, a rent tax (*jiawushui*) and a sales tax (*yingyeshui*), following the example of other provinces.[91] Faced with this request, all but one of the eighty-three assemblymen voted against Zhao's proposal. They pointed out that Zhao might be overstepping his power by asking for a rent tax and a sales tax specifically to fund the police. Citing as an example metropolitan Beijing, which had recently launched a shop tax (*pu juan*) and a vehicle tax (*che juan*) for "local public affairs" (*bendi gongyi*) but "not just for police expenditures," Sichuan assemblymen argued that the rent tax and sales tax proposed by Zhao, comparable in their eyes to the shop and vehicle taxes in Beijing, should be used for local public affairs rather than for the police.[92]

Zhao's attempts to guard the power of the provincial government by making the local people yield were countered by the assemblymen. They not only rejected Zhao's requests for more levies on the Sichuan people but also demanded more control over political matters.[93] In this monthlong period, they proposed thirty-seven bills, hoping to transform the way politics was conducted in Sichuan both by asserting their influence and by promoting self-governance. Among their initiatives was a proposal for setting up a Sichuan provincial bank in which the Sichuan gentry and merchants would be the shareholders and local self-government organizations would be used to obtain funds from the common people, a means of gathering Sichuan's extra capital into their own hands.[94] There was also a proposal to seize property from Buddhist and Daoist temples and local shrines to be handed over to local self-government organizations.[95] Yet another proposal involved setting up a revenue bureau at the county level (*difang caizhengju*) to be composed solely of local elite, tasked with accruing funds for their future self-governance activities.[96]

With regard to taxation, there was one proposal to change the way land tax was levied,[97] and another to change the way the other four taxes—the ones on property, pigs, liquor, and oil—were levied by the New Tax Bureau.[98] In these two proposals, assemblymen asked to have local gentry supervise all taxation in the county, which meant that the gentry would supervise not only collection of the land tax by the county magistrates and their clerks and runners but also the acts of the onerous New Tax Bureau—personally set up by Zhao Erxun to collect the lucrative four additional taxes in each county—and the bureau's county branches. In sum, the assemblymen made it clear that they wanted local self-governance to be something real and authoritative, and that they wanted to be given supervision over all taxation in Sichuan.

Was this vision for self-governance possible? In theory, there should be a demarcation between local administration (*difang xingzheng*) and local public affairs (*difang gongyi*). However, this distinction remained unclear throughout the entire constitutional reform. The 1906 "Memorial to Set Up the Principle of the Country" had called for "a clear delineation of the boundary between central and local government and the practice of self-governance," yet it did not clarify the relationship between local self-governance and local government.[99] Also, even though the central government document on constitutional reform, "Items of Preparation," stated that the scope of state tax (*guoshui*) and local tax (*dishui*) would be announced in 1911 and 1912 respectively, it was clear that until that time came, local elite and governors-general would each intend to do their best to protect potential resources for future revenue that they might eventually control. Thus, at the Sichuan Provincial Assembly, uncertainty provided a gray area in which the assemblymen and the governor-general were to compete.

The obscurity of the Qing taxation system was best revealed in the heated debate over the bill proposed by assemblymen "to demarcate the boundary between the main tax and the surcharge and to levy them separately." Taking a full month, this debate was one of the most protracted of all at the 1909 assembly. The bill was discussed among the assemblymen three times, sent to Governor-General Zhao twice, and both times rejected by him.[100] The initial November 8 proposal read:

> We find that when prefectures, subprefectures, and counties pay their main tax (*zhengshui*) to the provincial capital, they commonly obtain the money by a variety of means: taxing the slaughter of pigs, the sale of liquor, and the sale of oil. However, when they obtain money for their own local governments, they can use only one method: the surcharge (*fujiashui*) on taxing the slaughter of pigs.... However, because this tax is now levied by the New Tax Bureau [which is under the direction of the provincial officials], local governments ... can no longer get their surcharge.... The reason for this is that ... the New Tax Bureau constables use the surcharge tax collected to make up for the insufficiency of the main tax. This has led to a lack of funding for the localities. Now, various gentry have filed a complaint desiring the return of the surcharge tax, but they have received no reply.... In all countries in the world, the tax for the local governments and the tax for the central government are clearly divided. We have never heard of using the local government's money to fill a hole in the money for the center. So, we are in favor of demarcating the boundary between the local tax and the tax for the central and provincial governments.[101]

Here, "main tax" refers to state taxes paid to the central and provincial governments, and "surcharge" refers to local taxes paid to the county government.[102] From the Yongzheng period (1723–1735) on, the main tax would go to the central and the provincial treasuries and the surcharge (*huohao*, which in the late Qing was called *fujiashui*) stayed in the county yamen. As time progressed, expansion of both the main tax and the surcharge added to the people's burden. In Sichuan, for example, the property tax and the taxes on pigs, liquor, and oil were all added at various stages, with a portion of these taxes designated as the main tax and another portion designated the surcharge.[103]

In the early Qing, both the main tax and the surcharge were conventionally levied by county authorities, with local gentry and county tax secretaries playing an important role. After the Taiping Rebellion, the need to levy more new taxes led to the local gentry assuming an increased role in new tax collection. However, after Zhao Erxun became governor-general, the

New Tax Bureau began levying the new taxes, including the previous four, in place of the local gentry. The bureau would then collect taxes from Sichuan taxpayers directly; naturally, it clashed with the local gentry head-on.

Clearly, the subtext of the aforementioned proposal was the bitterness that Sichuan elites felt toward Zhao's New Tax Bureau, which had moved quickly to set up branches all over Sichuan, with branch personnel directly appointed by Zhao and his colleagues in Chengdu. In their revised proposal on November 16, the assemblymen laid out three reasons for going back to the old way of taxation and proposed two ways to fix the New Tax Bureau. First, they argued that because all surcharge taxes were originally levied for local public affairs and the local elite had been doing a fine job of collecting them, it made more sense to stick with the old way.[104] Second, they pointed out that the New Tax Bureau had always regarded the main tax as more important than the surcharge, leaving the local government in financial difficulty.[105] Third, they asserted that the expenditures of the New Tax Bureau were too great and that the salaries of its employees drained too much of the taxpayers' money.[106]

In sum, the assemblymen argued that the New Tax Bureau would exhaust the "wealth of the people" and cause large problems for their "constitutional and financial future" (*xianzheng ji caizheng qiantu*). The assemblymen believed that "the well-being of the local community is also part of state affairs" and thus deserved attention. To police the activities of the New Tax Bureau, assemblymen demanded that "no surcharge tax levied by the New Tax Bureau be used to fix shortages in the main tax, and that the main tax and the surcharge tax be recorded separately," so that "both officials and gentry can make an investigation when they need to."[107] In short, the assemblymen proposed that all surcharge taxes that had been levied by the local gentry still be levied by the local gentry, so that both local self-government and local public affairs would benefit.[108]

Not surprisingly, Governor-General Zhao rejected all of the assemblymen's arguments. First, Zhao claimed that the assemblymen were fabricating the historical record and that the surcharge had first been proposed in 1901 by the central government, presumably to pay for the Boxer Indemnity.[109] Second, he argued that there was a distinction between local government and local self-government. The building of a police force was under the purview of local government, not local gentry's self-government.[110] Third, the New Tax Bureau had been established because the central government was in great need of money. And, according to regulations drafted by the Institute of Constitutional Compilation, the issue of building the New Tax Bureau was outside the purview of the provincial assemblies.[111] Zhao Erxun quickly rejected the two fixes that the assemblymen proposed and stated that the New Tax Bureau was in truth one step in the constitutional reform. He also found no need to record the two taxes separately and argued that by posting the number publicly as he had done, he allowed "thousands of pairs of eyes to see" rather than "having only one or two persons" see the number written in the account books.[112]

In exasperation, the assemblymen wrote a rebuttal to Zhao's denial letter reasserting everything they had proposed previously. They challenged Zhao's distinction between local government and local self-government, arguing that both supported the welfare of the local community. In fact, it is at this juncture that the assemblymen first formulated a new principle centering on the rights of the local taxpayers. They argued:

> The tax for local government is tax levied by the state to administer the locality. The tax for local public affairs is tax levied by the locality to manage self-governance. These two differ only in their usages; their nature is essentially the same. . . . If the revenue for building the police all comes from the local people, then such revenue should be used for the local community. There should be no difference between the tax for local government and the tax for local self-government.[113]

From the point of view of these assemblymen, whoever paid for an administration's budget should control the expenditure of that budget; furthermore, whoever paid for an administration should have the rights to and power over its services. The power of the state did not come from the state, but from the people who paid for the state.

The assemblymen kept denying the right of the New Tax Bureau to levy local taxes and charged that the office was violating its role as an "agent" (*daishouzhe*).[114] They considered Zhao's refusal to make a separate account book for the surcharge tax a clear attempt to avoid supervision.[115] Predictably, after seeing this angry rebuttal, Zhao swiftly put forth his second denial. Like the assemblymen, Zhao reasserted everything he had said in his previous letter. For Zhao, the central and provincial governments always came first, and to best serve the state, he would do whatever was needed to preserve his tax bureau.

Both sides put up a good fight. In the process of debating, arguing, competing, and going head-to-head with Zhao Erxun, the Sichuan assemblymen developed a sharper understanding of the key elements of a constitutional state and of the relationship between the citizenry and the state. For them, the power and legitimacy of the state came from the people who paid for the state. The provincial government should not take precedence over the locality as the principal arbiter of public affairs. Rather, it was the taxpayers, by way of self-governance organs like county and local councils or the proposed revenue bureaus at the county level (*difang caizhengju*), who should be the heavy lifters of all public activity.

Meanwhile, Governor-General Zhao's position was revealed more clearly in these debates. When the question of who represented the state in daily politics came to the fore, the abstract and supreme entity of the state revealed its visible form. In actuality, the aim of Zhao's demands was to enhance the power of the central government by making the local people yield. Zhao's push to strengthen the state bureaucracy came at a time when the Qing empire was in the midst of serious internal and international crises. In his view, the interest of the central government trumped popular sovereignty.

NO TAXATION WITHOUT SUPERVISION

Zhao Erxun delivered the assembly's closing remarks as he had delivered his speech at the opening ceremony. He claimed that "the chief function of the Provincial Assembly is to assist (*fuzhu*) the administration."[116] He also emphasized that the only way to achieve self-government was for the people to actually possess the competence for it; otherwise, even if an assembly existed, it would still only be "empty talking."[117] After addressing the provincial assembly, Zhao evoked a lofty image of himself in contrast. He considered himself "always seeking truth with equanimity and fairmindedness," noting, "I do not feel sorrowful because of those who opposed me; nor am I pleased by those who flattered me." Zhao finished his speech by saying:

What I really hope from you is not only for you to supervise us, but more importantly, for you to exert all your energy to assist us. All those who support me I consider my helpful friends. All those who remonstrate with me I consider friends who hold me to high standards. You should all do the above.[118]

Even though the Qing was in the midst of a transition into becoming a constitutional state, it would seem that Zhao still considered the assemblymen to be, essentially, "censors," the traditional "officials with words" (*yanguan*) who in the monarchical system offered suggestions and assistance to the emperor.[119] However, in marked contrast to their vague assent at the opening ceremony, this time around the assemblymen reacted with strong opposition. First, Assemblyman Jiang Sancheng stepped up to the podium and challenged Governor-General Zhao. Jiang asserted that all matters under Heaven should be decided only by their own rightness or wrongness. Whether powerful men like Zhao approved or disapproved meant nothing. In other words, when facing truth, officials and the people should be equal.[120]

Right after Jiang's protest, Chairman Pu Dianjun went to the podium and defied Zhao's points on supervision:

> When Itō Hirobumi traveled in our country, he said that the Chinese were the most passive of all peoples. Being passive is the reason that our country is weak. Now that the provincial assemblies have been convened, if we assemblymen still insist on the principle of "do not give money and do not do things" (*bu chuqian bu banshi*), then our country cannot avoid the fate of being destroyed. However, prior to the provincial assemblies, there was no reason to blame the people. Why? Because we did give money in the past, but what things have been achieved and where did our money go? . . . If [you] do not allow the people to supervise you, [you] will surely receive no assistance from the people. This is the rule.[121]

In essence, Pu declared that "there would be no assistance without supervision," because all people who pay money deserve to know where their money is spent. Pu continued his closing remarks with this powerful rebuttal of Zhao's points:

> Now that the Provincial Assembly has been established, the parliament will follow suit. The imperial edict stated clearly that "various political issues should be solved by public opinion." . . . Therefore, today, we who represent the people should try our best to demolish old habits for the benefit of the people. And those who are in charge of things should try their best to put things straight. [We] are of assistance to administration, but we, following the law, also provide the supervision of administration. . . . To only pay taxes yet not participate in public affairs is the wrong way of doing things![122]

Indeed, Pu Dianjun and Jiang Sancheng were addressing a matter of great importance: what is a legitimate state and from where does its power come? Zhao pronounced that "all political power belongs to the state." Sichuan provincial assemblymen asserted otherwise, arguing instead that "we pay taxes, and thus we should have a say in politics." In their minds, it was the taxpayers who should be the masters of the state.

Both sides advanced their arguments in the name of constitutionalism, which for Governor-General Zhao was a legitimate reason to expand the power of the state, and for the assemblymen meant their transformation into stakeholders in the polity. In a practical sense, the assemblymen's constitutionalism meant that as taxpayers, the Sichuan people should have some say in the government and should occupy some sort of role in the decision-making process. These debates might appear mundane; nevertheless, they enabled these men—prominent Sichuan elite who would later lead the Railway Protection movement—to negotiate face-to-face with formidable representatives of the central government like Zhao Erxun. The emergence of Sichuan leaders like Pu Dianjun was no mere happenstance, but rather a logical development spawned by the reform agenda of Liang Qichao planted within a provincial political community that was ready to act—not in simple mimicry of Liang's ideas, but in local readings of concepts like legitimacy, sovereignty, and constitutionalism, which in turn took on great significance of their own.

Conclusion

While the Qing court was accelerating its preparations for constitutionalism, provincial officials were issuing orders to expand their modern bureaucracy, and constitutionalists began seizing the opportunity to occupy these newly founded organs and establish their own power base. The constitutional reform gave new legitimacy to local elite activism. The advocacy of local self-governance organizations emboldened the local elite to seek to control power and fight against the provincial governmental apparatus. As both local elite and statesmen wanted to considerably expand their control over local administration, conflict was inevitable. The unprecedented aggression of state infiltration into local affairs forced Sichuan gentry to confront officials head-to-head, honing their abstract ideas about people's rights and popular sovereignty into a true weapon for defending themselves.

As the contrast between the opening and closing ceremonies of the assembly shows, the confidence and poise of the Sichuan elite progressed tremendously in those six short weeks. The assemblymen's vague dissatisfaction with Zhao Erxun's argument that "all political power belongs to the state" was transformed into a focused and well-articulated counterargument. The beliefs that "if we pay the money, then we deserve to manage political affairs" and "as the representatives of the people, we need to supervise how taxes are levied and spent" became better articulated during the head-to-head struggles with Governor-General Zhao. To protect themselves, the Sichuan assemblymen had learned to express their arguments with vigor. Declaring themselves "the representatives of the people," assemblymen found power and justification in that assertion, and they gained solidarity, confidence, as well as a sense of righteousness in the idea of popular sovereignty. Even though not all of their proposals were successful nor did they officially represent the Sichuan people, they were still winners because of their newfound confidence, and because of their discovery of a way—at least in their minds—of relating to the Sichuan people.

The Provincial Assembly was a formative institution in the emergence of the possibility of a functioning constitutional state in China. It was also a staging area for the development of a new relationship between the citizenry and the state. The constitutionalists of Sichuan took Liang Qichao as their spiritual guide. Through serious political struggle with the powerful governor-general, they learned to formulate and express their political convictions; via taxation rights, the Sichuan assemblymen found a way to address the principle of popular sovereignty as they sharpened their ideas and rhetoric. In this process, Liang's principles about democracy and popular sovereignty became real, practical, and focused. Indeed, two years later, in the 1911 Revolution, these Sichuan elites utilized the same principles they had honed in the assembly and successfully mobilized a great number of followers. By then, they had become skilled orators who could convey their ideas powerfully and effectively.

5   *The Rhetoric of Revolution*
THE RIGHTS OF THE NATION, CONSTITUTIONALISM, AND THE RIGHTS OF THE PEOPLE

The Qing state's launch of the constitutional reform let loose a deluge of words—in print, in conversations, and in political meetings. Justified by the Guangxu emperor's edict declaring that "various political affairs are up for public discussion," political discourse flourished throughout the Qing empire during its last years. Political associations likewise proliferated at every level, and local electoral assemblies met continuously from the last years of the Qing through the first years of the Republic.[1] In Sichuan, just as in other places across the empire, talk was the order of the day. Few periodicals—and hardly any carrying what we would call news—were in circulation in Chengdu during the early 1900s; after the establishment of the Provincial Assembly in 1909, more than thirty new ones made their appearance.[2] In the Sichuan Railway Protection movement, words were invested with passion and meaning. In the most heated moments of the struggle, certain key words served as revolutionary incantations. Rights of the nation (*guoquan*) was perhaps the most universally accepted of these, but other words played a part as well, including constitutionalism (*lixian*), the rights of the people (*minquan*), and, more specific to the radicals, sovereignty of the people (*minzhu*), liberty (*ziyou*), and equality (*pingdeng*).

As they initiated the movement, leaders gave expression to their individual aspirations and interests, but a common purpose was generated by the rhetoric they created, which served to draw together people of different social statuses behind one cause. More than just an expression of an ideological position determined by socioeconomic interests, political language was a vibrant performative act that helped shape the perception of interests and hence the development of ideologies. This chapter delves into this revolutionary rhetoric, with a focus on the new forms of language that were developed, the collective identities and the common purpose that were created, and the novel means—newsletters, public speeches, and open meetings—by which revolutionary ideas were conveyed.

Movement Leaders and Their Clashes with the Qing Court

Sichuan provincial assemblymen—as recounted in the preceding chapter—had honed their principles and developed their potential for mobilization. Having enjoyed an indisputable status among the Sichuanese, they were looked to as a source of direction by local elites in county assemblies, professional groups, and railway tax branches of the Chuan-Han Railway Company. It was a ripe situation lacking only a revolutionary motive, which was to emerge rapidly following the unfolding of events in national politics after 1908. The deaths of Cixi and Guangxu in 1908 ushered in a new imperial regent: the headstrong, inexperienced, twenty-six-year-old Zaifeng. Under Zaifeng, the Qing court launched a series of centralizing and pro-Manchu policies that alienated virtually every important constituency with the exception of a small group of imperial relatives and Manchus. Ideological differences between officials and assemblymen that had been broached during the constitutional debates broke out into the open.

Between 1909 and 1910, China's provincial assemblymen put forth three petitions for establishing a parliament (*guohui*), a demand that owed much to their education at Hōsei University, where the Japanese constitutional scholar Minobe Tatsukichi taught his students that a constitutional government "is one that has a parliament."[3] On October 13, 1909, just before the close of the first meeting of the Jiangsu Provincial Assembly, Chairman Zhang Jian initiated the first petition for opening a parliament. Following Zhang's call, representatives of sixteen provincial assemblies gathered in Shanghai and submitted their request to the Censorate, demanding the opening of a parliament in 1911. The Qing court flatly rejected this first petition with the objection that "citizens are not well educated."[4] On June 16, 1910, a second petition, this time initiated by Zhili Provincial Assembly chairman Sun Hongyi, was submitted to the Censorate by 150 delegates. It, too, was rejected by the court, which this time cited "financial difficulty." Refusing to give up, the constitutionalists soon launched a third petition, this time convincing provincial officials to join their cause. On October 25, 1910, eighteen governors, governors-general, and Manchu garrison generals jointly sent a telegram to the Grand Council requesting that it urge the court to "establish a cabinet instantly and open a parliament the following year."[5] Under enormous political pressure, the court reluctantly agreed to "shorten the preparation period for constitutional government, open a parliament in 1913, and establish a cabinet."[6]

By the end of 1910, Chinese constitutionalists had divided into two groups.[7] Considering the third petition a success, the moderate group, including Zhang Jian, stopped action.[8] The radical group, among them Zhili's Sun Hongyi, Hubei's Tang Hualong, and Sichuan's Pu Dianjun, insisted on adhering to the original proposal that a parliament be opened in 1911 and began drafting a fourth petition. In addition to playing a key role in the fourth petition movement in January 1911, Pu Dianjun supported a movement by Sun Hongyi in the north and mobilized a mass movement in Chengdu. Together with Sun and Tang Hualong, Pu became a backbone member of the Xianyouhui (Association of the Friends of the Constitution)—the first political party of constitutionalists within China—upon its establishment.

On May 8, 1911, the "responsible cabinet" (*zeren neige*) was established, replacing the Grand Council to become the new executive organ after the constitutional reform. The cabinet, also dubbed the "prince cabinet," consisted of thirteen members, with seven of them belonging to the imperial lineage. Chinese constitutionalists, having completely lost faith in the Qing court, increasingly leaned toward revolution. They were again incensed when, on May 9, the court issued an official edict to nationalize the trunk lines of the commercially owned Yue-Han (Canton-Hankow) and Chuan-Han (Chengdu-Hankow) railways.[9] At the time of the announcement, Pu Dianjun and Xiao Xiang were in Beijing attending the founding meeting of the Xianyouhui. The provincial assembly leaders of the four affected provinces, who regarded the edict as both unjustifiable and unconstitutional, did their best to convince the court to change its decision. Their efforts were to no avail. In frustration, Pu confessed to a Hunan assemblyman before leaving the capital: "There is nothing we can do about Chinese politics nowadays. The government clearly has abandoned its people. If we still want to save China, there is no other way but revolution."[10]

While Pu's reaction was clearly political and revolutionary, it is important to note that not all Sichuanese concurred with this position. A wide range of other viewpoints on the nationalization policy were held by the leaders of the Chuan-Han Railway Company's headquarters in Chengdu, Sichuan-born officials who served in Beijing, and the company's Yichang branch leaders. It should be noted that at this time it was primarily the most radical of the Sichuanese, led by Pu Dianjun, who were opposed to the central government's will.

An argument could be made for the ample economic merit of nationalizing commercial railways. Germany and Japan were among many successfully industrialized nations in which the central government led the construction of railways, an advantageous arrangement given the state's capacity to systematically plan rail lines and leverage capital. Censor Shi Changxin, a Sichuan-born official serving in Beijing and a supporter of the policy, wrote in his memorial that the policy's rationale was "to accelerate the construction of the railways" and "lessen the huge burden it has laid on the people." Denouncing the heavy *zugu* tax on Sichuan commoners (*baixing*), Shi reminded the Qing court of the devastating loss of Chuan-Han Railway capital in a number of Shanghai banks under the leadership of "factious gentry" and urged the government to "quickly demarcate the trunk lines of the railways" so that they could be nationalized.[11]

Behind these certainly rational and justifiable reasons, however, lay a more urgent impetus for the nationalization policy: foreign lenders' repeated demands that the Qing court finalize the draft of the Huguang Foreign Loan Agreement that had been secretly signed by Governor-General Zhang Zhidong of Huguang in June 1909. According to the draft contract between Zhang and the banks of four nations—Britain, France, Germany, and the United States—not only had a total of six million British pounds been loaned to China by the foreign banks, with Hubei and Hunan's *likin* (transit tax) as security for the loan, but also these four nations held monopolistic rights to the construction of all trunk lines of the Chuan-Han railway in Hubei and the Yue-Han railway in Hunan and Hubei, and they furthermore retained priority rights to the construction of trunk lines of the Chuan-Han and Yue-Han railways in other provinces.[12] Notably, the Sichuan section of the Chuan-Han railway was not included in this original agreement.[13]

Understanding the subtleties involved in evaluating the role of foreign loans in railway building in China requires a look at the history. From 1903 to 1907 there was a strong trend in China for railways to be self-reliant, supported only by Chinese capital. However, as historian Ralph Huenemann shows, a number of the companies that had newly gained commercial status were struggling to an extent that deeply compromised their effectiveness. For example, the Yue-Han railway, redeemed from foreign control in 1905, set up provincial railway companies in Guangdong, Hunan, and Hubei to continue the work that had been started by the American China Development Company, but, plagued by factionalism and corruption, completed only about eighty kilometers of line. Similarly, in other provinces, Sichuan included, inadequate financing, factional bickering, and corruption were pervasive.[14] Under these circumstances, even the longtime governor-general of Huguang, Zhang Zhidong, who in 1905 had been supportive of redeeming the Yue-Han Railway from the foreigners, was willing to consider a foreign loan for the trunk lines of the Yue-Han and Chuan-Han railways. Discussions with bankers from England, France, and Germany began in 1908, and a preliminary agreement for the Huguang loan was reached in June 1909.[15]

Hence, even though there was agreement in public opinion that the imperialism of the industrialized nations left China with no choice but to carry out its own program of railway construction—which had inspired the rise of commercial railways—other views on how the railways should be financed and managed gained increasing popularity. By 1908, the central government was disenchanted with commercial railway companies. This sentiment, expressed in an edict on June 27, 1908, had three components. First, the companies were ineffectual *and* were causing popular discontent because of their tendency to rely on taxes rather than on voluntary investment. Second, some commercial railway companies were closely identified with Han nationalism. Third, railroads had great potential for generating profit, and at a time when the central government had a serious financial deficit, the possible revenues from railroads were an irresistible draw.[16] Soon, under the auspices of the Ministry of Posts and Communications, a rising tide of railway nationalization began.[17]

The economic drive from the court, compounded by the constant pressure to finalize the draft of the Huguang Foreign Loan Agreement, ultimately led to a decision to take over the Yue-Han and Chuan-Han railways. In March 1911, negotiations between the ministry and the four lenders began.[18] It was within this context that the nationalization policy was announced on May 9 and quickly followed on May 20 by the signing of the Huguang Foreign Loan Agreement. In a key change from Zhang Zhidong's original draft, clause 2 replaced the railway linking Jinmen and Hanyang (both in Hubei province) with the railway linking Yichang in Hubei and Kuizhou in Sichuan, thus subjecting Sichuan to the foreign loan agreement in a roundabout way.[19]

From May to early June of 1911, the Chuan-Han Railway Company leaders at the Chengdu headquarters, lacking much knowledge of the details of the foreign loan agreement and the nationalization policy, were uncertain about their response.[20] At the time, Pu Dianjun and other radical constitutionalist leaders were still on their way from Beijing to Chengdu. The issuance of the nationalization edict on May 9 triggered a frenzied exchange of letters between the leaders at the Chengdu headquarters and their informants in Beijing and other cities as they grappled with the true meaning of the policy.[21] In early June, the Chuan-Han Railway Company leaders finally formulated a response to the policy, using Deng Xiaoke, the chief editorialist of the assembly's newspaper, *Shubao*, as their main spokesperson in a widely circulated article titled "Methods of Dealing with the Sichuan Railway." In the article, which appeared in *Shubao*'s June 1 issue, Deng asserted, "If [the government] promises to quickly finish building the railway, . . . agrees to build an additional railway between Sichuan and Tibet, . . . gives precedence to using Sichuan's personnel and materials in building these railways, and lets Sichuanese keep the railway capital for developing Sichuan's industry, [then under these conditions] it would be all right to let the government have the railway lines."[22] Deferring comment on the issue of legality—namely, the question of whether, as a constitutional government, the court's decision to incur foreign loans without permission from the National Assembly was unlawful—Deng proposed, "Let us put it aside for now."[23] From this, it is clear that the main goal of the Chengdu leaders at that time was to keep the capital in their own hands. The rule of law was important, but striking a good deal was even more urgent.[24]

Other Sichuanese dignitaries disagreed. Sichuanese officials serving in Beijing, for example, disheartened and alienated by the mismanagement of the Chuan-Han Railway Company, had their own ideas on the matter. Among them, Gan Dazhang and Song Yuren both supported the appropriation of all of the existing railway capital by the central government and its transfer to Beijing. Gan and Song, who paid the railway tax as landowners yet were stationed at such a great distance that they had no control over the railway company, saw more safety in letting the central government manage the money than in leaving it in the hands of their compatriots in Chengdu, where it might be subject to disasters like the Shanghai stock-market losses.[25] Likewise, Li Jixun, manager of the Yichang branch of the Chuan-Han Railway Company, had over the years felt constrained by leaders at the Chengdu headquarters. As the manager of the only branch that was actually constructing railway lines, Li understood what it was like to have little power in allocating capital or appointing personnel. Having suffered from the bureaucratic working style of the Chengdu headquarters for years, Li had finally had enough.[26]

Attuned to the conflicts brewing, Sheng Xuanhuai, the minister of posts and communications, and Duanfang, the imperial commissioner of the Yue-Han and Chuan-Han railways, seized their opportunity, forming an alliance with the Beijing-based Sichuanese officials with the aim of advancing the nationalization policy and beginning to coax Li Jixun toward their point of view. In June 1911, Sheng and Duanfang launched an aggressive investigation into the financial accounts of the Yichang branch of the Chuan-Han Railway Company and demanded that the accounts of all other branches be investigated as well. They were confident that the issue in Sichuan would be resolved quickly, and that they would not only successfully nationalize the railways but also obtain all the capital of the Chuan-Han Railway Company for the center's coffers.[27]

The Rhetoric: The Rights of the Nation, Constitutionalism, and the Rights of the People

FOUNDATION OF THE RHETORIC: LUO LUN'S CRITIQUE OF THE TREATY

June 1911 was a daunting time for the leaders of the Chuan-Han Railway Company's headquarters in Chengdu. Sheng Xuanhuai and Duanfang had accelerated their efforts to nationalize the railway, making constant and unsympathetic demands on Sichuan acting governor-general Wang Renwen to "investigate and clarify the accounts of all Chuan-Han Railway Company branches." On June 1, their "*Ge* Telegram," referring to telegrams sent on the fifth day of a lunar month, ordered that all Chuan-Han Railway capital be nationalized and that no shareholders withdraw their investment capital.[28] This telegram indicated a different and harsher treatment of Sichuan than of all the other three provinces affected by the nationalization policy: while railway stockholders in Hunan and Hubei would get all of their capital back—though losing their interests—and railway investors in Guangdong would get 60 percent of their investment back, Sichuan was ordered to turn in all seven million taels of silver under its control to the central government. Sheng Xuanhuai and Duanfang also enlisted Yinliang, the Sichuan provincial treasurer and an ethnic Manchu, as their spy, thus obtaining an up-to-date and fairly accurate accounting of the activities of the leaders within Chengdu headquarters. Furthermore, Yichang branch manager Li Jixun, subjected to Sheng and Duanfang's constant urging, grew closer to the point of agreeing that the central government should own the railway. Taken together, these actions provided great momentum for Sheng and Duanfang's campaign to nationalize the Chuan-Han Railway Company.

With the central government's toughening stance on the nationalization issue, what could the Chengdu headquarters do to stem the tide? Guangdong and Hubei had been inactive for a while, and even in Hunan, the province where the Railway Protection movement had been initiated, the fervency had begun to subside. Responsibility for the entire railway movement seemingly had been placed solely in the hands of the Sichuanese, particularly those of the railway elite in Chengdu. In early June, the arrival in Chengdu of Pu Dianjun, whose reputation outshone that of any other literatus in Sichuan, served as a great reinforcement for the Chengdu headquarters. Pu's reputation was so extolled that, according to *Shibao*, "people would set up shrines for him," and "his name was well known by even women and children."[29] Pu and Luo Lun, another influential figure and vice-chairman of the Provincial Assembly, formed a solid leadership tandem for the Railway Protection movement. Under their joint leadership, the movement was able to appeal to nearly all of the important political constituencies in Sichuan, owing to Pu's connections to Sichuan's reform-minded officials, Luo's connections to the leaders of the Gowned Brothers, and their shared connections among the various local elites of Sichuan.

Opportunely for these Chengdu leaders, Sheng Xuanhuai and Duanfang's *Ge* Telegram was publicized on June 9, and the Huguang Foreign Loan Agreement arrived in Chengdu on June 13, providing the disheartened group with a chance to rally and formulate a vigorous argument against the central government. Not having previously seen the full version of the loan agreement or the *Ge* Telegram, Chengdu railway leaders had not had a good case against the nationalization policy on either legal or economic grounds. But once the agreement became known at a critical point in the struggle, the Chengdu leaders were solidly placed to make their case against the court.

The Chengdu elite quickly responded to the Huguang Foreign Loan Agreement with a critique of the treaty.[30] Although it listed Luo Lun as author, Pu Dianjun was generally believed to have been the mastermind behind the critique. In a lengthy analysis of the loan agreement, composed in purely legalistic language, Luo argued that the agreement "lost too many rights" (*sangquan taiduo*) to foreign lenders.[31] For example, in addition to the aforementioned change to clause 2, which subjected Sichuan to the loan agreement in a roundabout way, was a request in clause 9 subjecting the *likin* tax in Hunan and Hubei to the power of the four foreign nations. Likewise, clause 14 gave the right to manage investment for building the railway in Sichuan to the German Deutsche-Asiatische Bank and the right to manage investment for building the railway in Hunan and Hubei to the British HSBC Bank. Clause 17 specified that the Qing government select at least one Briton, one American, and one German as the chief engineers in building these railways, and clause 18 stated that these engineers would have the final say in buying railway materials.

Besides maintaining that the treaty would result in the loss of too many Chinese rights, the author also claimed that the treaty itself lacked legitimacy. For example, clause 3 demanded "a quick transfer of *all* capital of the railway company to a newly established Yue-Han and Chuan-Han Railways Official Bureau *without* shareholder approval," which was, according to the authors, clearly "unlawful." In a recapitulation of all of these points, Luo Lun wrote:

[The foreign loan treaty] mortgages the trunk lines for the loan. It offers the construction of railway, the management of capital, the appointment of personnel, the purchase of material, and the supervision of loan interest—in sum, all rights concerning the railway business—to the banks of the four foreign lending nations. Even though it is never clearly stated in the loan itself that the trunk lines themselves should serve as the security for the loan, all of the privileges that the banks have obtained regarding railway issues have led to damaging results. These privileges will impair our railway rights (*luquan*) and suffocate us. Once the loan agreement is signed, our railways will be forfeited.[32]

This lengthy, technical, and lawyerly critique elucidated all the key points of those who objected to the Huguang agreement, serving as the foundation for the more impassioned revolutionary propaganda that would follow. The Chengdu headquarters would soon introduce into the debate the key political principles of national rights, the people's rights, constitutionalism, and the rule of law, all of which extended far beyond the ownership rights of the railway lines.

RIGHTS OF THE NATION AND THE NEW MEANING OF *GUO*

The most innovative aspect of the Chengdu leaders' struggle was their invention of a fresh political discourse. They created a concrete rhetoric of rights, asserting the necessity of protecting the nation's rights in conjunction with protecting both the rights of the people and the rights of shareholders.

On June 17, 1911, *Shubao* published a widely circulated special issue presenting Luo Lun's arguments, couched in dramatic language and with memorable slogans printed in oversized type:

[The treaty] deprived our nation's people (*guoren*) [of the railway] and offered [it] to foreigners (*wairen*).

The people of our nation (*guoren*) should rise up [against it]; the people of Sichuan (*chuanren*) should rise up [against it].

[The treaty] snatched away our railway; [it] robbed us of our financial capital.

With such an act of robbery, however, there was no plan for building our railway.

The people of Sichuan should rise up [against it]; the people of our nation should rise up [against it].

If we fail to struggle, we will have no place to die![33]

The writer then accused Sheng Xuanhuai of ten crimes:

First, selling the railway.

Second, offering strategic railway lines to foreigners.

Third, relinquishing to foreigners the right to manage capital.

Fourth, relinquishing to foreigners the right to appoint personnel.

Fifth, relinquishing to foreigners the right to control the purchasing of materials.

Sixth, offering financial interest to foreigners.[34]

Seventh, cheating the emperor and bullying the citizens of the nation (*guomin*).

Eighth, snatching the railway away from the nation's citizens and giving it to foreigners.

Ninth, tyrannizing the people (*renmin*) and disobeying the edict.[35]

Tenth, robbing the railway and stealing its capital without planning to build further.[36]

Despite its dramatization of the accusations and the liberties it took in interpreting the treaty's clauses, the special issue of *Shubao* rewards analysis because of the way it showcased key changes in the concept of *guo*. The original notion of *guo* was "the fief of the feudal lord; or, the household of the lord," which was closely related to the head of the fief and the ruling house of the territory.[37] However, this document expressed a different notion of *guo*—the kind of *guo* that Mr. New People, Liang Qichao, had been talking about for years—which had more affinity with the people than with the ruling heads of the polity. Here, *guo* was frequently used in conjunction with the words "citizens" (*min*) or "people" (*ren*), such as in *guomin* and *guoren*, and it conveyed the meaning of being the opposite of foreigners.[38] *Guo* thus had become closely linked to *min* or *ren*, carrying the meaning of "nation" or "nation-state."

This new understanding of *guo* underwent further clarification as the railway movement continued. On June 21, the *Newsletter of the Sichuan Chamber of Commerce* published an article titled "The Foreign Loan Agreement Sells Out Our Nation's Rights" that clearly described the relationships among the nation (*guo*), the people (*renmin*), and the government (*zhengfu*). The author pitted the government against the people, stating, "Even though the *zhengfu* obtained unparalleled power, it could not repress the energy and the hearts of the *renmin*." He went on to say, "The *renmin* were deeply concerned about their *guo* being destroyed," which was why even though the nationalization policy actually decreased the tax burden on the people, they would still "exert their blood and sweat to build the railway on their own."³⁹ The writer argued that the railway had to be self-managed to realize the goal of being "entirely owned by the nation (*wanquan guoyou*)."⁴⁰ In short, *guo* was the people's *guo*.

CONSTITUTIONALISM AND THE RIGHTS
OF THE PEOPLE

Movement leaders also used the concepts of constitutionalism (*lixian*) and the people's rights (*minquan*) to rally supporters against the court, arguing that the procedure by which the foreign loan treaty was signed was unlawful and unconstitutional. For example, the aforementioned article in the *Newsletter of the Sichuan Chamber of Commerce* stated, "For a constitutional state (*lixian guo*), all financial policies should be discussed in the assembly and passed by the assembly. The National Assembly Regulations clearly states this!"⁴¹ Another writer argued along the same line: "If circumstances like government official Sheng Xuanhuai signing the treaty without submitting it to any assembly were to be tolerated and such violation of the law were to be condoned, how could it be guaranteed that one day China would be ruled by law?"⁴² And, as a corollary, how would people's rights be protected under this despotic government?

The point about the foreign loan agreement being signed without having undergone the proper legal procedure was also emphasized in an article published in the *Newsletter of the Sichuan Railway Association* on July 6, in which the author wrote:

The National Assembly was just convened, yet the first policy of the new cabinet disdained the law (*mieshi falü*). Clause 14.3 of the National Assembly Regulations clearly states that the National Assembly has the power to decide on public loans. Clause 12.1 of the Provincial Assembly Regulations clearly states that the Provincial Assembly has the power to decide on matters affecting provincial rights, which certainly include matters like nationalizing the railway. Why didn't the government wait for the result [of the assemblies]? According to the Commercial Code and the Company Code, all decisions concerning commercial railways should be made only by the shareholders.⁴³

A July 8 article similarly stated: "Those who are afraid of taking up struggle against Sheng Xuanhuai are not thinking about the matter of constitutionalism. All of the constitutional states in this world respect the liberty of their people (*renmin zhi ziyou*). . . . I now ask Sheng Xuanhuai, 'Has the foreign loan agreement been approved via legal procedure?'"⁴⁴

Once again writing about why Sichuanese needed to take action against the central government, leading propagandist Deng Xiaoke spelled out how the acts of signing the foreign loan treaty and issuing the nationalization policy damaged the nation. First, they destroyed the prospect of building a political system based on constitutionalism. Second, they gave Chinese citizens' railroads to foreigners, thus sacrificing national sovereignty. And third, they enabled the Ministry of Posts and Communications to disregard the people and violate the interests of the people.[45] Of these three reasons, Deng considered the first, constitutionalism, to be the most fundamental.[46] He continued, "If we believe that constitutionalism can strengthen the nation (*guo*) and we want to strengthen our nation, then we need to seriously attack the government, making it feel fearful so that it repents and knows that we the people (*wumin*) truly believe in following the laws." Only by doing so would the central government know that "by being autocratic and overbearing, it cannot go anywhere!"[47]

In addition to constitutionalism and the people's rights, popular sovereignty was another concept implicit in the rhetoric. By distancing *guo* from *zhengfu* and linking *guo* with *min*, the Chengdu leaders strongly implied that the legitimacy of ruling a *guo* should come only from its *min*, thus championing a nascent notion of popular sovereignty. This new relationship between *guo* and *min* was elaborated by Luo Yishi in another newsletter article, in which he argued that the interests of we the people (*wumin shenjia xingming*) should be the basis of all decisions made in the public sphere.[48] The *guo* was the people's *guo* and should serve the people's interests first and foremost.

Thus, leaders at the Chengdu headquarters had crafted a fresh political discourse to protect the rights of the nation, constitutionalism, and the rights of the people. This discourse enabled the slighted Chengdu elite to regain the momentum they needed to stand up to central government officials. With the gist of their rhetoric established, what remained for the movement leaders to do next was to convey their ideas to the public and organize their movement (Figure 5.1).

The Means: The Founding Meeting, the Organization, and the Key Slogan

THE FOUNDING MEETING

On June 17, 1911, an impassioned public meeting took place at the Chuan-Han Railway Company on Yuefu Street in Chengdu. Feeling "endangered and greatly pressured by the situation," the leaders at the Chengdu headquarters who organized the meeting could no longer wait for the formal shareholders' meeting, which was scheduled for August 4; they invited leaders of various professional associations and all shareholders

The Rhetoric of Revolution 151

FIGURE 5.1. Satirizing the Qing court for selling out the country. Sichuan bowuyuan (Sichuan museum), *Gonghe zhi guang: Xinhai qiu Sichuan baolu sishi bainian ji* (The glory of the republic: The one hundred anniversary of the death and sacrifice made for the Sichuan Railway Protection matter in the fall of 1911) (Chengdu: Sichuan jiaoyu chubanshe, 2011), 186.

who were then in Chengdu to "discuss and prepare" methods to help with their situation.[49] According to contemporary records, several agreements were reached at this founding meeting of the Sichuan Railway Protection Association. Writing on the same day as the meeting, Sichuan's acting governor-general Wang Renwen addressed the cabinet, the Ministry of Posts and Communications, and Imperial Commissioner Duanfang:

Early this morning, various professional associations came to the railway company and held a meeting. More than two thousand people came. The speeches were about the relationship of the foreign loan treaty to the life and death of the nation. People were crying so hard that it was earthshaking; some hid their heads behind tables and sobbed in private. In the end, it was determined that a railway protection association should be founded and that representatives should be selected by the association to go to Beijing, pay a formal visit to the Ministry of Posts and Communications, and find a solution. They asked that the investigation of the account books be carried out only after both sides reach an agreement. Fortunately, there was neither agitation nor commotion. Yet the predicament of sadness and pain was extraordinary.[50]

It was the respected Chengdu commissioner of education, Meng Gongfu, who cried the hardest at the meeting. Since Meng was the leader of the learned circles (*xuejie*) of Chengdu, his tears were effective: many of his students, as well moved to tears, decided to found a student association for protecting the railway.[51] The *Shubao* editorialist Deng Xiaoke also came to the meeting. Deng emphasized the terrible consequences the foreign loan would bring and delivered a heartrending critique of the treaty.[52] Of course, the master orator Luo Lun never missed a gathering like this. Luo asserted that it was definitely not enough to have only one association in Chengdu; rather, it was vital for all Sichuanese to understand that "the railway is a matter that concerns [us] all." Luo urged the seventy million Sichuanese not to be afraid of the "peremptory Sheng Xuanhuai and Duanfang" serving the "vicious foreign countries."[53] However, the most astounding scene at the founding meeting was created by Zhu Shan, the chief editor of *Shubao*. A man in his twenties, Zhu presented himself in a fashionable and "sharply tailored robe."[54] He claimed that two things had to be done to protect the railway: one was to call upon people in the outer counties to join the leaders in Chengdu, and the other was to mobilize an army of national citizens to fend off foreigners.[55] Requesting that he be assigned both tasks and displaying his determination, Zhu pounded his palms on the table and broke a teacup, the pieces of which cut up his hands as he was pounding.[56] The "bloodshed" of Zhu Shan added yet more drama to this already-emotional meeting. Those in attendance were moved.

Despite the sweltering heat, the turnout for the meeting was large. Even though there is some uncertainty over the exact number of the attendees, ranging from several hundred to five thousand in various historical accounts, there is no doubt that a considerable number of people attended.[57] Their enthusiasm was undeniable. Li Jieren wrote, "People from all different walks of life came, and it seemed that students and young artisans outnumbered other people and formed the majority."[58] Li continued, "The place was extremely crowded and even the street [where the railway company was located] was packed with people." The place reminded him of "a drama stage" (*xitai*).[59] After the meeting was adjourned, enthusiasm lingered as participants were encouraged to sign up for various branches of the Railway Protection Association. One student "had to wait for quite a while before he could finally grab a brush and sign his name."[60]

Following the meeting, the leaders marched to the provincial government to present their petition. The elite made a point of forgoing their privilege of traveling in sedan chairs; instead, they chose to walk in the open through the streets of Chengdu as a demonstration of their sincerity and determination. With police officers carving out a path in front, the procession marched from the railway company to the provincial yamen. According to onlookers, the entire scene was impressive. Wu Songsheng, aged eighty, of Hanlin Academy, led the parade, followed by a cluster of Sichuan provincial assemblymen who were also shareholders in the railway company. Next came a group from the railway company, immediately followed by a number of gentlemen of the learned circles. Famous people like Luo Lun, Deng Xiaoke, Meng Gongfu, and Zhu Shan were among those in the procession. These gentlemen, followed by their servants, secretaries, and clerks, formed an extraordinary spectacle for the people of Chengdu to behold.[61]

After this memorable day, protecting the railway became the most-talked-about subject in Chengdu. The Sichuanese would soon surprise officials like Yinliang, who was confident that their movement would quickly evaporate. Yinliang wrote on June 17: "I expect that in four or five days, the Sichuanese will humbly follow the edict.... In Sichuan, the power [of the people] is much weaker than in Guangdong and Hunan, and Sichuanese are simply following [the people of those two provinces]."[62] Much to the surprise of Yinliang, the movement did not die out; it became increasingly intense and powerful.

THE ORGANIZATION

The establishment of the Sichuan Railway Protection Association was followed by the launch of a highly effective campaign. The association employed new approaches to organizing, including sending its own representatives to counties throughout Sichuan and places outside Sichuan to ensure the message was conveyed accurately. Such expansion was achieved by establishing local branches of the association in Sichuan from which representatives were sent to various provinces outside of Sichuan, an activity that was painstakingly planned and executed by movement leaders in Chengdu.

Given that the leaders of the Railway Protection Association were also members of the Chengdu headquarters of the Chuan-Han Railway Company, they never lacked money. In fact, they appropriated as much as forty thousand taels of silver from the railway company. The Chuan-Han Railway Company Chengdu leader Peng Fen recollected years later:

In the middle of the fourth month of the third year of Xuantong [more likely the fifth month], Deng Xiaoke said to me, "We now need to issue magazines, vernacular newspapers, and newsletters and send representatives to Beijing, Shanghai, Hunan, Hubei, Guangdong, and various prefectures and counties in Sichuan. Without financial support, these things cannot be achieved." I then withdrew forty thousand taels of silver, which had been deposited by the Chuan-Han Railway Company in the Ri-Sheng-Chang Bank, and gave it to Li Qiulu and Li Wengeng for management.[63]

According to Peng Fen, the money was well spent. The diverted funds not only supported three newspapers but also allowed Liu Shengyuan to travel to Beijing and call on Prince Qing, bankrolled Xiao Xiang's journey to Shanghai to meet with the press, and supported other messengers' trips to Hubei, Hunan, and Guangdong. It also sustained students who returned to their hometowns and mobilized people from outlying counties in Sichuan.[64] In total, ten thousand taels of silver were used. Because of the immense impact of the activities funded by the railway company's money—"all Sichuan was restless and so was the entire country"—Peng Fen believed it was all worth it.

At one point when suspicions surfaced that the railway capital had been appropriated, a swift response by the association helped allay doubts. "The Expenditures of Our Association," published in the twelfth issue of the newsletter, explained by way of reply: "All the people working at the association do so voluntarily. They regard their work as a duty and even spend their own money on transportation. No one is taking any kind of salary; except for tea, water, food, brushes, ink, and expenses for printing, mailing, and sending telegrams, not a single penny is spent."[65] After this public reply, the Railway Protection Association continued to run smoothly, with no further questioning regarding expenditures.

The association's regulations described the basic structure of the organization. Its agenda was "to refuse to incur foreign loans, and to abandon the treaty and protect the railway" (*jujue yangkuan, feiyue baolu*).[66] There were four divisions under the association: General Affairs, Speech, Documents, and Public Relations. Under the leadership of Sichuan provincial assemblyman Jiang Sancheng, the General Affairs Division took up the general managerial role and held the seal of authority. The Speech Division, led by Assemblyman Cheng Yingdu and charged with promoting the association's chief causes, set up local branches of the association in various prefectures and counties and communicated with the groups outside Sichuan to ensure coordination. The Documents Division, responsible for producing all editorials and regulations relevant to railway issues as well as dealing with letters and telegrams addressed to the association, predictably was put under the direction of Provincial Assembly newspaper editorialist Deng Xiaoke. The assembly's vice-chairman, the master orator Luo Lun, ran the Public Relations Division, guiding its efforts to counter forces working in opposition to the association.[67]

The organizing principle of the association appeared to be democratic and inclusive. All people, not only Sichuanese but also those of other provinces, could join the association, and all members could freely choose to join any division. With respect to representation of the various counties in the association, the regulations stated: "Out of ten association members who come from the same county, one should be selected as the spokesperson of the ten. Out of five spokespersons who are selected, one should be elected as the chief spokesperson of the five."[68] These chief spokespersons were especially vital to the Documents Division because they would read and select articles from their home counties to be published in the newsletter.[69] All matters of import were to be discussed and decided collectively: "Each member should be present at important meetings," and "all decisions made by public meetings should be carried out without avoiding responsibility."[70] Another stipulation was that members of divisions should meet at least once a week.[71]

The two most important divisions of the association were the Documents Division and the Speech Division. The former "exerted all the powers of the pen to guarantee that the association's messages were communicated clearly and powerfully."[72] Its chief publication—the *Newsletter of the Sichuan Railway Protection Association*—provided a crucial means of keeping the people of the outer counties up to date with events in Chengdu. For example, a request that came from the Tibetan Border Education Bureau expressed hope that the newsletter would "mobilize public opinion and sentiment in the border region too."[73] In Zizhou prefecture, a teahouse owner was so moved after reading the newsletter that he commenced ardently delivering his own speeches on railway issues at the teahouse, "with the newsletter in hand."[74] Besides the newsletter, the Documents Division also produced the important newspaper *Xigubao* (literally, *Western Concerns Newspaper*), which had a vast circulation in Chengdu and served as another vital platform for discussing railway issues.[75]

No less influential in the spread of the railway movement than the output of the Documents Division were the efforts made by the Speech Division. On a nearly daily basis, at least one speech organized by the division was delivered in Chengdu. Specially designed advertisements announcing the place, time, and names of the lecturers for the meetings urged gentry, merchants, and ordinary Chengdu residents to attend. Prominent movement leaders such as Luo Lun delivered these speeches in public spaces such as the Three Righteousnesses Temple, Fire Deity Temple, and God of Literature Temple so that ordinary Chengdunese all around the city could easily attend.[76] The Speech Division was also in charge of sending people to build branches of the association in the outer counties of Sichuan, a key activity to be discussed in detail in Chapter 6.

THE KEY SLOGAN: "TO PROTECT THE RAILWAY AND BREAK THE TREATY"

Two weeks after the launch of the movement, the leaders found it necessary to clarify their purpose, and a manifesto elaborating on the objectives of the association was published on July 6 in the *Newsletter of the Sichuan Railway Association*. Their rhetoric again emphasized the dual aim of preserving constitutionalism and the rights of the nation. With regard to constitutionalism, the manifesto asked:

> Why are thousands of people calling upon constitutionalism with devotion? Is it not because "with a constitution, the government cannot arbitrarily carry out policies that betray the people"? . . . Even if the motive of the treaty was justifiable, its content good, and even if the policy was favorable and caused no shareholders to lose anything, we would still fight against it because, if we did not, we would never be able to talk about building constitutionalism, opening a parliament, and meeting in the National Assembly and provincial assemblies![77]

On the rights of the nation, the manifesto claimed:

> The foreign loan treaty has strangled the people. Its clause 25 clearly puts all business regarding the 3,600-li railway into foreigners' hands. The purchase of a nail or even the use of a clerk cannot be decided by our countrymen (*guoren*). . . . We national citizens (*wu guomin*) should know that wherever the foreign railway goes, the power and rule of foreigners follow. We have had enough examples of this kind, and this is why in order to survive we have to resist [the treaty] at the cost of our lives.[78]

By this point, the railway movement had established its significance in constructing constitutionalism and preserving national rights. Following the foregoing declarations, the proclamation coined a key slogan—"to protect the railway and break the treaty" (*baolu poyue*)—and then clarified which railway they were protecting and which treaty they were breaking:

> To protect the railway is to protect a Chinese railway from being owned by foreigners, not to protect the privately owned Sichuan railway from being owned by the state. To break the treaty is to break a treaty that was selling out [a Chinese railway's] interests . . . and a treaty that was produced via unlawful procedures, without being submitted for discussion in the National Assembly.[79]

Put succinctly, the constitutionalist movement leaders had channeled their political demands into a concrete slogan that was used to draw broad participation in the movement and give people a common, concrete purpose. The scholarship on collective movements proposes many explanations for choices individuals make to affiliate with social movements.[80] However, as Sidney Tarrow observes, "While it is true that some movements are marked by a spirit of play and carnival while others reveal the grim frenzy of the mob, there is a much more common and prosaic reason why people band together in movements: to mount common claims against opponents and authorities."[81] There are considerable risks and costs involved in acting collectively against authorities; people do not sacrifice their time or risk their lives unless they think they have good reason to do so. Common purpose is that reason, and in "protecting the railway and breaking the treaty," the movement leaders had found a way to articulate and promote that common purpose.

Evoking Emotions: Celebrities, the Popularization of New Concepts, and the Use of Old Symbols

CELEBRITIES

Even with a common purpose established, it was still essential for movement organizers to disseminate their propaganda in a convincing way. In 1911, leaders in Chengdu invented, adapted, and combined various forms of collective action to stimulate support from the local people. In their search for tangible symbols and examples to drive home their points, they created two sensations: Sichuan opera (*chuanju*) actor Yang Sulan and movement martyr Guo Huanwen.

Yang Sulan first appeared in revolutionary propaganda when he reportedly donated sixty *mu* (four hectares) of land to the Railway Protection Association on June 24.[82] Yang, one of the most famous and widely known Sichuan drama performers of the 1900s, was idolized in Chengdu. Love affairs between Yang Sulan and his ardent fans (including many Sichuan provincial officials) provided ample grist for publicly traded rumors among Chengdu residents.[83] Yang brought star power and celebrity appeal to the table when he joined the movement. In an article titled "The Patriotism of a Little Performer" that appeared in the third issue of the association's newsletter, Yang expressed his devotion to the cause:

Sulan is a member of the Sichuan people. Even though I am ashamed of belonging to the lower class (*xialiu*), I still understand the great righteousness (*dayi*). Even though I cannot serve to the fullest extent, I want to donate my entire savings of sixty *mu* of land to your association to help preserve railway rights and resist foreign loans. I am simply assuming my duty as a Sichuanese. And [if we] can invoke the emotion of our compatriots, [our power] will be like little streams congregating into an ocean and tiny mosquitoes amassing into a mountain. If every single one of us struggles against this dangerous situation, then our situation will be transformed from danger to safety. . . . Losing the railway is destroying our country.[84]

Yang then transferred twenty-three *mu* of land in the name of Tieding Temple and thirty-seven *mu* of land in Pengxi county in the name of the Railway Protection Association. Yang's act was popularized in the newsletter at least once every few days; for example, a local literatus composed a folk song (*qu*) about Yang, praising his nationalistic action.[85] Yang Sulan's story was also used by some radicals to reinterpret the meaning of "lower class" and "upper class." One commentator wrote that Yang was at heart a "high class" (*shangliu*) gentleman, even though he was an actor. By contrast, the behavior of Sheng Xuanhuai and Duanfang was characterized as "low class" (*xialiu*), even though they were officials of a high class.[86] Thus, the "Yang Sulan incident" kicked off a colorful propaganda campaign and successfully generated a great deal of enthusiasm among the people of Chengdu.[87]

Following the Yang Sulan phenomenon, Guo Huanwen's suicide provided an even more dramatic and effective propaganda tool. The sixth issue of the newsletter published, in large type, an editorial about the incident, "The Early and Unexpected Death of Gentleman Guo." The editorial disclosed the details of Guo's dramatic death:

After Guo heard that Sheng Xuanhuai was selling the railway, he was so infuriated that he suffered a severe illness. On the night of the twenty-eighth day of the fifth month [June 24], he rushed out of his apartment hall and shouted: "Our country is about to be destroyed. At least we comrades of Sichuan have the passion and tenacity to break the treaty and preserve our railway. But I am worried that our movement will end too soon even though it started out so strong. I shall die today in order to solidify the determination of our comrades."[88]

The editorial continued:

When we first heard Guo screaming and calling upon people, we all thought he was crazy, and we did not take him seriously. However, two days later, Mr. Guo was nowhere to be found. On the morning of the first day of the sixth month [June 27], the superintendent of his apartment suddenly discovered a body floating in the well . . . and that was the body of Mr. Guo, who decided to die first so that the determination of the Sichuan people would not be deterred![89]

The spectacular death of Guo Huanwen made him the patriot dying for his country par excellence.[90] Soon after, the newsletter started a massive campaign centering on Guo's story. In the propaganda, Guo's tragic suicide was described in increasingly intimate detail. Even a farewell letter from Guo was posthumously "discovered," wherein Guo allegedly urged every one of his comrades to strengthen their determination and succeed in "preserving the railway and breaking the treaty."[91] Copies of the seventh issue of the newsletter were distributed to the public at no charge as a means of commemorating the great martyr Guo Huanwen.[92] From that moment on, nearly every issue of the newsletter included some mention of Guo, constantly reminding readers of his patriotic action. Stories of the "Guo Huanwen incident" were also incorporated into speeches recited all over Sichuan, and writers from various counties responded by paying tribute to and writing articles in mourning for their martyr.[93]

People's hearts were so deeply touched by Guo Huanwen that many were moved to take issue with Sheng Xuanhuai and the central government. As Li Jieren recalls, Guo's story led several Chengdu apprentices to realize that "caring for the country and caring for Sichuan actually had something to do with us." One apprentice commented: "Before [Guo Huanwen's suicide], we cared only about doing our own business. However, after seeing that someone [like Guo] did not hesitate to sacrifice his life . . . we all agreed that we should form our own branch of the Railway Protection Association."[94] The two sensational stories of Yang Sulan and Guo Huanwen galvanized public support for the movement to such an extent that the agenda to preserve national sovereignty and people's rights became well established.

THE POPULARIZATION OF NEW CONCEPTS

To achieve their aim of preserving constitutionalism, national sovereignty, and the rights of the people, movement leaders drew people into collective action by adapting familiar repertoires such as local folk songs, couplets, poems, and dramas in innovative ways and applying familiar metaphors to advance and popularize these concepts. With the need to protect the nation (*guo*) indisputably established as the top priority, propagandists made ample use of folk songs to convey a sense of urgency. In the folk song "On the Foreign Loan Treaty," which appeared in the second issue of the newsletter, the rhymester wrote:

Nowadays, there is a noisy crowd,

boisterous and loud,

The people of Sichuan are a band of comrades.

A band of comrades? Why?

The destruction of the nation is nigh!

The nation destroyed? How can that be?

Foreigners and traitors and conspiracy!⁹⁵

To make sure ordinary Sichuanese understood that the treaty was "selling out" to foreigners, the folk song conveyed its points in the simplest of terms:

The Qing state borrowing six million pounds is like a landowner borrowing money while mortgaging his land. . . .

Clause 8 shows that when it can't repay a loan, the state will just borrow more.

This is like an unlucky country fellow encountering a drought.

He mortgages the harvest of his grain to pay interest on the loan.

Even though the drought makes it impossible for him to pay the interest he has to repay it, even at the cost of selling his wife and children.

The most evil clause is clause 17.

It is as when building a house, one grants complete freedom to the lender, letting him appoint the manager, accountant, and all apprentices.

Then, long before the house is finished, these men steal the money and claim that the money has disappeared.⁹⁶

The arguments in this example replicated the points in the polemic published by Luo Lun half a month earlier. But here, in lively jingles, rhyming colloquialisms, and simple metaphors that used relevant examples from Sichuan commoners' daily activities, movement leaders made Luo's technical arguments accessible to a larger audience. Concurrently, the *Newsletter of the Sichuan Railway Protection Association* serialized the original foreign loan treaty, making it available to the public so that people could become acquainted with the original document, thus educating them on the political situation and bringing it within the grasp of their understanding.⁹⁷

Of course, the important issue of the people's rights and popular sovereignty did not go unaddressed. The third verse of "On Nationalizing Railways," which appeared in the fifth issue of the newsletter, tackled this issue and spelled out the relation between state (*guojia*) and the people (*renmin*):

Let's talk about *guojia* and *renmin*. *Guojia* is like a house and *renmin* are its masters.

If the house didn't exist, then where would people hide?

A house should be built on a piece of land. If the land didn't exist, where would we build the house's walls? . . .

If the land and the house were both mortgaged to a lender and he suddenly decided to withdraw his capital, then the only outcome [for the debtor] would be losing everything.

All this is due to the debtor's reckless borrowing; the debt never goes away.⁹⁸

These metaphors, referencing Liang Qichao's familiar and homely analogy of the state as a village or company and the people as the masters of the village or company (see Chapter 2), were explicitly employed to convey points about power and the rights of the people to the larger population beyond the elite. In doing so, they also brought about a crystallization of Liang's understanding of the relationships between the state (*guojia*) and the people (*renmin*), asserting that "the people are the masters of the state."

Movement leaders also called attention to the rule of law for protecting the rights of the people, as in the folk song titled "On Legal Protection":

The lyrics of this folk song are very unusual, and the title of it is admittedly bookish.

Let us pause for a moment and explain the title: "Law is an extremely important matter for each person's life." . . .

Law has regulatory power over the Son of Heaven and all officials; law also prevents the people from behaving subversively.

According to the spirit of constitutionalism, all matters should be conducted under the framework of law and as a result, all things will remain peaceful.

If we think about the effects of the law in protecting the people—their life and property remain intact—then we should recognize that "law" is incomparably splendid.[99]

The rhetoric in these lyrics about supporting the rule of law is unmistakable. The principle of equality before the law—the idea that every citizen, even the emperor, has to be put under the law—was especially noticeable. If the people's rights and constitutionalism had been the watchwords of the Chinese political elite in the first decade of the twentieth century, in 1911 they acquired concrete substance. In particular, ensuring the rights of the people in 1911 became a legally obtainable goal within the existing political framework: once the National Assembly and provincial assemblies were established, people had a legitimate process by which they could pursue their political rights. The writer of "On Nationalizing Railways," for example, wrote, "We should count on assembly members to deal with national affairs because they are elected by the people and thus they represent the people's participation in politics."[100] Chengdu movement leaders avoided resorting to violence to get what they wanted; rather, they stressed the nonviolence of their struggle and referenced the authority of the law to buttress their view.

Still, for many, the concepts of nation (*guo*) and the people (*renmin*) were still too abstract to relate to. To address this problem, another concept, the people of Sichuan (*chuanmin* or *chuanren*), was utilized to help bridge the gap between *guo* and individuals. The terms *chuanmin* and *chuanren* appeared frequently in propaganda publications. For example, a propaganda article in the sixth issue of the newsletter regularly linked the character "Sichuan" (Chuan) with the character "we" (*wo*). Phrases like "our Sichuan" (*wo Sichuan*) and "we, the people of Sichuan" (*wo chuanmin*) appeared side by side with ones like "our life and property" (*wo shengming caichan*) and "our rights" (*wo quanli*).[101] The propagandist was savvy enough to tap into the robust and long-lasting sentiment of loving one's native land as a way of binding the people together into "the people of Sichuan" and, eventually, into the people of the nation.

Likewise, in the eleventh issue of the newsletter, a columnist drew on the time-honored sentiment of loving one's home to evoke an attitude of loving one's nation by linking together the concepts of *chuan*, *min*, and *guo*: "Ever since the preparation for constitutionalism, wise people have repeatedly talked about loving one's nation. However, for us to love our nation (*guo*), we should start by loving our homeland. Our homeland is Sichuan (*chuan*), and the Sichuan railway is the common property of the seventy million Sichuan people (*chuanmin*)."[102] The columnist criticized the Qing government for strangling the Sichuan people and pitted the despotic government against *guo*, *min*, and *chuan*. In his argument, *chuanren* (the people of Sichuan) were part and parcel of *guoren* (the people of the nation): their interests were the same, and *chuanren* could certainly represent *guoren*. To be clear, in this conception, Sichuan was subordinate in the hierarchy of an individual's multiple political allegiances, with the pinnacle being national loyalty: "The Sichuan Railway Protection Association is for all national citizens, not just for the people of Sichuan. Its goal is to preserve all the railways in all four provinces, yet our goal does not stop there. We are standing up for all the people in our nation."[103]

With these key arguments firmly deployed, the new relationship among *guo*, *min*, and *chuan* became increasingly unmistakable. *Guo* was made of *min* (the people); thus, the loss of the rights of *guo* (*guoquan*) affected every single citizen. Also, protection of the rights of the people (*minquan*) was ensured by the constitution, as was punishment of anyone who violated those rights—no matter who that person might be.[104] Thus, movement leaders had effectively put forth the concept of a new polity built on the consent of the people. They challenged the traditional basis of monarchy—now, even the Son of Heaven was subject to the law and possessed no sacred supremacy over it—and had opened up the essential questions about the locus of political authority and sovereignty.

OLD CONCEPTS AND SYMBOLS MADE NEW

The movement's leaders continued to develop their campaign to solicit more participation. They appropriated old cultural symbols like those of the traitor (*hanjian*), loyalty (*zhong*), and treacherousness (*jian*) to lend their ideas familiarity and stir people's emotions. Often, a movement needs a perfect target—such as, in the case of France, Marie Antoinette—to foster solidarity by directing the emotional fervor of its participants toward something concrete. In the Sichuan Railway movement, that perfect target was Sheng Xuanhuai. In Chengdu in 1911, Sheng was deemed the devil incarnate and a symbol of the "unlawful and presumptuous government" (*qiangheng de zhengfu*).[105] The movement's rhetoric depicted a devious Sheng pitted against the Sichuan people and the Guangxu emperor.[106] It wrote:

> We Sichuan people have been saving and putting our hard-earned money [into the railway company] to preserve our province . . . hoping only that no foreign power would ever coerce us. . . . However, there was this white-faced, treacherous official, who cheated the emperor and the people. He came from the Ministry of Posts and Communications and had the name "Sheng Xuanhuai." He is evil and dangerous, conceited and crooked, pitiless and corrupt. He sneakily borrowed hundreds of thousands of pounds in foreign loans and behaved as a traitor (*hanjian*) working for Britain, France, Germany, and the United States. . . . All of us Sichuanese who live and have property in Sichuan should regard Sheng Xuanhuai as our archenemy![107]

Among the many conventional tropes employed to demonize Sheng and evoke resentment against him was the adoption of the Sichuan opera symbol of the "white face" for the treacherous official, which came close to making the whole movement seem like a kind of show. The most frequent referents for Sheng were "traitor" (*hanjian*) and "renegade" (*maiguonu*).[108] An article titled "Blind People's Patriotism," for instance, made allusions to familiar examples from Chinese history of the type of despicable person Sheng was. As stand-ins for Sheng, the author trotted out the infamous traitor Qin Hui of the Southern Song dynasty, the notorious ministers Yan Song and Wei Zhongxian from the Ming dynasty, and the villainous Manchu official Qishan, of the Qing dynasty.[109] These stories and cultural symbols, drawn from the common lore of the people, were to readily provoke contempt among ordinary Chinese.

In their propaganda, movement leaders set up the bravest and most moral and bravest of Sichuan natives, Liu Shengyuan, in direct contrast to Sheng Xuanhuai. Liu was selected to petition against the foreign treaty before the central government. On July 1, 1911, a huge public meeting was held to send off the hero as he headed for Beijing. At South Square in Chengdu, at "nine o'clock in the morning . . . ten thousand people had already congregated."[110] Undeterred by pouring rain, the chairmen of the meeting adhered to the original plan and continued the gathering. Liu bowed in front of his Sichuan compatriots and delivered the following speech:

Today I come here to say my final goodbye to you. This time I am going to Beijing; I have determined to "cry for seven days in the Qin courtyard"[111] to persuade the Qing court to change its mind and achieve our goal of breaking the treaty and recovering the railway. If the treaty is not broken, I will choose to die and will never come back alive. My only wish is that after I die, our railway protection comrades will continue to carry out our struggle and do so in a peaceful and orderly way.[112]

As Liu spoke, "people, on and off the stage, were all crying." In one touching scene, an old farmer "held his hands in front and kept bowing to Liu, saying 'We thank you; we thank you (*women ganxie ni; women ganxie ni*)!'" People were "clapping and crying their hearts out."[113] Liu seemed to have effectively rallied the pride of the Sichuan people. In several issues of the newsletter following the meeting, Sichuan literati overwhelmed the editors with letters, praising their great hero Liu Shengyuan. If the notorious traitor Qin Hui was a fitting proxy for Sheng, then the historical figure most analogous to Liu was Jing Ke, the righteous warrior who rose up against the tyrannical Qin emperor. To laud Liu's utter determination and courage to resist the central government and break the treaty, local literati drew parallels to the famous poem that Jing Ke wrote before making his assassination attempt on the Qin emperor.[114]

Public meetings like the one for Liu Shengyuan mobilized people beyond just the elite. Guo Moruo, a middle school student at the time, attended one such meeting and would later recall: "All the crying and screaming has greatly stirred people. . . . Luo Lun was crying on the stage, railway shareholders were crying offstage, even the coolies and clerks working for the railway company were crying. Of course, all of us onlookers were crying too." It was again an "earthshaking" gathering, wherein "the land trembled for twenty to thirty minutes."[115] Significantly, meetings like this brought commoners and elites together into one organization, for one purpose. Now, at least in these meetings, they could relate to one another as equal political participants.

Observations on the role of old cultural symbols in evoking people's emotions offer evidence for the efficacy of drawing on such symbols, as movement leaders did. David Kertzer writes that collective action is "not born out of organizers' heads" but is "culturally inscribed and communicated."[116] In a similar vein, Charles Tilly notes that people cannot "employ routines of collective action of which they are ignorant; each society has a stock of familiar forms of action that are known by both potential challengers and their opponents."[117] If it can be assumed that the people of Chengdu, like any society, had available knowledge of their own, then it becomes clear that movement leaders were drawn to a known repertoire of collective symbols that they successfully used to render the railway movement concrete.[118]

Conclusion

It is true that the Sichuan constitutionalists and the leaders of the Chengdu branch of the Chuan-Han Railway Company were only a small fraction of "the Sichuan people," and that they, to a large degree, initiated the movement to serve their own political aspirations and economic interests. Nonetheless, their campaign raised significant issues that extended well beyond their own interests and introduced into public discourse issues of nationalism, constitutionalism, popular sovereignty, and the rights of the people, all of which had far-reaching implications.

The revolutionary rhetoric focused on defending the rights of the nation (*guoquan*), constitutionalism (*lixian*), and the rights of the people (*minquan*), with *minquan* and *guoquan* inextricably linked to one another. *Guo* (nation) was the totality of *min* (the people), and the well-being of *min* determined the fate of *guo*. Moreover, *min* possessed important political rights and held an important political stake in *guo*; the rights of *min* were protected by the law and were both legitimate and virtuous. With such emphasis on the equality of citizenship, this new political rhetoric held particular appeal for those who had had no political stake in the previous political system; in turn, the rhetoric depended on those very people for its further spread. As mentioned earlier, Guo Moruo indicated that the good and even magical feeling that the concept of equality held for students, small merchants, coolies, and young apprentices might be the reason it was they who formed the majority of the participants in the movement in Chengdu.

Besides these key concepts, movement leaders also adapted various forms of collective action in stimulating support from the people. They created intermediate, approachable collective identities, for example, the people of Sichuan (*chuanren*), and a concrete goal, to protect the railway and break the treaty (*baolu poyue*), to draw diverse groups of people into one collective action. The movement elite further excited participants by invoking old symbols—traitors (*hanjian*), loyalty (*zhong*), and treacherousness (*jian*), all serving to heighten people's emotions. Taken together, the political concepts centering on rights and the protest repertoire—including meetings, speeches, processions, propaganda, and political theater—were introduced to a wide-ranging Sichuanese audience for the first time. Once learned, they would leave a deep impression in the minds of the Sichuan people and be used in their future political struggles.

6 *The Practice of Revolution*

ORGANIZATION, MOBILIZATION, AND RADICALIZATION

Up to this point, the Sichuan constitutionalists, leaders of the Railway Protection Movement, had made potent use of the power of ideas to effect political change by putting into play a persuasive rhetoric and a robust set of repertoires with broad appeal. Presented with the opportunity in the summer of 1911, how did the leaders in Chengdu mobilize an even larger base of support? How did they spread the revolution beyond the city of Chengdu and into the outlying counties of Sichuan? And, after the court exerted extra pressure, how did the movement maintain its solidarity, sustain its challenges against enemies, and, finally, transform itself from a peaceful protest into an open revolt?

Unlike the 1911 Revolution in other provinces, where violence was limited to cities and lasted only a matter of days, the revolution in Sichuan spanned more than six months and extended well beyond urban centers such as Chengdu and Chongqing. The movement inspired thousands of Sichuanese throughout the province to participate in the uprising. Movement leaders did not simply debate the classical questions of government; they sang songs about rights and popular sovereignty in the open streets and acted on their revolutionary ideas in new and unexpected ways. For the first time, ordinary people joined together with the elite in a single, unified political movement and interacted as equal citizens. In the heat of political conflict, the old structure of the polity collapsed under the impact of increasing political participation and popular mobilization, and as a result, the very notion of the political expanded and changed shape as well.

Public Mobilization: Local Branches of the Railway Association

After June 17, 1911, the Sichuan Railway Protection Association set its sights beyond the development of rhetoric alone as it turned its attention toward new methods of organization. As described in the previous chapter, the forty thousand taels of silver that the leaders of the Railway Protection Association obtained from the Chuan-Han Railway Company were used not only to fund three newspapers but also to sustain students who returned to their hometowns in the outlying counties of Sichuan in order to mobilize the people there.[1]

The Railway Protection Association's Speech Division, which was responsible for sending representatives to build county-level association branches, dispatched ten to twenty students from each county back to their hometowns during the summer vacation months of June and July to spread the principle of protecting the railways and breaking the treaty. Equipped with at least ten silver dollars in travel money each, the students, who were selected because they were "eloquent in speech," delivered passionate speeches back in their hometowns. These students, most of whom came from influential gentry and landlord (*shenliang*) families, used personal connections to set up local branches of the Railway Protection Association. In Xinjin county, for example, it was Chen Wenqing, a Xinjin native studying at the Chengdu School of Law and Politics (Chengdu fazheng xuetang), who linked up with the famous local strongman Hou Baozhai and helped Hou establish the Xinjin branch of the Railway Protection Association.[2] In Yibin, Li Lelun, a Yibin native studying at the Sichuan School of Industry (Sichuan gongye xuetang), rushed back to his hometown to mobilize his fellows after hearing Luo Lun's passionate speech and witnessing Zhu Shan's "blood-shedding" action at the founding meeting of the association. Whenever the local market convened, Li would step up on a chair and speak about the treasonous behavior of the Qing government, and how it had snatched the railway from the Sichuanese and sold out Chinese rights to foreigners.[3] Through extensive print media and powerful oration, the same propaganda and collective action routines designed by the movement leaders in Chengdu were replicated across Sichuan.

On July 15, after local mobilization had gone on for some weeks, the Speech Division published an article titled "Concrete Methods of Making Speeches and Organizing Branches," explaining once again its specific process for setting up local branches:

First, local professional associations (*fatuan*) should set up a general organization to receive our Speech Division messengers sent from Chengdu. The organization should then send people to distribute reports and daily newspapers to market towns and post them in suitable places.

Second, members of the Speech Division should send letters to market towns, addressing those in local associations (*tuanti*). They—local militia leaders (*tuanzong*), academic gentry (*xuedong*), village leaders (*xiangyue*), *baojia* leaders (*baozheng*), native-place association leaders (*kezhang*), and others—should be invited by name and respectfully asked to attend our meetings.

Third, as for how to write the letters, the speakers (*yanjiangyuan*) should be consulted.

Fourth, in terms of where to deliver the speeches, it will be necessary to select spacious public offices (*gongsuo*) and never make use of empty squares (*kongkuo bazi*). It is important that everyone should register in order to attend these meetings.

Fifth, at each meeting, receptionists should be present to receive the people mentioned in the second point, and a watchman should be hired to make sure there is no chaos.

Sixth, as for the content of the speeches, we should first explain how the railway company started as an officially owned enterprise but became a privately owned one. Then we should explain the nationalization policy. Last, we should elaborate upon the failures of Sheng Xuanhuai's treaty with the foreigners and explain the relevance of the treaty to the future of Sichuan. This should be the order used in delivering speeches.

Seventh, after the speaker from our Speech Division has delivered his speech, he should immediately organize a Railway Protection Association branch. The speaker should explain that a branch of the association is the only means of action and discuss the concrete methods of organizing it with local leaders.

Eighth, after making the speech and finishing the organization of the local branch, the speaker should persist in persuading people concerning the association's principles, help local officials keep order, and make sure to find a place where he can post the regulations and copies of the *Newsletter of the Sichuan Railway Association*.

Ninth, speechmaking and branch organizing have to be done in consultation with the local officials. We have to invite local officials to attend the meetings and ask local police and guards to keep order.

Tenth, it is crucial to both be independent of and at the same time be reliant upon local officials.[4]

This detailed ten-point directive, distributed by the Speech Division to its members, reveals the determination of the Chengdu leaders that their message—protecting the railways and breaking the treaty—not only was spread to the outlying counties, but also was conveyed in a very specific way.

As the directive mandated, the movement mainly used local elites to carry out the mobilization. On the same day it published the "ten-points" directive, the Railway Protection Association sent out a formal letter urging all leaders in the local associations to be both ardent in promoting their nation and supportive in establishing local branches of the association.[5] In addition, besides local elites, the directive's ninth and tenth points made clear that local officials should also be relied on in carrying out the objectives of the movement. In July 1911, for example, the *Newsletter of the Sichuan Railway Association* published an open letter to "all prefecture, department, and county governments," in which movement elites clarified their allegiance to the emperor and assured the local governments that the railway association was looking neither to "create trouble for the emperor" nor "attack foreigners."[6] Reassured, Sichuan's local officials responded by tolerating the actions of the association, allowing messengers from Chengdu to travel freely to local counties, and exercising extra vigilance to ensure that meetings concerning railway matters took place without disorder by providing police or guards.[7]

With the association's meticulous program and the support of local elites and the official circles (*zhengjie*), the railway movement expanded rapidly.[8] For example, "more than four thousand people" showed up at the founding meeting of the Railway Protection Association branch of the important eastern Sichuan metropolis, Chongqing.[9] A letter from the Chongqing branch to the Chengdu headquarters reported the founding of the branch, declaring that the Chongqing people supported the cause "for they cannot accept the railway being mortgaged to foreigners."[10] Similarly, a report from Chengkou district—Chengkou being a suburb of Chongqing—proclaimed, "We are all furious and grieved about the behavior of Sheng Xuanhuai, who, in a time of constitutionalism, has been overbearing. . . . Our magistrate also knows that [the railway matter] is important, and he has created no trouble for us as we set up our branch. . . . The only thing we worry about is that we are far away from Chengdu, and it is hard for us to hear news. . . . We then decided to send people to Chengdu to learn about everything."[11] Thus, although Chongqing had often been at odds with Chengdu—their clash of opinions on which section of the railway should be built first being one example—Chongqingese supported the Chengdu headquarters in the railway movement. Nationalism had enabled them to set aside their differences and join forces with the movement leaders in Chengdu.

A letter to Chengdu from Yang Ruirao, a messenger from the Speech Division, depicts in detail the establishment of a branch in Chengdu city's neighboring Chongning county, offering insight into common characteristics of the approach to setting up local branches on the ground. First, branches throughout the province, as was the case with the branch in Chongning, were set up nearly exactly as the Chengdu leaders wanted: under the leadership of the headquarters of the Sichuan Railway Protection Association in Chengdu with regulations mimicking those of the Chengdu headquarters and with an organizational structure modeled after Chengdu's.[12] Second, forming the backbone of the Railway Protection Association branches were the gentry of various local self-governance organizations, which, as shown in Chapter 4, were booming after the constitutional reform.[13] With local elites serving as their social base, the branches tapped into a broad network of preexisting organizations that held sway in local affairs and were poised to set in motion the powerful forces of mobilization.[14] A third common characteristic was the peaceful manner in which mobilization was carried out, with most local officials supporting the Railway Protection Association. Magistrates were present at the meetings; some even delivered speeches, concurring with the points about nationalism made by the elite.[15]

As was the case in Chongning, Emei, Fengjie, Yongchuan, Mingshan, Chongqing, and Mabian counties the support of local officials helped to disarm opposition to the branches.[16] With the establishment of various levels of the Railway Protection Association across Sichuan, diverse and geographically separated Sichuanese were linked together into a single political community that began to recognize an alternative source of authority separate from the central and provincial governments. A Chengdu participant in the movement recalled, "At that time, we Sichuan people paid no attention to the grand announcements (*gaoshi*) issued by the acting Sichuan governor-general, even though they carried his intrusive red stamp. On the other hand, we paid keen attention to the propaganda (*xuanchuan wu*) crafted by the Railway Protection Association. Even a small piece of paper with a few words on it, if posted in the streets, would gain enormous attention and attract a crowd."[17]

The organizational structure of the Railway Protection Association branches played an essential role in mobilizing various kinds of people into one political movement. In Chengdu, for example, branches affiliated with specific neighborhoods, occupations, social groups, and genders mushroomed at an astonishing rate. The Children's Street Branch, the Women's Branch, the Students' Branch, the Mechanical Workers' and Printers' Branch, the Silk Guild Branch, and even the Beggars' Branch were all set up in less than a month's time.[18] Chengdu residents eagerly joined the branches. Though they represented different social strata, their shared sentiment brought them together; in that moment, at least, the gap between social classes receded in importance.

The movement also crossed ethnic and religious boundaries. On June 28, more than four hundred Chengdu Muslims created their own branch, announcing, "Chinese Muslims (*huimin*) are also national citizens (*guomin*)."[19] Meanwhile, a Qiang minority tribal leader (*tusi*) by the name of He Xiegong from Maozhou donated the money he obtained from the sale of grain and horses, noting, "If we put all of our needles together we will have an ax. . . . If we feel strongly about this now, we will in the future avoid the fate of losing our country."[20] In Hanzhou, after the nationalization policy was announced, Christians headed to churches and prayed for Sichuan for more than twelve days in a row.[21] And in Chengdu, Buddhist and Daoist monks had been committed participants from the very beginning of the movement.[22]

This newfound sense of community inspired those Sichuanese who had never been part of public affairs to participate in politics. Elementary school students, for example, were an active part of the railway movement. In late June, Huang Xuedian and Huang Bin initiated the Children's Branch of the Railway Protection Association in Chengdu, drawing three hundred of their fellow elementary school students into membership.[23] In Jiading, a ten-year-old girl with the surname Ni donated her savings of five silver dollars, asking her teacher to mail the money to the Chengdu Railway Protection Association to support its struggle.[24] In Huayang, elementary school students Tang Shijun and Tang Shiqing personally delivered their savings of five hundred copper coins to the secretary of general affairs, Jiang Sancheng, insisting that he take the money.[25]

Women, who had not participated in politics before, joined the movement as well. On June 28, 1911, the Women's Branch of the Railway Protection Association was created. Its founder, Zhu Li (the wife of Zhu Shan, the emotional orator who shed blood while making his speech at the founding meeting of the Railway Protection Association on June 17), successfully imparted to this branch the original association's principles, calling upon "all Sichuan women to take politics passionately to heart, and to contribute their strength to the movement." Activist women declared, "No matter how people look at us and talk about us, we swear not to change our principles."[26] Undeterred by heavy rain on the day the Women's Branch was established, the female attendees trudged to the meeting, at which representatives were nominated to be sent off to Beijing, Hunan, Hubei, and Guangdong, "covering their heads with their hands, wading through mud, their dresses soaked by the rain and dampened by water." Zhu Li willingly accepted the position as head of the branch, vowing, "Whether diving into hot water or walking through fire, I will do the job without hesitation."²⁷ Afterward, sub-branches of the Women's Branch continued to spread.²⁸

For the first time, lower-class people also had a taste of engagement in political activism. A sedan-chair carrier donated his hard-earned money, contending that "coolies are citizens too, and we shall not sit and wait to die."²⁹ Shopkeepers in Chengdu organized the "One Cash Association" (Yiqianhui), with each member contributing one wen daily to the Railway Protection Association.³⁰ To join the Yiqianhui, one did *not* have to be a shareholder of the railway company or own property or have status; rather, it was their common political agenda that linked these people together.

In Li Jieren's 1937 novel *Great Wave*, the experience of the humble merchant Boss Fu, who sold umbrellas in Chengdu for a living, is an exemplification of Foucault's thesis about revolution as spectacle. Exhilarated by the movement, Boss Fu, having put aside his umbrella business in the summer of 1911 to follow the lectures given by movement leaders, finds that "those big gentry (*da laoye*), who have never been respectful to people like me, now stand side by side with me." Previously, they "always used a language that was so opaque and incomprehensible. Now, they are talking to *us* in a way we understand! They treat us as equals!"³¹ Boss Fu then joins the Railway Protection Association branch on his street and remains a solid supporter throughout the course of the entire movement. In real life it would have been unlikely for a small-time merchant like Boss Fu to have been a shareholder of the Chuan-Han Railway Company, because the railway tax was a surtax on land tax and most shareholders were landholders. But Fu is passionate about the railway movement because it offers him the opportunity to deploy his rights as a political citizen and to be the big gentry's equal.

Boss Fu's story is emblematic of real-life experiences during the movement. Guo Moruo, then a middle-school student, recorded a similar kind of political leveling effect in his experience attending meetings organized by the association.³² At least during meetings, people like Boss Fu were transformed from passive subjects of the empire into active citizens of an emerging nation-state, an experience that imbued lower-class people with a sense of possessing equal citizenship status with the educated elite. Thus, in extending its purview well beyond the protection of constitutionalism and the promotion of nationalism, which were its stated objectives, the railway movement also became a vehicle for political enlightenment and personal empowerment.

The ideas of the railway movement not only prompted people to view politics in new ways but also helped forge political solidarity among

Sichuanese. An article in the *Newsletter of the Sichuan Railway Association* summed up the situation:

> From June 25 to July 1, the General Affairs Division received 226 letters and sent out 260. Altogether, the four divisions received more than one thousand letters and sent out nine hundred. Of course, the enthusiasm and hot blood that our people have is infinite, and not all of that passion can be expressed within the limitations of those publications. If we take into consideration those who could not write to express their feelings, we know that the impact of the movement is huge. It is not an exaggeration to say that in this half-month, not a single day went by without meetings. There was not a single meeting that was attended by fewer than a thousand people. . . . Men or women, youngsters or the elderly, people rich or poor, smart or stupid, virtuous or flawed, insiders or outsiders, they all expressed that they share one heart and have one goal. We know that the treaty is selling out the country, and we must break the treaty and recover the railways! . . . Though passionate, we are not engaging in unruly behavior but are acting properly. We have kept order. Long live the nation! Now, the people of our country are finally the great national citizens of a constitutional and civilized state![33]

Hyperbolic as this depiction might be, it does convey a sense of Sichuan people's passionate engagement with the movement. The common purpose it provided united people from different walks of life and drew them into one community, and common political ideas and activities forged a new sense of social connection. Although the propaganda and revolutionary language were not a reflection of the realities of many Sichuan people's economic interests (for example, Boss Fu), the revolutionary rhetoric helped shape the people's perception of their interests and hence became a powerful call to action.

Secret Expansion: Personal and Secret Linkages

Propaganda and formal organizations were not the only means employed by the movement's leaders to promote solidarity among the Sichuan people; they also sought support from Sichuan's preexisting secret society network, the Gowned Brothers. Notably, it was not just the Tongmenghui that had connections with the Gowned Brothers, as many historians have argued. Leaders of the Sichuan Railway Protection Association also had close and direct relationships with the leaders of the Gowned Brothers. Even those Gowned Brothers leaders who might have also joined the Tongmenghui received direct orders from the Railway Protection Association.[34]

The nature of the connections between the associations and the Gowned Brothers can be demonstrated through examples in various counties. The late June 1911 publication in *Shubao* of Luo Lun's speech at the founding meeting of the Railway Protection Association aroused such excitement in the famous Gowned Brothers leader Wu Qingxi from Wenjiang that he wrote to Luo of his determination to send his troops to help Luo establish "an independent Sichuan."[35] In July 1911, Xiang Dizhang, a student at the Sichuan School of Law and Politics (Sichuan fazheng xuetang), received explicit orders from Railway Protection Association leaders to return to his hometown in Shuangliu county to establish a branch of the association *and* make connections with all possible Gowned Brothers members there.[36] In Huayang, it was the famous Gowned Brother and militia leader Qin Zaigeng who set up a branch of the Railway Protection Association there.[37] And in Chongning, it was another famous Gowned Brothers leader, Gao Zhaolin, who made an ardent public speech at the opening meeting of the Chongning branch of the association.[38]

It is important here to recall the prowess of the Sichuan Gowned Brothers. As discussed in Chapter 1, by the 1870s, the Gowned Brothers had emerged as a powerful social force in Sichuan, drawing members from a wide variety of occupations, including soldiers, sailors, miners, laborers, salt smugglers, unemployed vagrants, actors, yamen runners, artisans, small shopkeepers, pawnbrokers, and sedan-chair carriers. In the 1890s, the Gowned Brothers became a leading force of the anti-Qing and anti-foreign resistance, and they continued to proliferate and expand their reach. A Gowned Brothers branch might be found in any village, *bao*,[39] or temporary lodging in Sichuan, as indicated in a popular saying in Sichuan at the time: "There were no illiterates at the end of the Ming dynasty, nor anyone who was not a Gowned Brother at the end of the Qing."[40] As it turns out, Sichuan Gowned Brothers were not actually that "secret."[41] Nor, as historian Wang Chunwu has shown, did Sichuan Gowned Brothers—in particular, those on the Chengdu Plain—have any connection to the Society of Heaven and Earth (Tiandihui) in South China, an underground anti-Manchu society that was growing in influence in the late Qing.[42]

The direct link between Chengdu's Railway Protection Association and the Gowned Brothers is hard to deny. In particular, Luo Lun, a principal leader of the association, had major ties to the Gowned Brothers. Born in 1876 into a powerful family in Xichong county, Luo became a *juren* at the age of twenty-three and was said to be a leader of the Gowned Brothers in his hometown. Although not a member of the Tongmenghui, Luo was sympathetic to its radical, republican principles.[43] During the railway movement, Luo gained a reputation in Sichuan as a hero because of his passionate speeches, biting commentaries, and radicalism. Nevertheless, stepping beyond just the delivery of stirring speeches and the publication of provocative articles, Luo at an early stage of the railway movement established connections with the Gowned Brothers and local militia leaders. Even though his secret link with the Gowned Brothers was less well documented than his role as a public figure, evidence suggests that Luo was the one primarily responsible for the extensive involvement of secret societies in the movement.

Even Acting Governor-General Zhao Erfeng sensed it. Zhao claimed to have discovered a letter in Pu Dianjun's home, written by Luo Lun, indicating that he was involved with the Gowned Brothers and prepared for rebellion. Later, when providing justification for the arrests of the Chengdu elite, Zhao singled out Luo Lun as the "rebellious gentleman" (*nishen*) who had connections to bandits. Zhao wrote, "All of these rebel leaders claimed that they came over to Chengdu to save Luo Lun's life. Such a secret link [between Luo Lun and the bandits] is not known by people outside of Chengdu. Even some who are in the Railway Protection Association in Chengdu do not know. The reason I arrested Luo Lun is because he was rebelling against the dynasty. . . . Railway protection is just a cover-up."[44]

Not coincidentally, Duanfang, the imperial commissioner of the Yue-Han and Chuan-Han railways, also believed that Luo Lun was defying the dynasty, noting that "Luo was the most radical and rebellious leader in the Railway Protection Association."[45] Foreign accounts similarly documented Luo Lun's leadership over the Gowned Brothers in Sichuan. The British acting Chongqing customs commissioner E. von Strauch informed his superiors in Beijing that Luo was considered "the leader of the rebellious forces"[46] and "the most dangerous figure in the Railway Protection Association."[47] On the basis of his interviews of Gowned Brothers leaders Sun Zepei and Wu Qingxi, Sichuan historian Huang Shou offered further substantiation for these claims, stating that Sun and Wu "admired and listened only to Luo Lun."[48]

Among the many Gowned Brothers leaders with whom Luo Lun and the Railway Protection Association coordinated their activities, the most crucial figure was Hou Baozhai, whose Gowned Brothers network was a key resource for the Railway Protection Association leaders. Hou was born in 1851 and raised in a household that had one room and ten *mu* (less than a hectare) of land in Xinjin county. To make ends meet, he had smuggled salt, sold tung oil, and transported timber. Hou eventually became the leader of the swift-hand (*kuaiban*) yamen runners and the police (*buban*) yamen runners and organized a Gowned Brothers organization called the New West Leader (Xinxigong). In Xinjin, Hou had a reputation for being "righteous (*yi*), generous (*zhangyi shucai*), and warmhearted (*rexin*)." Hou was "always willing to help people" and "did not shirk responsibilities," and "whoever encountered a lawsuit, no matter if he knows Hou well or not, [could count on] Hou to offer him money and support."[49] In 1878, Hou became the chief training officer of the Xinjin militia bureau.[50] From that point until his tenure ended in the early 1900s, Xinjin was always "peaceful."[51]

In 1904, Hou united nine groups of Gowned Brothers that were then referred to as "the Nine Groups" (Jiucheng tuanti), assuming leadership of the alliance. In the fall of 1907, he was accused of "conducting a rebellion" but was excused because of lack of evidence following an investigation by troops sent in by the Sichuan governor-general.[52] In late June and early July 1911, as the railway movement extended into the outlying counties of Sichuan, Xinjin also formed a branch of the Railway Protection Association. Summarily elected chairman of the branch, Hou became an ardent supporter of the railway movement from that point on. Xinjin county archival sources show that Hou joined the railway movement because of his "wrath" (*fen*) over the way the Qing court was treating Sichuan. Outraged when the Qing took away the "railway rights" (*luquan*) of the people of Sichuan, he responded to Luo Lun's call and formed his force out of "honorable anger" (*yifen*).[53]

By mid-July, Hou Baozhai was already engaged in rebellious action. Using his sixtieth birthday celebration as a pretext to invite the Gowned Brothers leaders from all nine groups to his home, Hou took the opportunity to discuss plans for a rebellion against the Qing. He and other important Gowned Brothers leaders—the most radical of whom was Qin Zaigeng, a prominent Gowned Brother and militia leader from Huayang county—had already developed their ideas. After much discussion, the group agreed to return to their home counties, to "be prepared and get ready as called upon," and to "carry out the matter uniformly" (*yizhi jinxing*). If they "could not gather enough people to attack Chengdu all at once," they would first "occupy southern and eastern Sichuan, seize control of this rich area, and then devise ways to get Chengdu later."[54] At this meeting, Qin emerged as the leader who would be in charge of attacking eastern Sichuan, and Hou was put in charge of the southern attack.[55]

In late August, when asked by an illiterate man to explain Zhao Erfeng's announcement, which in reality spoke simply about "keeping order," Hou purposely misconstrued the meaning, telling the man instead that Zhao was about to "kill people" (*kai hongshan*). Even today, a local ballad from Xinjin rants, "Hou Baozhai looked at the announcement: inauspicious, inauspicious, and inauspicious!" (*Hou Baozhai kan gaoshi: xiong xiong xiong!*)[56] After a massacre in Chengdu on September 7, which is discussed later in this chapter, it was in Hou's base, Xinjin county, that the most heated battle between the Qing armies and the Sichuan railway protection armies was fought.

All in all, the Railway Protection Association had formed a strong, direct union with the local Gowned Brothers. Although it is unclear to what extent the discourse propagated by the Chengdu leaders had motivated these Gowned Brothers—some, such as Wu Qingxi, were excited by the notion of self-determination (*zizhu*) hinted at in these publications—they had been exposed to it, to say the least.[57] The ties forged by the association with Gowned Brothers leaders served to strengthen its alliance with the local people.

Pressures from Beijing

As the Chengdu elite were building solidarity among the people in Sichuan (via both public and "secret" organizations), their relationship with Beijing was becoming increasingly strained. After the founding of the association on June 17, struggles between Chengdu and Beijing intensified, with the Railway Protection Association and the court locked in competition for support from the Sichuan provincial officials in Chengdu, the Sichuan metropolitan officials based in Beijing, and the Yichang branch of the railway company.

The Railway Protection Association was successful in securing support from the acting Sichuan governor-general, Wang Renwen. Wang, who had been provincial treasurer during Zhao Erxun's tenure, became the acting governor-general in January 1911, following Zhao's departure to assume the post of governor-general of Manchuria. A native of Yunnan who had served in Sichuan for a number of years, Wang was on good terms with the Sichuan gentry. On June 17, when movement leaders Luo Lun, Deng Xiaoke, Wu Songsheng, Meng Gongfu, Zhu Shan, and others marched to the provincial government to present their petition, Wang received them and proclaimed: "My position as governor-general is to look after the people. As my people have a grievance, I shall raise the problem with the court on my people's behalf. If I cannot succeed, I will resign!"[58] After the founding of the Railway Protection Association, Wang began speaking up on behalf of the Sichuan elites even more aggressively. In his June 19 memorial to the court, Wang impeached (*tanhe*) Sheng Xuanhuai, asking the court to "punish him seriously, using the most severe law of the dynasty."[59] He also forwarded Luo Lun's critique of the foreign loan treaty to the court.[60] In the memorial sent along with the critique, Wang reiterated his position: "If the Ministry of Posts and Communications coerces the people of Sichuan into following its orders, the only fate left for Sichuanese is death."[61]

Needless to say, Beijing was not thrilled. The court criticized everything Wang wrote and accused him of "constantly sending in rude memorials" (*yizai duzou*). It threatened Wang that "if any chaos occurred, [he] would be singled out as fully responsible."⁶² In addition, the court rushed Zhao Erfeng back to Chengdu from the Sichuan-Tibet border, both to "extinguish the people's agitation" and to "punish the troublemakers."⁶³ Meanwhile, Sheng Xuanhuai and Duanfang were successful in marshaling support from the Sichuanese metropolitan officials. Among these were Gan Dazhang and Song Yuren, who supported the court's takeover and the transfer of all existing railway capital to Beijing. In June, Song sent the Ministry of Posts and Communications a petition, stating that "the nationalization of the railway will bring benefits for both the state and the people." Also in June, Gan and Song issued two petitions that decried the heavy burden of the railway tax (*zugu*) borne by the Sichuan people and the lack of progress in railroad construction. To mitigate the conflict between Beijing and Chengdu, Gan and Song proposed that the seven million taels of silver reportedly held by the Railway Protection Association be used to build the section from Chengdu to Kuizhou. In this way, at least some part of the railway would be built with the "people's capital" (*mingu*).⁶⁴

Upon hearing of the petitions from Gan and Song, the exasperated Railway Protection Association leaders in Chengdu denied that Gan and Song were "appointed by the Sichuan people" and argued that "the numerous Sichuan shareholders and their opinions could not be reduced to the selfish words of a dozen people."⁶⁵ A vicious campaign against Gan and Song followed.⁶⁶ The Chengdu leaders organized support from other Sichuan-born metropolitan officials, such as Zhao Xi and Hu Jun, who joined them in condemning Gan Dazhang and his clique.⁶⁷ The Chengdu headquarters labeled all the supporters of Sheng Xuanhuai "traitors" to Sichuan, and the hometown organizations (*tongxianghui*) of Gan Dazhang and Song Yuren voted to strip them of their membership. For example, the hometown organization of Suining, which was Gan Dazhang's home county, threatened to dig up Gan's ancestral tombs, expropriate his family's properties, and take his wife and children hostage so that the public "would know about all the evils he has perpetrated on the Sichuanese."⁶⁸ Recognizing the depth of the hatred directed toward him, Gan asked the Department of Posts and Communications to order Acting Governor-General Wang Renwen to protect his home and his ancestral tombs.⁶⁹ The campaign against "traitors" became increasingly violent.

Realizing the futility of trying to win over all of the metropolitan officials, Sheng Xuanhuai and Duanfang shifted their focus to converting

Li Jixun, the manager of the Yichang branch of the Chuan-Han Railway Company, to their cause. Li was perhaps the most valuable figure in the railway company, as Yichang was the only branch that actually carried out railway construction. Li, whose work and achievements elevated the importance of his voice in the struggle, was summoned to Beijing by Sheng Xuanhuai and Duanfang. On July 5, 1911, Li agreed to accept Beijing's proposal to appropriate the seven million taels of silver in Chengdu.[70] On July 13, Duanfang recommended that Li remain as the chief manager of the Yichang branch of the company. Three days later, on July 16, Duanfang followed up with another telegram, asking Sheng to support Li and his continuing construction of the Kuizhou-Zigui section of railway; subsequently, on July 27, Li's appointment was confirmed after he and Duanfang met in person.[71] Following his decision to support the nationalization policy, Li served as one of its major proponents.[72]

Sheng and Duanfang, by then allied with Li Jixun and a group of Beijing-based Sichuan officials, were confident that the issue in Sichuan would be resolved quickly and in their favor. A systematic investigation into the accounts of the Yichang branch had begun in early July, and it was also demanded that the accounts of all other branches of the Chuan-Han Railway Company be inspected. Under these circumstances, the Chengdu railway elite realized that they would have to take radical action to win their battle.

Radicalization: From Protecting the Railways and Breaking the Treaty to Open Revolt

THE SPECIAL SHAREHOLDER MEETING (JULY 31–AUGUST 24)

The decision to convene an all-Sichuan shareholder meeting—known as the Special Shareholder Meeting (Tebie gudong hui)—on August 5 had been made on May 22, following the announcement by the court of the decision to stop levying the railway tax; however, by August the situation had become increasingly urgent, and Chengdu leaders were determined to take the opportunity presented by this meeting to reenergize and put up resistance to the central government.

In the days leading up to the meeting, the Chengdu elite worked hard to develop their rhetoric. On July 31, they drafted "Our Opinions on Following the Previous Emperor's Edict and Keeping the Railway Commercially Managed," an outline for the August 5 meeting enumerating the key reasons the Sichuanese had to fight for their railways.[73] In the outline, Chengdu leaders underscored over and over how the treaty violated the rights and the interests of the shareholders, which would eventually violate the rights of the nation and its citizens as a whole.

The outline also proposed four action items for discussion at the shareholder meeting. The first was to beseech the court to let Sichuan people privately manage their railways. The second was to appeal to the court to cease levying the old and new "voluntary surcharge taxes" (*juanshu*) so that Sichuan could have money to help build the railways. The third was to propose the levying of a "one-cash tax" (*yiwen juan*) to raise money for building the railway, and the fourth was to set up a bureau to investigate and clear up the accounts of the company.[74]

At the same time, Beijing was doing its best to obstruct Chengdu's moves. Concurrent with the Chengdu elite's attempt to organize their forces, Sheng Xuanhuai and Duanfang were engaged in a full-tilt effort to marshal forces against them. On July 28, Duanfang telegraphed Sheng Xuanhuai with a request that he order Sichuan officials to prevent any "hostile mass gatherings." He further proposed: "We should let the police department and the office of the Sichuan treasurer check up on the meeting. If the meeting is a legal shareholder meeting, then it will be allowed to convene. If the meeting is for the Railway Protection Association, which has been well propagandized in newspapers and would rally ten or twenty thousand people to resist the government, then we should strictly forbid it."[75] In a second telegram to Sheng that same day, Duanfang urged him to rush Zhao Erfeng to Chengdu to control the elites, whom he accused of sending out pamphlets that were "unreasonable and rebellious."[76] Both telegrams were also sent to Prince Zaize, ensuring that the cabinet supported their stand. On July 30, the central government issued an edict ordering Zhao Erfeng to arrive in Chengdu before the day of the shareholder meeting and declaring a ban on all meetings other than the shareholder meeting.[77]

This flurry of attempts from Beijing to disrupt the meeting did little to impede the Sichuanese. Well prepared and well organized, the Chengdu elite opened the Special Shareholder Meeting on August 5 at the railway company on Yuefu Street with seven hundred people in attendance. They voted Luo Lun the chairperson and Zhang Lan and Yan Kai the vice-chairs of the meeting. That afternoon, freshly arrived Acting Governor-General Zhao Erfeng attended the meeting and delivered a speech (Figure 6.1). After consulting with Sichuan officials Wang Renwen and Zhou Shanpei, both supportive of the Chengdu elite, Zhao claimed that he would "do the best within his power to help sort things out."[78]

FIGURE 6.1. Acting Governor-General Zhao Erfeng. *Wikipedia.*

After August 5, Chengdu's struggle with the central government intensified. On August 7, after representatives at the shareholder meeting received Duanfang's telegram asserting that "all of the activists are local troublemakers and the fair and righteous gentry managers are not supporting them," they were infuriated. Chengdu leaders quickly drafted a telegram to Duanfang, accusing him of "arbitrarily interfering with the operation of the shareholder meeting." They claimed that only those who were following public opinion (*yulun*) such as themselves could be considered "fair" and "righteous." Notably, Zhao Erfeng threw his support behind the railway leaders, concurring with them that Duanfang's telegram was "truly unreasonable." Furthermore, Zhao agreed to forward the Chengdu elite's rebuttal to Duanfang and in an expression of solidarity underscored his personal disagreement with Duanfang's stand.[79]

August 8 marked the emergence of a new point of contention, which resulted from Zhao's revelation that Li Jixun, the manager of the Yichang branch, had switched to the side of Duanfang and Sheng Xuanhuai. Reacting to this news with "huge anger" (*da fen*) and refusing to back down, the organizers of the shareholders' meeting clashed with Beijing head-on. Opening the agenda on August 9 was discussion of "the Li Jixun problem." Luo Lun and seven others marched to Zhao Erfeng's office to entreat Zhao to forward to the court their request to impeach Sheng Xuanhuai and Li Jixun. Li Jixun was fired as a collective decision by all shareholders, who then asked Zhao Erfeng to order Li to hand in all railway paperwork within ten days. After August 9, Li's behavior in "selling out the rail line" was widely publicized in propaganda newspapers in Chengdu, and the increasingly vicious verbal attacks against Li and his "treacherous behavior," initiated by the Chengdu headquarters, made Li the second archenemy of the Sichuanese after Sheng Xuanhuai. For example, *Xigubao* reported that the Youyang Hometown Organization—Youyang being Li's home county—had passed a motion to withdraw Li's membership, to expropriate all his properties, and, most radically, to assassinate (*an'sha*) Li Jixun in Beijing.[80] Outrage over the Li Jixun problem pushed the Sichuan people in an increasingly radical direction.

Meanwhile, the shareholder meetings lost no time in taking up the key issue on which to challenge the court—the voluntary surcharge tax (*juanshu*)—just as they had planned on July 31. On August 11, the shareholders discussed declining to submit the old and new *juanshu* tax as a way of alleviating the financial pressure on the Sichuanese while at the same time boosting the availability of money for building the railway. Anticipating that the magistrate might tell the gentry and landowners that they could not submit the standard tax (*dingliang*) before submitting the *juanshu*, they decided that in this case the gentry and landowners should submit their standard tax first and send it directly to the county seats, making it impossible for their actions to be construed as rebellion.[81]

While fighting against the Qing government over the issue of *juanshu*, the gentry at the shareholders meeting were not shy about levying their own tax on the Sichuan people. In August 12's discussion, the shareholders came up with the concrete method of having local gentry assemblies, urban and rural, levy a one-cash tax (*yiwen juan*) to raise money for the railway: "People . . . no matter rich or poor, male or female, should voluntarily contribute one copper coin every day to help the railway construction. . . . Once people contribute money, they will be considered shareholders."[82] The levy and collection responsibilities were assigned to city and town councils and, in rural areas, to the countryside gentry. In essence, these Sichuan elite were devising ways to take over taxation from the central and the provincial governments by using new self-governance organs, such as the local assemblies that had emerged in the constitutional reform, in achieving their goal.

The Special Shareholder Meeting was a turning point for the Railway Protection movement. Each attempt at interference by the central officials served only to amplify the anger of the Sichuanese. With their increasing alienation from the court, the Sichuan elite went on to employ a new self-governing apparatus to combat the central state. They capitalized on the growing radicalization, fueled people's heightened emotions during the meeting period, and successfully solidified the unity of the movement. In the wake of the Special Shareholder Meeting, Sichuanese became more emboldened than ever, and the movement quickly passed the stage of building constitutionalism and promoting the people's rights via peaceful petitioning and memorializing to become an open revolt focusing on the very legitimacy of the state.

MARKET STRIKES AND TAX RESISTANCE (AUGUST 24–SEPTEMBER 6)

The struggles between Beijing and Chengdu continued. Refusing the demand of the Special Shareholder Meeting attendees to fire Li Jixun as the Yichang branch manager of the railway company, Sheng Xuanhuai, Duanfang, and Huguang governor-general Ruicheng countered with a request to the court that Li be retained in his position and Zhao Erfeng be ordered to quickly suppress the agitation in Sichuan.

On August 23, when Zhao Erfeng received the edict ordering Li Jixun to remain in his post, he immediately forwarded it to the Special Shareholder Meeting. Upon hearing it announced by the vice-chair Yan Kai, people at the meeting were incensed. They "cried, shouted, cursed, hit their chests, stamped on the floor, and made speeches. . . . Some were shouting about carrying out a market strike, some talked about letting students organize a school strike, some insisted that Sichuanese should not pay the transit tax, and others proposed using the land tax to replace the railway tax."[83] At the end of the day, the shareholders resolved to carry out a market strike and a school strike.

The response of Chengdu residents to the call announcing the strikes was enthusiastic. Commoners took part in the market strike; all shops were closed and all trade discontinued in support of the movement, despite the heavy financial cost to the strikers. As historian Wang Di vividly depicts in his book *Street Culture in Chengdu*, the city had never known such stillness:

> The sound of gongs and drums in Joy Teahouse and Elegant Garden, the pure singing in other teahouses, the cries of business on Drum Tower Street, and the waiters' voices in restaurants all disappeared. Even the noise of the weaving machines on Half Street and Horse Riding Street, and the jingling of hammers in the jewelry stores on Golden Ware Street, which could be heard throughout the day, were stopped. The hawkers also stripped the goods from their sheds and stalls.[84]

The Qing court, ever watchful of what was happening in Chengdu, ordered Zhao Erfeng to "suppress the movement effectively."[85] Zhao and his subordinates did their best to persuade the Chengdu people to reopen the market. However, because, as he put it, "the suspicion and misunderstanding of the people were already so strong . . . they could not be persuaded by any reasons."[86]

To deter possible accusations that they were engaged in rebellion, Chengdu leaders devised clever ways to safely conduct their strikes. Commoners occupied the streets and with the elite's support built altars to the Guangxu emperor (*xianhuang tai*), who had died in 1908 but was still considered an important proponent of the commercial ownership of Sichuan railroads. Within days, memorial tablets for the late emperor (*shengwei pai*) were also displayed in households and shops in Chengdu. Likewise, matching couplets pasted on commoners' doors read "Various political affairs are up for public discussion; railways should be run by the local people"—a phrase taken from the Guangxu emperor's edict. On every street, people burned incense and worshiped at the altars and tablets day and night.[87] Officials did not dare show disrespect for the deceased emperor by traveling past them. As Zhao Erfeng acknowledged: "Any attempt to travel in sedan chairs or with horses on the street will give the commoners an excuse to oppose their officials. They have the Guangxu emperor's tablets as their amulet."[88]

Thrilled that the people were now mobilized, the Chengdu elite took care to keep the movement under control. A public announcement was directed at restraining the masses. First, there was to be no gathering on the street; second, no rebellion; third, no attacking the churches; fourth, no humiliating of officials or the government; and fifth, oil, salt, firewood, rice, and all other basic household necessities should be sold just as usual.[89]

The market and school strikes soon expanded beyond Chengdu, with Sichuanese from outlying counties joining in by staging their own strikes. After a September 2 meeting of the Learned Circles Association in Chengdu, students from Fushun, Ziyang, Youyang, Hejiang, Neijiang, Santai, and other counties returned to their homes to organize strikes.[90] The learned circles and the commercial circles decided that unless their goal—to protect the railways and break the treaty—was achieved, they would never go back to school or reopen their shops. The strikes spread quickly to Qiongzhou and Yazhou in the south, to Mianzhou in the west, to Shunqing in the north, and to Rongxian and Longchang in the east. It was said that for a radius of a thousand *li* (576 kilometers) from Chengdu, shops were closed in market towns and county seats.[91] In Xindu, shops were closed, with half the people in the county seat having joined the

Railway Protection Association at that point. In Chongning and Xinfan counties, all shops, except for those that sold basic necessities, were closed. Market strikes were also under way in Deyang, Suiding, Xuzhou, Jiading, Renshou, Ziyang, Chongqing, Wanxian, Qianwei, and Zigong.[92]

Xigubao, the influential propaganda newspaper controlled by the Railway Protection Association, later published a summarizing commentary (*shiping*) that praised the political consciousness exhibited by the Sichuanese in their strikes and raved about the persistence, enthusiasm, and ability to maintain order on display during such a dangerous time. The reporter commended the Sichuanese for their selfless participation in the railway movement, even though "many have had to sacrifice their meager income," while criticizing their treatment at the hands of the Qing government: "The government has always used the excuse that Sichuan is far away and its people are close minded [to bully the Sichuanese]. . . . Now, the ability of the Sichuan people in organizing such an orderly movement has even gained praise from Europeans. The quality of the Sichuanese is thus by no means worse than that of the government. It is only because Sichuanese have suffered under autocracy (*zhuanzhi*) for too long that their true quality has never [before] had a chance to be seen."[93]

While mobilizing commoners to take part in the strikes, the leaders at the Special Shareholder Meeting themselves were also becoming increasingly radical. The decision to not pay the *juanshu* was made before the Special Shareholder Meeting, but it was only after the strikes began that it was fully implemented. The movement elite composed popular ballads to make sure commoners understood the meaning of the *juanshu* resistance. One particularly revealing song, titled "The Song about Stopping the Submission of the *Juanshu*" (*Tingban juanshu ge*), not only challenged the Qing government by decrying its taxation policy but also questioned its very legitimacy to tax the people. The song also explored, in bold language, why the people of Sichuan had always been so frightened of government officials.

The songwriter began by exposing the origin of the *juanshu* as a "voluntary" surcharge, the levying of which began during the Tongzhi reign when officials urged commoners to submit money to help suppress the Taiping Rebellion. However, long after the suppression of the Taipings, the Sichuanese were still forced to pay the *juanshu* and it was thus "not voluntary at all." In this way, Sichuanese had been "bullied by the untrustworthy government."[94] The songwriter then analyzed the Sichuan people's fear: "The people who have suffered under the despotic system are scared. And these scared men are naturally wary of an act that is seen as 'resisting the *juanshu*.'"[95] On this point, the writer lamented, "To think in this way is truly deplorable."[96] He pointed to "people's eternal fear of officials" as the crux of the issue and encouraged the Sichuanese to participate in the anti-*juanshu* resistance with the following lyrics:

We should not be afraid of officials, not be afraid of officials (*bupa guan, bupa guan*); we should shout this slogan a thousand times (*lianshuo yiqiange bupa guan*).... The reason that we should not be afraid of officials is that we are in a constitutional state.... If we do not violate any laws, we should, with perfect assurance, not be afraid of officials....

We thus have determined not to pay the *juanshu*.... If officials insist on levying the *juanshu* ... we will, by all means, use the law to question the justice of their actions. If they still decide to violate the law, we will certainly rebel against them!

Why do we dare to exert such resistance? It is because we are national citizens in a constitutional state and we have the rights and freedoms a citizen in a constitutional state has.... All constitutional states have set examples for us in dealing with similar issues. They have followed one principle: "No taxation without representation!"

In contrast, the Qing government did not consult with the National Assembly or the Provincial Assembly but signed the foreign loan treaty and issued the nationalization policy. Such acts violated the regulations of the National Assembly and the Provincial Assembly. If we still pay the *juanshu*, the energy of the people (*minqi*) will never develop![97]

By its clear reasoning, the song made explicit an abstract political principle first set forth by theorists like Liang Qichao, namely, that sovereignty lies with the people, by applying it to a concrete political action, namely, whether to pay the *juanshu* tax or not. Along with this principle, which was used for mobilizing people, the Chengdu leaders also skillfully employed the concept of the rule of law as a key weapon to establish popular sovereignty as the new basis for a legitimate government. In contrast to political legitimacy in the old regime, which justified the rule of the emperor in collaboration with scholar-officials in the name of Heaven, the new discourse on legitimacy emphasized the notion of rights, stressed the principle of "no taxation without supervision," and encouraged the power of regular citizens and the people.

The energized Chengdu movement leaders made an even bolder decision at the Shareholder Meeting's August 29 session: they called upon the Sichuan people not only to stop paying the *juanshu* but also to cease payment of *all* forms of taxes and surcharges, including the standard tax, in hopes of forcing the central government to abandon the idea of nationalizing the railways.[98] Luo Lun was again the mastermind behind this idea,[99] which he and his colleagues framed not as an act of rebellion against the dynasty but as a way to recoup their loss in interest of the *zugu*—which they calculated as six hundred thousand taels per year (6 percent of ten million taels' investment)—by withholding the standard tax and the *juanshu*.[100]

No matter how it was phrased, however, such a proposal was blatantly rebellious. The increasingly radicalized movement elite soon set up organizations to carry out tax resistance with full awareness that resisting the standard tax would in the eyes of the Qing court be a "great disobedience" (*dani*). They encouraged one another in this behavior with rationalizations such as the following, which was put forth by one shareholder: "For all taxes, it is our right to pay them or not. . . . As for the *juanshu*, we always have the ultimate right to pay it or not!"[101] Rather than being a responsibility of all subjects "gratefully living on the ruler's land and eating the grain growing on that land" (*shimao jiantu*), the decision of whether or not to pay taxes was considered "a right we have."

Inspired by this attitude, increasing numbers of Sichuan people were moved to demand more. The movement leaders' declaration that people had the ability to act for themselves rather than having to follow what the administration told them to do was, in Chengdu commandant Yukun's eyes, too much to condone. Yukun wrote: "Even though they say that they are not rioting . . . the intentions of these organizations—the Shareholder Meeting, the Railway Protection Association, the Official-Gentry Allied Association, and the Order-Keeping Organization—are extremely evil. . . . Taxes that were supposed to be submitted cannot be put into the provincial treasury. This is truly like a real rebellion! A falling-out between the government and the Chengdu leaders will soon come."[102]

On September 1, the announcement of the shareholders' tax-resistance decision was posted all across the city.[103] To launch the campaign to resist the payment of taxes, the Sichuan Railway Protection Association also made strategic use of newspapers and pictorials. Writers for the *Xigubao* composed a rhyming ballad to help people memorize the principles:

First, as we find our *zugu* interest nowhere, we deduct the land tax. They rob us of money; we do not give them any.

Second, the surcharge tax (*jintie*) and voluntary surcharge tax (*juanshu*), we do not pay them anymore. The salt tax, to remove it sounds good.

Third, if we stop buying land and houses, members of the New Tax Bureau will have no food.

Fourth, all taxes are removed, we do not care if [the government] has huge debts or not.

Keeping these four things in mind, we have our song to resist the government.[104]

In the end, the writers maintained cheerfully, "If the officials have no money, how can they be threatening? If they have no food, how can they be repressive? If they are hungry, they will be afraid of us and they may abandon the dynasty. At that moment, we Sichuanese will obtain our 'human rights' (*renquan*)!"[105]

This deluge of propaganda directed at the Qing government and officials proved effective in mobilizing the Sichuan people. An increasingly impassioned and unified Sichuanese opposition emerged, determined to "break the treaty and protect the railways" and to resist all taxes they deemed illegitimate. The *Veritable Records of the Qing Dynasty in the Xuantong Reign* recorded that "several dozen counties across Sichuan also participate in the movement, collectively. They do not pay the land tax or the *juanshu*, and they all take part in market and school strikes. . . . People are not thinking about living a better life; rather, they are ready to die if they have to in order to achieve their goals. Sichuan is in great danger."[106] Responding to Chengdu leaders' calls to resist taxes, people in outlying counties attacked the New Tax Bureau branches and police bureaus in an open display of opposition to Qing policies. On August 30 in Peng and Xinfan counties, on September 2 in Guan county, and in early September in Zizhou, Jintang, and Zhongjiang counties, emboldened local people assaulted bureau personnel, unleashing their frustration with the Qing and their anger over these much-reviled bureaus that had appeared in the New Policies era.[107]

Faced with this escalating movement, Sichuan provincial officials, led by Acting Governor-General Zhao Erfeng, chose at first to collaborate with the Chengdu movement elite in an effort to keep things under control.[108] On August 27 and 28, Zhao and other officials sent telegrams, drafted by Zhou Shanpei in consultation with Pu Dianjun, asking the cabinet to let the national and provincial assemblies decide how the railway issue should be handled, to permit the railway to remain privately managed, to abolish the loan treaty, and to fire Li Jixun.[109] In these telegrams, Zhao fully adopted the reasoning that had been laid out at the Special Shareholder Meeting. He then aligned himself even further with the railway movement, to the point of deploying the rhetoric of constitutionalism in a telegram to the cabinet on August 30: "Ever since the constitutional reform, in provinces, the power of officials has declined every day and the power of the people has expanded. . . . Every time [the people] discuss a matter, as it concerns their rights (*quan*), they will not want to compromise. This trend has been there for a while. . . . The Sichuan people consider themselves citizens in a constitutional state. . . . The signing of the foreign loan treaty is a matter of national importance; however, the decision to sign it was not made by the National Assembly, and that violated the constitution."[110]

The court did not respond favorably to the missives from Zhao Erfeng. A series of telegrams exchanged between August 30 and September 4 raised the specter of "foreign disputes" if the nationalization policy were to be rescinded and threatened Zhao: "If you fail to suppress the chaos . . . you will be severely punished! Be careful!"[111] Indeed, by this point, any kind of peaceful solution to the railway matter seemed to be out of the question. The court had resolved to crush the Sichuan Railway Protection movement, mostly as a result of constant pressure from Duanfang and Sheng Xuanhuai. Beginning on August 27, Duanfang fired off a series of telegrams to Sheng Xuanhuai and Zaize accusing Zhao Erfeng of "allying with the Sichuan bandits" and urging them to pressure the court to send in other officials to replace Zhao as a way of bringing the railway movement under control. Having come to view Zhao with disfavor (in large part because of Duanfang's repeated slanders), on September 2 the court decided to appoint Duanfang to "help" Zhao suppress the Sichuan Railway Protection movement.[112] Along with his official appointment on September 6, Duanfang was also given command of all of the Qing armies in Sichuan.[113] Finding himself under tremendous pressure, Zhao was pushed into an act of desperation.

THE SEPTEMBER 7 CHENGDU MASSACRE

The massacre in Chengdu on September 7 was the catalyst that catapulted the movement into a full-fledged revolt against the Qing. The incident that touched off the crisis occurred early in the morning on September 5, when an unidentified man showed up at the gate of the Special Shareholder Meeting hall and began distributing copies of a printed pamphlet. The pamphlet, *Suggestions to the Sichuan People for Preserving Themselves* (*Chuanren zibao shangque shu*), stated: "The [Qing] government is corrupt, engaging in bribery, and selling out the nation. . . . The only way for the Sichuanese to survive is to stand up for themselves."[114]

The pamphlet called upon the Sichuanese to do two things: first, to use local assemblies in townships and the countryside (*zhen xiang yishihui*) to collect taxes—including the land tax, meltage charges, the *juanshu*, and all other charges—that would then be kept by the assemblies; and second, to rely on local assemblies to select and organize men from the area into a citizen army (*guomin jun*) and to manufacture weapons. Deflecting suspicion with the claim that "we are simply assisting the government," this pamphlet in actuality called on the Sichuanese to engage in the defiant acts of resisting taxes and organizing armed forces. The writer closed the pamphlet with an unequivocal statement: "Officials or members of the gentry, whoever is treacherous, we Sichuanese will treat them as the enemy, an enemy we will never reconcile with."[115]

Having already lost favor with the court while suffering through Duanfang's political attacks, Zhao Erfeng was livid upon receiving this pamphlet. Convinced of the need to preserve his position as acting governor-general and redeem himself after Beijing had chastised him, Zhao resorted to a rash course of action. Citing *Suggestions to the Sichuan People* as evidence of railway movement leaders' "rebellious acts," on September 7 Zhao accused the leaders of building a republican government (*gonghe zhengfu*). That morning, under the pretext of wanting to show them telegrams from Beijing, Zhao invited to his yamen the Railway Protection Association leaders Luo Lun, Deng Xiaoke, and Zhang Lan; the Provincial Assembly leaders Pu Dianjun and Jiang Sancheng; and the Chuan-Han Railway Company elite Yan Kai, Wang Mingxin, Ye Bingcheng, and Peng Fen. Upon their arrival, Zhao placed them all under arrest and locked them up.[116] Zhao Erfeng then quickly dispatched police and guards to search the railway company. He also sealed the railway school and closed down the company's guesthouse. In addition, he banned the *Newsletter of the Sichuan Railway Protection Association*, *Xigubao*, *Enlightening Pictorials*, and all of the other propaganda publications.[117]

News of the arrests shocked the entire city, prompting groups of Chengdu residents to immediately gather at Zhao's yamen to demonstrate. They were soon followed by thousands of people, their voices raised in the same angry cry. Wang Di describes the memorable scene, in which men, women, and children, "with sticks of lighted incense in one hand and yellow paper spirit tablets of the Guangxu emperor in the other, pressed toward Zhao's yamen to petition for their leaders' release, as they wept, wailed, and cried: 'Give us back our Luo Lun; give us back our Luo Lun.'"[118] On the streets, police officers responded with sympathy toward the petitioning commoners. In the procession to Zhao's yamen, policemen led the way, followed by gentry, and behind them large numbers of commoners. That day, Chengdu witnessed a political drama played out on the public stage, acted out by elites and commoners together.

The demonstration that had begun as such an earnest outpouring of public support came to a tragic end. Although the people peacefully presented their appeal by "begging and kowtowing," Zhao ordered his soldiers to open fire in front of his yamen. By the time the forecourt had been cleared of demonstrators, it was left littered with more than twenty bleeding bodies and scattered debris that included broken memorial tablets. Most of the participants were laborers and other members of the lower classes. Of the twenty-six victims identified, sixteen were humble folk such as weavers, carvers, apprentices, tailors, and peddlers.[119] To prevent a provincewide rebellion and to cut Chengdu off from communication with the outside world, Zhao imposed martial law and shut the city gates. He also sent his soldiers to guard street corners to prohibit people from coming and going. But the people resolutely defended their heroes Pu and Luo. Historian Wang Di translated from an eyewitness's account: "The ferocious New Army depended on guns to maintain order, but this only made people so angry that they snatched the guns from them, fighting without fear."[120] This was the Chengdu massacre of September 7 (Figure 6.2).

To put the day's events into perspective, it is important to consider the divergent positions, perceptions, and ideas that the Qing court and the Sichuan people held regarding the actions of the railway movement leaders, beginning with the attitude of the Qing officials and the court. On September 7, the day of the massacre, Zhao Erfeng reported to the court that the Sichuanese had openly confronted the dynasty. In Zhao's telegram to Duanfang that same day, he quoted the objectives listed in the pamphlet—namely, to resist taxes and to build armed forces—as evidence of the railway movement leaders' rebellious acts.[121] Concurring, the court summarily issued two edicts, one endorsing Zhao's decision and the other sending him the Hubei Army as reinforcements.[122] On September 11, Zhao posted a comprehensive public announcement enumerating the reasons he had arrested the railway movement leaders. Aimed at solidifying Zhao's authority among Chengdu's antagonistic subjects, the announcement, written in

FIGURE 6.2. Victims of the Chengdu massacre of September 7, 1911. *Gonghe zhi guang: Xinhai qiu Sichuan baolu sishi bainian ji*, 261.

colloquial language, alleged that the railway movement leaders had committed two illegal acts: they had "resisted taxes," and they had "organized independent forces and freely moved about (*zizou*) and enjoyed their freedom (*ziyou*)." In doing so, they had committed the greatest crime of all, rebellion (*moufan*).[123]

The people of Chengdu saw this matter differently. Commoners supported their leaders and declared that they had done nothing wrong. Soon after Zhao posted his announcement, in some back streets and alleys, residents tore down the public notices or spattered them with red paint. In one case, the entire notice was overwritten with comments and rebuttals. Where Zhao had said that the leaders were rebels and had connections to bandits outside of the city wall, there appeared the comment: "It is only because you, Zhao Erfeng, killed the kind people on September 7 and arrested the righteous gentry that angry commoners rushed to Chengdu on September 8, holding that such a view about the gentry was unfair!"[124] Repudiating Zhao's statement that the leaders "organized independent forces and freely moved about and enjoyed their freedom" was the retort: "If you claim that these behaviors were so rebellious, you could have used other means to stop them. Why do you have to use barbaric methods?"[125] "It was the government that made the people rebel (*guanbi minfan*)!"[126] "All disasters and wrongs were done by officials! Starting with Sheng Xuanhuai, Li Jixun, and Duanfang! And today's disaster should be imputed to Zhao Erfeng, Zhou Shanpei, and Tian Zhengkui!"[127] This anonymous commentator gave voice to the belief in an alternative legitimacy to that of the government, raising the question: who had acted legitimately here? In his eyes, it was the government that had violated the rights of the people and wronged the people, not the other way around.

The opinions of the Chengdu people had no influence on the court's decision. On September 12, the court issued another edict, declaring that the railway matter and the rebellion were separate issues and ordering Zhao to suppress the rebellion. As for the railway matter, the court stated that the nationalization policy would continue.[128] In a telegram to the cabinet, Zhao claimed to have turned up hard evidence proving that Luo Lun and Pu Dianjun were openly rebelling: a letter he found in Pu's home, written by Luo, stated, "It is now time for us to rise in great righteousness, and I hope that you can support us by giving us two thousand guns."[129] While the Qing authorities were convinced that the movement leaders were organizing a rebellion, the Sichuan people believed in their innocence, dismissing out of hand all of the evidence Zhao had presented against them. The Sichuanese remained unshaken in their belief that it was the government that had wronged the people.[130]

Conclusion

Returning to the questions posed at the beginning of this chapter, given the opportunity before them in the summer of 1911, how were the Chengdu leaders able to mobilize an even larger base of support? How did the movement expand beyond the city of Chengdu? And, after more pressure was put on the movement leaders by the Qing court, how did the movement change from a peaceful protest into an open revolt? Coordinating people in collective action against powerful targets at strategic moments in history requires a social support and cultural imagination. At the base of any movement are the social networks and cultural symbols through which relationships are organized; the denser the former and the more familiar the latter, the greater the likelihood that a movement will spread and be sustained. Yet it is the participants' *perceptions* of their common interests—rather than the realities of their common interests—that translate the potential for movement into collective action. If people are convinced they have a shared stake in the outcome, then they will join in revolution.

The Chengdu leaders were very effective in stimulating and building a consensus and motivating broad participation in their challenge to the Qing. As the most potent demonstration of value and belief, actions become the line demarcating the "good" from the "bad," as demonstrated in the case of Li Jixun. In opting not to confine their mobilization to the initial issues, the movement leaders strategically expanded their political rhetoric and actions. From the slogan "to protect the railways and break the treaty," they turned to market strikes and school strikes. From market strikes and school strikes, they turned to resisting the *juanshu* and then all taxes. And after the issue of resisting taxes was broached, they expanded their rhetoric and discussion to include the leadership of the country, the legitimacy of the state, popular sovereignty, and the establishment of a republican government. As seen in this chapter, the Sichuan Railway Protection movement continued to gain momentum as leaders tapped into some of the more widely held and deeply rooted feelings of the Sichuanese. Besides spreading suspicion of foreigners, the leaders dwelt on matters of taxation, using the issue of the *juanshu* in particular to incite the local gentry and militia leaders to resist.

However, rather than provoking the people to challenge the sheer level of the tax burden, the movement leaders took pains to educate people on questions of legitimacy regarding the power to levy taxes, encouraging them to see themselves as the masters of the country and citizens who had rights, possessing the authority to choose whether or not to pay taxes. In doing so, the leaders spread the notion of popular sovereignty. In this vital sense, the 1911 Revolution was an enlightening movement, and the fostering of a political culture and discourse around rights was its invention. As the revolution gained traction and moved forward, the very notion of the political expanded and changed shape—from one that only involved officials and elites who collaborated in solving problems for the emperor to one that invited commoners to act as equal citizens in an emerging nation.

7 The Expansion and Division of Revolution
DEMOCRATIC POLITICAL CULTURE IN ACTION

The Chengdu massacre of September 7, 1911, triggered an open rebellion throughout the entirety of Sichuan. Upon hearing of the arrest of key movement leaders, organized hordes of local militiamen and Gowned Brothers rushed from neighboring counties to Chengdu. Their immediate aim: to save their leaders, especially Luo Lun, who had been arrested by Zhao Erfeng. After the most important leaders were all arrested on September 7, how did the movement sustain itself? That is, how did the movement hold its common purpose, maintain its solidarity, and continue its challenging actions? Who were the participants in the revolution after September 7, and why did they decide to take up arms against more powerful enemies, such as Acting Governor-General Zhao Erfeng, at the risk of their lives?

In the 1911 Revolution in Sichuan, popular power arose quickly and reached a peak. While protesting the Qing state, the participants of 1911 differed from previous rebels by engaging in a new political discourse that concerned not only their immediate well-being but also the very legitimacy of the state. Figuring prominently in a number of local rebellious proclamations were concepts of self-rule and self-determination, and the idea of popular sovereignty. Moreover, as the revolution gained momentum, the struggles on the Chengdu Plain created opportunities for the rise of other players: Tongmenghui members and radical students in eastern Sichuan, officers in the New Army, and also, unfortunately, bandits across the province. By October the revolution in Sichuan had become potent enough to have severely threatened the provincial authorities, prompting them to seek intervention from outside. The dispatch of New Army troops from Hubei further destabilized an already-volatile situation. The tipping point occurred when the Wuchang uprising broke out, and it was within this mix of forces that drew China together—even as it seemed to be falling apart—that Sichuan gained its independence.

Attacking Chengdu

ENCIRCLING THE CITY (SEPTEMBER 8–15)

Early in the morning of September 8, attackers from neighboring counties assembled on the outskirts of Chengdu in groups as large as several thousand each (see Map 7.1). These men, armed with swords and spears and carrying red flags, were poised to take control of the city. Considering the speed with which these organized forces showed up at the city gates from as far as thirty kilometers away, William Wilkinson, the British consul-general in Chengdu, construed it as sure evidence that the Railway Protection Association leaders had indeed been guilty of plotting rebellious acts as charged by Zhao Erfeng.[1]

Zhao reported:

> Outside of Chengdu city, there were militias (*mintuan*) of several thousand people.... Right outside [east] of the city, at Damianpu and Niushikou, there were more than a thousand militiamen who claimed to have been called by the Railway Protection Association to come to Chengdu. Among those who had arrived at Chengdu from the west, there were militias from Wenjiang, Pi, Chongqing, and Guan counties. Coming from the south, there were militias from Chengdu, Huayang, Shuangliu, Xinjin, Qiongzhou, Pujiang, and Dayi counties.[2]

Wilkinson's account gives a similar description, corroborating that the attacks on the city of Chengdu were from three directions: west, south, and east.[3] That morning was the moment when the railway movement exploded into an armed uprising.

The swiftness of their gathering is attributable in part to an innovative contrivance—"river telegraph"—used by insurgents inside Chengdu to communicate with the outside world. On the evening of September 7, tens of thousands of small wooden boards, on which were written accounts of what had happened in Chengdu, were put afloat into the rivers. Owing to Sichuan's extensive waterway system, these "telegrams" traveled all over the province (Figure 7.1). The river telegrams carried impassioned calls to action: "Zhao Erfeng first captured Pu and Luo; next he will crush all Sichuan. All comrades across Sichuan, we must quickly get organized and save ourselves!"[4] And another river telegraph read: "The railway protection representatives in Chengdu were arrested. Now, compatriots, broth-

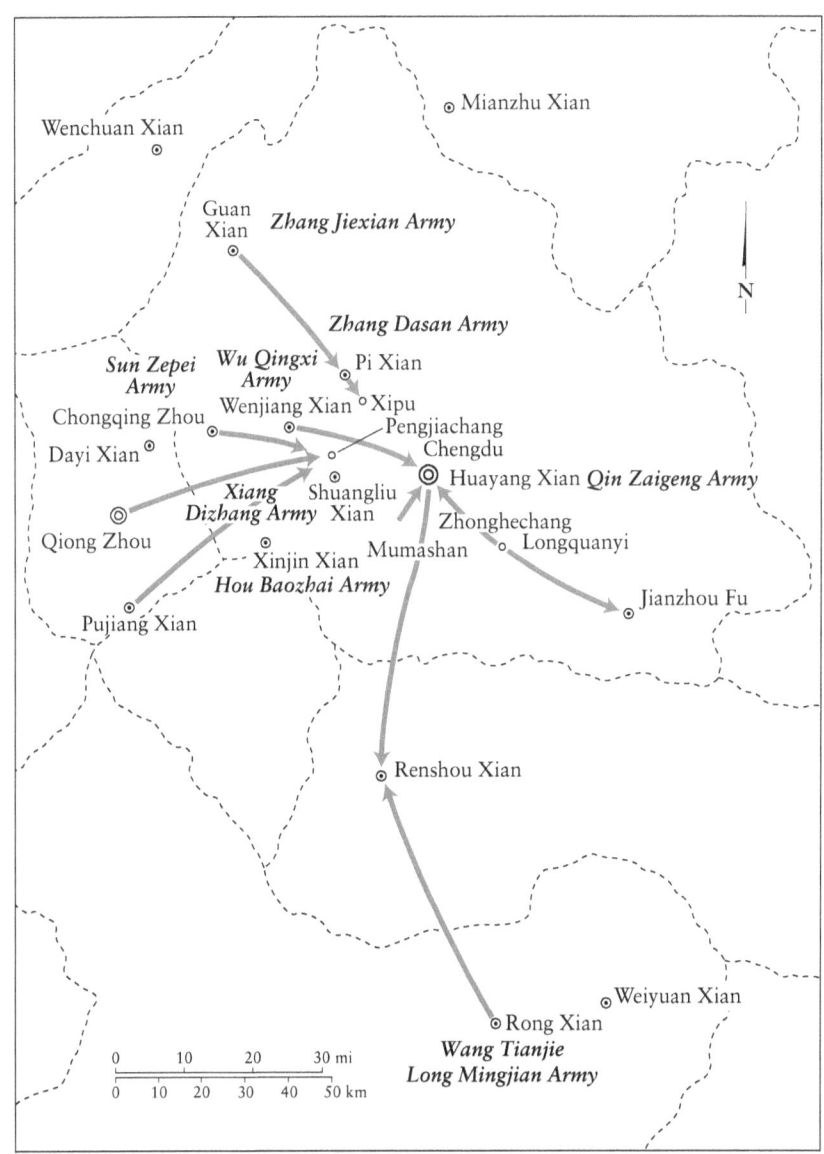

MAP 7.1. Attack on Chengdu after September 7, 1911. Based on Dai Zhili, ed., *Sichuan baolu yundong shiliao huizuan* (Taipei: Zhongyang yanjiu yuan jindaishi yanjiusuo, 1994), 1143.

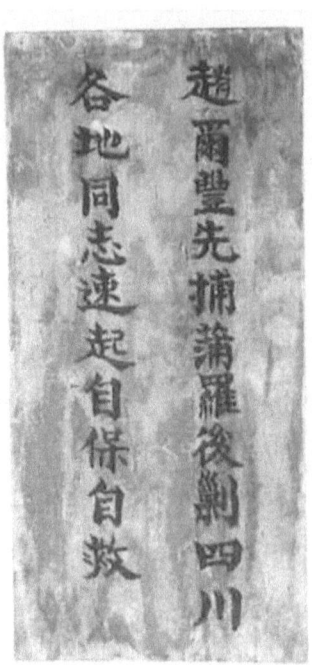

FIGURE 7.1. Replica of a river telegram. *Gonghe zhi guang: Xinhai qiu Sichuan baolu sishi bainian ji*, 266.

ers, people of all backgrounds, heroes, should prepare arms and quickly rush to Chengdu to save [them]."[5]

Hundreds of these river telegrams reached Sichuan's various counties. In some places, after people read them, they put them back into the river for more people to see. In other places, local Sichuanese created their own adaptations of the original river telegrams, adding these to the rivers and further expanding the spread of the news. Praised by foreign observers as a "smart" invention, the river telegrams played a critical role in passing on information from the city of Chengdu to the rest of Sichuan. Thus, in spite of Zhao's closure of the Chengdu city gates and his prohibition of the use of telegraph lines to talk about railway issues, the news of the Chengdu massacre made its way out to the populace in Sichuan at large.[6]

Innovative and essential as they were, however, river telegrams were not the only means used to send out the call urging people to rush to Chengdu. As discussed in Chapter 6, Gowned Brothers leaders like Hou Baozhai had been allied with railway movement leaders for a long time. Indeed, without prior planning it would have been nearly impossible for militias as far as thirty kilometers away from Chengdu to have formed an army, found provisions, and traveled all the way to Chengdu's city gates as quickly as they did upon receiving news of the massacre. Who, then, were the attackers taking part in the siege of Chengdu that began on September 8?

Acting Governor-General Zhao Erfeng observed, "Among the people who rushed to Chengdu, local militias and bandits were mixed together.... Even those who came from one county belonged to different leaders." Their origins varied: "Some said they were called upon by leaders in the Sichuan Railway Protection Association and had begun mobilizing before September 6. Others claimed that they came after receiving river telegrams, which directed them to come to Chengdu to save Luo Lun and Pu Dianjun."[7] Zhao thus concluded, "There were rebels and there were 'stupid commoners' (*yumin*) among the attackers."[8] Further supporting the acting governor-general's judgment, foreign accounts also suggested the involvement of these two different types of attackers: local militiamen who, after hearing the news or reading the river telegrams, gathered to save their arrested movement leaders; and pre-organized "bandits," who had long been linked to Luo Lun and been organized to promote "rebellion."[9]

As both the acting governor-general and the British consul-general maintained, the earliest attackers on Chengdu came from the east, led by the famous Gowned Brother and militia leader of Huayang county, Qin Zaigeng. Upon hearing about the massacre on September 7, Qin led his East Route Railway Protection Army (Donglu baolu tongzhi jun) to rush to Chengdu and fight against Zhao Erfeng's army at the city's eastern gate, in what was considered the "first battle" of the armed revolution in Sichuan. Soon defeated by Zhao, Qin's men retreated to Longquanyi, an eastern suburb of Chengdu, where they remained a persistent threat to Zhao.[10] Notably, Qin Zaigeng himself had multiple roles within the movement. First, he led a powerful local militia of Huayang, the Anji Militia, and was the Railway Protection Association branch leader of Huayang. Second, Qin was an influential Gowned Brothers leader known as "the civilized gentleman" (Wenminggong). Having long been associated with the Nine Groups founded by Hou Baozhai (see Chapter 6), Qin was one of the attendees of Hou's July 1911 sixtieth birthday celebration in Xinjin (also called the Xinjin meeting), which established a plan for Gowned Brothers leaders to organize their members, manufacture and collect weapons, and prepare for rebellion. Lastly, Qin had befriended the Tongmenghui's Chengdu branch leader Long Mingjian and was sympathetic to his anti-Manchu sentiment, although there is no reliable evidence that Qin ever actually joined the Tongmenghui.[11]

Attackers from the south were led by local strongmen with similar dual identities as militia and Gowned Brothers: they were Xiang Dizhang from Shuangliu county and Hou Baozhai from Xinjin county. Undeterred by a downpour of rain on September 8, Hou Baozhai led his troops in a rush to the southern suburbs of Chengdu, heedless of being "totally soaked and caked with mud."[12] Hou Baozhai quickly combined his force with that of Xiang Dizhang, who was also leading his militia en route to Chengdu. Together, Hou and Xiang fought a number of battles against Qing forces and launched a fresh attack on Chengdu on September 17, occupying the area around Muma Mountain in Shuangliu county. As discussed in Chapter 6, Hou Baozhai had developed close connections with the Railway Protection Association, as had Xiang Dizhang. Xiang came from an influential household of Shuangliu and had been educated in several Chengdu schools— first in the Normal School, then in the Commercial School, and last in the School of Law and Politics before 1911. After the railway movement erupted, Xiang returned to his hometown and connected with gentry and Gowned Brothers leaders in compliance with the directives of the Railway Protection Association leaders. Xiang also quickly set up a Shuangliu branch of the association and began socializing with Gowned Brothers in his hometown, and on September 8 ended up leading a militia to join the fight.[13]

The third major force that attacked Chengdu came from the west, and also consisted of both Gowned Brothers and local militias. Of the militias, those from Wenjiang, west of Chengdu, were the most prominent. In the early morning of September 8, carrying aloft in the heavy rain their banner inscribed "Wenjiang Railway Protection Army," militia leaders Huang Maoxun and He Zuyi gathered their men and proceeded to the Chengdu city gates.[14] On September 9, Li Xianzhou, a militia leader from the Heshengchang district of Wenjiang county, led a similar group to Chengdu.[15] It was these forces that Zhao Erfeng called "local militias."[16] In addition, among those attacking from the west was a longtime Gowned Brothers ally of Luo Lun, Wu Qingxi of Wenjiang.[17] He and other key Gowned Brothers leaders—Zhang Zun from Pi county, Sun Zepei from Chongqing county, and Zhang Xi from Guan county—constituted the leadership group of the West Sichuan Railway Protection Association (Chuanxi tongzhihui), as identified by the *Pi County Gazetteer*.[18] Most of these leaders had been mobilized well in advance of the siege of Chengdu.

If Huang Maoxun, He Zuyi, and Li Xianzhou rose up mainly in response to the Chengdu massacre and mainly to save their Chengdu leaders, the reason their fellow Wenjiang county man Wu Qingxi rose up was more complex. Wu was a famed Gowned Brother in Wenjiang. In some records, he is described as a "great bandit" (*jufei*). Long before the Chengdu massacre, Wu had formed an alliance with Luo Lun. On September 8, upon hearing of the Chengdu massacre, Wu Qingxi and his cousin Wu Zhisan

(Wu Congying), also a militia leader, rushed to Chengdu. On September 11, the two Wus combined their militias from Wenjiang. On September 18, Wu Qingxi joined Sun Zepei in Wenjiang county; they attacked the Qing New Armies in an ambush at Sandushui and captured hundreds of rifles and numerous bullets. In addition to the Wus and Sun Zepei, other rebels attacking Chengdu because of the preexisting Gowned Brothers link included Zhang Zun, a Gowned Brothers leader from Pi county who had been mobilized ahead of time.[19] The entire Chengdu Plain was in rebellion and "riots were breaking out like thunderstorms."[20]

What sense can be made of the attacks on Chengdu launched by this mix of forces? In his September 10 announcement to the Chengdu people, Acting Governor-General Zhao Erfeng claimed that the local militias had been "tricked" by the Railway Protection Association leaders, who, clutching the railway issue as a pretext, were actually rebelling against the dynasty. Zhao wrote, "It is only for their own sakes that the leaders are sacrificing the lives of the ordinary Sichuanese."[21] On September 14, Zhao posted another announcement, urging local militias to stay away from the rebels: "All of your militia leaders should not in the first place have gathered people and instigated disturbances. However, [your behavior] is understandable. First, you were tricked by Luo Lun, who was conducting a rebellion but called it protecting the railway.... Second, some of you were coerced to join [the rebellion]."[22] Zhao then released the "stupid commoners" and issued an order to "send them back home."[23]

Even if the militias had been tricked into joining the rebellion, the question remains of why they were tricked so willingly. Writing on September 20, for example, Yukun, the Chengdu commandant, placed most of the blame on the tax program of the New Policies reform:

The Sichuan rebellion this time could be thought of as "officials forcing people to rebel" (*guanbi minfan*). In recent years, the state had taxed the Sichuan people so heavily; it was like sucking the blood from their body. The Sichuanese became poor and lost their wealth. Hence, they developed a strong antagonism toward the administrative leaders (*xingzheng zhugong*). Merchants, peasants, gentry, and commoners all harbored hatred toward these men.... The New Policies reform of recent years has led to many bureaus and all sorts of taxes. All had to be paid by the people, which surely made their hearts rebellious.[24]

However, unlike a traditional tax revolt centering on pure economics, in 1911 in Sichuan, the idea of the people's rights was a powerful tool for mobilizing supporters. Chongqing circuit intendant Zhu Youji, while writing to the Ministry of Posts and Communications on September 19, was convinced that the widely promoted idea of the people's rights was the key to this insurgency:

This rebellion was something initiated by the gentry and learned circles, then infiltrated by bandits, and later joined by stupid commoners. Even though it was triggered by the railway matter, it was actually something beyond that. . . . The lectures made by those leaders, all about resisting officials and not respecting the emperor, were planted like seeds in the hearts of the people. Easily ten thousand people gathered to attack governmental offices. Officials were constrained [facing the gentry], and could not say a word about this. . . . In recent years, talk about the people's rights has become so prevalent, it is something that not only Sichuan people, but all people in China, have picked up.[25]

Acting Chongqing customs commissioner E. von Strauch concurred with Zhu's verdict on the gentry's leadership in the movement: "The attackers of Chengdu were no bandits. . . . [They] were under the leadership of the local gentry. . . . Even though it is extremely hard to understand and make sense of all of the conflicting phenomena, I believe that the movement was supported by public opinion (*yulun*) in Sichuan and dominated by one authority, that is, the Railway Protection Association."[26]

Nonetheless, despite the movement's extensive organization, the poorly equipped rebels were no match for Zhao Erfeng's professional soldiers. By September 15, all attackers had been repelled from Chengdu.[27] Still, they cut down telegraph lines, seized important intersections, and stopped mail delivery, successfully disrupting the entire communication system of the Qing administration. They went back to their counties, where they continued their fight, seized county seats, and freed local prisoners. These combined actions threw Sichuan into great chaos, and the revolution soon extended beyond the Chengdu Plain.[28]

REACTIONS OF THE SICHUAN PEOPLE

Inauspiciously for Zhao Erfeng, ordinary Sichuanese sympathized with the rebels. As Zhao himself stated: "The stupid commoners, lacking judgment, take the rebels as the righteous ones. When they see the rebels, they offer them food. When they see the soldiers, they treat them like enemies."[29] Posing an even greater threat to Zhao, the Sichuan New Army had also come to sympathize with the rebels. Sheng Xuanhuai wrote to Huguang governor-general Ruicheng on September 12, informing him that most of the New Army soldiers in Chengdu were resisting orders: "Among the troops in the New Army, there are only three battalions that follow orders. All the rest have their hearts with the rebels."[30] As a measure of self-defense, Zhao set up a new bureau on September 12 in an effort to recruit his own militias in Chengdu, an effort that was, however, to no avail.[31]

As soon as Chengdu's situation was stabilized on September 15, the previously aloof Zhao resorted to the political repertoire of the Railway Protection Association, employing vernacular announcements, public lectures, and newspaper propaganda to convey his points. On September 16, Zhao ordered the Sichuan Militia Headquarters in Chengdu to propagandize his suppression of the uprising, spreading his message to the militias in various counties and urging the people "not to believe the rumors."[32] When issuing this order, Zhao also provided the militia headquarters with four thousand copies of posters written in the vernacular to explain his message.[33] The militia headquarters also implored local elite and militia leaders to "truly understand right and wrong, to join the officials to rule together with them, and to bring out the happiness of the people."[34] Another poster from Zhao, again in the vernacular, asserted that "the matter of protecting the railway" (lushi) and "the matter of rebelling" (luanshi) were two different things, and asked the Sichuanese not to be tricked by the Railway Protection Association.[35]

Appropriating yet another tactic used by the movement leaders, on September 16 Zhao issued an elaborate "exhortation song" (quanmin ge) to further spread his message. This song condemned the "evilness" of the Railway Protection Association leaders, especially Luo Lun, for exploiting the people's trust through deception and leading them to betray the court. In a direct attack on the principles underlying the revolt, Zhao chastised Luo Lun for his subversive act of "not respecting the emperor and the father" and criticized the "one-cash tax" scheme as a vehicle for promoting Luo's own ambition.[36]

To follow up this musical piece of propaganda, Zhao turned to public lectures—another format that had been masterfully exploited by the movement leaders to mobilize the masses—and ordered county officials near Chengdu to organize lectures explaining why he had imprisoned Luo Lun.[37] In a report to Zhao on his compliance with this order, Chengdu magistrate Shi Wenlong described how he recruited eight men of the gentry to join him at eight local markets to explain Zhao's directives to the people:[38]

> On September 14, 16, and 26, I went to various townships (xiang) in Chengdu. I asked reputable and righteous gentry to join me, and we went to different baos to give lectures. We explained to the people the leniency of the dynasty and the kindness of the acting governor-general. We explained to them the origin of the riot and the methods of dealing with it. We explained to the people the difference between the railway protectors and the rebels.... The people understood our intention and all taxes were levied just as before.[39]

Efficacious as it sounded, Shi nonetheless admitted that the local gentry were reluctant to comply, noting tactfully, "I feel that it is easier for officials than for the gentry to make these lectures."[40] He then made a suggestion, which Zhao accepted, that the lectures be given by officials with gentry serving only as assistants.⁴¹ Subsequently Zhao ordered magistrates to personally give the lectures, spreading the "kindness of the dynasty."⁴² Following that up with another directive on October 15, Zhao ordered the magistrates to make one point particularly clear, namely that when suppressing the revolt he would differentiate the militias from the bandits and refrain from meting out as severe a punishment to the militias.⁴³

Having witnessed how successful the movement elite had been with their newspapers, the acting governor-general Zhao Erfeng also conscripted newspapers for his propaganda campaign. Not only did he use the official *Chengdu Daily* to spread his views in colloquial language, he also established a new vernacular-language newspaper, *Zhengsu baihua bao*, as a propaganda mouthpiece.⁴⁴ Though Zhao adapted the medium from the railway movement's repertoire, his message was more reminiscent of his brother Zhao Erxun's "statist" lecture to the 1909 Provincial Assembly (see Chapter 4). Beginning with its first issue, the new paper printed consecutive installments of a lengthy article titled "The Response of the Emperor to the Minister and the People," which entreated the people to stay away from politics and regard the management of public affairs as the monopoly of the emperor and officials, asserting: "All people under Heaven—gentry, peasants, artisans, and merchants—should fulfill their own duty and do their own job. As for public matters under Heaven, the emperor and the officials will handle them."⁴⁵

Nevertheless, Zhao's exclusive and nondemocratic stance in conducting politics could not scare or deter Chengdunese anymore. As the idea of *minquan* had unleashed the political energy of the Chengdunese, who were resolved to defend their political rights, Zhao Erfeng found it extremely difficult to reestablish his authority again.⁴⁶ Lending further credence to the argument that ideas rather than tactics were driving people's behavior, Zhao's imitation of the political repertoire of the Railway Protection Association met with no success. The people of Chengdu were "very suspicious of Zhao's words [and] were unwilling to buy the newspapers that Zhao put out." His announcements suffered an even worse reception. Some Chengdunese tore down the public notices or spattered them with red paint as soon as Zhao posted new ones.

Among the expressions of opposition to Zhao were two typical denunciations by locals on the Chengdu Plain. The first, written in formal, literary Chinese, was penned by an elite in the Railway Protection Association:

Nowadays, the court has set up the principle of constitutionalism and all people under Heaven should follow it. However, some officials did not obey the imperial directive and even killed earnest people. They, then, are the true traitors. If we look at all of the European countries, we see that there is no way that a parliamentary representative can be arrested, much less the chairpersons of the parliament. Today, Sichuan Provincial Assembly leaders Pu Dianjun and Luo Lun were detained, solely because they were trying to save the country and protect the railway. Governor-General Zhao committed barbaric acts against them![47]

The other denunciation, written in the vernacular and issued by the rebels fighting on the Chengdu Plain, is equally revealing:

In October, we attacked Chengdu. We have militias (*mintuan*) of several tens of thousands and local secret society members (*huidang*) of several thousands. We do not want to disturb the local people, loot, rape, attack churches, or take money. . . . The reason that we rise up is that we do not wish the demise of our country. We fight for our railway rights. . . . Our Sichuan is a civilized province and we Sichuanese are righteous people. Every time the *juanshu* was increased, we obediently paid it. But such taxes were exploited by officials. . . . They treated us worse than they treat sheep and cows![48]

Despite their divergent styles, the common, refreshing aspect of these two documents is the clear articulation of the reasons for the revolt—the defense of constitutionalism and the legitimate use of taxes. The emphatic message that Sichuanese were *not* resisting taxes but, quite to the contrary, would willingly pay their taxes if the taxes were used properly, conveys the extent to which Sichuanese had learned to question the assumptions of the prevailing political milieu. Their newfound sense of justice engendered a desire to punish the guilty party; the upheavals in Sichuan were in truth fights over political legitimacy. In this, they spawned a new mode of politics based on new principles.

Observers from other provinces drew inspiration from the Sichuan revolution. In his commentary for the September 14 issue of *People's Independent Daily* (*Minlibao*), famous Tongmenghui leader Song Jiaoren praised the Sichuanese for their fearless opposition to autocracy and their determination to participate in politics, extend the power of public opinion, and protect the people's rights.[49] Lauding the Sichuanese for "helping out all of the people of China," Song encouraged them to further liberate their thinking, to truly raise the banner that "politics should be decided by public opinion," and to "more completely fight against autocracy."[50] On September 20, Song again published a special issue on Sichuan, encouraging all the people of China to follow in the footsteps of the Sichuanese in order to establish a real democratic polity in China.[51]

In fact, Sichuanese were already doing what Song Jiaoren had hoped they would do. They took things into their own hands and refused to be ruled as they formerly were, like "sheep and cows." The previously imperious acting governor-general Zhao Erfeng, left dependent on popular support, found himself enmeshed in a political process in which an increasingly confident popular front wielded authority and did not shy away from dissent. He was forced to recognize public opinion and adopt the methods of the Railway Protection Association in hopes of swaying the people to his side. A new polity recognizing the power of the people was in the making.

Revolts Across Sichuan

THE MAIN STORY: THE STRUGGLE AROUND CHENGDU (SEPTEMBER 16–NOVEMBER 27)

The groups laying siege to Chengdu, having been dispersed by Zhao Erfeng's armies by September 16, had returned to their home counties but had not given up the fight. In Pi, Chongqing, Xindu, and Hanzhou counties, and in fact across the entire Chengdu Plain, revolts were expanding.[52] In Qiongzhou, on the perimeter of the Chengdu Plain, Gowned Brothers leader Zhou Hongxun, who was also an officer of the Patrol and Defense Forces, revolted against the Qing and moved his forces to Xinjin.[53] As a result, in the second half of September, "the entire area west, south, and north of Chengdu was occupied by rebel armies."[54]

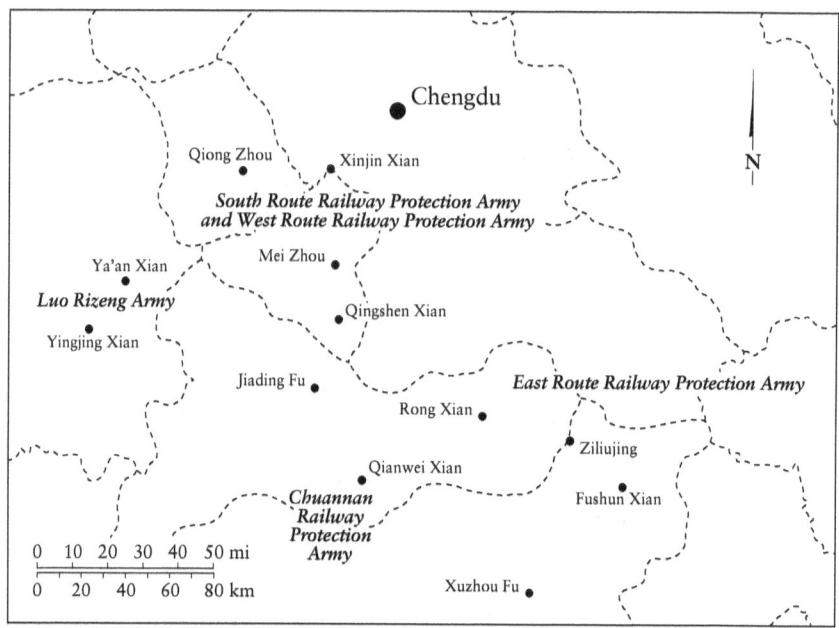

MAP 7.2. Battles on the Chengdu Plain, 1911.

Observers continued to struggle with differentiating the militias from bandits, for all identified themselves as belonging to the Railway Protection Association, thereby suggesting a shared common purpose. Behind the chaos that engulfed Sichuan, it is possible to discern four distinct groups of organized rebels that were responsible for the majority of the uprisings from September through November. These four groups posed the most serious threats and engaged in the most heated battles against the Qing armies. All were concentrated on the Chengdu Plain, and all shared a similar social network—their Gowned Brothers link (see Map 7.2).

The first group was the potent South Route Railway Protection Army (Nanlu tongzhijun) combined with the West Route Railway Protection Army (Xilu tongzhijun). They spread widely across the sixteen counties of Chengdu prefecture, sometimes extending to Qiongzhou, Meishan, Qingshen, and Meizhou, extending to the outer ring of Chengdu Plain. This group was led by Gowned Brothers leaders Hou Baozhai and Zhou Hongxun from the South Route and Gowned Brothers leaders Wu Qingxi, Sun Zepei, Zhang Zun, and Zhang Xi from the West Route. Situated close to Chengdu and well connected by their Gowned Brothers identities, this first group presented the most dangerous threat to Zhao Erfeng.[55]

The second group was the East Route Railway Protection Army (Donglu tongzhijun), which occupied Fushun and Ziliujing, the rich salt-producing region of southeastern Sichuan. The leaders of this group were Qin Zaigeng from Huayang county and Wang Tianjie and Long Mingjian from Rong county. Having been defeated by the Qing army after attacking Chengdu, Qin Zaigeng retreated to the eastern suburbs of Chengdu, where he met and combined forces with Wang Tianjie and Long Mingjian, who had mobilized the "Rong County Comrade Army" and were en route to Chengdu. Of these three men, both Qin and Wang were members of the Gowned Brothers and local militia leaders with a record of long and active involvement in the Railway Protection movement, while Long was a new-style gentleman who had studied in Japan, had served as a provincial assemblyman, and had been a longtime member of the railway movement as the shareholder representative of Rong county. Although Long was a member of the Tongmenghui, it should be noted that his anti-Manchu stance was given no expression in the East Route's declarations.[56]

The third group comprised the Railway Protection armies in Ya'an and Yingjing counties. Led by Gowned Brothers leader Luo Rizeng (Luo Zizhou) of Ya'an county and local militia leader Li Yongzhong of Yingjing county, this group successfully prevented Zhao Erfeng's Patrol and Defense Forces, led by Fu Huafeng, from immediately rushing back to Chengdu from the Sichuan-Tibet border, a delay that provided a superb opportunity for the protesters to extend their rebellion.[57]

The fourth and final group was the Railway Protection Army of Southern Sichuan (*Chuannan tongzhijun*, hereafter the Chuannan Army). Led by Gowned Brothers leader Hu Tan (Hu Chongyi) of Qianwei, this group consisted of the combined forces of Hu's Gowned Brothers associates and included some of the armies active in the other three groups: the Railway Protection Army led by Li Wuchu from Xuzhou prefecture, the Railway Protection Army led by Luo Rizeng from Ya'an county, and a division of the South Route Railway Protection Army led by Zhou Hongxun. Together, they attacked the Qing forces in Xuzhou, Jiading, and Qianwei in southern Sichuan.[58] Despite their different places of origin, all four of these groups identified themselves as the "Railway Protection Army." By concentrating their attacks on the Chengdu Plain, they severely diminished Zhao Erfeng's military dominance of Sichuan.

A closer look at the four major organized rebel groups reveals complex convergence of motives driving the revolution in Sichuan. Consider first the South Route Railway Protection Army centered on Xinjin. It was in Xinjin that the most determined railway protectors assembled, marched to Chengdu, and most effectively threatened the Qing forces. Xinjin's railway protectors were led by the influential Gowned Brothers and militia leader Hou Baozhai, whose active participation in the railway movement dated back to its early days. At the mid-July Xinjin meeting, Hou and other Gowned Brothers leaders discussed the creation of a new Sichuan polity in which Sichuanese would have their own stake. After marching to Chengdu and losing the fight with the Qing soldiers there, Hou returned to Xinjin.[59] Upon his return, Hou Baozhai was joined by Zhou Hongxun, a fellow Gowned Brothers leader who was also a Qing Patrol and Defense Forces officer. Having served as a police officer in Chengdu, Zhou had been forced to flee to Yunnan after begin charged with indiscipline. In Yunnan, Zhou had been offended by the way that the French treated the Chinese populace.[60] Upon returning to Sichuan, Zhou joined the Patrol and Defense Forces, became an officer, and recruited his subordinates and fellow soldiers into his Gowned Brothers organization.[61] When the railway movement broke out, Zhou urged his fellow Gowned Brothers to support the revolutionary cause. On September 12, Zhou led 160 of them against the Qing, killing the commander of the Eighth Battalion of the Patrol and Defense Forces in Qiongzhou and assuming leadership. Afterward, he steered his troops to Xinjin.

Under the combined leadership of Hou and Zhou, Xinjin became the most vital stronghold for rebels in Sichuan. On September 30, they launched attacks on the New Army base in Xinjin, seized weapons, and freed prisoners. On October 1, Zhao Erfeng ordered a counterattack, dispatching the top commanders of both the new and the old armies of Sichuan—the New Army commander-in-chief Zhu Qinglan and the Green Standard chief officer Tian Zhenbang—to attack Xinjin. Lasting over ten days, the Battle of Xinjin drew the strongest force that Zhao Erfeng could deploy at the time, and the consequent absence of troops in other parts of Sichuan proved a great benefit to the rebellions in the rest of the province. A careful analysis of Hou and Zhou's announcements sheds light on the persuasive message that drew local military leaders in western Sichuan to support the revolts. Hou Baozhai issued the following announcement in October:

The traitors to us people, / will soon be captured. / We only want Zhou Shanpei and Zhao Erfeng; / we do not want others. / The great matter is settled; / do not listen to rumors. / All we Sichuan people / should happily lead our lives.[62]

The spirit of patriotism and the responsibility Hou felt toward the Railway Protection Association leaders were at the heart of his decision to rebel. Hou's announcement made an appeal to a general sense of duty, while specifically targeting grievances directly at Zhao Erfeng, who had captured the Chengdu leaders and killed Sichuanese, and at Zhou Shanpei, who was rumored to have helped Zhao trick the Chengdu leaders into going to the provincial yamen on September 7. In Hou's eyes, they were the "traitors to the people."[63]

As for Zhou Hongxun, his was a revolution that had at its center slogans of republicanism, liberty, equality, and the people's rights. One of his proclamations stated: "We should all join forces, so that no one dares to bully us Chinese. We also should establish a new polity, a republic (*gonghe guo*), where all people enjoy equality (*pingdeng*). Let us destroy [the Qing's] power and enjoy true liberty (*ziyou*)!"[64] Another one, deploying the idea of the people's rights, boldly declared:

The reason that we comrades set up the Railway Protection Association to protect the railway and to protect Sichuan was all because of the people's rights (*minquan*). . . . Here I urge all of us Sichuanese to be independent and to not rely on officials. . . . Zhao Erfeng will kill us all. The only thing we can do is to kill those traitors, so as to win our people's rights and to protect our people's safety.[65]

Documents such as these tapped into and voiced the strong anti-autocracy sentiment of the times, calling on commoners to escape the yoke of the Qing and look to their own resources to protect themselves, thereby promoting a new kind of empowerment and legitimacy. As leaders in Xinjin, Hou and Zhou drew on both traditional virtues such as loyalty and novel ideas such as the people's rights as they devised rhetorical tools to sway the populace and to inspire and organize their forces.

Other forces shared key commonalities with Xinjin. Both the West Route and the Chuannan Army identified with Gowned Brothers sensibilities, and the cause motivating the rise of each group was that of saving the arrested movement leaders. The West Route leader Sun Zepei, for example, issued this announcement in November: "The reason we have the Railway Protection Army is to recover our railway and to protect our Sichuan people. We have rushed to Chengdu, hoping that Zhao Erfeng would release Luo and Pu."[66] Indeed, the slogan "to protect the railway and save Pu-Luo" and the notion of Sichuanese self-governance unified all of these groups into a single force with a common purpose.

Along with the ideas of Sichuanese self-governance, protecting the railway, and saving Pu-Luo, concepts such as liberty and independence were also appropriated by rebel leaders. The third major group, the Railway Protection soldiers in Ya'an and Yingjing counties, is one example. When their leader Luo Rizeng rallied his forces and attacked the county seat of Qianwei on September 17, he claimed that he would "ring the liberty bell and fly the independence flag" (*zhuang ziyou zhong, shu duli qi*).[67] Though the extent to which these local leaders actually understood the full implications of liberty and independence is open to question, it is obvious that they were exposed to and sufficiently well versed in the deployment of these concepts. They also used these concepts as slogans to justify their actions, and perhaps, with the hope to mobilize more followers.

The East Route Army gave expression to both components described earlier. The idea of Sichuanese self-governance was also a slogan for the East Route leaders, as is evident in an announcement from Qin Zaigeng that stated: "All Sichuan rose up to protect the railway. . . . Our Railway Protection Association considers protecting our locale to be the most important principle. . . . The reason that we rose up was to protect our Sichuan."[68] The attention paid by the East Route Army to "extending the energy of the people" (*shenzhang minqi*) also demonstrated its intention to promote a sense of democracy, another focus held in common by the rebels.[69]

Hence, all four major rebel groups shared a common goal, "to protect the railway and save Pu-Luo," and a common identity, "Sichuanese." At the same time, terms such as "liberty," "independence," "the rights of the people," and "the energy of the people" were also extensively utilized throughout the 1911 Revolution in Sichuan. A movement as widespread as this one seldom remains under the control of one single organization, and in due course, beginning in late October, other rebels engaged in battles of their own. Whatever their differences were, unhappy with the old way of ruling, the Sichuanese had decided to throw off the yoke of the Qing and fight for a Sichuan that would be ruled by Sichuanese themselves, with a bold sense of self-determination as an essential component underlying all of these rebellious acts.

MAKING SENSE OF THE STRUGGLE
AROUND CHENGDU

With this understanding of the motives, stated intentions, actions, and networks of the major players involved, one can better appreciate what the 1911 Revolution meant for the people of Sichuan. In addition, contemporaneous accounts from Qing officials provide detailed analyses of the movement, as well as observations on the people's feelings about the movement. For example, as noted earlier, Commandant Yukun opined on September 20 that one reason for the steadfast resistance was excessive taxation.[70] On October 30, Yukun repeated his view that it was officials who had made people into bandits, suggesting that the railway movement tapped into an "old hatred" that had been accumulating over an extended time.[71]

An even less sympathetic official, Zhao Erfeng, noted on October 12 that the ordinary people of Chengdu prefecture overwhelmingly supported the rebels, observing: "The trend of rebellion in Sichuan was like a fire burning. People, especially those from western and southern Sichuan, roused by the maxim that 'the loss of the railway will lead to the demise of Sichuan,' joined the rebels. There was serious talk among the people from eastern and southern Sichuan about setting up an independent regime and taking matters into their own hands."[72] As Zhao wrote, this time around "the rebels were different from ordinary robbers" in that "they are especially ambitious (*biehuai dazhi*) and have contemplated their plans for a long time."[73]

Foreign observers' accounts also provide extensive documentation on the spirit of the Sichuanese. In a report to London on the market and student strikes, the British ambassador Sir John Jordan reported that the students and merchants of Chengdu were determined in resisting the government's orders, and their announcements showed that fearless spirit of resistance.[74] In southern Sichuan, a Catholic priest noted that the Railway Protection Army was supported by local power holders: "The army was initiated by gentry, landowners, and militia leaders, and in Qianwei, in almost every market town there was a Railway Protection Association branch."[75] They "all demanded Luo Lun's life be preserved."[76]

In a similar vein, the correspondence of the bishop of the Chuandong episcopate also documented the organized resistance that was wresting control of the Chengdu Plain away from Zhao Erfeng: "Among the nine thousand soldiers that Zhao commanded, half of them were stopped by the Railway Protection comrades." In another letter, the bishop reported that "from Jiading to Chengdu, all areas were controlled by the rebel groups."[77] And Chongqing's acting customs commissioner E. von Strauch informed his superiors in Beijing that "public opinion in Sichuan was clearly on the side of the rebelling gentry."[78] Similarly, the British consul-general at Chengdu, William Wilkinson, wrote to Ambassador Jordan that "the real power here was in the hands of the local people. The officials were helpless."[79] It is clear from these foreign observers' descriptions that the loss of authority by the governor-general—as well as by many county officials—was apparent to all. On November 1, von Strauch predicted, "It is only a matter of time before the Qing rule of Sichuan is overthrown."[80]

As the movement expanded, some bandits also became involved on the side of the Railway Protection armies, and it was often impossible to distinguish them from the rebelling Railway Protection soldiers. Even so, most Sichuanese chose to support the rebels.[81] Despite the involvement of bandits, the people's sympathies remained with them.[82] A spirit of self-determination, a notion of taking things into their own hands, and a raw sense of democracy had taken root, and Sichuanese exposure to and practice of some of these ideas—especially the idea of the rights and the power of the people—all made the 1911 Revolution something different in Chinese history.

THE SIDE STORY: THE TONGMENGHUI AND THE BATTLES NEAR CHONGQING (OCTOBER 29– NOVEMBER 27)

Indisputably, the main battles of the Railway Protection movement were fought on the Chengdu Plain, where the Railway Protection Armies, comprising local militia and Gowned Brothers, severely diminished Zhao Erfeng's military dominance of Sichuan.[83] It was on the Chengdu Plain that the Railway Protection armies tied down Zhao Erfeng's main forces, fought the most stubborn battles, and successfully prevented Zhao's Patrol and Defense Forces from rushing back to Chengdu from the Sichuan-Tibet border. Also of note, these especially arduous battles were fought mainly in September and October, when national politics was still very much unsettled. As the movement expanded, other aspiring groups—in particular, the Tongmenghui—joined in, spreading the revolution across an increasingly wide area. The Tongmenghui, however, should be viewed as only a dependent variable in the calculus of revolution, important only in that it was part of a coalition with more powerful partners such as the Gowned Brothers, militia leaders, and other kinds of local elites and local strongmen.

The first Tongmenghui battle was in Rong county, which involved two Tongmenghui members, Long Mingjian and Wu Yuzhang, both natives of Rong. On September 15, upon hearing the news of the Chengdu massacre, Rong county militia leader Wang Tianjie mobilized an army of five thousand peasants, the Rong County Comrade Army, for the purpose of attacking Chengdu. Wang's father was "one of the richest men in Rong," and he "willingly gave out his wealth to support Wang's troops."[84] A Gowned Brother of renown in southern Sichuan, Wang, soon joined by Sichuan provincial assemblyman and Tongmenghui member Long Mingjian, led his five thousand men on a march toward Chengdu. On their way to Chengdu, they joined forces with the famed Gowned Brothers leader Qin Zaigeng, who had just been defeated by Acting Governor-General Zhao Erfeng's army near Chengdu.[85] With Qin Zaigeng as the commander and Wang Tianjie as the vice-commander, the combined forces, known as the East Route Railway Protection Army, occupied the rich salt-producing region of southeastern Sichuan for a time but ultimately failed to consolidate their gains. After Long Mingjian's death from illness on October 6, Wang Tianjie decided to return to Rong.[86] Upon his arrival, the county magistrate fled, and Rong county's independence was established on October 29 by Wang Tianjie and Wu Yuzhang—another Rong county native who was a Tongmenghui member and new-style student who had returned from Japan.[87] Rong thus became the first Tongmenghui regime in Sichuan, and, in its declaration of independence, the first to propagate an anti-Manchu message.

Although the Rong county battle was often hailed as the first Tongmenghui revolt in Sichuan, and Wu Yuzhang, who was politically influential after 1949, had often declared that the Rong battle preceded the Wuchang uprising, the reality was much more complicated and considerably less glorified. Not only was the battle later than Hubei's Wuchang uprising, it can hardly be viewed as a Tongmenghui victory. First, the real power in the Rong battle was the Rong County Comrade Army organized by Wang Tianjie, who was leading the county militia. Beyond that, it was the common Gowned Brothers identities of Wang Tianjie and Qin Zaigeng and the personal bond between Long Mingjian and Qin Zaigeng that formed the link between the Rong County Comrade Army and the East Route Army, and there is no clear evidence that either Wang or Qin had joined the Tongmenghui. Furthermore, Long Mingjian—a former student in Japan, a Sichuan provincial assemblyman, and the head of the Chengdu Four Sages Temple (Sishengci) School of Law and Politics—had been a longtime member of the Railway Protection movement as the shareholder representative of Rong county. He had ample motive to oppose the Qing even had he not been a Tongmenghui leader. Tellingly, Long Mingjian did not declare his anti-Manchu stance while with either the Rong County Comrade Army or the East Route Army. Last, even Tongmenghui member Wu Yuzhang found it necessary to join the Gowned Brothers ranks to gain enough authority to lead the rebels. It was connections from other networks—not the control of the Tongmenghui—that led to the Rong rebellion.

Complexities related to the launching of the Rong rebellion aside, in its aftermath there was an outbreak of a series of Tongmenghui rebellions, concentrated in places near the city of Chongqing. Unlike Chengdu, which was the political center of Sichuan, Chongqing was a commercial port, where Qing control was looser and the Tongmenghui branch more vibrant. From the time that the railway movement erupted, the Chongqing branch members had been waiting for just the right moment. By mid-November, news of the Wuchang uprising reached Chongqing, not far from Hubei. Emboldened, Tongmenghui members near Chongqing launched a rebellion, first in Changshou.

In Changshou, as in most other Sichuan counties, a Railway Protection Association branch had been established not long after the railway movement began. While local gentry participated in the railway branch, underground Tongmenghui members also organized themselves. Tu Defeng, a Changshou native who had joined the Tongmenghui while studying in Japan, returned to his hometown at a time when "hundreds of Mauser rifles and thousands of bullets, purchased by the county authorities, were being transferred to Linzhuang Primary School to train student armies and local militias."[88] Joined by Liao Shuxun, the trainer of the student soldiers at Linzhuang Primary School, and by other Tongmenghui members, Tu raised the anti-Manchu banner and led a revolt against the Qing authorities in Changshou on November 18.

The Changshou revolt led directly to an uprising in Fuzhou. On November 21, with reinforcements from the newly independent Changshou rebels, Fuzhou Tongmenghui members Gao Yaheng, Li Weiru, and Guo Xianghan led men in an attack on the Fuzhou county seat that forced the magistrate to capitulate and turn in his seal. Like Tu Defeng of Changshou, Gao had also studied in Japan and joined the Tongmenghui while there. After November 21, a republican regime was set up in Fuzhou, under which a separate judicial branch was established, and ideas of equality and liberty were welcomed by the local people, though often "misunderstood" by them at first.[89]

In a similar fashion, radical students in Jiangjin, led by Cheng Deyin and Xia Fengxun, united all available forces and rebelled against the Qing. These students, who since November 17 had been engaging in subversive acts against the local Qing military units and the county magistrate, joined forces with the local Gowned Brothers to spark an uprising on November

21. As the county gazetteer recorded: "We had only dilapidated rifles and shoddy cannons, and we organized our forces in haste. . . . It was because the hearts of the people were all with us that the old regime quickly and utterly collapsed. . . . How fearful our power is!"[90] The Jiangjin rebellion was swift, smooth, and successful.

Another important county-level Tongmenghui revolt was that of Guang'an county, masterminded by Zeng Du (Zeng Shengzhai), a seasoned Tongmenghui revolutionary. Zeng had participated in a number of important Tongmenghui actions in Sichuan before 1911, including an uprising in Guang'an in 1909. On October 27, after spending a period of time hiding in the guise of a high school teacher, Zeng gathered militias in neighboring Dianjiang county, ready to rebel against the Qing. Zeng was soon joined by local strongmen—such as the leader of the Xiaoyihui (Society of Piety and Virtue), Li Shaoyi, and Guang'an militia students Lu Yuqing, Wang Jubo, Hu Menghui, and Tang Zhiping—and together the rebel troops passed through Dazu, Quxian, Linshui, and Yuechi, instigating uprisings along the way, before finally arriving in Guang'an.[91] On November 10, Guang'an Tongmenghui member Hu Menghui, together with Zeng Du's militias, encircled the Guang'an county seat. On November 21, they established a Tongmenghui-controlled military government.[92] Pengxi, Shehong, and Yingshan counties soon followed Guang'an's example.[93]

The most important Tongmenghui uprising was no doubt that in Chongqing. On November 5, Tongmenghui member and New Army platoon commander Xia Zhishi instigated a revolt at Longquanyi. Leading four platoons of the Sichuan New Army, Xia killed the New Army commander and wounded the chief staff officer. Xia soon became the main revolutionary leader of the area and rushed his troops to Chongqing. Along the way, Xia was joined by other New Army soldiers stationed in Jianzhou and Lezhi, expanding his forces to nearly one thousand. On November 22, reinforced by Xia's newly arrived forces, a public meeting was convened in Chongqing at which the three hundred representatives from the official, gentry, commercial, and learned circles in attendance determined that Chongqing be declared independent from the Qing. On the same day, they established the Sichuan Military Government (Shujun zhengfu). Chongqing residents responded enthusiastically to this change of regime. Foreigners reported: "On that day, white flags were flying across the city; people were exhilarated and in high spirits. . . . The entire city was in a festive mood."[94] Quickly, dozens of eastern Sichuan counties followed suit and revolted. In the week following Chongqing's declaration of independence, Nanchuan, Neijiang, Wanxian, Kuizhou, Yunyang, Dongxiang, Suiding, and Luzhou all rose up against the Qing.[95]

The motivations that led so many counties in eastern Sichuan to turn against the Qing had much in common with the reasons adduced by the rebels on the Chengdu Plain. A number of the declarations issued in these counties mentioned such tax relief measures as reducing the voluntary surcharge tax and the standard tax and repealing various other taxes.[96] There was also a strong emphasis on local people taking control of local politics. For example, in Nanchuan, all of the Qing officials—the magistrate, the chief of police, and the leader of the New Tax Bureau—were captured, and the new government "established new bureaus, where local gentry and students who had studied abroad took things under their control."[97] Equally important, "republicanism" was an oft-invoked slogan in these announcements.[98] In Chongqing in particular, the revolutionaries used newly established presses to spread ideas of democracy and republicanism, indoctrinating people in the fundamentals they considered necessary for the making of qualified republican citizens.[99] Economic distress, self-governance, and new principles such as republicanism all factored into the 1911 Revolution in Sichuan.

MAKING SENSE OF THE ROLE OF THE TONGMENGHUI

In studies of the 1911 Revolution, the role of the Tongmenghui is always a sensitive and fraught subject. As a corollary, the actual importance of anti-Manchuism also remains uncertain. Sichuan historians Dai Zhili and Wei Yingtao, to name but two, have uncovered important sources for and made substantial contributions toward illuminating the 1911 Revolution in Sichuan. Their scholarship, which has noted the crucial role played by the constitutionalists and evaluated them in a generally positive light, is, however, compromised by the still-restrictive political conditions in China. As a result, Dai and Wei must echo points originally made by political leaders such as Mao Zedong and Wu Yuzhang—one of them being the leading role of the Tongmenghui in the 1911 Revolution—and emphasize certain conclusions, such as the "incomplete and unsuccessful" nature of the 1911 Revolution.[100]

Compounding the difficult task of understanding the revolutionary process is the existence of many knotty "historical" sources, produced in mass quantities both by the Nationalists after 1928 and by the Communists starting in the 1950s. These materials, often taking the form of memoirs, emphasize the revolutionary leadership of the Tongmenghui. In the case of Sichuan, *Record of the Campaigns of Sichuan Martyrs* (*Shuzhong xianlie beizhenglu*), published in 1928, and *Memoirs of the 1911 Revolution* (*Xinhai geming huiyilu*), published in 1961, are typical examples. Although these sources provide some good insights into the historical moment, their accounts contain stories that often cannot be verified by other primary or secondary sources. The question of when and how Gowned Brother Qin Zaigeng joined the Tongmenghui, for example, remains unclear.

Arguments made in the past emphasizing the leadership of the Tongmenghui have been based primarily on claims that the involvement of the Gowned Brothers in the 1911 Revolution was solely due to the organizational work of the Tongmenghui. Evidence for ties between the Tongmenghui and the Gowned Brothers on the Chengdu Plain came almost entirely from the 1928 *Record of the Campaigns of Sichuan Martyrs* and the 1961 *Memoirs of the 1911 Revolution*, with the latter supplying the single piece of evidence that supports the argument that the Tongmenghui led the armed rebellion. According to the exceedingly detailed account found in the 1961 *Memoirs*, it was Tongmenghui member Long Mingjian who persuaded the Gowned Brothers leader Qin Zaigeng, who was also the East Route Railway Protection Army commander, to join his cause, and the two together masterminded the entire rebellion. In this account, Qin and Long called a meeting of the Sichuan Gowned Brothers leaders on August 4 in Luoquanjing at which these leaders allied themselves with the revolutionary forces and renamed their troops the Railway Protection Comrade Army.[101] This meeting, which appears in almost every history book about the 1911 Revolution in Sichuan, is considered a turning point at which the "Tongmenghui replaced the constitutionalists as the leaders of the 1911 Revolution."[102] However, this piece of evidence is highly problematic. First, some of the Gowned Brothers leaders said to be present at the meeting might not have been there, as demonstrated by other sources,[103] and second, the two writers of this piece were unlikely to have attended the meeting either, one of them being only twelve years old at the time. It is even questionable whether such a meeting took place at all.[104] Those who emphasize the importance of Tongmenghui leadership in the revolution, despite the highly problematic nature of the only piece of evidence on which their entire argument is based, have in turn dismissed clear evidence for the involvement of the constitutionalists in the rebellion and their direct link to the Gowned Brothers.[105]

Likewise, in past scholarship, once someone had rebelled against the Qing during the 1911 Revolution, he was often described as "having been influenced by the Tongmenghui," and the identification of a movement participant as a Tongmenghui member invariably was construed as an example of the Tongmenghui's leadership, whether or not that conclusion was warranted by the evidence. That said, it is true that Tongmenghui members participated in the railway movement. For example, Zhu Zhihong, a member of the Tongmenghui's Chongqing branch, participated in the railway movement starting from his arrival in Chengdu as a shareholder representative, and Long Mingjian, a member of Tongmenghui's Chengdu branch who was also a Sichuan provincial assemblyman and head of the Sishengci School of Law and Politics in Chengdu, joined the movement as a shareholder representative of Rong. However, in these cases, it was because of their elite social identity that these men joined the movement. Most Tongmenghui members came from well-to-do families and generally belonged to at least one of three influential groups—the gentry circles, the learned circles, or the commercial circles—and in some cases more than one. Their membership in the Tongmenghui aside, these men had ample motive to join the railway movement, and within the revolutionary process it was not their Tongmenghui affiliation that positioned them to command influence and power, but rather their link to either the local elite, as in the case of Long Mingjian, or the Gowned Brothers, as in the case of Wu Yuzhang.

Hence, an argument can be made that the Tongmenghui was a latecomer to the situation and contributed little to the halting of Qing troops, and that argument is stronger than the one previously put forth by scholars emphasizing the leadership role of the Tongmenghui and the importance of anti-Manchuism in the revolution. Furthermore, Tongmenghui membership was not the critical factor in railway movement involvement. The constitutionalists, the gentry in the Railway Protection Association branches, the Gowned Brothers, the local militia leaders, and the Tongmenghui all paid their dues. In the course of the 1911 Revolution in Sichuan, they all helped put into practice concepts of self-determination, the people's rights, or republicanism. Ideas like liberty and equality spread during the revolution, and Sichuanese of different backgrounds seized the chance to make a collective bid to control their own destiny.

The Independence of Sichuan

QING OFFICIALS RESPONDED: DUANFANG AND ZHAO ERFENG VERSUS THE PEOPLE

How did Qing officials respond to the pervasive uprisings in Sichuan? Duanfang, who had been sent by the court on September 2 to "quickly exterminate" the movement, changed his stance after arriving in Chongqing on October 13, as battles raged across the Chengdu Plain. Initially bent on "exterminating the rebels," Duanfang, following in-depth interactions with the Sichuan elite, was convinced of the impossibility of crushing the movement and advocated a shift in strategy to "pacifying them."[106] The court took his advice. In mid-October, Duanfang condemned Zhao Erfeng, accusing him of "conducting matters unfairly" and requesting that Pu Dianjun, Luo Lun, and other leaders be set free.

Duanfang's campaign to mollify the people and sway public opinion through announcements posted across Chongqing met with a hostile reception. By this time, the reputation of Qing officials had deteriorated to such a low point that his announcements suffered a fate similar to those of Zhao Erfeng. One defiant commentary, written on Duanfang's actual announcement placards and running alongside each of Duanfang's claims, ran like this:

"I shall set Pu, Luo, and all nine people free"—not likely!

"I shall punish Tian, Zhou, Wang, and Rao for their crimes"—you'd better!

"I do this because you have earnestly asked me to"—we never did!

"If the will of Heaven is finally the same as yours"—nonsense!

"You kind people should all go back to your homes"—only in your dreams!

"Bandits should all be dispersed quickly"—will not!

"If there are still people conducting armed fights"—there sure will be!

"Official soldiers will come and kill you; don't complain then"—just come, whatever![107]

The authority of the Qing rulers had by now reached a nadir, leaving no chance for the Qing officials to "pacify" the movement. On November 27, in Zizhong, the Hubei New Army officers led by veteran Tongmenghui revolutionary Chen Zhenfan launched an insurrection and killed Duanfang. The rioting soldiers also decapitated Duanfang's brother Duanjin. Their heads were immersed in oil in two large containers and traveled with the Hubei New Army, which proceeded on a march through Neijiang, Dazu, Longchuan, Rongchang, and Yongchuan, ultimately reaching Chongqing, where the army was given twenty thousand taels of silver from the newly established revolutionary government. The army then traveled back to Wuchang.[108]

Meanwhile, in Chengdu, Zhao Erfeng's situation was no better. Facing an unprecedented level of opposition, Zhao had no recourse but to appeal to Beijing for reinforcements.[109] On October 19, Zhao asked Beijing to send the Hunan Army to Sichuan.[110] And on October 21, he requested that the Shaanxi Army also be sent.[111] On October 28, the court offered military funding of one million taels of silver, specifically for suppressing the rebellions in Sichuan.[112]

By the end of October, the acting governor-general was losing the court's trust day by day, despite relative success on the battlefield. On

October 26, his condemnation by Duanfang caused the court to chastise Zhao for "being incapable of curbing [the rebels'] power before the rebellion and incapable of exterminating it afterward." Zhao was ordered to let the cabinet decide the fate of the railway movement leaders and to "persuade the railway protection armies to dissolve themselves."[113] On November 6, the court ordered Duanfang to replace Zhao as the new acting governor-general of Sichuan once he reached Chengdu, sending Zhao back to the Sichuan-Tibet border.[114] Assuming an increasingly harsh stance, on November 15, the court ordered Duanfang to "cuff and send Zhao and all the culprits back to the capital" so that "they can be properly tried by the Office of Central Judicial Affairs (Daliyuan) in accordance with the law."[115] At this point, knowing about the uprising in Wuchang, having suffered from Duanfang's backstabbing, and having been virtually abandoned by the court, a distraught Zhao Erfeng released the nine railway movement leaders on November 15.[116]

Negotiations between Zhao and the gentry soon followed. On November 18, a plan for Sichuan independence—initiated by Zhou Shanpei, who sympathized with the gentry, and Chen Chongji, a Sichuan gentleman—was worked out, under which Zhao would turn his power over to the Sichuanese. Zhou Shanpei then convinced military officer Wu Bihua and Sichuan gentleman Shao Cong'en to persuade Zhao Erfeng and the railway movement leaders to throw their support behind the plan.[117] After days of cajoling, on the night of November 21, a dispirited Zhao agreed to the plan, having decided that it was time he "thought for himself."[118] On November 22, Zhao convinced the Qing Sichuan officials to reach an agreement with the Sichuan gentry, the "Thirty Regulations on Sichuan's Independence." The document contained several resolutions of significance. First, the Sichuan people were to have independence in deciding on all political affairs in Sichuan, with Pu Dianjun temporarily taking charge. Second, Zhao Erfeng was to go to the Sichuan-Tibet border and resume his job of defending Sichuan. Each year, Zhao would receive 1.2 million taels of silver from the new government for provisions. Third, except for the Patrol and Defense Forces, led by Zhao Erfeng, all other armies were to be under the control of the Sichuan New Army's commander-in-chief Zhu Qinglan.[119] Pu became the new Sichuan governor-general and Zhu the new vice-governor-general (Figure 7.2).

Hence, Zhao Erfeng, a high-powered official with an impeccable record of service in several different provinces of the Qing empire and a good reputation for his service on the Sichuan-Tibet border, withdrew his allegiance to the Qing. When Zhao agreed to give up his power, he still had at his disposal twenty thousand well-trained soldiers and six million taels

FIGURE 7.2. Governor Pu Dianjun, *left*, and Vice-Governor Zhu Qinglan. Personal collection of the Johns family. Photo by Alfred Johns. Used with permission of Ken Johns of the Johns family.

of silver. As Zhou Shanpei put it, Governor-General Zhao was a "man of strength and determination." Zhao had been impelled to side with the Sichuan gentry by the actions of Duanfang and the court, and, having been boxed into a corner, had no choice but to defect from the Qing.[120] After months of fighting, Sichuan finally gained its independence.

THE DECLARATION OF INDEPENDENCE: THE GREAT HAN SICHUAN MILITARY GOVERNMENT (NOVEMBER 22–DECEMBER 7)

The ceremony celebrating the founding of the new regime, the Great Han Sichuan Military Government (Dahan Sichuan junzhengfu), was set for November 27 (Figure 7.3). At noon on that day, the new military government declared Sichuan's independence from the Qing. According to a foreign observer, the ceremony was "brief and simple." A new flag was raised: a white background emblazoned with the red character "Han" in the center, surrounded by eighteen black stars in a sun-shaped pattern, representing the eighteen provinces of China proper. The new governor-general, Pu Dianjun, delivered a short speech, followed by addresses from

FIGURE 7.3. Public gathering in Chengdu on November 27, 1911, for the Great Han Sichuan Military Government. United Church Archives, Toronto. 98.083P/22N.

other leaders of the new regime. The new government issued the Sichuan Declaration of Independence (Sichuan duli xuanyan), which declared:

The founding principle of the Great Han Sichuan Military Government is based on universal principles (*shijie zhi gongli*) and humanitarianism (*rendao zhi zhuyi*). We shall organize a republican constitution (*gonghe xianfa*) to preserve and solidify the foundation of our Han federalist empire (*gonggu wo dahan lianbang zhi diguo*) and to connect with the world. We want make sure that all seventy million people in Sichuan obey and follow these principles.[121]

This declaration is notable in several regards. The organizing principles of the polity were not traditional Chinese principles, but rather "universal" principles. Although not endorsing the overthrow of a weakened emperorship, the declaration made clear that it was the Sichuanese who must rule Sichuan, under the tenets of federalism. The new polity envisioned by the Sichuan leaders was a radical departure from the prior hierarchical imperial rule, the Confucian-Legalist hegemony. With the emergence of a new political paradigm in which citizens confronted their leaders face-to-face, political equality was a core value and an everyday practice, standing in stark contrast to the inequality and hierarchism that had long been the backbone of China's social and cultural order. The strong sense of self-determination and resolve for self-governance is impossible to mistake.

At the same time, the declaration is riddled with contradictions. Mixed in with aspirations for organizing a "republican constitution," the term "empire" appears, presumably in an attempt by the leaders to accommodate too many viewpoints or satisfy too many factions at the same time. It also runs into a Tocquevillian paradox, that a revolution would level society to enhance the power of the state. The new polity, which "encompassed all of the seventy million people of Sichuan," had to take orders from the new state, with all of the people of Sichuan bound to "obey" the principles set forth by the state. Yet overall, the revolutionary nature of this new regime still shines, with a constitutionalist agenda being the crux of the declaration. The establishment of a constitution, and of a constitutional regime based on the consent of the people, lay at the core of the new polity. The enduring thinking of Pu Dianjun and his colleagues is reflected in the new revolutionary order set forth in this declaration. As Chapters 2 and 4 demonstrated in detail, the goal for the majority of the Chinese constitutionalists, as represented by the Sichuan reformers, was to promote the rights and power of the people. That is, Chinese constitutionalism was a tool for realizing popular sovereignty.

Having helped formulate a new political culture and unleash the energy of the people, Pu Dianjun had to contend with the exigencies of establishing a functioning state. On November 27, Pu issued a joint public announcement with Luo Lun, "Humbly Telling Our Brothers of Sichuan." The announcement asserted that with both purposes of the movement—to

FIGURE 7.4. Reading revolutionary proclamations dated November 27, 1911, of the Great Han Sichuan Military Government. Personal collection of the Johns family. Photo by Alfred Johns. Used with permission of Ken Johns of the Johns family.

protect the railways and to break the treaty—having been achieved, the Sichuanese should focus on the more important matters of maintaining peace and preparing to build a constitutional future, and it pleaded with the Sichuan people to put down their weapons, return home, and till their lands (Figure 7.4).[122] However, after the extensive mobilization of the people, the movement had reached a stage at which it could no longer be controlled by the constitutionalist elite. Although much of the power of the railway movement derived from the movement leaders' thorough activation of the people, the power of the leaders did not extend beyond the purview of promoting collective action. The movement lacked the resources to control its own fate, and this time not only were the orders of the leaders not heeded, but they were contradicted. In late November, heartened by the release of Pu and of Luo in particular, the fighting escalated.[123]

Conclusion

After the railway movement leaders were arrested on September 7, the revolution continued to expand. While expanding, the movement also diverged from its original course. In Sichuan in 1911, it was the constitutionalists who shaped public opinion, transformed it into a potent political force, and created the revolutionary repertoire that successfully mobilized the people, all of which helped to promote the key notions of equality, rights, self-rule, and popular sovereignty. However, once those ideas and repertoires had circulated widely, they gained a life of their own and could be appropriated by anyone.

The mantra of "liberating the people from the yoke of the Qing" together with the newly embraced concept of popular sovereignty led to the emergence of an uncontrollably political force: the people. Revolutions create opportunities for all kinds of political actors. As the number of people involved in the movement grew, and as those people increasingly diverged from one another, they would also, within the capacity of their understanding, utilize the new slogans and concepts to lend legitimacy to their own individual struggles. At this stage of the revolution, revolutionary ideas such as the people's rights, liberty, and equality continued to be utilized by various political actors as they were staging uprisings. These concepts, though voiced during this stage of the movement as much for their value as revolutionary catchwords as for the principles they stood for, were still a pivotal force underpinning the movement.

8 *The End of Revolution*

THE RISE OF REPUBLICANISM AND THE FAILURE
OF CONSTITUTIONALISM

After months of propagandizing, mobilizing, and armed fighting, the 1911 Revolution in Sichuan had turned itself into a true mass movement. It was the Chengdu elite's pursuits for their own economic and political interests that initiated the Railway Protection movement; however, the movement was made possible only because of a well-crafted political culture centering on the ideas of rights and popular sovereignty. As demonstrated in Chapters 5–7, during the revolutionary process, hundreds of thousands of Sichuanese joined forces driven by the new rhetoric of rights and popular sovereignty, which was again fortified by their preexisting social networks and fueled by their long-lasting taxation-related frustrations. At the same time, the revolution also gave birth to a new political culture, with the consent and the participation of the people being an inalienable part of that.

The declaration of Sichuan's independence was, however, only a beginning. The discourse of the revolution was all about empowering the previously powerless people. After months of mass mobilization, a greater number of Sichuanese were left with the ideas that the people have rights, that the nation is the people, and that the people are the nation. This democratic political culture centering on rights was an effective force in overthrowing the old regime. But the real challenge was this: to build a constitutional state ultimately involves limiting power through checks and balances, not growing it. Now, with many Chinese being mobilized into a new polity of citizens and political leaders having the opportunity to expand their own power in the name of "the people," would they all be willing to let go of some power in the interests of constitutionalism? Would they be able to negotiate and reach an agreement with one another? In other words, would the 1911 Revolution give rise to a functional constitutional state, that is, a viable constitutional republic with a set of republican institutions at work: a genuine representative assembly, a potent independent judiciary, a real system of checks and balances with limits constraining yet protecting the power of each of the three branches of government?

Popular Sovereignty and the Rise of Yin Changheng: The Chengdu Mutiny and the Death of Zhao Erfeng

The new revolutionary government, the Great Han Sichuan Military Government (Dahan Sichuan junzhengfu), struggled to survive, but the prospects of its becoming a functional state were bleak. Even before its inauguration ceremony on November 27, problems threatening the formation of the new government had begun to emerge. First of all, the legitimacy of the new government was challenged. The Chongqing Military Government (Shujun zhengfu), established on November 22 with the "ambition to control the entirety of Sichuan," had since its inception been actively reaching out to Wuchang revolutionary commander Li Yuanhong and the leader of the Tongmenghui, Sun Yat-sen.[1] Declaring themselves the sole revolutionary government of Sichuan, the Chongqing leadership had organized a force of three thousand men in readiness to take over Chengdu, and they asked for reinforcements from the Yunnan, Hubei, and Guizhou New Armies to come and support their action. As a result, serious conflicts between the Sichuan native armies and the "guest armies" were to arise. Chongqing also launched a bitter, nationwide propaganda campaign against Chengdu. In newspapers, the Chongqing leaders harshly criticized the agreement between Zhao Erfeng and the constitutionalists, arguing that Pu Dianjun, Luo Lun, and the other constitutionalists were "selling out the interests of the Sichuanese," and branding the constitutionalists as "traitors," "cowards," and "fools."[2]

Also troublesome were the conflicts within the ranks of the Sichuan armies in Chengdu. The competition between the old army (the Patrol and Defense Forces in particular) and the New Army had long been a problem. After the revolution, conflicts *within* the New Army became predominant. The Sichuanese in the New Armies, emboldened by the notions of Sichuan being ruled by the Sichuanese and self-governance, became serious contenders for power. Headed by Yin Changheng, a Sichuanese officer in the Sichuan New Army who was the deputy of the Sichuan Army Elementary School at the time, some low-ranking Sichuan New Army officers were extremely unhappy that Zhu Qinglan (a Zhejiang native) and other non-Sichuan officers had taken control of the Sichuan New Army and demanded that the new government create an additional division of the New Army for the Sichuanese.[3]

Most disheartening of all, perhaps, was factionalism within the new government's leadership. Serious differences existed between Pu Dianjun and Luo Lun, the two most respected constitutionalists who had collaborated in leading the railway movement. According to William Wilkinson, Pu aimed to establish a German-style constitutional monarchy that would retain the emperor, but Luo desired a more radical, American-style republican government. The two leaders, though appearing as a united front in public, were thinking along different lines in private.[4] Furthermore, there was competition both between the constitutionalists and the Tongmenghui members who had joined the movement later, and between the former Qing officials who stayed on and the Sichuan elites who led the new government.[5] Thus, in a situation already rife with tensions, problems emerged even before the November 27 inauguration. On the night of November 26, following a day of agitation by Yin Changheng's supporters in the New Army, three unidentified men went to Zhao Erfeng's yamen to demand that he give his seal to Luo Lun, not Pu Dianjun.[6]

With antagonism and discontent accumulating rapidly, rumors of a mutiny circulated widely in the streets of Chengdu. Shortly after independence was declared on November 27, Yin began making excessive demands of the new government. He wanted to be the military minister of the new regime and insisted that an additional division of the New Army be created just for Sichuanese. In early December, Yin led a group of his associates to the seat of the new government, demanding promotions and the additional army division. They drew guns and pointed them at the new government leaders, shouting that they, the Sichuanese, were not treated well and threatened that if their demands were not met they would carry out extreme acts.[7] Having been nonrevolutionaries during the first six months of the revolution, they were now out to grab power and pursue their own agenda.

Buoyed by the support of his fellow Sichuanese in the New Army, Yin Changheng would do whatever it took to achieve success. It is worth noting that Yin had no revolutionary credentials. He neither was a Tongmenghui member nor had contributed to the railway movement in Sichuan.[8] He had no prior connections to the Gowned Brothers, nor was he from a powerful elite family himself. What he had was an oversized ambition, a degree of support from Sichuanese soldiers, and a marriage link to the Chengdu gentleman Yan Kai, the shareholder board chairman of the Chuan-Han Railway Company. Nevertheless, Yin had taken swift action to seize his opportunity in this chaotic Chengdu political milieu and he did so precisely with the newly crafted discourse about the consent and the rulership of the people, the Sichuanese.

To appeal to as broad a political constituency as he could, Yin joined the Tongmenghui eight days after Sichuan declared independence and subsequently started socializing with Tongmenghui members in Chengdu.⁹ Yin also turned himself into a Gowned Brother, naming himself the "Grand Han Gentleman" (Dahangong), wining and dining with the Gowned Brothers leaders, dressing as a Gowned Brother, and opening new Gowned Brothers lodges in Chengdu. Yin fostered and fully capitalized on his connection with Yan Kai and other Sichuan gentry, never failing to act humbly in their presence. Finally, to expand his influence into the Patrol and Defense Forces—himself being an officer of the Sichuan New Army who had no prior liaisons with the Patrol and Defense Forces—Yin used his Sichuanese identity and his newly obtained Gowned Brothers persona to forge new alliances. Specifically, relying on his New Army battalion commander Peng Guanglie, whose cousin was a platoon commander in the Patrol and Defense Forces and an influential Gowned Brothers leader, Yin was in position to command the Patrol and Defense Forces and carry out a mutiny. On December 7, Gowned Brothers members from both the Patrol and Defense Forces and the New Army held a secret meeting, attended by Yin's confidants Peng Guanglie and Sun Zhaoluan, at which they planned the mutiny for the following day. They would first demand an extra three months' pay; if it were not granted, they would fire shots and start raiding: first the official treasury, then the banks, and finally the shops in Chengdu's commercial areas.[10]

Despite the strong sense of hope that the Great Han Government had brought to the Sichuanese, it was not a functioning state. The emergence of competing centers of power created a situation that Pu Dianjun was unable to control. Having put much of his energy into matters such as deciding on the right style of hair and clothes, Pu failed to foresee the most urgent threats to the new state. Ignoring all of the obvious signs of danger, he insisted on inspecting the armies on December 8, naively believing that after personally reviewing the soldiers he would gain their trust and they would gratefully follow the new government's orders.[11]

On December 8, as Pu Dianjun and Zhu Qinglan were inspecting soldiers at the East Field in Chengdu, a solider from the Patrol and Defense Forces suddenly fired a shot. Immediately following that, New Army soldiers also opened fire. Pu and Zhu frantically fled as the situation veered out of control. Soldiers from both the old and the new armies rushed to the provincial treasury, banks, and shops and commenced looting at once, just as they had planned. After attacking the Great Qing Bank, one of Chengdu's largest, as well as two other large banks, soldiers plundered the Center for Promoting Commerce and Industry. Historian Wang Di presents a vivid description of the looting: "In an incredibly short time, the mob headed by the soldiers had cleared every shop on the street, upstairs and down."[12]

The mob shattered glass display cases and tossed much of their contents into the street. Later that afternoon, soldiers ransacked East Great Street, Chengdu's most prosperous district. Their main goal was money: "Late into the evening, smaller bands of soldiers, still carrying their rifles and bandoliers of cartridges, demanded and received dollars or lump silver."[13] At night, pawnshops became common targets for these soldiers, who set fifteen or sixteen fires throughout the city. The pillaging lasted for an entire day, from morning until night. The city gates were not closed during the night, and many soldiers fled with their booty.[14] Chengdu suffered extensive damage as a result: the six million taels of silver in the provincial treasury were completely gone.[15] The total estimated loss on December 8 was more than ten million taels of silver.[16]

When the looting had nearly died down, Yin Changheng led his New Army troops in a rush to Chengdu to "pacify the mutiny" as planned. On the second day, organized hordes of Railway Protection Army troops marched into the city. Supported by Luo Lun, who had great influence over the Gowned Brothers troops, Yin "stabilized" the situation. Despite Yin's attempt to conceal his plot under the guise of restoring order, detailed memoirs by Wang Youyu and Huang Shou have exposed Yin's deliberate planning of the chaos. The person firing the first shot on December 8, an officer from Zhao Erfeng's Patrol and Defense Forces, was also the cousin of Yin's confidant Peng Guanglie and had in fact been ordered to fire by Peng.[17] Luo Lun, who shared Yin's strong desire for Sichuanese self-governance and who, as Zhou Shanpei alleged, did not get what he had hoped for after independence, chose to throw his support behind Yin and let go of Pu Dianjun.[18] On December 9, the new Sichuan Military Government (Sichuan junzhengfu) was established in Chengdu with Yin as the new governor and Luo the vice-governor.

Yin's rise, in addition to his knack for wheeling and dealing, also owed much to his deployment of the new political discourse of popular sovereignty. Taking a page out of the Chengdu elite's book, Yin purloined the mantle of leadership at rifle point. However, a critical factor that enabled Yin to take a leading role in Sichuan was the newly valorized notion of "the people." This concept, first cultivated and promoted by the constitutionalists to mobilize a force for the railway movement, now helped give rise to Yin Changheng, who at that moment was the preeminent manifestation of "the people" to protect the rights of the Sichuanese. Pointedly, Yin issued a stream of public announcements with emphasis on the notions of popular rule and self-rule. A typical announcement by Yin ran like this:

Ever since September 7, Sichuan has been in great chaos; unexpectedly, the December 8 incident again created much agony for the Sichuanese. How ill-fated we

Sichuanese are! . . . We have struggled bravely to gain back power from the Manchus, but after that, our Sichuan was given to outsiders (*wairen*)! . . . It was for the happiness of all seventy million Sichuan people that we, Yin Changheng and Luo Lun, came to assume the responsibility of ruling Sichuan.[19]

In another announcement, Yin emphasized that it was because of "popular demand" (*renmin huyu*) that he and Luo Lun were chosen to be the leaders of all Sichuanese.[20] Yin's repeated invocation of self-governance and popular rule played a key role in legitimizing his power; the Chengdunese regarded Yin as someone whose thinking resonated with their own, and they accepted him as the new governor of Sichuan. At that particular moment in Sichuan politics, leaders had to be responsive in the face of the people's demands, and Yin's rise confirms the strength of the new polity and the vibrancy of the new political discourse.

Having obtained his position with the help of "public demand," Yin Changheng was now also subject to it, compelled to continue rallying support via public opinion to solidify his power. In particular, Yin needed a public enemy for the Sichuanese to unite against, and as fate would have it, he found one in Zhao Erfeng. The entirety of the blame for the December 8 mutiny was placed squarely on Zhao's shoulders, due to the indisputable fact that a soldier in Zhao's Patrol and Defense Forces had fired the first shot. The rumor in Chengdu was that Zhao still wanted to overthrow the new government and that he had mobilized the mutiny as part of a conspiracy.[21]

Such rumors, unsurprisingly, were carefully formulated and spread by Yin. The actual history of the event runs quite to the contrary. First of all, as Consul-General Wilkinson observed, Zhao Erfeng had no motive for carrying out such a mutiny, especially considering that he had put almost all of his savings in the Great Qing Bank.[22] Second, there exists no hard evidence that Zhao was planning to overthrow the new government. The only two pieces of "evidence" against Zhao—one being the claim that Zhao had ordered his subordinate Fu Huafeng to rush to Chengdu with reinforcements and the other that Zhao had used the title "governor-general" as he issued an announcement ordering the rioting soldiers to go back to their camps after December 8—do not stand up to careful scrutiny.[23]

However, given the hatred that had long festered between Zhao and the Sichuanese, rumors like these were readily believed. Yin Changheng used those emotions to create an opportunity for himself. He framed Zhao Erfeng for partaking in the conspiracy to overthrow the new government and laid out his "evidence." Then, on December 22, Zhao was tricked by Yin into an ambush and was publicly executed. After Zhao's death, his head was put on display by Yin at one of the Chengdu city gates for days. Yin, having shown his "ability" to execute "the enemy of the people," earned a leading position in the Sichuan Military Government and was hailed as the "hero" and "savior" of Sichuan. This act was considered at the time the "most important and correct" decision made by the new revolutionary government, for it helped Yin stabilize the situation in Chengdu.[24] It even gained Yin some respect from the Tongmenghui leaders in Chongqing (Figure 8.1).

In this intensely politicized situation, the Sichuan people were engaged in radicalization that led to violence, defection, and, finally, repression. Yin's attempt to maintain his base of support led to the death of Zhao Erfeng. Yin won power because he easily rode the momentum that the movement had created. By merging himself with "the people," standing up for "public opinion," and crushing Zhao's "conspiracy," Yin gained popularity, while the Sichuanese felt that it was their moment too, and they too claimed a stake in this new order of self-rule. To a great extent, it was "the people of Sichuan" who endowed Yin with power, because he made himself into someone who had the greatest appeal for the Sichuan people, including the Sichuanese soldiers, the Gowned Brothers, the Chengdu elite, and many of the mobilized commoners of Sichuan.

FIGURE 8.1. Bodyguards of Sichuan's new provincial leaders, 1911. Personal collection of the Johns family. Photo by Alfred Johns. Used with permission of Ken Johns of the Johns family.

The Rise of Republicanism: The End of Absolute Monarchy

From an idealistic perspective, Yin Changheng's seizure of power on December 8 signaled the failure of the 1911 Revolution in Sichuan, for Yin was hardly a revolutionary. The rise of Yin, however, foretold what was to come. Military power would soon become the most important political capital in the ensuing power struggles, as long as the person in command could also speak to the people in the language of revolution. At the same time, the discourse of rights, the fervor of the people, and the consent of the public were real, and they lent power and authority to political figures locked in struggle. As a testament to the potency of revolutionary political culture, with the new notion of popular sovereignty as its core principle, the rise of Yin Changheng signaled the trend of future politics.

Buoyed by his New Army supporters and espousing the much-hailed rhetoric of self-rule, Yin nonetheless faced the same formidable challenges of state making that had diminished Pu Dianjun's power. Following the collapse of the Qing in late November, the unleashed zeal of the local people ushered in a new wave of regime change at the county level. At the outset, the Railway Protection Army, local militias, bandits, and Gowned Brothers remained powerful. As but one example of the similar scenarios that played out in a number of counties, in Qianwei the Railway Protection Army entered the county seat, destroyed the prison, drove out the magistrate, and established a new government, emulating the structure of the military government in Chengdu.[25] Before long, former Qing officials entered the fray. In Leshan and Hanyuan, for example, the former Qing county magistrates adopted the title "military governor" (*dudu*) in imitation of the provincial governor in Chengdu and remained in their posts.[26] Political mobilization of the local gentry was also rampant. In Deyang, when the new provincial regime sent "inspecting delegates" (*xuanweishi*) to the county, Deyang gentry seized the occasion and jettisoned the Qing magistrate.[27] A local observer opined, "All counties were rising up and all [rioters] advancing the idea of being self-governing tyrants."[28] The new revolutionary ideas and mantras unleashed an intense desire for power as gentry and bandits alike jockeyed for the opportunity to be the "masters" of the new republic.

To make things worse, the Sichuan Military Government, by then headed by Yin and Luo Lun in Chengdu, also faced challenges from outside. The Chongqing Military Government and the Yunnan Army, which was invited by Chongqing to attack Chengdu, launched the most strenuous challenge to the legitimacy of the Chengdu government, which, owing to its close connection to the Gowned Brothers, was maligned as being a Gowned Brothers government rather than a genuine republican one.[29] Beginning in late December, hordes of Yunnan soldiers clashed with local Sichuan troops, and brutal conflicts between the native and the guest armies led to a number of deaths of Sichuan leaders, including the famous South Route Commander Zhou Hongxun and the veteran Tongmenghui adherent Huang Fang.[30] The brutal death of Huang Fang on January 21, 1912—his belly slashed open and his heart torn out—shocked Sichuanese from Chengdu and Chongqing alike. The incident tempered the hostile attitude of Chongqing toward Chengdu, raising awareness that uniting to protect the interests of Sichuan as a whole took precedence over competition and factionalism.[31]

On January 29, 1912, Chengdu initiated a merger proposition wherein Chengdu would remain the political center of Sichuan while Chongqing would lead an independent division of the army and be granted a certain degree of autonomy. Yin Changheng would be the governor of Sichuan and Zhang Peijue, the governor of Chongqing, would be the vice-governor of Sichuan. Luo Lun and Xia Zhishi—the vice-governors of Chengdu and Chongqing—would serve, respectively, as the chairman of the Military Council and the commander of the Chongqing Division. Chongqing accepted the plan, and on March 11 the leaders of the new government took office. Hailing the merger, Sichuan newspapers effused that it "embodied the spirit of republicanism" and "served the happiness of all Sichuanese."[32] Hyperbolic as these words might have been, the sovereignty of the people as a political concept had established itself as the fundamental principle of the new Republican regime, and the merger signaled the denouement of the 1911 Revolution in Sichuan.

While the Sichuan New Army, Tongmenghui members, and constitutionalists were striving to create a republic in Chengdu, the situation nationwide paralleled that of Sichuan, as the political elites in the rebellious southern provinces similarly worked together to bring an end to the absolute monarchy, with the constitutionalists once again playing a key role. In November 1911, the dominant constitutionalists from Jiangsu and Zhejiang provinces, Zhao Fengchang, Zhang Jian, and Zhuang Yunkuan in particular, proposed a plan for uniting all of the southern forces into one polity under the principle of republicanism, taking the United States of America as their model:

Ever since the Wuhan uprising and the uprisings that followed in various provinces, republicanism has been accepted by public opinion (*yulun*) in China. Yet, if we wish to successfully establish our state, we need to take lessons from those countries that have done so fruitfully. Among them, the federalist system of the United States of America should be our model. . . .

We should immediately emulate the United States of America in calling a national convention, regarding it as our temporary authoritative legislature, and using it to draft plans for all of the domestic and international issues.... Our aim is to maintain our territorial integrity, uphold humanitarianism, and keep peace. With great urgency, we ask you, all the provinces, to elect delegates and send them to meet in Shanghai.³³

Listed as the initiators of the proposal were nineteen representatives from twelve provinces, including former Qing official Cheng Dequan, constitutionalists Zhao Fengchang, Zhang Jian, and Tang Shouqian, and revolutionaries Song Jiaoren and Yu Youren (Figure 8.2).³⁴ The proposal laid out a concrete model for selecting delegates whereby in each province the prior Qing provincial assembly and the new provincial military governor should each send one delegate, clearly demonstrating an intention to bring together the three types of southern political elites—the constitutionalists, the reform-minded Qing officials, and the anti-Manchu revolutionaries. It specified that "the agenda of the convention should be, first, to elect delegates to cope with foreign powers, second, to come up with solutions to military affairs, and third, to find a solution to the dilemma of how to handle the fate of the Qing ruling house."³⁵

Constitutional in nature and national in scope, this proposal served as an instruction manual for the series of key events that followed. The convention it created, the United Convention of the Delegates of Provincial Governments (Gesheng dudufu daibiao lianhehui)—which traveled from

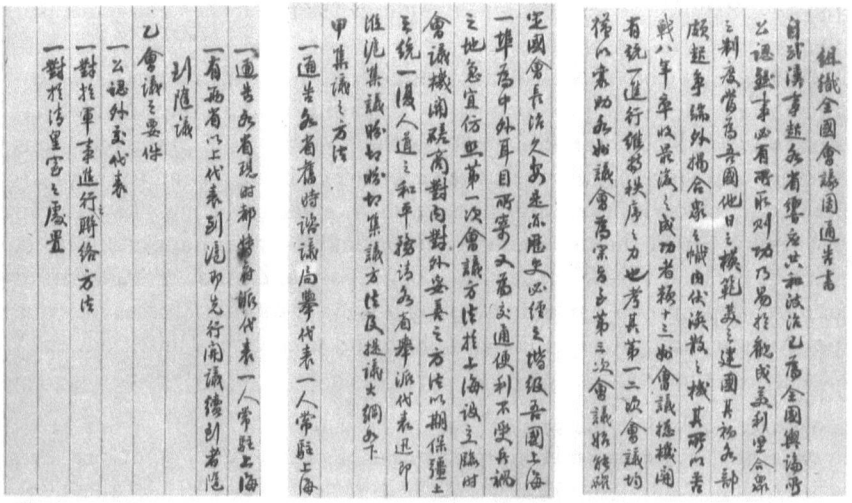

FIGURE 8.2. Call to organize a united convention on the model of the United States of America, (ca. October 1911). Guojia tushuguan shanben bu, ed., *Zhao Fengchang cangzha* (Beijing: Guojia tushuguan chubanshe, 2009), vol. 3, 582–84.

Shanghai to Wuhan and eventually settled in Nanjing before becoming the Nanjing Provisional Senate (Nanjing linshi canyiyuan)—supported the truce between the Beiyang Army and the Hubei Revolutionary Army, elected the southern delegates sent to negotiate with Yuan Shikai at the South-North peace talks, voted Sun Yat-sen the provisional president of the Republic of China, and drafted the Provisional Constitution. It was this convention—composed of constitutionalists, officials, and anti-Manchu revolutionaries alike—that brought the end of the absolute monarchy and the birth of the Chinese republic.

The proposal was welcomed by all southern political elites. On November 11, taking the proposal word for word, Jiangsu governor Cheng Dequan and Zhejiang governor Tang Shouqian issued a public statement to the Tongmenghui Shanghai governor Chen Qimei, extending an invitation to all the southern provinces to dispatch delegates for the formation of a united legislature. Chen immediately endorsed the plan. Four days later, delegates from Shanghai, Jiangsu, Zhejiang, and Fujian arrived in Shanghai and created the United Convention of the Delegates of Provincial Governments.[36] The proposal was also accepted by the revolutionaries in Hubei. On November 24, at the request of the Hubei Military Government, which regarded itself as the first revolutionary regime, the United Convention moved to Wuhan. Between late November and early December, twenty-three delegates from twelve southern provinces arrived in Hubei. While the majority of the delegates continued to meet in Wuhan, a minority stayed in Shanghai to "support their Hubei comrades from afar."[37]

The United Convention—now representing the unified southern political elites—soon became the key player in negotiating with the northern power of Yuan Shikai and his Beiyang clique. On November 26, the Beiyang Army seized Hanyang. On November 30, facilitated by the British ambassador and the British consul-general at Hankow, secret negotiations between Yuan Shikai and Li Yuanhong began.[38] On the same day, the United Convention opened its first formal meeting, electing Li Yuanhong as the commander of all southern provinces.[39] On December 3, the United Convention passed the "Outline for the Organization of the Provisional Government of the Republic of China." While maintaining that republicanism as a political principle was nonnegotiable, it agreed to give the presidency to Yuan Shikai if he would support republicanism and convince the Qing to abdicate.[40] On December 8, five days after the ceasefire between Beiyang and Hubei, Yuan Shikai appointed Tang Shaoyi as his envoy, and the United Convention elected their delegates for the peace talks: Wu Tingfang was the chief deputy, with Tongmenghui members including Wang Jingwei and Wang Chonghui as consuls and the Hubei's Hu Ying and Wang Zhengting as special representatives.[41]

The election of Li Yuanhong as the commander of the southern provinces and the dominance of Hubei representatives, however, agitated the Jiang-Zhe elite. While delegates were meeting in Hubei, on December 4, Shanghai governor Chen Qimei, Jiangsu governor Cheng Dequan, and Zhejiang governor Tang Shouqian called a meeting of the remaining United Convention representatives in Shanghai, where the decision was made to name Nanjing the new capital of the provisional government, another display of the Jiang-Zhe elite's ambition to control national affairs. Following the cease-fire, Li Yuanhong's role was no longer crucial, and the final outcome of the competition between Jiang-Zhe and Hubei was a Jiang-Zhe victory. The United Convention began moving to Nanjing on December 8, and by late December, forty-four delegates from seventeen provinces had arrived in Nanjing to meet.[42]

The peace talks between the North and the South, which at the insistence of the Jiang-Zhe elite had also moved out of Hubei, resumed on December 18 at the Shanghai Municipal Council of the International Settlement.[43] Five rounds of negotiations took place between December 18 and 31. While formal negotiations were going on at the Municipal Council during the day, at night, secret talks took place at Zhao Fengchang's home, Xinyin Hall. In fact, the morning talks were more or less a performance of what had been settled in the previous night's talks, at which Zhao was the key spokesperson for the South.[44] As the South-North negotiators were meeting, Sun Yat-sen, after years of exile abroad, made his return to China on December 25. On December 29, the United Convention, now relocated to Nanjing, elected Sun the provisional president. Forty-three delegates from seventeen provinces voted, giving Sun sixteen out of seventeen votes.[45] Sun's election to the provisional presidency did not, however, alter the course of the negotiations. Aligning with its earlier resolution of making Yuan Shikai the president once he supported republicanism, the United Convention in Nanjing decided that if Yuan could convince the Manchus to abdicate, Sun Yat-sen would hand over his presidency to Yuan.[46] The fear of a possible foreign invasion, the desire to maintain territorial integrity, and the hope of avoiding bloodshed had already set the tone for the talks.

By mid-January, the Jiang-Zhe constitutionalists had collectively penned a draft of the Manchu Abdication Edict in the name of the Qing court.[47] And the rest, as they say, is history. On February 12, the Qing ruling house abdicated. Claiming that "the power to govern is now transferred to all in the country" (*tongzhiquan gongzhu quanguo*) and that "a constitutional republic is now the state system of our country" (*gonghe lixian guoti*), the edict signaled the end of the monarchy and the birth of the Chinese republic, which seemed to have occurred overnight. On February 13, the following day, Sun Yat-sen resigned as provisional president; by March 1912, the initial arrangement of the republic had been laid down: the Manchus abdicated, the governments of the south and north were combined into one, Yuan became the head of the new republic, and Beijing was the new capital. Noteworthy was the critical role played by the constitutionalists, who created a culture that helped dismantle the old political order, mobilized the masses in the revolution, and masterminded a grand compromise that brought together the political elites in China and created the Republic of China in 1912.

Following the fall of the Qing empire, celebration of republicanism filled public life in China.[48] As David Strand and Henrietta Harrison have compellingly demonstrated, a new political culture with republicanism at its core emerged in early twentieth-century China. As elucidated by Harrison, the notion of republican citizenship manifested itself through rituals, speeches, fashions, gestures, symbols, and other actions in the wake of the revolution.[49] In addition, Strand shows that the Revolution of 1911 engendered a new political life: as Chinese citizens confronted their leaders face-to-face, the leaders found themselves dependent on popular support and citizens became enmeshed in the political process.[50] When students across the country began to move out of their family schools, they developed new political subjectivities and seized onto the hope that they would be able lead China toward a future where more citizens could be involved in the political decision-making process.

After 1911, Sichuan too felt the fundamental change that the revolution brought to the local people. In Luzhou prefecture in southern Sichuan, the republican era "ushered in a new society."[51] Its gazetteer recorded that "ever since the establishment of the Republic, people of the traditional four classes (gentry, peasants, artisans and merchants) came to be equal to one another: the society was forever changed."[52] In An county in northern Sichuan, traditional gentry wrote with great anxiety: "After the first year of Republican China, about six or seven out of ten people supported the old values. The rest of the people mistakenly believed in the notions of equality and liberty. Gradually, the old morals would wither and die out."[53] The gazetteers demonstrated that a significant number of people in Sichuan were exposed to new ideologies and that many accepted the new political legitimacy. Furthermore, the relation between the ruler and the ruled was seriously altered: "Nowadays, as county chief executives try a case, the people stand rather than kneel. The county chief executives thus have no authority that keeps the ruled in awe."[54] In the private space of the lives of ordinary people, the 1911 Revolution ushered in a new way for them to relate to and to interact with one another. The hierarchical distinctions between elder and younger, male and female, became obscured: "The order was lost. There was no distinction between masters and servants or between the upper and lower groups. This situation was more severe than in the late Qing."[55] People bowed and shook hands when addressing each other. No kneeling was allowed. To say the least, in rituals, customs, and discourse, greater equality prevailed. The language enshrining the preservation of nationalism and the people's rights, the values of republican citizenship, and the public gestures affirming equality all verified the rise of a democratic political culture and the coming of a new Chinese republican polity.

The Failure of Constitutionalism

This emergent and flourishing republican political culture was, nonetheless, insufficient, for political leaders had to forge a consensus on an adequate system of representation both symbolically and institutionally. The revolution had empowered people in new ways, and especially those who previously had no political power or participation in politics. Now, with a greater number of people believing in the idea that they were the "masters" in a polity called China, and with political leaders believing that they deserved to assert their will to the fullest extent, was there a mechanism for adjudicating competing claims made on behalf of the people? To answer this question, it is necessary to scrutinize the activities of the major players in early republican politics.

As we have seen, the swift regime change from a monarchy to a republic was based on the common principle of republicanism, the desire to maintain territorial integrity, and the belief that it was imperative that all five ethnicities—the Han, the Manchus, the Mongols, the Hui, and the Tibetans—be brought together in union. Following the Qing abdication, however, the political elites who had together created the republic could neither let go of what they believed to be right nor limit their own power in the new regime. Although all agreed that Yuan Shikai should be the president of China, they disagreed on how powerful this president should be. Although all agreed that China must be united and be republican, they disagreed on how and why the republic actually came to be. While Yuan emphasized the continuity between the republic and the Qing, citing the Manchu Abdication Edict, the Tongmenghui leaders stressed the revolutionary origins of the new regime.[56]

Compounding the fundamental disagreement with respect to the legitimacy of the republic—as each regarded their own group as having made the most contributions to creating the republic—were problems stemming from the process by which the 1912 Provisional Constitution was drafted. First, the constitution was written by southern elites in the Nanjing Provisional Senate, with no input from the north. It stipulated that the composition of the cabinet and "any treaties that would add financial request to the national treasury" be approved by the Provisional Senate, a clear move to limit the power of the executive branch, namely, Yuan Shikai.[57] Second, within the Nanjing Provisional Senate, the Tongmenghui members and the constitutionalists, and even the Tongmenghui members among themselves, were divided. Song Jiaoren and most of the constitutionalists, trained at the French-influenced Hōsei University, advocated parliamentarism, but Sun Yat-sen, a longtime admirer of the political system of the United States, wanted presidentialism. Consequently, the final version of the Provisional Constitution contained elements of both presidentialism and parliamentarism, an ambiguity that diminished the document's effectiveness and guaranteed future conflict.[58]

In 1912, the political alliance of the Beiyang clique, the Tongmenghui, and the constitutionalists was superficially maintained, and political debates and discussions about constitutions and parliamentary elections dominated China's elite circles.[59] Three parties were particularly influential at the outset as parliamentary politics was in the making: the radical Nationalist Party (Guomindang), which had just been reconstructed using the Tongmenghui as its base; the Democratic Party (Minzhudang), which consisted of constitutionalists led by Liang Qichao and Tang Hualong; and the Republican Party (Gonghedang), whose members came from five different political groups, including the Jiang-Zhe constitutionalists like Zhang Jian and Zhao Fengchang, notables like Li Yuanhong and Zhang Binlin, and former Qing officials like Cheng Dequan and Xiong Xiling. The Democrats and the Republicans stood between the Nationalists and the Beiyang clique. Like Yuan, they aimed to build a strong central government; like the Nationalists, they were committed to republicanism.[60]

Beginning in January 1913, an estimated forty million Chinese voters participated in two rounds of elections. In the first round, eligible voters chose electors, who would in turn elect the actual provincial assemblymen, the parliamentary representatives, and the senators in the second round. On February 24, when the election results were declared, the Nationalist Party had won 269 seats out of 569 in the parliament and 123 seats out of 274 in the senate, a clear indication that no single party would be able to compete with the Nationalists. As one would expect, the Nationalists' victory brought to light the conflicts dividing the republican state makers, especially the conflicts between the Beiyang clique and the Nationalists.[61] Flush from their victory in the elections and more emboldened than ever, the Nationalists aggressively set out to optimize their political advantages. Beginning in 1913, the acting chairman of the Nationalist Party, Song Jiaoren, gave a number of anti-Yuan speeches in provinces along the Yangzi River.[62] The attitude of the Nationalist Party was clear. It was ready to compete against the Beiyang clique for control of the Beijing government. On the other side of the political divide, however, Yuan had made great progress both in securing foreign loans to run his state and in separating the civic and the military powers of various provincial governments, which helped centralize power in his own hands.[63] The tension between the two sides reached a tipping point when Song Jiaoren was assassinated at the Shanghai train station on March 20, 1913. With this event that finally severed the collaboration between Sun Yat-sen and the Beiyang clique, parliamentary politics eluded China.[64]

If the national union represented a fragile compromise, the combined republican government of Sichuan was a no less flimsy contrivance. On paper, both the constitutionalists and members of the Tongmenghui occupied chief positions in the new government.[65] In reality, however, neither had the acumen to solve Sichuan's knotty political crises, the most urgent of which was the Yunnan Army problem. From this vacuum emerged Hu Jingyi. Through connections with both the Yunnan and Sichuan armies, Hu successfully made a deal with the Yunnan officers: once Sichuan offered two hundred thousand taels of silver in provisions to the Yunnan Army, the Yunnan Army would leave Sichuan.[66] In the months that followed, Hu became increasingly indispensable to Yin Changheng. Yin appointed Hu the new Chongqing Division army commander so as to tighten his control there, a job that Hu carried out effectively. Gradually, even Yin's confidant, the First Division commander Zhou Jun, who had come to power with Yin after the Chengdu mutiny, shifted his allegiance to Hu. Meanwhile, Hu made connections with Yuan Shikai and gained his backing. On July 12, 1912, two days after Yin was ordered by Yuan to march to the Sichuan-Tibet border to suppress uprisings there, Hu Jingyi was appointed the acting governor of Sichuan by Yuan. In September 1912, the Sichuan Tongmenghui vice-governor Zhang Peijue was ordered to Beijing by Yuan. By this time, Hu had transformed himself into the de facto power holder in Sichuan.[67]

Given the divergent political orientations of the Sichuan Army, the constitutionalists, and the Tongmenghui, reaching agreement on a common political framework was equally impossible, as had been the case in national politics. In August 1912, with Hu's explicit support, the Sichuan branch of the Republican Party was founded with the aim of "strengthening the central government and attaining unification." A great number of Sichuan army officers joined the Republican Party, making it almost Hu's own party.[68] In September 1912, the Sichuan branch of the Nationalist Party was established, and veteran Tongmenghui members in Sichuan quickly regrouped and campaigned for it. In October 1912, after Liang Qichao returned to China, the rejuvenated Sichuan constitutionalists restructured their association into the Democratic Party, counting as members all the famed constitutionalists we have met earlier, including Pu Dianjun, Luo Lun, Deng Xiaoke, Zhang Lan, and Shao Cong'en.[69] Mirroring its victory at the national level, the Nationalist Party dominated the 1913 election for the Sichuan Provincial Assembly.[70] Conflicts among the three parties ensued at the assembly meetings. Finding a political consensus became impossible.

Back in the national capital of Beijing, the first parliament of the Republic of China began meeting on April 8, 1913. The 1913 parliament was rife with conflicts and power struggles, and a political consensus was more difficult to reach than ever. The Nationalists, bitter about the assassination of Song Jiaoren, regularly clashed with Yuan Shikai. The constitutionalists, wishing to form a party large enough to compete with the Nationalists, on May 29 combined the Democratic, Republican, and Unification Parties into a single party: the Progressive Party (Jinbudang).[71] Liang Qichao and the Progressive Party were in favor of a strong executive with a more centralized government. This was in contrast to the Nationalists, who wanted a stronger parliament and a weaker executive once Yuan had become the provisional president.[72] By the fall of 1913, Yuan Shikai had effectively suppressed the Nationalist-led insurrection against him, the Second Revolution. On October 6, with support from the Progressive Party, Yuan was elected president.[73] The struggle between Yuan and the Nationalists only intensified after that.

In October 1913, the completion of a new constitution known as the Temple Draft Constitution (Tiantan xiancao)—so named because the drafting committee met at the Temple of Heaven—further fueled the conflict. Defying Yuan Shikai's desire for the new constitution to extend the power of the president, the Constitution Draft Committee, dominated by Nationalist experts, had instead emphasized enlarging the power of the parliament, thus turning the president into a virtual figurehead.[74] Compared to the Provisional Constitution, the Temple Draft radically expanded the power of the legislative branch: first, a parliamentary standing committee was set up to exercise the power of the parliament when it was in recess; second, the parliament became the sole authority in interpreting the constitution; and third, the prerequisites for the parliament to impeach the president and the cabinet were lowered. Of these three items, the third was perhaps the most aggravating to Yuan Shikai.

Legal scholar Zhang Yongle gives an example to illustrate the overwhelming extent of legislative power according to the Temple Draft. The parliament could topple the president's cabinet if half of the attending members decided to do so; however, given that no quorum for parliament meetings was set and past practice was that meetings could be held if half of the parliament was present, in the most extreme case, a quarter of the parliament could oust a cabinet![75] The Temple Draft also further reduced the power of the president. During the drafting process, Yuan tried to negotiate with the committee about two particular presidential powers—the power to appoint the members of the State Council and the power to dismiss the parliament—but failed to get his way on either count. For example, the Temple Draft stipulated that the president could dismiss the parliament only if two-thirds of the senators agreed with him, virtually making this presidential right "meaningless."[76] As summed up by historian Yan Quan, the system under the Temple Draft was hardly a checks-and-balances system; rather, the legislative branch was disproportionally dominant to the extent that it was almost exclusive.[77]

Establishing a constitution that is accepted by *all* of the political elites is a difficult task. Building a constitutional state involves clearly defined limits on power; it requires that all players be willing to compromise to reach an agreement. Upon examination of the path by which the Provisional Constitution and the Temple Draft were created, we see political elites in early Republican China failing to create a system of checks and balances: the Provisional Constitution had been forced upon Yuan Shikai with no chance for him to take part in its creation, and the Temple Draft, though having been written with the nominal inclusion of Yuan in the discussion, did not give Beiyang the share of power it deserved. The Temple Draft in effect signaled the final break that ended the two parties' attempts at working together. Finally, in November 1913, Yuan Shikai, with consent from the Progressive Party, purged all Nationalist Party members from the parliament and in January 1914, Yuan dismissed the entire parliament.[78]

Within two short years, the union of China's political elites had collapsed. Before the end of the Qing, differences among elites about how to construct a constitutional state and who should have power in that state had been put aside. Their differences did not matter much so long as they had the common goal of opposing the absolute monarchy. However, once the Qing was gone, conflicts instantly came out into the open. The rhetoric of republicanism did not in and of itself provide a mechanism to resolve these conflicts. In fact, precisely because the revolution had been built upon a mass political culture that valorized "the people" as the only source of political authority, creating a functional state became even more difficult following the revolution, as now everyone could speak on behalf of the people and claim to fight for the people's rights. Chinese constitutionalists, though called "constitutionalists," were in truth revolutionaries who created that mass political culture but could not control it: the advocacy for constitutionalism, as demonstrated in Chapter 2, had primarily been used as a means for realizing popular sovereignty in the face of absolute monarchy. It was a revolutionary ideology rather than a program for effective state making.

The leading Chinese constitutionalists in November 1911 took the United States of America as their model, yet Chinese constitutionalism differed significantly from the American counterpart. First, unlike in the Anglo-American case, where there was already an existing and historical precedent for limiting and diffusing the power of the head of the state, and a functioning constitutional state—in England—that served as an example for the earliest American state builders; in China, as has been said, constitutionalism was a means for opposing an entrenched absolute monarchy and realizing popular sovereignty. In the process of the revolution, important parts of constitutionalism—limited government and checks and balances, for example—were ignored from the very beginning of political activism because of this priority.

Also, related to this, the Founding Fathers of the United States tempered their understanding of popular sovereignty with concern about the potential dangers of majority rule.[79] The constitution they wrote was in many ways antimajoritarian, since they worried not just about the tyranny of the king but also about the tyranny of the majority, with both understood to be potential threats to constitutionalism. In China, however, "the people" were conceptualized into a necessary political discourse for activism, and "the people' rights" mattered only when it could mobilize people. As demonstrated in the course of the 1911 Revolution, minorities were readily deprived of their rights, and that was considered perfectly legitimate as long as the majority of the people agreed. Like their French counterpart, their concern was not about protecting the rights of every individual but about opposing the absolute monarchy.

These dilemmas persisted. In 1916, after the death of Yuan Shikai, the parliament first seated in 1913 was back in action; meanwhile, the Constitution Draft Committee resumed its regular meetings. To avoid factional struggles along party lines, both the Nationalists and the Progressives chose to dissolve themselves. The key members of the Progressive Party reorganized themselves into the Constitution Research Group (Xianfa yanjiu hui), whereas the Nationalists broke into several smaller political organizations. Still, the individuals who had previously belonged to the two parties could not reach an agreement. They fought unremittingly, this time mainly over the issue of how the central government and the provincial governments should relate to each other. The clash became increasingly physical, with pens, paperweights, and ink boxes flying across the meeting hall.[80]

Another chance for China to practice constitutionalism and parliamentary politics briefly emerged in 1917, when political events of that year enabled the constitutionalists to garner more power. In parliament, the Constitution Research Group gave Prime Minister Duan Qirui much-needed support for his decision to declare war against Germany. In July, when Xuzhou warlord Zhang Xun attempted a coup d'état to restore Puyi, the last emperor, the Constitution Research Group stood by Duan, and together they prevailed. Liang Qichao suggested to Duan that he dismiss the parliament and call for new elections, a move that required setting up a temporary senate to serve until the new parliament was ready. However, to Liang's great disappointment, Duan manipulated the senate election by having provincial electors vote for his personal faction, the Anfu clique. In the senate election in November 1917, the Constitution Research Group suffered a bitter defeat at the hands of the Anfu clique.[81]

By 1918, an increasing number of China's political elite, Liang Qichao included, had come to believe that constitutionalism and parliamentary politics would not work for China.[82] A dozen years after the late Qing constitutional reform, China found itself with three forces in play: a politically active citizenry, an insurgent military, and a divided political elite. The failure of the political elite to find a consensus and to keep the military in check essentially led to the decline of the republican state. Despite having experimented with constitutional politics since 1906, China still lacked a permanent constitution, a potent parliament, and a working republican state. As Pu Dianjun put it several years later when reflecting on this period, "We brought about the triumph of a fake republic."[83]

Conclusion

By inventing a new mass political culture utilizing the idea of rights and popular sovereignty, the political elites were able to mobilize the previously marginalized people to join the movement and oppose the old regime. This mass mobilization empowered people in new ways, which was most effective in overthrowing the Qing, but people also became intoxicated by the idea that they all had power and all deserved to assert their power and will in the political arena. In fact, this new culture made it even more difficult for competing factions to resolve their differences, as it encouraged people to fight for their rights to the fullest extent.

Although successful in helping to depose the Qing, that revolutionary political culture did not possess the resources to resolve the various differences that had long existed. A change in focus from revolutionary mobilization to constitutional state making did not occur in early Republican China. Building a functional constitutional state required that all of the aspiring political leaders in postrevolutionary China be prepared to concede some degree of their newly acquired power, since the key features of constitutionalism—limited government and checks and balances—demand that no single government agency have too much power. This, however, was not the desire or goal of our 1911 players. The seeds of discord were already planted.

Conclusion

THE LEGACY OF THE 1911 REVOLUTION

For the Chinese constitutionalists, the ending of the 1911 Revolution was a particularly unfulfilling one. Was the revolution a success or a failure? Did the revolution have an impact beyond its short-lived mobilization? What was the legacy of the revolution? These troubled questions have haunted students of the 1911 Revolution for more than a hundred years. The 1911 Revolution included all manner of actors, from high-level administrators in Beijing to local Gowned Brothers and militiamen in rural Sichuan, and from famous revolutionaries like Sun Yat-sen to cultural figures such as the vernacular opera performer Yang Sulan, who helped sing the revolution into existence. A revolution might fail in the most narrow, political sense, but despite its failure, it can still have lasting effects and set in motion major political change.

The 1911 Revolution occurred within the context of the wider political transformations that were playing out at the end of the Qing dynasty. In 1900, Chinese elites were still dutifully serving their emperor in Beijing, providing him with resources and maintaining his monarchical legitimacy; in 1912, these same elites became advocates of the political principles embodied by a newborn republic. By the end of the revolutionary decade, they had learned a new political discourse: the concept of rights had gained currency, ideologies of equality and political participation had challenged the traditional cosmology of hierarchy and harmony, and mass propaganda had been deployed as a powerful tool for political change. The revolution had demonstrated the mobilizing potential of democratic republicanism and mass nationalism. Marking the rise of a new political consciousness, thousands of men and women gained firsthand experience in the public arena: they talked, read, and listened in new ways; they voted, protested, and joined political parties.

The 1911 Revolution was a fundamental political change spearheaded by new ideas about rights (*quan, quanli, minquan*, and *guoquan*), equality (*pingdeng*), and popular sovereignty (*minzhu, zhuquan zai guomin, guomin zhi zhuquan*, and *minquan*), which furnished a powerful stimulus for the Chinese elite to abandon the old imperial order. A defining feature of the revolution was the creation of a rhetoric that centered on rights and a political repertoire that included mass media, speeches, demonstrations, and public meetings. The filtering of the revolutionary experience through the media created a new community, transforming how politics was conducted. Looking at the 1911 Revolution through the lens of political culture reveals the crucial role played by the constitutionalists. Contrary to the dominant tendency in the historiography of the 1911 Revolution to focus on the Tongmenghui, this book instead has foregrounded the popularity of constitutional reform among the Chinese gentry. In the two decades leading up to the collapse of the Qing, it was this group of men who mobilized political activism; fostered the learning, translation, and promulgation of the new, revolutionary ideas; and created schools, legal codes, and mechanisms to transform Chinese society in accordance with those ideas. Their potential as a political constituency capable of turning one way or another was contingent on the circumstances they faced. During the revolutionary turmoil in 1911, the movement leaders in Sichuan, who were counted among the constitutionalists, voiced an alternative legitimacy to that of the old regime, created a new, democratic political culture, and gave life to the revolution.

The revolution had a mixed legacy. That the Chinese constitutionalists failed to establish a constitutional order had much to do with the ways the revolution unfolded. To begin with, Chinese constitutionalists had their own understanding of constitutionalism. For them, constitutionalism was a means to achieve popular sovereignty. It was aimed not necessarily at establishing a limited government but at strengthening state power, on the condition that the state would be led by them, or that sovereignty would lie with them. In reflecting the assertion that "constitutional politics is the politics of public opinion," they sought to rely on "public opinion" to achieve constitutionalism.[1] During the revolution, claiming to represent the people, these leaders' exercise of power was often unlimited and oppressive, and the valorization of "public opinion" spawned further scrambles for public office, with all contenders maintaining that they embodied the people. After the revolution, movement leaders were neither able to reach a consensus about the setup of the new state, nor to control the military or local powers once the Qing was deposed. The revolution failed to build a viable, constitutional state; however, the core of revolutionary experience, that is, the emergence of a new, democratic political culture, has survived.

Rather than attempting to determine long-term social and economic origins or outcomes, this book has concentrated on identifying the source of unity in the revolutionary process. From a consideration of the various types of power that arose in the revolution, it is clear that socioeconomic interests were an important part of the story, but they were not the decisive factor. Movement leaders held that every person was a citizen of the nation, and that rhetoric effectively mobilized multitudes to join the revolution, making the experience of the revolution all the more dramatic and all the more drastic.

. . .

The interaction of structure and ideas is an underlying theme of the story told in this book. To be concrete, up until 1900, although the effectiveness of the old regime had been challenged, neither elites nor commoners had called into question the political principle of imperial China. For example, in 1875, when Yuan Tingjiao rebelled against the gentry and landowners (*shenliang*) in Dongxiang, he talked about "clearing the emperor's name" and "restoring the emperor's rule." In 1897, the flamboyant Dayi Gowned Brother Yu Dongchen rose up to "repel the foreigners and restore the Qing." While Yu and his cohorts began questioning the Manchus' otherness, they did not question the sacredness of the emperorship or the legitimacy of the old regime. As influential as Yu was, he collaborated with the local officials and elites without questioning the justice of the local power structure. The old pattern of legitimacy survived, and fate was in the hands of Heaven, not his own.

Endorsement of the old regime was also natural for the elite. Chinese elites gained their status and prestige from the state. They were neither agents of self-governance nor representatives of the people. Up until the early 1890s, they had been willing to partner with the state in return for access to the limited number of official positions, and confirmation of local elite status through degrees, honorifics, and privileges of all kinds. This partnership with the state was also evident in their all-important role in negotiating and collecting the taxes that the dynasty relied on for its sustenance. In Sichuan, *shenliang* and local officials determined administration and shared control of local society. Tension and conflict arising between them did sometimes function as stimuli for change, but the maximal returns secured by the *shenliang* under the existing system blunted their desire to alter the status quo. They had no respect for insurgents like Yuan Tingjiao who rose up to correct the evils of the old regime; that is, the *shenliang*, with the acquiescence of local officials, cheated and imposed extra taxes on peasants, asserting that Yuan deserved to "die more than ten thousand times," for he had shown the "greatest defiance and had no basic morality."

Missionary cases seriously challenged and stressed the old regime in the 1890s. In Sichuan, local officials shared with elites and commoners' repugnance for Christians and animosity against foreign missionaries. Despite the solidarity Sichuan officials achieved with the *shenliang* and the Gowned Brothers, imperial orders from Beijing threw them into a quandary. They had to obey Beijing to maintain their posts, but as they did so, their alliance with the *shenliang* was collapsing. It was in moments like these that the local Sichuanese lost their trust in the state, and over time their support of the Qing eroded. The missionary cases left the alliance between local officials and the elite shaken, while a new alliance—between the *shenliang* and the Gowned Brothers, as demonstrated by the Yu Dongchen Rebellion—grew stronger.

While local power structures were being renegotiated, new ideas also came to Sichuan. In the 1900s, the passionate writings of "Mr. New People," Liang Qichao, spread across the province. In essence, Liang's writings offered a new discourse on rights. Through them, ideas such as equality, the people's rights, and popular sovereignty became known among a new generation of Sichuanese. The sense of ownership in public affairs, the belief that the people were stakeholders in the polity, and the notion of political participation also became prevalent and gained popularity. Before long, statements that "all were masters of the nation" were chanted in many classrooms across Sichuan, propelling students to see politics in new and different ways. Among them, a democratic impulse and a desire for equality were rising.

In one of the most influential constitutionalist essays of this period, Liang Qichao compared the state to a company, and citizens to owners, not employees. The Chinese people seem to have read Liang's analogy of citizenship as ownership as the literal truth. Before this, Chinese subjects, especially the Confucian gentry, would have conceded that although the emperor had no "right" to rule, all under Heaven belonged to him. Landowners held land and other forms of wealth at the emperor's sufferance. This, together with a shared set of hierarchical values keyed to obligation and obedience, protected the money in one's own pocket and the flow of taxes to the capital. But now the state wanted more than was customary in terms of wealth, and citizens wanted more power from the state than it was accustomed to giving. This new circumstance made what had been an obligation a right and what had been informal, formal.

It is important to note that the concept of rights was inclusive of political as well as economic rights. Economic considerations were of particular importance in understanding how the commitment of the state to modernizing China (e.g., dominating railway development in Sichuan and elsewhere) and its attempts to accommodate foreign interests in the meantime, in order to gain breathing space for its own development (e.g., yielding to Western demands in railway investment), led large numbers of gentry in a relatively isolated province like Sichuan to become constitutionalists and then revolutionaries, who could deploy ideas like the people's rights and equality with confidence and abandon.

The political terms were new, but they well described the mounting challenges the Sichuan elite faced. In the Sichuan political vernacular, the cry was not "no taxation without representation" but rather "no taxation without supervision." The expense of developing railways, police forces, and schools had led statist reformers to centralize and formalize taxation, thus running roughshod over gentry-landlord interests and the past practice of negotiating taxes in ways that balanced elite interests with those of the dynasty. The elite wanted back into the political process, and constitutional reform—which relied on formal institutions rather than informal connections—appeared to be a means of ensuring that. For the elite, constitutionalism was a new path between old-style protests escalating to open rebellions on the one hand, and long-standing expressions of loyalty to a dynasty now at the end of its run on the other. In the case of railways, if Sichuan was to have railways and pay for them via taxes or investment capital, then Sichuanese—that is, the elite—should control and supervise them. Private ownership, as long as the people—or some subset of the people—of Sichuan were the owners, was considered more trustworthy than national ownership that lacked local supervision.

Establishing the Provincial Assembly was an important formative event in the emergence of the revolution in Sichuan. In their clashes with the new tax bureaus, the Sichuan elite found a way to address the principle of popular sovereignty as they refined their ideas and rhetoric. "No taxation without supervision" became a key notion that helped pave the way for the railway movement that was to come. In the course of their economic and political struggles against the state, the Sichuan elite also became increasingly influential, consolidating their political power in the Provincial Assembly and in the Chuan-Han Railway Company, where the reins of the economy were in their hands. After the assembly meeting, a strong constituency was formed through this convergence of social, political, and economic powers. The free-floating political ideas that had been in circulation for years among the disaffected Sichuan elite finally coalesced into a formidable political movement.

When the revolution came to Sichuan in the summer of 1911, the leaders of the movement in Chengdu wielded the rhetoric of rights as a weapon and quickly deployed the political repertoire that had already been practiced in the Provincial Assembly—meetings, speech making, newspaper propagandizing—to mobilize supporters. On occasion, revolutionary leaders employed familiar cultural symbols from the past to stimulate people's emotions and at times appropriated traditional values such as loyalty (*zhong*) and righteousness (*yi*) to give people a sense of moral purpose. But more important, new concepts such as the rights of the nation, constitutionalism, and the rights of the people circulated in Sichuan. Sichuanese learned to organize, propagandize, apply peaceful yet firm tactics to achieve their goals, and articulate their opinions on national and public affairs. These experiences gave them a taste of what it was like to participate in politics, an understanding of political equality, and growing confidence in their ability to give voice to a new political authority.

Springing from the political elite's desire to establish a constitutional government and maintain economic interests, the 1911 Sichuan Revolution was more than an old-style protest. During the revolution, the pressing need to mobilize commoners was the impetus for the creation of a new, democratic political culture. As the revolution continued, radicalization was engendered by the constitutionalists, and their actions diverged from their originally proposed goals. The initial discourse about rights was augmented with slogans of equality, freedom, republicanism, and self-governance. The people in Sichuan were encouraged to learn about these new ideas, identities, and modes of collective action. As a result, they left a long-lasting impact on the working of modern Chinese politics.

. . .

To be sure, the immediate outcome of the 1911 Revolution was not a triumph. The revolution achieved its goal of overthrowing the monarchy, but deposing the Qing did not give birth to a functioning constitutional republic. The secret to making a republic work is not the promulgation of a radical political discourse but the channeling of the energy of the citizens into stable institutions. In recent years, legal scholars in China have returned to this important topic and reflected on the failure of Chinese constitutionalism. Zhang Yongle, for example, emphasizes above all the prerequisite of a viable state as the foundation for a working constitutional order. He notes the conditions militating against China establishing a viable state following the collapse of the Qing: the uncontrollable military, the encroaching imperialist powers, and the breakdown of the relationship between the central and the local governments. In addition to these material reasons, he attributes the miscarriage of constitutionalism to the political elite's failure to achieve a consensus when drafting constitutions.[2]

Indeed, the inability of the political elite to reach agreement on the basic structure of the state had been a long-running theme in China's constitutional history. Between 1906 and 1911, Qing central officials and the provincial elite disagreed, and the Qing's resistance to the idea of constitutional monarchy gave rise to the elite's demand for republicanism. In 1913, the failure of the Progressives and the Nationalists to reach an accord in effect led to the failure of the parliament. In 1917, as another chance for China to achieve parliamentary politics briefly emerged, the former Progressives and Nationalists were still unable to work together, and the new military strongman Duan Qirui manipulated the senate election to advance his Anfu clique. After 1918, as parliamentary politics was losing popularity among politically minded Chinese, a new political ideal, that is, the politics of the masses, became the more appealing alternative. Mass movement and socialism, as Li Dazhao articulated in his 1918 seminal article "The Victory of the Masses," became the future for China.[3]

While scholars like Zhang Yongle correctly point out the material and structural reasons for the failure of constitutionalism in China, this book stresses instead the democratic impulse and the fixation on popular sovereignty—which again led to the obsession with expanding the power of the legislative branch—of the Chinese constitutionalists. The greatest number of Chinese constitutionalists studied at Hōsei University in Japan, where they were educated in the French political tradition, infused with concepts such as equality, rights, and popular sovereignty. It was these radical, egalitarian values rather than the mediated, hierarchical ones of mainstream Japanese constitutionalism that shaped their imagining of a Chinese constitutionalism. Contrary to the tenets in the Meiji Constitution (1889), which emphasized the authority of the emperor and claimed that "sovereignty lies with the emperor," constitutional law professor Minobe Tatsukichi taught Hōsei's Chinese students that constitutionalism was first of all to realize freedom and equality.[4] Sovereignty, he insisted, must reside with the people. Being a liberal, he viewed constitutionalism as "the politics of public opinion," and as a corollary, he emphasized the importance of a parliament in the polity and at times equated constitutionalism with "a political system that has a parliament."[5]

Tang Hualong, Song Jiaoren, Pu Dianjun, Wang Jingwei, Shen Junru, Yang Du, and Ju Zheng, to name but a few leading Chinese constitutionalists and legal talents in the Tongmenghui camp, were all trained at Hōsei. Forty-eight chairs, vice-chairs, and resident representatives of the provincial assemblies and twenty-one national assemblymen among the core group of the late Qing constitutionalists had studied at Hōsei.[6] In addition, the most important of the early Republican lawmakers, who created the Provincial Constitution, had also been trained there.[7] The training at Hōsei coincided with Liang Qichao's widespread idea that "people are the masters of a nation" and reinforced Liang's argument that constitutionalism is a means for realizing popular sovereignty. These students came back to their home provinces and disseminated knowledge about constitutionalism to the rest of the educated elite. They brought back with them the principles of democracy and popular sovereignty, but far less of the administrative know-how for running a constitutional state, or the values of separation of powers or limited government.

The experience of studying in Japan, in addition to a tradition of elite activism, created a Chinese constitutionalism that was full of contradictions. While claiming to represent the people, Chinese constitutionalists were the most aggressive agents in imposing state-building projects on local communities. Deploying the rhetoric of rights, Sichuan constitutionalists took over the railway company but ended up demanding more taxes from the people. Legitimized by the late Qing constitutional reform, these constitutionalists strove to be power holders in the newly enhanced state. As the movement became ever more radical, the demand for constitutionalism shrank. After 1911, the same, persistent focus on popular sovereignty and the role of the legislature also helped explain the troubled process of building constitutionalism in early Republican China. Historian Zhang Yong, for example, demonstrates that both the Provisional Constitution and the Temple Draft embodied the spirit of parliamentarism of the French Third Republic; both placed the parliament in a supreme position and considerably limited the power of the executive branch.[8] The French emphasis on the power of the legislature, though better able to speak to the hearts of the Chinese constitutionalists, also included aspects that were not conducive to the making of a viable, working constitutional republic.

. . .

As messy and unfulfilling as the immediate outcome of the 1911 Revolution was, the people of China subsequently lived under a republican government. From 1912 onward, notwithstanding political turmoil, factionalism, civil wars, invasions, and revolutions, the polity of China has remained, at least in name, republican. Whether it was the Beiyang warlords, the Nationalists, or the Communists in power, selections of the head of state have invariably been "by the people," and the popular will of the nation has steadfastly remained the declared basis of state sovereignty. The mantra "liberation of the people from the yoke of the Qing," combined with the newly embraced concepts of political rights and self-determination, led to the emergence of an unprecedented political and moral force—"the people"—as a recognizable political constituency. This was, in effect, the birth of modern politics in China: the establishment of the ideal and the discourse that the state should be built for "the people" and that "the people" should have sovereignty over the state (Figure CON.1).

FIGURE CON.1. In Memory of the Martyrs of the Railway Protection Movement. Photo taken by the author in 2004. Monument erected in 1913 in Chengdu, located in today's Renmin gongyuan (The People's Park) at the center of the city. The caption reads "Monument to commemorate the death and sacrifice for the Sichuan Railway Protection matter in the fall of 1911."

The 1911 Revolution changed Chinese political culture in ways that were irrevocable. The revolution shows that the value of rights was often protean, fungible, and translatable, but while being translatable it was still accruing momentum, and while subsiding, it still had the potential to erupt like a volcano at the right moment. After the revolution, a new polity emerged in China, and in that new polity, the principle of popular sovereignty and the ideas, lexicon, symbols, and rituals of republicanism became widespread in Chinese society. Even though politicians oftentimes manipulated republican rhetoric to pursue interests of their own that were far from the noble principles they espoused, rather than simply labeling Chinese republicanism as "fake" and proffering as evidence a handful of short-lived examples, it is more illuminating to analyze the impact of republican values in the *longue durée*.[9] Political change is often preceded by an ideological paradigm shift. The establishment of democracy is often a process spearheaded by a new conceptual framework, and its content remains to be gradually filled.

Furthermore, if we view the political transformation in 1911 in the longer time frame of twentieth-century Chinese revolutions, we see that the concept of rights rather than obligations is a paradigm shift that began among the elite but continued to gradually take root in the broader population. That shift laid the foundation for the subsequent popular revolutions in twentieth-century China. It is precisely the emphasis on equality and popular sovereignty that deepened the revolution's hold further down in Chinese society, leading to the ultimate success of mass movement in China. A consistent theme running through constitutional reform, the 1911 Revolution, the Campaign to Defend the Republic, the Nationalist Revolution, the Communist Revolution, and finally, the Cultural Revolution, was a fundamental belief that "the people are the masters of the nation." For many political leaders and activists, ideas about equality and rights were central to the values and expectations that shaped their intentions and actions.

Thus, when we look at what the 1911 Revolution brought to the people of China, we see a sea change resulting from new ideas and practices that transformed perceptions about government and the role of the state. The revolution established the mobilizing potential of democratic republicanism. During the revolution, more Chinese learned about their rights and their power and learned to deploy a new repertoire of protest. The language of preserving the nation, the gestures of equality and fraternity, and the emotion-filled songs and public parades were not soon forgotten. The repertoire of movement politics and the values of promoting national and popular sovereignty, rights, and the rule of law would not easily disappear. A revolution attracts people's enthusiasm in an exhilarating way. It connects the elite with commoners, shakes people's prior beliefs, and destabilizes old lifestyles. It creates powerful stories and puts on a good show on open streets, and in doing so touches people's hearts and exerts a profound impact. Through movements like this, key notions fundamental to modern Chinese politics were spread among a larger group of Chinese people for the first time. After 1911, political institutions had to be based on a new form of legitimacy, and new political values continued informing Chinese politics and setting discursive rules for it. Even though the new political language has been appropriated, subverted, and distorted by various powers, the legacy of the 1911 Revolution remains. After the revolution, China has never again been the same.

Appendix
THE PU FAMILY OF GUANG'AN COUNTY

广安蒲氏族人身分表（第七世以降）

辈行·支派	名	生殁年	身份	辈行·支派	名	生殁年	身份	
(7)	应现	1633-1671			春澍	1830-?	廪贡生	
	恺	1634-1697	明儒生	(13) III	春铭	1835-1879	进士	
	性	1666-1746	明儒生	III	春泽	1837-?	从九品	
(8) III	遇贵	1662-1729	业儒	III	绍昆	1857-?	库生	
IV	遇霖	1677-1746	监生	(14) I	绍楷	1833-1901	附贡生	
(9) III	葵	1683-1749	武生	III	绍诚	1814-1864	监生	
(10) III	永盛	1706-1768	增生	III	绍桢	1832-?	监生	耆员
III	永信	1714-1805	库生	III	绍宸	1837-?	库生	
III	永智	1730-1764	业儒	III	绍谦	1843-1891	增生	
IV	永宗	1737-1774	业儒	III	绍洋	1818-1879	监生	
(11) III	景	1731-1797	业儒	III	绍璁	1850-1909	监生	
III	元	1744-?	业儒	III	绍琦	1873-?	监生	
III	全	1748-1821	业儒	(15) I	金门	1869-?	监生	
III	春	1738-1764	业儒	III		1880-?		试名云卿

Ⅲ	昺	1747-1797		业儒		金吾	1852-1909	廪生	业儒
Ⅲ	香	1773-1850		耆员	Ⅱ	金柩	1838-1872	例贡生	
(12) Ⅱ	坤才	1763-1845	职员		Ⅲ	金品	1845-1897	从九	
Ⅱ	坤植	1769-1837	职员		Ⅲ	金琳	1855-1898	监生	
Ⅱ	坤焘	1778-1831	监生		Ⅲ	金瑗	1859-?	庠生	
Ⅲ	坤晋	1804-1839	庠生		Ⅲ	金鹏	1859-?	监生	
(13) Ⅰ	盛春	1827-1896	监生		Ⅲ	金科	1867-?	监生	
Ⅱ	成春	1813-1872	监生		Ⅲ	金峤	1863-?	监生	
Ⅲ	正春	1778-1846	监生		Ⅲ	金槐	1849-?	庠生	业儒
Ⅲ	洪春	1795-1835	庠生		Ⅲ	金麒	1836-1909	庠生	
Ⅲ	晋春	1818-1879	监生		Ⅲ	金琛	1840-1902	监生	
Ⅲ	宇春	1837-1883	监生		Ⅲ	金麟	1844-?	岁贡生	
Ⅲ	含春	1793-1866		业儒	Ⅲ	金万	1869-?	举人	
Ⅲ	象春	1796-1880	恩贡生		Ⅲ	金彤	1871-1904	庠生	
Ⅲ	锦春	1823-1864	廪生		(16) Ⅲ	殿俊	1876-1934	进士	
Ⅲ	鋼春	1826-1864	从九品						

表 I 广安蒲氏族人身分表（第七世以降）

辈行/支派	名	身份	配	女
(7)	恺	[明]儒生		长适庠生陈靖
(8) Ⅲ	裙贯	业儒		长适庠生李拱极
Ⅳ	裙橚	（监生）		（次适修职郎刘海）
(9) Ⅲ	荸	武生	监生武善政生	适考廉邓简临长子以仁
(10) Ⅰ	永长		增生骆国彦次女	
Ⅲ	永信	庠生	庠生胡璧三女	
Ⅲ	永年		贡士姜谱文三女	
Ⅲ	永三		河南永亭县知县合阳张玉龄孙女	长适江南华亭县知县李源长孙宗絮次适台湾副将丁豢孙耀先
Ⅲ	永明		继配品邑庠生郑纯修女	
Ⅲ	永智	业儒	岳邑监生任职重三女	长适贵州龙泉县知县刘元主子贡生刘人桂
Ⅲ	永聪		刘谈次女云南蒙化府普理塘千总刘广聪妹继配合阳吏员杨文英妹	
Ⅲ	永眷			次适大竹县原任湖北当阳知县黄仁三适太学生杨广信
Ⅲ	永哲			
Ⅳ	永宗	业儒	廪生杨天俞长女	长适庠生邓仁滋
Ⅳ	永亮		监生显锺长女	

(11) III	景		贡生王亮女，继配山西绛县城县知县南充宋时平孙女	
III	全	业儒	监生徐士通六女	
III	岗	业儒	监生郭县长女	次适顺庆千聪张杭子士俊
III	昱	业儒	山东济南府掖县分县邓以伊四女	
III	晙		太学生朱兴宗长女	三适监生李尚品
III	映		顺庆千总张杭五姝	
IV	瀛		廪生黎寿女	适诰封奉直大夫杜绍顺
IV	济			
IV	政			
(12) II	坤琇		太学生郑人敏次女	次适庠生周范岐
III	坤秀		庠生杨长宁三女	适庠生贺代盛
III	坤维		成都什邡县教论渠县雷思愁女	
III	坤佐		监生袁伸女	
III	坤兴		庠生刘履清四女	适庠生周克宽
III	坤轼			
III	坤荣		诰授修职郎熊光远三女	次适廪生杜云铭

(continued)

表 I 广安浦氏族人身分表（第七世以降）

辈行-支派		身份	配	女
III		坤芳	庠生凌秀屏次女	适庠生丁鼎臣
III		坤晋	庠生	
(13) I		盛春	太学生	次适庠生邓建业
III		洪春	太学生	长适同知衔舒人吉，次适监生王天年，三适监生李明德
III		桂春	庠生杜芳次女	
III		孚春	太学生	长适监生陈聘三，次适优贡生周兑壁次子
III		含春	业儒	
III		春泽	从九·让叙盐大使	庠生周之瀚女	
(14) II		绍芝		

Source: Masao Nishikawa, "Shisenshō kōanken bibōroku: Shinmatsu minkoku shoki no kyōshin" [Notes on Guang'an county of Sichuan province: Gentry of the late Qing and early Republican China], *Kanazawa Daigaku Bungakubu Bungakubu ronshū shigaku-ka hen*, no. 15 (1995): 83–92. Historian Xu Yao modified and combined Nishikawa's charts into this current one. Xu Yao, "Guang'an Pushi zuren shenfen biao" [Identity chart of the Pu Family of Guang'an county], in "Qingmo de miaochan xingxue yundong: yi qingmo Sichuan difang wei zhongxin de yanjiu," (PhD diss., Sichuan University, 2008), 188–90. My special thanks to Xu Yao for sharing his table with me. Reprinted with permission.

Notes

INTRODUCTION

1. There are many intellectual historians who have studied the fluid and sometimes interchangeable concepts of *minquan* and *minzhu*. The first significant elite references to *minquan* and *minzhu* both appeared in Guo Songtao's diary, *London and Paris Diaries* (*Lundun yu Bali riji*), published in 1879. Guo was the first Chinese diplomat to live in Europe for an extended period of time, and when he described the democratic systems of government and the various forms of elections in the West, he used the phrase "the rule of the people" (*minzhu*) in opposition to "the rule of the monarch" (*junzhu*), and "the power of the people" (*minquan*) in opposition to "the power of the monarch" (*junquan*). *Minzhu* appeared in his entry from April 6, 1878, and *minquan* appeared in his entry from May 26, 1878. See Guo Songtao et al., *Lundun yu Bali riji*, in *Guo Songtao deng shixiji liuzhong* [Six diaries of the journey to the West by Guo Songtao and others] (Shanghai: Zhongxi shuju, 2012), 90 and 125.

Generally speaking, *minquan* has two meanings, "the power of the people" and "the rights of the people." Between 1895 and 1898, after the first Sino-Japanese War, *minquan* became a rallying cry, and the term was frequently used by intellectuals like Yan Fu, Kang Youwei, and Liang Qichao. During this time, *minquan* was understood in an anti-autocratic sense and more or less referred to the power of the people as a counterpart to *junquan*, the power of the emperor. In this sense, *minquan* was close to the same meaning of the term *minzhu*, "the rule of the people." After 1898, the Japanese word *minken* entered the Chinese political discourse, referring to "the political rights of the people." Because of the promotion of this term by intellectuals like Liang Qichao, the Chinese word *minquan* increasingly came to be used in this sense. Also due to influence by the Japanese intellectual environment, the Chinese character *quan* was used more frequently in the sense of rights (*quanli*) rather than simply power. *Minquan* more frequently referred to the political rights of the people. After the foundation of the Tongmenghui in 1905, Sun Yat-sen also used the term *minquan* in his revolutionary rhetoric. Sun's usage had a different sense, primarily referring to popular sovereignty. In this book, I pay particular attention to the meaning of the term by putting it in its specific context. As this work directly deals with the 1911 Revolution in Sichuan, I emphasize the meaning of *minquan* as it was understood and used in the context of the revolution, where it referred, most commonly, to the rights of the people.

Likewise, the term *minzhu* had a number of meanings when it was introduced to China. First, it referred to the rule of the people, as in the case of Ambassador Guo Songtao's first mention of the term. *Minzhu*, for Guo, meant the kind of rule in a particular political system. The second meaning of the term concerns the location of state sovereignty and carries the meaning of "popular sovereignty." The third meaning of the term refers to the head of the state, as in *minzhu lixian*, denoting a constitutional political system with the head of the state being elected by the people, or *junzhu lixian*, meaning "constitutional monarchy." For a comprehensive summary of the terms *minzhu* and *minquan* and bibliographical references, please contact Xiaowei Zheng for her article in progress, "On *Minquan* and *Minzhu*." *Guomin zhi zhuquan* and *zhuquan zai guomin* will be elaborated in Chapter 2.

Another important term in this book is "republicanism." "Republicanism" is used here as an ideology of being a citizen in a state as a republic under which the people hold popular sovereignty. Classical republicanism emphasizes that mixed government was an important element and that virtue and the common good were central to good government. In this sense, monarchy was compatible with republicanism. During the Enlightenment, antimonarchism extended beyond the civic humanism of the Renaissance. Liberalism and republicanism were frequently conflated during this period, because they both opposed absolute monarchy. Also in the late eighteenth century, there was convergence of democracy and republicanism. Democracy means "rule by the people." Republicanism is a system that replaces or accompanies inherited rule: there is an emphasis on equality and a rejection of corruption, which strongly influenced the American Revolution and the French Revolution in the 1770s and 1790s, respectively. A defining moment for the development of the concept of republicanism was the execution of Louis XVI on January 21, 1793. After that, modern republicanism could not be compatible with monarchy: in a republic, the head of the state could not be inherited rule, and republicanism held that kings and aristocracies were not the real rulers, but rather the whole people were. Noteworthy, exactly how the people were to rule was an issue of democracy; republicanism itself did not specify a means. My sincere thanks to Manuel Covo for the long conversations we had, which helped me tease out the meaning of these knotty terms.

2. In Dai Zhili, ed., *Sichuan baolu yundong shiliao huizuan* [Collection of historical materials on the Sichuan Railway Protection movement] (Taipei: Zhongyang yanjiuyuan jindaishi yanjiusuo, 1994), 695–729, 1015–79.

3. Wang Di, *Street Culture in Chengdu: Public Space, Urban Commoners, and Local Politics, 1870–1930* (Stanford, CA: Stanford University Press, 2003), 213. See also *Baolu tongzhihui baogao* (hereafter *Baogao*) [Newsletter of the Sichuan Railway Protection Association], no. 21, July 21, 1911.

4. "Mawang miao laodongzhe juankuan yuanshu" [Letter from laborers at the Mawang temple pledging to donate], *Baogao*, no. 33, August 14, 1911.

5. Zhao Erfeng, "Zhao Erfeng zhi Zhao Erxun shu jubu Pu Dianjun deng ji tongzhijun weigong Chengdu dian" [Telegram from Zhao Erfeng to Zhao Erxun on the capture of Pu Dianjun and others and the encirclement of Chengdu by railway protection armies], in Dai, ed., *Sichuan baolu yundong shiliao huizuan*, 1160.

6. In this book, the term "revolutionaries" refers to the people who participated in the revolutionary process. It is not necessarily limited to Tongmenghui or other anti-Manchu groups aiming to violently overthrow the dynasty, which is how

contemporaries were using the term. When discussing the Tongmenghui or other anti-Manchu revolutionaries, I use "anti-Manchu" to stress their racial sentiment. Also, in this book, the term "constitutionalists" refers to the political elites who actively campaigned for the establishment of a constitutional monarchy in Qing China. Many of these constitutionalists had been reform-minded scholar-officials who precipitated the Hundred Days' reform in 1898, then became earnest constitutionalists in the early twentieth century. As historian Hou Yijie observes, after the Russo-Japanese war, "the reformers had now changed their name to 'constitutionalists'" (see Chapter 2).

7. For the 1911 Revolution in Hubei and Hunan, see Joseph Esherick, *Reform and Revolution: The 1911 Revolution in Hunan and Hubei* (Berkeley: University of California Press, 1976).

8. Feng Feng, "Shaanxi junzhengfu yu xinhai geming" [The Shaanxi military government and the 1911 Revolution], in Zhongguo shixuehui, ed., *Jinian xinhai geming yibai zhounian guoji xueshu yantaohui lunwenji* [Papers commemorating the hundredth anniversary of the 1911 Revolution] (Wuhan: 2011), 347–55.

9. Li Xizhu, "Xinhai dingge zhiji defang dufu de chuchu jueze" [The course of action chosen by local governors in the 1911 Revolution], in Li Xizhu, *Difang dufu yu qingmo xinzheng: Wanqing quanli geju zai yanjiu* [Local governors and the New Policies reform: A further study of the power structure in the late Qing] (Beijing: Shehui kexue wenxian chubanshe, 2012), 424–25.

10. Zhang Pengyuan, *Lixianpai yu xinhai geming* [Constitutionalists and the 1911 Revolution] (Taipei: Zhongyang yanjiuyuan jindaishi yanjiusuo, 1969), 143–47.

11. Ibid., 159.

12. Zhang, *Lixianpai yu xinhai geming*, 151–57.

13. Li, "Xinhai dingge zhiji defang dufu de chuchu jueze," 420–21.

14. Ibid., 425.

15. Zhang, *Lixianpai yu xinhai geming*, 137–38.

16. Li, "Xinhai dingge zhiji defang dufu de chuchu jueze," 422–23.

17. Zhang, *Lixianpai yu xinhai geming*, 134–35.

18. Ibid., 160–61. See also Li, "Xinhai dingge zhiji defang dufu de chuchu jueze," 423–24.

19. Zhang, *Lixianpai yu xinhai geming*, 135–37.

20. Li, "Xinhai dingge zhiji defang dufu de chuchu jueze," 426.

21. "Zuzhi quanguo huiyi tuan tonggao shu" [Announcement for organizing a national United Convention], in Guojia tushuguan shanben bu, ed., *Zhao Fengchang cangzha* [A collection of Zhao Fengchang's letters] (Beijing: Guojia tushuguan chubanshe, 2009), vol. 3, 584.

22. Zhao Zunyue, "Xiyin tang xinhai geming ji" [Chronicle of Xiyin Hall's 1911 Revolution], in Jindaishi yanjiusuo jindaishi ziliao bianji bu, ed., *Jindaishi ziliao* [Sources on modern Chinese history] (Beijing: Zhongguo shehui kexue chubanshe, 2002), vol. 102, 246–57.

23. "Xuantong 3 nian 8 yue 27 ri neige fazhiyuan canyiyuan Wu Tingxie zouzhe" [Memorial by Wu Tingxie on October 18, 1911], in Zhongguo shixuehui,

ed., *Xinhai geming* [The 1911 Revolution] (Shanghai: Shanghai renmin chubanshe, 1957), vol. 5, 428.

24. "Zhang Jian zhi Tieliang han" [Letter from Zhang Jian to General Tieliang], in Zhang Kaiyuan, Luo Fuhui, and Yan Changhong, eds., *Xinhai gemingshi ziliao xinbian* [New compilation of historical documents on the 1911 Revolution] (Wuhan: Hubei renmin chubanshe), vol. 2, 46.

25. Winston Hsieh, *Chinese Historiography on the Revolution of 1911: A Critical Survey and a Selected Bibliography* (Stanford, CA: Hoover Institution Press, 1975).

26. Zou Lu's *Zhongguo guomindang shigao* [Draft history of the Chinese Nationalist Party], published in 1929, is a typical example of this interpretation. Even in collecting historical sources, activities of the Tongmenghui were the only consideration for these historians. For example, the source collections compiled by the Guomindang (GMD) on the Sichuan Revolution, *Zhongguo guomindang Sichuan dangshi cailiao* [The history of the GMD in Sichuan] and the collection *Shuzhong xianlie beizhenglu* [A record of the campaigns of Sichuan martyrs], trace only the activities of Tongmenghui members. As Winston Hsieh argues, this Sun-centered interpretation emerged when Sun urgently needed to build up his reputation. See Hsieh, *Chinese Historiography on the Revolution of 1911*, 18.

27. After Chiang Kai-shek came to power in 1928, this Sun-centered narrative became dominant. In the GMD's history books, Sun Yat-sen was described as the "father of the nation." When the Nationalists retreated to Taiwan, it became even more crucial to rely on the myth of Sun Yat-sen to restore legitimacy. The Communists also revered Sun Yat-sen as a "pioneer of the revolution," though in a more modest role than those of Marx, Lenin, and Mao Zedong. Sun was portrayed as the exclusive leader of the revolutionary movement up until the appearance of the Communist Party in 1921. See Marie-Claire Bergère, *Sun Yat-sen* (Stanford, CA: Stanford University Press, 2000), which demystifies Sun Yat-sen and his contributions to the Chinese revolution. Bergère maintains that the exaltation of Sun by the Communists was intended to create the basis for an entente with the Taiwan regime and prepare the way for the island's return to the mother country. Such a gesture was obvious in the 2011 Wuhan Conference on Commemorating the Centennial of the 1911 Revolution. In the official speeches about the 1911 Revolution, President Hu Jintao and President Ma Ying-jeou both credited Sun Yat-sen as the leader of the revolution, with Hu Jintao emphasizing Sun's role in "reviving the greatness of the Chinese nation" and Ma Ying-jeou emphasizing Sun's contribution to "leading China toward democracy." Both claimed that their party was the true heir of Sun.

28. Harold Schiffrin, *Sun Yat-sen and the Origins of the Chinese Revolution* (Berkeley: University of California Press, 1968). Schiffrin systematically challenges the "greatness" of Sun Yat-sen and critically interprets the first forty years of his life. See also K. S. Liew, *Struggle for Democracy: Sung Chiao-jen and the 1911 Chinese Revolution* (Berkeley: University of California Press, 1971); Michael Gasster, *Chinese Intellectuals and the Revolution of 1911: The Birth of Modern Chinese Radicalism* (Seattle: University of Washington Press, 1969); Mary Rankin, *Early*

Chinese Revolutionaries: Radical Intellectuals in Shanghai and Chekiang, 1902–1911 (Cambridge, MA: Harvard University Press, 1971); Zhang Yufa, *Qingji de geming tuanti* [Revolutionaries of the late Qing period: An analysis of groups in the revolutionary movement, 1894–1911] (Taipei: Zhongyang yanjiuyuan jindaishi yanjiusuo, 1982); and Joseph Esherick, "1911: A Review," *Modern China*, vol. 2, no. 2 (1976): 141–84.

29. Mao Zedong first argued in his article "Xin minzhu zhuyi lun" [On the new democratic revolution], "The 1911 Revolution was a great revolution, and . . . its failure lies in the weakness of the nationalist bourgeois class." After this claim, Wu Yuzhang's *Xinhai geming* [The 1911 Revolution], first written in 1960, was among the first historical works that defended the Maoist interpretation of the 1911 Revolution. This set the tone for the study of the 1911 Revolution in mainland China before the 1990s. The very comprehensive and high-quality historical works, such as Wei Yingtao's *Sichuan baolu yundong shi* [History of the Sichuan Railway Protection movement], Li Xin's *Zhonghua minguo shi* [History of Republican China], and Jin Chongji and Hu Shengwu's *Xinhai geming shigao* [Draft history of the 1911 Revolution] all make great efforts to examine the situation of the cities and the newly emergent bourgeoisie of China at that time. Wu Yuzhang, *Xinhai geming* (Beijing: Renmin chubanshe, 1960); Wei Yingtao, *Sichuan baolu yundong shi* (Chengdu: Sichuan renmin chubanshe, 1981); Li Xin, *Zhonghua minguo shi* (Beijing: Zhonghua shuju, 1981); and Jin Chongji and Hu Shengwu, *Xinhai geming shigao* (Shanghai: Shanghai renmin chubanshe, 1991).

30. Zhang Kaiyuan, "Xinhai geming de bainian xiasi" [Reflecting on the 1911 Revolution after one hundred years], in William Kirby and Zhou Yan, ed., *Bu queding de yichan: Hafo xinhai bainian luntan jiangyan lu* [Uncertain legacy: Harvard lectures on the 1911 Revolution after one hundred years] (Beijing: Jiuzhou chubanshe, 2012), 20. See Zhang Kaiyuan and Tian Tong, *Zhang Jian yu jindai shehui* [Zhang Jian and modern society] (Wuhan: Huazhong shifan daxue chubanshe, 2001); Ma Min, *Shangren jingshen de shanbian: Jindai Zhongguo shangren guannian yanjiu* [Transformation of the Chinese merchant spirit: Studies on modern Chinese merchant concepts] (Wuhan: Huazhong shifan daxue chubanshe, 2001); Zhu Ying, *Jindai Zhongguo shangren yu shehui* [Merchants and society in modern China] (Wuhan: Huazhong shifan daxue chubanshe, 2001); Yan Changhong and Xu Xiaoqing, *Guimao nian wansui: 1903 nian de geming sichao yu geming yundong* [Long live the year of Guimao: Revolutionary thought and movement in the year of 1903] (Wuhan: Huazhong shifan daxue chubanshe, 2001); and Luo Fuhui, *Xinhai geming shiqi de jingying wenhua yanjiu* [Study on the elite culture during the 1911 Revolution] (Wuhan: Huazhong shifan daxue chubanshe, 2001). See also Zhang Kaiyuan and Tian Tong, "Xin shiji zhichu de xinhai gemingshi yanjiu (2000–2009)" [Review of studies on the history of the 1911 revolution from 2000 to 2009], *Zhejiang shehui kexue*, no. 9 (2010): 89–93.

31. Chūzō Ichiko, "The Role of the Gentry: A Hypothesis," in Mary Wright, ed., *China in Revolution: The First Phase, 1900–1913* (New Haven, CT: Yale University Press, 1968). See also Mary Wright, introduction to *China in Revolution*; Joseph Esherick, *Reform and Revolution: The 1911 Revolution in Hunan*

and Hubei (Berkeley: University of California Press, 1976); and Edward Rhoads, *China's Republican Revolution: The Case of Kwangtung, 1895–1913* (Cambridge, MA: Harvard University Press, 1975). Other scholars of this group also help us understand elite activism of the late Qing: Mary Rankin, *Elite Activism and Political Transformation in China: Zhejiang Province, 1865–1911* (Stanford, CA: Stanford University Press, 1986); John Fincher, *Chinese Democracy: The Self-Government Movement in Local, Provincial, and National Politics (1905–1914)* (Canberra: Australian National University Press, 1981); and Keith Schoppa, *Chinese Elites and Political Change: Zhejiang Province in the Early Twentieth Century* (Cambridge, MA: Harvard University Press, 1982).

32. Mary Rankin, John Fairbank, and Albert Feuerwerker, "Introduction: Perspectives on Modern China's History," in John Fairbank and Albert Feuerwerker, eds., *Cambridge History of China* (Cambridge: Cambridge University Press, 1986), vol. 13, 9.

33. Ibid., 49–50.

34. Alexis de Tocqueville, *The Ancien Régime and the Revolution*, trans. Gerald Bevan (London: Penguin Classics, 2003).

35. Philip Kuhn, *Origins of the Modern Chinese State* (Stanford, CA: Stanford University Press, 2002), 43.

36. Other scholars adopting this approach include Li Enhan, "Wanqing shouhui liquan yundong yu lixian yundong" [The sovereignty-recovery movement and the constitutional movement in the late Qing], in Li Enhan, *Jindai Zhongguo shishi yanjiu lunji* [Articles on modern Chinese history] (Taipei: Taiwan shangwu yinshuguan, 1982), vol. 2, 84–100; Kristin Stapleton, *Civilizing Chengdu: Chinese Urban Reform, 1895–1937* (Cambridge, MA: Harvard University Press, 2000); and Li Xizhu, *Difang dufu yu qingmo xinzheng: Wanqing quanli geju zai yanjiu* [Local governors and the New Policies reform: A further study of the power structure of the late Qing] (Beijing: Shehui kexue wenxian chubanshe, 2012).

37. Joseph Levenson, *Confucian China and Its Modern Fate* (Berkeley: University of California Press, 1958). Starting from Benjamin Schwartz on Yan Fu, Jung-pang Lo and Hsiao Kung-chuan on Kang Youwei, and Chang Hao on Liang Qichao, luminary thinkers of the late Qing have received great attention from intellectual historians. In addition, both Wong Young-tsu and Charlotte Furth have published studies on Zhang Binglin. See Benjamin Schwartz, *In Search of Wealth and Power: Yen Fu and the West* (Cambridge, MA: Harvard University Press, 1964); Lo Jung-pang, ed., *K'ang Yu-Wei: A Biography and a Symposium* (Tucson: University of Arizona Press, 1967); Hsiao Kung-chuan, *A Modern China and a New World: K'ang Yu-wei, Reformer and Utopian, 1858–1927* (Seattle: University of Washington Press, 1975); Chang Hao, *Liang Ch'i-ch'ao and Intellectual Transition in China, 1890–1907* (Cambridge, MA: Harvard University Press, 1971); Tang Xiaobing, *Global Space and the Nationalist Discourse of Modernity: The Historical Thinking of Liang Qichao* (Stanford, CA: Stanford University Press, 1996); Joshua Fogel, ed., *Late Qing China and Meiji Japan: Political and Cultural Aspects* (Norwalk, CT: EastBridge, 2004); Wong Young-tsu, *Search for Modern Nationalism: Zhang Binglin and Revolutionary China, 1869–1936* (Hong Kong:

Oxford University Press, 1989); Charlotte Furth, "The Sage as Rebel: The Inner World of Chang Ping-lin," in Charlotte Furth, ed., *The Limits of Change: Essays on Conservative Alternatives in Republican China* (Cambridge, MA: Harvard University Press, 1976), 22–53. A comprehensive intellectual history regarding modern Chinese thought is the four-volume book of Wang Hui, *Xiandai Zhongguo sixiang de xingqi* [The rise of modern Chinese thought] (Beijing: Sanlian shudian, 2008).

38. Zhang Pengyuan, *Liang Qichao yu qingji geming* [Liang Qichao and the late Qing revolution] (Taipei: Zhongyang yanjiuyuan jindaishi yanjiusuo, 1982).

39. Joan Judge, *Print and Politics: "Shibao" and the Culture of Reform in Late Qing China* (Stanford, CA: Stanford University Press, 1997); Barbara Mittler, *A Newspaper for China? Power, Identity, and Change in Shanghai's News Media, 1872–1912* (Cambridge, MA: Harvard University Press, 2004); Juan Wang, *Merry Laughter and Angry Curses: The Shanghai Tabloid Press, 1897–1911* (Vancouver: University of British Columbia Press, 2012); and Peter Zarrow, "Anti-Despotism and 'Rights Talk': The Intellectual Origins of Modern Human Rights Thinking in the Late Qing," *Modern China*, vol. 34, no. 2 (2008): 179–209, *After Empire: The Conceptual Transformation of the Chinese State, 1885–1924* (Stanford, CA: Stanford University Press, 2012), and *Educating China: Knowledge, Society and Textbooks in a Modernizing World, 1902–1937* (Cambridge: Cambridge University Press, 2015).

40. Henrietta Harrison, *The Making of the Republican Citizen: Political Ceremonies and Symbols in China, 1911–1929* (New York: Oxford University Press, 2000); and David Strand, *An Unfinished Republic: Leading by Word and Deed in Modern China* (Berkeley: University of California Press, 2011).

41. The Foucauldian concept of eventalization, that is, the phenomenon in history whereby various dispersed elements and practices coalesce to the point at which they form an event or rupture, neatly encapsulates what I do in this study. "Eventalization means making visible a singularity at places where there is a temptation to invoke a historical constant, an immediate anthropological trait or an obviousness that imposes itself uniformly on all. . . . It means uncovering the procedure of causal multiplication: analyzing an event according to the multiple processes that constitute it." Michel Foucault, "Impossible Prison," in Michel Foucault, *Foucault Live: Interviews, 1966–84* (Los Angeles: Semiotext(e), 1996), 277.

42. Esherick, *Reform and Revolution*, 256.

43. Lynn Hunt, *Politics, Culture, and Class in the French Revolution* (Berkeley: University of California Press, 1984), 10–11.

44. Michel Foucault, *The Politics of Truth* (Los Angeles: Semiotext(e), 2007), 90.

45. Ibid.

46. Song Jiaoren, "Lun chuanren zhenglu shi" [On Sichuanese fighting for the railway], *Minlibao*, September 14, 1911, in Wei Yingtao, Li Youming, Li Runcang, Zhang Li, Liu Chuanying, and Zeng Shaomin, *Sichuan jindaishi* [History of modern Sichuan] (Chengdu: Sichuan shehui kexue chubanshe, 1985), 593.

47. *Xuxiu daxianzhi* [Continued Da county gazetteer], vol. 9, "Fengsu" [Customs], in Wei et al., *Sichuan jindaishi*, 595.

48. *Luxianzhi* [Lu county gazetteer], vol. 3, "Fengsu" [Customs], in Wei et al., *Sichuan jindaishi*, 595.

49. *Hechuanxianzhi* [Hechuan county gazetteer], vol. 25, "Zhengfa" [Politics and laws], in Wei et al., *Sichuan jindaishi*, 595.

50. Yunnan sheng zhengxie, ed., *Wenshi ziliao xuanji* [Selected personal histories of Yunnan province] (Kunming: Yunnan renmin chubanshe, 1982), vol. 4, 245.

CHAPTER 1. SICHUAN AND THE OLD REGIME

1. S. A. M. Adshead, *Province and Politics in Late Imperial China: Viceregal Government in Szechwan* (London: Curzon Press, 1984), 2.

2. Wang Di, *Kuachu fengbi de shijie: Changjiang shangyou quyu shehui yanjiu, 1644–1911* [Striding out of a closed world: A study of society in the upper Yangzi region, 1644–1911] (Beijing: Zhonghua shuju, 1993), 81. Wang Di believes that Sichuan's population in 1910 was forty-five million.

3. Shanhezidi, "Shuo juansheng" [On Sichuan], in Zhang Nan and Wang Renzhi, eds., *Xinhai geming qian shinian jian shilun xuanji* [Anthology of editorials from the decade before the 1911 Revolution] (Beijing: Sanlian shudian, 1963), vol. 2, 564.

4. Adshead, *Province and Politics*, 2.

5. Xiliang, *Xiliang yigao zougao* [Posthumous papers and memorials of Xiliang] (Beijing: Zhonghua shuju, 1959), vol. 1, 323 and 326.

6. Ferdinand von Richthofen, *Baron Richthofen's Letters 1870–1872*, 2nd ed. (Shanghai, 1903), 177, in Adshead, *Province and Politics*, 2.

7. *Report of the Mission to China of the Blackburn Chamber of Commerce 1896–1897* (Blackburn, 1898), 321, in Adshead, *Province and Politics*, 2–3.

8. Richthofen, *Baron Richthofen's Letters*, 206, in Adshead, *Province and Politics*, 5.

9. Adshead, *Province and Politics*, 3.

10. Richthofen, *Baron Richthofen's Letters*, 176, in Adshead, *Province and Politics*, 4.

11. Ibid., 164–65, in Adshead, *Province and Politics*, 4.

12. Alexander Hosie, *Report by Consul-General Hosie on the Province of Ssuch'uan*, in British Parliamentary Papers on China, no. 5 (1904), 4, in Adshead, *Province and Politics*, 4.

13. Wang, *Kuachu fengbi de shijie*, 35.

14. Deng Shaoqing, *Jindai chuanjiang hangyun jianshi*, 122, in Wang, *Kuachu fengbi de shijie*, 41.

15. Adshead, *Province and Politics*, 8.

16. Richthofen, *Baron Richthofen's Letters*, 163, in Adshead, *Province and Politics*, 6.

17. *Daqing jinshen quanshu* [Complete directory of the gentry of the great Qing] (Beijing: Ronglu tang, 1911 edition), vol. 1, 17a.

18. Richthofen, *Baron Richthofen's Letters*, 163, in Adshead, *Province and Politics*, 6.

19. Hosie, *Report by Consul-General Hosie on the Province of Ssuch'uan*, 28, in Adshead, *Province and Politics*, 6.

20. Adshead, *Province and Politics*, 6–7. See also William Skinner, "Marketing and Social Structure in Rural China: Part 1," *Journal of Asian Studies*, vol. 24, no. 1 (1964): 3–43.

21. Adshead (*Province and Politics*, 7) cites the population in 1900 as forty-five million; Wang Di (*Kuachu fengbi de shijie*, 80) gives the number as forty-one million in the same year.

22. Adshead, *Province and Politics*, 7.

23. Joseph Needham, *Science and Civilisation in China* (Cambridge: Cambridge University Press, 1954), vol. 4, 296, in Adshead, *Province and Politics*, 7.

24. Richthofen, *Baron Richthofen's Letters*, 173, in Adshead, *Province and Politics*, 9; Lothar von Falkenhausen, http://www.hsozkult.de/event/id/termine-5675.

25. In 1903 Governor-General Xiliang was behind the proposal to build a railway company and in 1908 Governor-General Zhao Erxun proposed buying steamships to strengthen Sichuan's links on the Yangzi River, both with the intention of developing the economy of the province.

26. Following Ch'ü T'ung-tsu in *Local Government in China Under the Ch'ing* (Cambridge, MA: Harvard University Press, 1962), I use the term "government" to encompass both formal and informal institutions. Formal government refers to the bureaucracy; informal government to the social institutions beyond the bureaucracy, including elite organizations as a mechanism of ruling.

27. A. C. Graham, *Disputers of the Tao: Philosophical Argument in Ancient China* (Chicago: Open Court, 1989), 1–8.

28. On the continuity of the bureaucratic state, see Étienne Balazs, *Chinese Civilization and Bureaucracy: Variations on a Theme* (New Haven, CT: Yale University Press, 1964). Yuri Pines has a series of writings on Qin political thought and its imperial descendants. Yuri Pines, *Envisioning Eternal Empire: Chinese Political Thought of the Warring States Era* (Honolulu: University of Hawai'i Press, 2009), and Pines, *The Everlasting Empire: The Political Culture of Ancient China and Its Imperial Legacy* (Princeton, NJ: Princeton University Press, 2012).

29. Graham, *Disputers of the Tao*, 315.

30. Zhao Dingxin, *The Confucian-Legalist State: A New Theory of Chinese History* (Oxford: Oxford University, 2015), 277–78.

31. S. N. Eisenstadt, "Frederic Wakeman's Oeuvre in the Framework of World and Comparative History," in Frederic Wakeman Jr., *Telling Chinese History: A Selection of Essays* (Berkeley: University of California Press, 2009), xii–xiii.

32. Ibid., xiii.

33. Ibid.

34. Yan Buke, *Shidafu zhengzhi yansheng shigao* [A history of the development of scholar-officials] (Beijing: Beijing daxue chubanshe, 1996), 491.

35. Ibid., 448.

36. Ibid., 22 and 468.

37. Thomas Barfield, *The Perilous Frontier: Nomadic Empires and China 220 BC to AD 1757* (Oxford: Blackwell, 1989), ix. See also Jinping Wang, "Between

Family and State: Networks of Literati, Clergy, and Villagers in Shanxi, North China, 1200–1400" (PhD diss., Yale University, 2011).

38. Peter Bol, *Neo-Confucianism in History* (Cambridge, MA: Harvard University Press, 2008), 272–73.

39. Ibid., 273–75.

40. Hok-lam Chan and Wm. Theodore de Bary, eds., *Yuan Thought: Chinese Thought and Religion Under the Mongols* (New York: Columbia University Press, 1982), 1–25.

41. Bol, *Neo-Confucianism in History*, 277. See also Benjamin Elman, *From Philosophy to Philology: Intellectual and Social Aspects of Change in Late Imperial China* (Berkeley: University of California Press, 2001); and Benjamin Elman, *Civil Examinations and Meritocracy in Late Imperial China* (Cambridge, MA: Harvard University Press, 2013).

42. Kai-wing Chow, *The Rise of Confucian Ritualism in Late Imperial China: Ethics, Classics, and Lineage Discourse* (Stanford, CA: Stanford University Press, 1994), 1–6.

43. Eisenstadt, "Frederic Wakeman's Oeuvre," xv; Yan, *Shidafu zhengzhi yansheng shigao*, 4 and 22.

44. Historians have reflected on important transformative moments in Chinese history—the Tang-Song, the Song-Yuan-Ming, and the Ming-Qing transitions—beginning with Naitō Konan's hypothesis on the Tang-Song transition. Naitō believes there are significant differences between the culture of Tang and that of Song: Tang marks the end of the medieval era, whereas Song represents the beginning of the modern age. Naitō's viewpoint was reiterated by Miyazaki Ichisada in *Tōyōteki kinsei* [China's modern age] (Osaka: Kyōiku taimususha, 1950), in which he argues that the modern age started with the unification of China under the Song. Scholars of the Tang-Song transition focus on China's explosive development of urbanism, commerce, paper currency, literacy, science, and technology during the Song. On the Tang-Song transformation, see also Bao Bide [Peter Bol], "Tang song zhuanxing de fansi: Yi sixiangshi de bianhua wei zhu" [Reflecting on the Tang-Song transition: From an intellectual history perspective], *Zhongguo xueshu*, vol. 3, no. 1 (2000): 63–87. In recent years, China scholars have also studied the Song-Yuan-Ming transition and looked at the important role the Mongol conquest played in Chinese history. See Paul Smith and Richard von Glahn, eds., *The Song-Yuan-Ming Transition in Chinese History* (Cambridge, MA: Harvard University Press, 2004). In the field of Ming and Qing history, the Ming-Qing transition has long been of interest to historians. See, for example, Frederic Wakeman Jr., *The Great Enterprise: The Manchu Reconstruction of Imperial Order in Seventeenth-Century China* (Berkeley: University of California Press, 1986); and William Rowe, *China's Last Empire* (Cambridge, MA: Harvard University Press, 2012). Nonetheless, the basic Confucian-Legalist structure in the administrative apparatus and imperial ideology in ruling China proper remained throughout these eras.

45. On the multicultural Qing emperorship, see Evelyn Rawski, *The Last Emperors: A Social History of Qing Imperial Institutions* (Berkeley: University of California Press, 1998), and Pamela Crossley, *A Translucent Mirror: History and Identity in Qing Imperial Ideology* (Berkeley: University of California Press, 1999).

46. Eisenstadt, "Frederic Wakeman's Oeuvre," xvi.
47. Edward Rhoads, *Manchus and Han: Ethnic Relations and Political Power in Late Qing and Early Republican China, 1861–1928* (Seattle: University of Washington Press, 2000), 45.
48. On the Qing garrisons, see Mark Elliot, *The Manchu Way: The Eight Banners and Ethnic Identity in Late Imperial China* (Stanford, CA: Stanford University Press, 2001).
49. Wang, *Kuachu fengbi de shijie*, 349.
50. Joseph Levenson, *Confucian China and Its Modern Fate* (Berkeley: University of California Press, 1965), vol. 2, 12.
51. Ibid.
52. Zhou Xun, *Shuhai congtan* [Collected talks about Sichuan] (Chongqing: Chongqing dagongbao bu, 1948), vol. 1, 53b–64b.
53. Ibid., 53b–54b.
54. Ibid., 58a–59b.
55. Ibid., 59b–60b.
56. Ibid., 56a–57b.
57. Ibid., 53b–54b.
58. Ibid., 36b–37a.
59. Ibid., 39a–40a.
60. Wang, *Kuachu fengbi de shijie*, 408–9.
61. Zhao Erxun, ed., *Qingshigao* [Draft history of the Qing dynasty] (Beijing: Zhonghua shuju, 1998), vol. 14, 3943–44.
62. Zhou, *Shuhai congtan*, vol. 1, 54b–55b.
63. Wang, *Kuachu fengbi de shijie*, 349.
64. Zhou, *Shuhai congtan*, vol. 1, 65a–66b.
65. Ibid., 67a–76b.
66. Pu Xiaorong, *Sichuan zhengqu yan'ge yu zhidi jinshi* [Historical and contemporary analyses of regions administered by Sichuan] (Chengdu: Sichuan renmin chubanshe, 1986), 423.
67. Wang, *Kuachu fengbi de shijie*, 357, 361. On magistrates, see also Ch'ü T'ung-tsu, *Local Government in China Under the Ch'ing*, chap. 2.
68. Ibid.
69. On clerks, see ibid., chap. 3; and Bradley Reed, *Talons and Teeth: County Clerks and Runners in the Qing Dynasty* (Stanford, CA: Stanford University Press, 2000), chap. 2.
70. On runners, see Ch'ü, *Local Government in China Under the Ch'ing*, chap. 4; and Reed, *Talons and Teeth*, chap. 4.
71. On servants and secretaries, see Ch'ü, *Local Government in China Under the Ch'ing*, chaps. 5–6.
72. *Daqing huidian shili* [Examples from the Qing Code], vol. 157, "Hubu: hukou" [Board of revenue: households]; *Qingchao wenxian tongkao* [A comprehensive study of Qing institutions], vol. 19, "Hukoukao 1" [Households 1], 5026, both in Wang, *Kuachu fengbi de shijie*, 420.
73. "Ba xian tuan shou pai tuan tiaoli" [Regulations on *pai* and *tuan* in Ba county], in Wang, *Kuachu fengbi de shijie*, 377–78.

74. Zhou, *Shuhai congtan*, vol. 1, 59b–60b.

75. Wang, *Kuachu fengbi de shijie*, 310.

76. Wang Chunwu, *Paoge tanmi* [Exploring the secrets of the Gowned Brothers] (Chengdu: Bashu shushe, 1993), 96.

77. Wang, *Kuachu fengbi de shijie*, 376. See also Yang Guoqiang, "Yang Guoqiang tan wanqing de shenshi yu shenquan" [Yang Guoqiang on the gentry and the power of the gentry in late Qing China], http://book.sohu.com/20090327/n263043062.shtml (viewed on July 1, 2009).

78. *Minguo daxianzhi* [Da county gazetteer in the Republican era], vol. 4, "Lisu 8" [Customs 8] "Fengsu: shixi" [Local customs: gentry], in Wang, *Kuachu fengbi de shijie*, 383.

79. *Daqing lüli huiji bianlan* [Collected regulations and statutes of the Qing dynasty] (1876), 29/2b and 29/1a, in Chang Chung-li, *The Chinese Gentry: Studies on Their Role in Nineteenth-Century Chinese Society* (Seattle: University of Washington Press, 1967), 35.

80. Gu Yanwu, "Tinglin wenji," *Tinglin yishu shizhong* [Ten posthumous papers of Gu Yanwu], 1/27b–18a, in Chang, *Chinese Gentry*, 43.

81. Wang Fengsheng, "Shenshi" [On the gentry], in Xu Zhichu, ed., *Mulingshu* [Handbook for administration] (1848), 16/26b, in Chang, *Chinese Gentry*, 32.

82. *Minguo Yunyangxianzhi* [Yunyang county gazetteer in the Republican era], vol. 9, "Lisu: fengsu" [Rituals: customs], in Wang, *Kuachu fengbi de shijie*, 379.

83. *Minguo Nanxixianzhi* [Nanxi county gazetteer in the Republican era], vol. 2, "Caifu 3: tianfu" [Revenue and taxation 3: land tax], in Wang, *Kuachu fengbi de shijie*, 379.

84. *Minguo chongxiu Nanchuanxianzhi* [Revised Nanchuan county gazetteer in the Republican era], vol. 4, no. 1, "Shihuo: tianfu (1): diding" [Economy: land tax (1): *diding*], in Wang, *Kuachu fengbi de shijie*, 379.

85. "Bianlian baojia hukou tiaogui gaoshi" [Announcement of the regulations to group people into *baojia*] (1810), in *Baxian dang'an* [Ba county archives], in Wang, *Kuachu fengbi de shijie*, 377.

86. Ibid.

87. *Daxianzhi* [Da county gazetteer], vol. 7, "Guanzheng men: minzhi" [Category of the officials: civil officials], in Wang, *Kuachu fengbi de shijie*, 378.

88. Wang, *Kuachu fengbi de shijie*, 378.

89. Wu Gou, "Cong minjian zifa dao guanfu jieru: xiangyue zizhi qiannian liubian" [From local spontaneity to governmental intervention: The changing history of the xiangyue and self-governance in the past one thousand years], http://history.sina.com.cn/bk/gds/2015-09-11/1053125459.shtml (viewed on December 12, 2015).

90. Fu Chongju, *Chengdu tonglan* [Investigation of Chengdu] (Chengdu: Chengdu shidai chubanshe, 2006), 129.

91. Ibid.

92. Adshead, *Province and Politics*, 10.

93. Ibid., 12; Wang, *Kuachu fengbi de shijie*, 81.

94. *Kangxi Sichuan tongzhi* [Provincial gazetteer of Sichuan in the Kangxi reign], vol. 5, "Tianfu" [Land tax], in Wang, *Kuachu fengbi de shijie*, 421.

95. *Qingchao wenxian tongkao*, vol. 1, "Tianfukao 1" [Land tax 1], in Wang, *Kuachu fengbi de shijie*, 421.
96. Ibid., vol. 2, "Tianfukao 2" [Land tax 2], in Wang, *Kuachu fengbi de shijie*, 422.
97. Anonymous, *Sichuan caizheng kao* [A study of the financial history of Sichuan], 1, in Wang, *Kuachu fengbi de shijie*, 422.
98. Wang, *Kuachu fengbi de shijie*, 80.
99. Robert Entenmann, "Migration and Settlement in Sichuan, 1644–1796" (PhD diss., Harvard University, 1982), 261–62.
100. Yan Zhongping, *Zhongguo jindai jingjishi tongji ziliao xuanji* [Selected statistical materials in modern Chinese economic history] (Beijing: Kexue chubanshe, 1955), 37.
101. Wei Yingtao et al., *Sichuan jindaishi* [History of modern Sichuan] (Chengdu: Sichuan shehui kexue chubanshe, 1985), 164–73.
102. *Minguo Dayixianzhi* [Dayi county gazetteer in the Republican era], vol. 14, 3, in ibid., 163.
103. Judith Wyman, "The Ambiguities of Chinese Antiforeignism: Chongqing: 1870–1900," *Late Imperial China*, vol. 18, no. 2 (1998): 90.
104. *Baxian dang'an* [Ba county archive], "Junshi" [Military affairs] 3001, no. 4, "Governor-General Ding Baozhen to Ba county magistrate" (January 26, 1883) (the quotation, slightly revised here, is in Wyman, "Ambiguities of Chinese Antiforeignism," 91). The *guolu*, bandits in the Daba Mountains area of Sichuan, first appeared around the Kangxi and the Yongzheng reigns. In the Qianlong reign, their number increased dramatically. They participated in the White Lotus Rebellion. After the Jiaqing and the Daoguang reigns, they merged with and became a significant component of the Gowned Brothers. See Wang, *Kuachu fengbi de shijie*, 535–37.
105. Adshead, *Province and Politics in Late Imperial China*, 17.
106. Ibid., 11.
107. Ibid., 12.
108. Wei et al., *Sichuan jindaishi*, 45. On militias in general, see Philip Kuhn, *Rebellion and Its Enemies in Late Imperial China: Militarization and Social Structure, 1796–1864* (Cambridge, MA: Harvard University Press, 1970).
109. Zhao Shuji, *Cunwushan fang shucao* [Writings and drafts compiled in the room called Cunwushan], vol. 1, 19, in Wei et al., *Sichuan jindaishi*, 45–46.
110. *Donghua xulu* [The continued records of the Donghua Gate], "Xianfeng chao" [Xianfeng reign], vol. 21, in Wei et al., *Sichuan jindaishi*, 46.
111. Wang Di, *The Teahouse: Small Business, Everyday Culture, and Public Politics in Chengdu, 1900–1950* (Stanford, CA: Stanford University Press, 2008), 97.
112. Fu, "Chengdu zhi paoge hua" [Chitchat about the Gowned Brothers in Chengdu], *Chengdu tonglan*, 275.
113. Chen Shulong, "Sichuan paoge yu xinhai geming" [The Gowned Brothers of Sichuan and the 1911 Revolution], in *Xinhai geming huiyilu* [Memoirs on the 1911 Revolution], vol. 3, in Wang, *Kuachu fengbi de shijie*, 549.
114. Luo Zhitian et al., *Shanyu yulai* [The coming of the storm] (Shanghai: Shanghai shudian chubanshe, 2011), 116. Scholars have long debated the origin

of the Gowned Brothers (*Paoge*) and their relation to the Elder Brothers Society (*Gelaohui*). Both developed from Sichuan's native bandits. *Paoge* was used to refer to this group in most places in Sichuan (including Chengdu Plain, the center of this study), while *Gelaohui* was often used to refer to this group in eastern Sichuan. As this book concerns itself with Sichuan as a whole, Gowned Brothers (*Paoge*) is the primary term used here.

115. Li Rong, "Bing Zeng zhongtang Li zhijun Peng gongbao Liu zhongcheng" [Letter to Zeng Guofan, Li Hongzhang, Peng Yulin, and Liu Kunyi], in *Shisanfeng shuwu* [Bookstore of the thirteen mountains], vol. 1, in Wang, *Kuachu fengbi de shijie*, 544.

116. Wang, *Kuachu fengbi de shijie*, 547.

117. Sichuan sheng ziyiju [Sichuan provincial assembly], *Sichuan ziyiju diyici yishilu* [Transcripts of the proposals by the first Sichuan provincial assembly], in Wei Yingtao and Zhao Qing, eds., *Sichuan Xinhai geming shiliao* [Collected historical materials of the 1911 Revolution in Sichuan] (Chengdu: Sichuan renmin chubanshe, 1982), vol. 1, 134–35. As a Sichuan magistrate noted: "By the time of the Guangxu reign, both the Gowned Brothers and the *guolu* existed in many places in Sichuan. . . . These people join up with each other. If one rises up, a group of people will follow. . . . Their lodges are to be found everywhere. They are innumerable. . . . The Gowned Brothers mobilize thousands of people, who have guns and [other] weapons and are able to put up an effective resistance against officials and soldiers" (ibid.).

118. "Dubutang zixun zhijian: Jiesan huidang" [Proposals by the governor-general for consultation: Disbanding the sworn brotherhood], in Wei and Zhao, eds., *Sichuan Xinhai geming shiliao*, vol. 1, 134.

119. *Sichuan guanbao*, vol. 9 (1911), in Wang, *Kuachu fengbi de shijie*, 546.

120. Hou Lishi [Wife of Hou Baozhai], "Hou Baozhai fuzi can bei mouhai yuanbai" [Petition on the brutal murder of Hou Baozhai and his son], in *Xinjin dang'an* [Xinjin county archives], "Minguo" [Republican period] 138, no. 12 (1911).

121. Wang Chaoyue, "Wang Chaoyue bing" [Memorial by Wang Chaoyue], in *Xinhai geming qian shinian minbian dang'an shiliao* [Historical materials on popular uprisings in the decade before the 1911 Revolution] (Beijing: Zhonghua shuju, 1985), vol. 2, 792.

122. Richthofen, *Baron Richthofen's Letters*, 179, in Adshead, *Province and Politics in Late Imperial China*, 22.

123. *British Foreign Office Records*, F.O. 405/145, Little to Satow, 19 August 1904, in Adshead, *Province and Politics*, 22.

124. Adshead, *Province and Politics*, 22.

125. Yangwu zongju [Bureau of Foreign Affairs], ed., "Sichuan tongsheng waiguo guanyuan shangmin tongji biao" [Statistics on all Sichuan foreign officials, merchants, and citizens] (Chengdu: 1909). I thank Professor Dai Zhili for providing me with this original document.

126. Wang, *Kuachu fengbi de shijie*, 671.

127. Ibid., 665.

128. Ibid., 684–85.

129. Ibid.

130. Paul A. Cohen, *China and Christianity: The Missionary Movement and the Growth of Chinese Antiforeignism, 1860–1870* (Cambridge, MA: Harvard University Press, 1967). Cohen provides a wonderful depiction of the anti-Christian riots from the early period (1860–1870s). In this groundbreaking study, he argues that anti-Christian incidents in the 1860s moved beyond simple xenophobia. He stresses social factors, especially the missionary encroachment upon the cultural, social, economic, and political power structure of the local Chinese elite.

131. Wang, *Kuachu fengbi de shijie*, 686.

132. "Houxuan zhixian Feng Wenyuan zao jiaomin wukong cheng" [Legal case filed by magistrate candidate Feng Wenyuan on him being stigmatized by Chinese Christians], September 19, 1865, in Sichuan sheng dang'an guan, ed., *Sichuan jiao'an yu yihequan dang'an* [Archival records on missionary cases and the Boxers in Sichuan] (Chengdu: Sichuan renmin chubanshe, 1985), 345.

133. Wang, *Kuachu fengbi de shijie*, 684.

134. "Chongqing fu zhuanchi geshu zhizhao Faguo siduo suokong ge'an yi zhuxiao buying fankong zha" [Chongqing prefect notifying the subdistricts on not retrying religious cases—brought up by the French priest—that have been concluded], April 29, 1879, in Sichuan sheng dang'an guan, ed., *Sichuan jiao'an yu yihequan dang'an*, 409.

135. "Chengdu jiangjun Sichuan zongdu ying Faguo gongshi qingqiu zixing quecha jiao'an chiping chuli zha" [Edict by the Chengdu commandant and the Sichuan governor-general on dealing impartially with religious cases], September 3, 1879, in Sichuan sheng dang'an guan, ed., *Sichuan jiao'an yu yihequan dang'an*, 410–11.

136. "Chaban Chongqing jiao'an shangyu" [Imperial edict on solving the Chongqing missionary case], August 1886, in Sichuan sheng dang'an guan, ed., *Sichuan jiao'an yu yihequan dang'an*, 426.

137. "Chengdu jiangjun Sichuan zongdu chaofa chuli Chongqing jiao'an peikuan zouzhe zha" [The Chengdu commandant and the Sichuan governor-general on dealing with the indemnity initiated by the Chongqing missionary dispute], January 11, 1887, in Sichuan sheng dang'an guan, ed., *Sichuan jiao'an yu yihequan dang'an*, 456.

138. "Zuifan xiongxing" [Violent crimes], 1886, in Sichuan sheng dang'an guan, ed., *Sichuan jiao'an yu yihequan dang'an*, 429–35.

139. "Shouhai shi qin kongzhuang" [Accusations by relatives of those who were killed], 1886, in Sichuan sheng dang'an guan, ed., *Sichuan jiao'an yu yihequan dang'an*, 417–20.

140. "Ba xian chengbao Luo Yuanyi juzhong xingxiong niangcheng zhong'an xiang" [Report by Ba the magistrate on the crimes of Luo Yuanyi], September 6, 1886, in Sichuan sheng dang'an guan, ed., *Sichuan jiao'an yu yihequan dang'an*, 438–45.

141. "Luo Yuanyi jingkong" [Luo Yuanyi's metropolitan accusation], in Sichuan sheng dang'an guan, ed., *Sichuan jiao'an yu yihequan dang'an*, 422.

142. "Sichuan buzhengshi fengzhi chufen Ba xian zhixian zha" [Sichuan provincial treasurer punishes Ba magistrate according to edict from Beijing], January 22, 1887, in Sichuan sheng dang'an guan, ed., *Sichuan jiao'an yu yihequan dang'an*, 468.

143. "Ba xian xiaoyu shiqin huijia tinghou jiejue wu zai zuoshou zishi paishi" [Ba magistrate notifies the relatives of those killed to go back home and wait for the result and not to bring trouble], October 24, 1886, in Sichuan sheng dang'an guan, ed., *Sichuan jiao'an yu yihequan dang'an*, 449.

144. "Chengdu jiangjun Sichuan zongdu chaofa chuli Chongqing jiao'an peikuan zouzhe zha" [The Chengdu commandant and the Sichuan governor-general on dealing with the indemnity initiated by the Chongqing missionary dispute], January 11, 1887, in Sichuan sheng dang'an guan, ed., *Sichuan jiao'an yu yihequan dang'an*, 460.

145. "Chuandong zhen, Chuandong dao, Chongqing fu ji Ba xian huixian wei shengyuan minjiao qixin xiaoyu yanjin dajiao gaoshi" [Announcement jointly issued by Chuandong zhen, Chuandong daotai, Chongqing prefect, and Ba xian magistrate on not following the path of the people of Chengdu and attacking missionaries], June 20, 1895, in Sichuan sheng dang'an guan, ed., *Sichuan jiao'an yu yihequan dang'an*, 476–77.

146. "Meiguo chuanjiaoshi He Zhongyi tan Chengdu jiao'an" [American missionary He Zhongyi on the Chengdu case], in Sichuan sheng dang'an guan, ed., *Sichuan jiao'an yu yihequan dang'an*, 499.

147. Wang, *Paoge tanmi*, 96.

148. "Yu Dongchen chou jiao ji" [Chronology of Yu Dongchen hating the missionaries], in Sichuan sheng dang'an guan, ed., *Sichuan jiao'an yu yihequan dang'an*, 513.

149. "Chongqing haiguan daili shuiwusi Watson gei haiguan zongshu (ying) zong shuiwusi Hede de baogao" [Report from Chongqing customs officer Watson to Beijing customs officer Hart], December 31, 1901, in Sichuan sheng dang'an guan, ed., *Sichuan jiao'an yu yihequan dang'an*, 629.

150. Wyman, "Ambiguities of Chinese Antiforeignism," 91.

CHAPTER 2. THE IDEAS OF REVOLUTION

1. Zhao Erfeng, "Zhao Erfeng zhi Zhao Erxun shu jubu Pu Dianjun deng ji tongzhijun weigong Chengdu dian" [Telegram from Zhao Erfeng to Zhao Erxun on the capture of Pu Dianjun and others and the encirclement of Chengdu by railway protection armies], in Dai Zhili, ed., *Sichuan baolu yundong shiliao huizuan* [Collection of historical materials on the Sichuan Railway Protection movement] (Taipei: Zhongyang yanjiuyuan jindaishi yanjiusuo, 1994), 1160.

2. Jiang Liping and Lin Weiping, "Deng Xiaoke yu Sichuan baolu yundong" [Deng Xiaoke and the Sichuan Railway Protection movement], *Shucheng* (April 2009): 36–37.

3. Huang Shou, "Baolu yundong zhong de Luo Lun" [Luo Lun in the Railway Protection movement], in Sichuan sheng zhengxie wenshi ziliao weiyuanhui, ed., *Sichuan wenshi ziliao jicui* [Selected personal histories of Sichuan province] (Chengdu: Sichuan renmin chubanshe, 1996), vol. 1, 165–66.

4. Zou Xinshi and Hu Gongshu, "Yan Kai shilüe" [A short biography of Yan Kai], in Chengdu shi zhengxie wenshi ziliao weiyuanhui, ed., *Sichuan xinhai fenglei* [Thunder and wind in Sichuan in the 1911 Revolution] (Chengdu: Chengdu chubanshe, 1991), 197–99.

5. Xie Zengshou, *Zhang Lan nianpu xinbian* [A new chronicle of Zhang Lan] (Beijing: Qunyan chubanshe, 2011), 9, 11, 13–14.

6. Nishikawa Masao, "Shisenshō kōanken bibōroku: Shinmatsu minkoku shoki no kyōshin" [Notes on Guang'an county of Sichuan province: Gentry of the late Qing and early Republican China], *Kanazawa Daigaku Bungakubu ronshū shigaku-ka hen*, no. 15 (1995): 9–92.

7. Xiao Xiang, "Guang'an Pu Dianjun xingzhuang" [The life of Pu Dianjun of Guang'an county], in Wei Yingtao and Zhao Qing, eds., *Sichuan Xinhai geming shiliao* [Collected historical materials of the 1911 Revolution in Sichuan] (Chengdu: Sichuan renmin chubanshe, 1982), vol. 2, 612.

8. "Established literati," historian Philip Kuhn's term, are those who held provincial-level degrees and by virtue of their regularly gathering in Beijing could be termed a "national elite" in the late Qing. Philip Kuhn, *Origins of the Modern Chinese State* (Stanford, CA: Stanford University Press, 2002), 43.

9. I use the term "constitutional" here as Philip Kuhn does: "constitutional" means something politically fundamental; a constitution is the fundamental political principle according to which the state functions. Ibid., 2. See the first endnote of the Introduction for *minzhu* and *minquan*. *Zhuquan zai guomin* appeared in Liang Qichao's "Yao Shun wei Zhongguo zhongyang junquan lanshang kao" [A study of Yao and Shun as the source of centralized imperial power in China], *Qingyibao* (1901), in Liang Qichao, *Yinbingshi heji* [Collected essays from an ice-drinker's studio] (Beijing reprint: Zhonghua shuju, 1989), *wenji* vol. 6, 23. *Guomin zhi zhuquan* appeared in Liang Qichao's "Lusuo xue'an" [Notes on Rousseau], *Qingyibao* (1901), in *Yinbingshi heji*, *wenji* vol. 6, 104. These two terms were used to covey the idea of popular sovereignty. See also Mao Haijian, "Lun wuxu shiqi Liang Qichao de minzhu sixiang" [On democratic ideas of Liang Qichao around the Hundred Days' Reform era], *Xueshu yuekan*, vol. 49, no. 4 (2017): 142–43.

10. Wei Lianchen [Alexander Williamson], "Tongwen shuhui zhangcheng zhiyuan mingdan faqishu he siku baogao" [The regulations, personnel list, initiation report, and auditing report of the Chinese Book and Tract Society] (1887), in Chen Yushen, *Wanqing baoye shi* [The history of the late-Qing press] (Ji'nan: Shandong huabao chubanshe, 2003), 21.

11. Hong Liangji, "Zheng xiejiao shu" [Memorial on suppressing the cult], in Kuhn, *Origins of the Modern Chinese State*, 6.

12. Benjamin Elman, *Classicism, Politics, and Kinship: The Ch'ang-chou School of New Text Confucianism in Late Imperial China* (Berkeley: University of California Press), 319–23.

13. Kuhn, *Origins of the Modern Chinese State*, 39.

14. Ibid., 48.

15. Ibid., 54–56.

16. Ibid., 60–62.

17. Ibid., 66.
18. Ibid., 64–66.
19. Ibid., 72.
20. Ibid., 61.
21. Ibid., 69.
22. Ibid., 70–71.
23. Of course, commoners for Madison were male, nonslave, European-descended commoners.
24. Kuhn, *Origins of the Modern Chinese State*, 76.
25. Ibid., 76–77.
26. Kang Youwei, *Kang Nanhai zibian nianpu* [Self-selected chronicle of Kang Youwei], Guangxu sinian [1878], age twenty-one, in Tang Zhijun, *Wuxu bianfa shi* [The history of the 1898 reform] (Shanghai: Shanghai shehui kexue chubanshe, 2003), 60–61.
27. Chen, *Wanqing baoye shi*, 3.
28. Ibid., 12.
29. Ibid., 16.
30. Lin Lezhi [John Young Allen], "Yi minzhuguo yu geguo zhangcheng ji gongyitang jie" [Defining the terms of constitutions and parliaments in democratic and various nations] (June 1875), in Zhu Weizheng ed., *Wanguo gongbao wenxuan* [Collected essays from *Wanguo gongbao*] (Beijing: Sanlian shudian, 1998), 437.
31. Ibid.
32. Chen, *Wanqing baoye shi*, 21.
33. Ibid., 22.
34. Ibid., 26–27.
35. Ibid., 29–30.
36. Zhang Hairong, "Gongche shangshu ji zuozhe "Hushang aishi laoren weihuanshi" jiujing shishui?" [Who is the author for the *Account of the Petition of Metropolitan Candidates*?], *Qingshi yanjiu*, no. 2 (2011): 138–44.
37. Su Huilian [William Soothill], *Litimotai zhuan* [Timothy Richard of China], trans. Guan Zhiyuan et al. (Nanjing: Guangxi shifan daxue chubanshe, 2007), 227.
38. Chen, *Wanqing baoye shi*, 30.
39. Ibid., 31.
40. Ibid., 54.
41. Xiong Yuezhi, *Xixue dongjian yu wanqing shehui* [Western Learning and Late Qing Society] (Beijing: Renmin daxue chubanshe), 408–9.
42. Zhang Zengyi, "Jiangnan zhizaoju de yishu huodong" [Translation activities by the Jiangnan Arsenal], *Jindaishi yanjiu*, no. 3 (1996): 212.
43. Wang Tao, "Zhong min xia" [The emphasis of the people and commoners], in Chen, *Wanqing baoye shi*, 60.
44. Guo Songtao et al., *Lundun yu Bali riji*, in *Guo Songtao deng shixiji liuzhong* [Six diaries of the journey to the West by Guo Songtao and others] (Shanghai: Zhongxi shuju, 2012), 90 and 125.
45. Tang, *Wuxu bianfa shi*, 61.

46. Chang Hao, *Liang Ch'i-ch'ao and Intellectual Transition in China, 1890–1907* (Cambridge, MA: Harvard University Press, 1971), 35–47.
47. Tang, *Wuxu bianfa shi*, 63.
48. Kang Youwei, *Shili gongfa quanshu* [Complete book of true principles and public laws], in Zhang Ronghua, ed., *Zhongguo jindai sixiangjia wenku: Kang Youwei juan* [Anthology of modern Chinese thinkers: Kang Youwei] (Beijing: Zhongguo renmin daxue chubanshe, 2015), 25.
49. Tang, *Wuxu bianfa shi*, 65.
50. Ibid., 71.
51. Chang, *Liang Ch'i-ch'ao and Intellectual Transition in China*, 48.
52. Murao Susumu, "Wanmu sensen: Shiwubao shiqi de Liang Qichao jiqi zhouwei de qingkuang" [Growing trees: Liang Qichao around the time of the *Chinese Progress*], in Hazama Naoki, ed., *Liang Qichao, Mingzhi Riben, Xifang* [Liang Qichao, Meiji Japan, the West: Report of the joint research of the Institute in the Humanities, Kyoto University, Japan] (Beijing: Shehui kexue wenxian chubanshe, 2012), 37. See also Mao Haijian, "Lun wuxu shiqi Liang Qichao de minzhu sixiang," 124.
53. Chang, *Liang Ch'i-ch'ao and Intellectual Transition in China*, 50–51.
54. Murao, "Wanmu sensen: Shiwubao shiqi de Liang Qichao jiqi zhouwei de qingkuang," 58.
55. Ding Wenjiang and Zhao Fengtian, eds., *Liang Qichao nianpu changbian* [Chronicle of Liang Qichao's life] (Beijing: Zhonghua shuju, 2010), 15.
56. Kang Youwei, *Kang Nanhai zibian nianpu* (also published as *Nanhai xiansheng zibian nianpu*) [Self-selected chronicle of Kang Youwei], in ibid., 23. See also Mao Haijian, *Wuxu bianfa shishi kao erji* [A study of historical facts of the reform movement of 1898, vol. 2] (Beijing: Sanlian shudian, 2011), 86.
57. Kuhn, *Origins of the Modern Chinese State*, 123. See also Tang, *Wuxu bianfa shi*, 149, and Mao Haijian, *Cong jiawu dao wuxu: Kang Youwei 'Woshi' jianzhu* [From 1895 to 1898: The textual research and annotations on Kang Youwei's autobiography (My history)] (Beijing: Sanlian shudian, 2009), 100.
58. Kuhn, *Origins of the Modern Chinese State*, 123.
59. Ibid., 124.
60. Hsiao Kung-chuan, *A Modern China and a New World: K'ang Yu-wei, Reformer and Utopian, 1858–1927* (Seattle: University of Washington Press, 1975), 202.
61. Yan Fu, "Pi Han" [In refutation of Han Yu], in Huang Ko-wu ed., *Zhongguo jindai sixiangjia wenku: Yan Fu juan* [Anthology of modern Chinese thinkers: Yan Fu] (Beijing: Zhongguo renmin daxue chubanshe, 2014), 17–18.
62. Mao Haijian, *Zhang Zhidong dang'an yuedu biji: wuxu bianfa de lingmian* [Readings of the Zhang Zhidong archive: A study of the other side of the reform movement of 1898] (Shanghai: Shanghai guji chubanshe, 2014), 1–2.
63. Liang Qichao, "Lun bubianfa zhihai" [On the harms of not reforming], *Shiwubao* (1896), in *Yinbingshi heji, wenji* vol. 1, 2.
64. Liang Qichao, "Xixue shumubiao houxu" [Epilogue to the bibliography of Western scholars' works], *Shiwubao* (1896), in *Yinbingshi heji, wenji* vol. 1, 128.
65. Liang Qichao, "Xuyi lieguo suiji zhengyao xu" [Preface to the translation of *Lieguo suiji zhengyao*], *Shiwubao* (1897), in *Yinbingshi heji, wenji* vol. 2, 59.

66. Liang, "Xixue shumubiao houxu," *wenji* vol. 1, 128.

67. Su Yu, ed., *Yijiao congbian* [Collection of writings by the reformers], vol. 5, in Zhang Pengyuan, *Liang Qichao yu qingji geming* [Liang Qichao and the late Qing revolution] (Taipei: Zhongyang yanjiuyuan jindaishi yanjiusuo, 1982), 56.

68. Mao Haijian, "Lun wuxu shiqi Liang Qichao de minzhu sixiang," 120–44. In this article, Professor Mao systematically studies Liang's ideas of democracy between 1895 and 1898. Unfortunately, I am unable to fully incorporate all of his arguments in the book due to time constraints.

69. Fan Zhui, "Kaicheng pian," *Xiangbao*, no. 24, 1898, in Chen, *Wanqing baoye shi*, 97.

70. He Laibao, "Shuo si," *Xiangbao*, no. 33, 1898, in Chen, *Wanqing baoye shi*, 98.

71. Bi Yongnian, "Cunhua pian," *Xiangbao*, no. 34, 1898, in Chen, *Wanqing baoye shi*, 98.

72. Su, ed., *Yijiao congbian*, vol. 5, in Zhang, *Liang Qichao yu qingji geming*, 61–62.

73. Ibid., 62.

74. Ibid.

75. Mao Haijian, *Zhang Zhidong dang'an yuedu biji*, 25.

76. Li Xizhu, *Zhang Zhidong yu qingmo xinzheng yanjiu* [A study of Zhang Zhidong and the late Qing New Politics reform] (Shanghai: Shanghai shudian chubanshe, 2003), 287.

77. Su, ed., *Yijiao congbian*, vol. 5, in Zhang, *Liang Qichao yu qingji geming*, 63.

78. An excellent study of the cultural meaning of the 1898 reform is Rebecca Karl and Peter Zarrow, eds., *Rethinking the 1898 Reform Period: Political and Cultural Change in Late-Qing China* (Cambridge, MA: Harvard University Press), 2002.

79. Wu Yuzhang, "Jiawu zhanbai yu bairi weixin de huiyi" [Memories of the defeat in the first Sino-Japanese War and the Hundred Days' Reform], in Sichuan sheng zhengxie wenshi ziliao weiyuanhui, ed., *Sichuan wenshi ziliao jicui*, vol. 1, 3–16.

80. Xu Xiaoqing, "Liuri xuesheng kanwu de chuanbo wangluo" [Circulation network of the magazines by the Chinese students in Japan], *Zhongzhou xuekan*, no. 6 (2001): 92–96. Rune Svarverud, "The Notions of 'Power' and 'Rights' in Chinese Political Discourse," in Michael Lackner, Iwo Amelung, and Joachim Kurtz, eds., *New Terms for New Ideas: Western Knowledge and Lexical Change in Late Imperial China* (Leiden: Brill, 2001), 125–44.

81. Liang Qichao, "Benguan di yibaice zhuci bing lun baoguan zhi zeren ji benguan zhi jingli" [Celebrating the 100th issue: Our responsibility and our experiences], *Qingyibao* (1901), in *Yinbingshi heji, wenji* vol. 6, 54.

82. Svarverud, "Notions of 'Power' and 'Rights' in Chinese Political Discourse," 136.

83. Liang Qichao, "Caomao weiyan" [An outsider's words of warning], *Qingyibao* (1899), in *Yinbingshi heji, zhuanji* vol. 2, 12.

84. Wang Yao, "Lusuo yu wanqing Zhongguo sixiang shijie (1882–1911)" [J.J. Rousseau and the Intellectual World in China (1882–1911)] (PhD diss., East China Normal University, 2014), 32.

85. Wang Yao, "Lusuo yu wanqing Zhongguo sixiang shijie," 34.

86. Liang Qichao, "Wenye sanjie zhibie" [The demarcation between the civilized and uncivilized people], *Qingyibao* (1899), in *Yinbingshi heji, zhuanji* vol. 2, 8–9.

87. Liang Qichao, "Pohuai zhuyi" [Destructivism], *Qingyibao* (1900), in *Yinbingshi heji, zhuanji* vol. 2, 25.

88. Liang Qichao, "Guojia sixiang bianqian yitong lun" [The similarities and differences in the changing ideas of the state], *Qingyibao* (1901), in *Yinbingshi heji, wenji* vol. 6, 12–22.

89. Ibid., 12.

90. Ibid., 19.

91. Ibid., 20.

92. Ibid., 22.

93. Liang Qichao, "Notes on Rousseau" [Lusuo xue'an], *Qingyibao* (1901), in *Yinbingshi heji, wenji* vol. 6, 97–110. See also Hazama Naoki, "Nakae Chōmin *Minyaku yakkai* no rekishiteki igi ni tsuite" [Nakae Chōmin's translation of Rousseau's *Social Contract*], in Ishikawa Yoshihiro, Hazama Naoki, eds. *Kindai higashi ajia ni okeru hon'yaku gainen no tenkai* (Kyoto: Kyoto daigaku jinbun kagaku kenkyūjo, 2013), 1–53; and Hazama Naoki, "Dongyang Lusuo Zhongjiang Zhaomin zai jindai dongya wenmingshi shang de diwei" [The role of Nakae Chōmin—Rousseau of the East—in the history of East Asian civilization], in Sha Peide [Peter Zarrow] and Zhang Zhejia, eds., *Jindai Zhongguo xinzhishi de jiangou* [The construction of new knowledge in modern China] (Taipei: Zhongyang yanjiu yuan, 2013), 53–68.

94. Liang Qichao, "Lun zhengfu yu renmin zhi quan xian" [On the boundary of power between the government and the people], *Xinmin congbao* (1902), in *Yinbingshi heji, wenji* vol. 10, 1–5.

95. Ibid., 5.

96. Ibid.

97. Tsuchiya Hideo, "Liang Qichao de xiyang shequ yu quanli ziyou lun" [On "Western" influences on Liang Qichao: His theory on rights and liberty], in Hazama Naoki, *Liang Qichao, Mingzhi Riben, Xifang*, 135.

98. Ibid., 135–38.

99. Liang Qichao, "Xinmin shuo: lun guojia sixiang" [On the New People: on ideas about the nation], *Xinmin congbao* (1902), in *Yinbingshi heji, zhuanji* vol. 4, 16–17.

100. There are several versions of *Zhongguohun* circulating today. The first version was published in 1902, by Shanghai's Guangzhi shuju, and consists of two volumes. I have seen Guangzhi shuju's 1903, 1905, 1907 and 1913 editions. The 1903 edition, for example, on the back cover is stated "printed for the third time" and "sold at forty cents (*si jiao*)." The 1905 edition contains two volumes; on the back cover is stated "printed for the fifth time," "sold at thirty cents (*san jiao*),"

and "can be obtained from all big bookstores in China's provinces." Guangzhi shuju combined the two volumes and published a one-volume edition, although its date is unidentifiable. Besides the Guangzhi shuju version, Shanghai's Yunji shuzhuang also published it in 1903, and is in one volume. In addition, there are numerous hand-written copies of *Zhongguohun* circulating in China, for example, http://book.kongfz.com/21177/590794502/. All these indicate the great popularity of this pamphlet.

101. Liang Qichao, "He pangguanzhe wen" [Chastising onlookers], *Qingyibao* (1900), in *Yinbingshi heji, wenji* vol. 5, 69–75.

102. Liang Qichao, "Shaonian Zhongguo shuo" [On a young China], *Qingyibao* (1900), in *Yinbingshi heji, wenji* vol. 5, 7–8.

103. Ibid., 9.

104. Liang Qichao, "Lun jinshi guomin jingzheng zhi dashi ji Zhongguo qiantu" [On recent trends in the competition between national citizens and the future of China], *Qingyibao* (1899), in *Yinbingshi heji, wenji* vol. 4, 56.

105. See note 100.

106. On pirated books and journals, see also Zhang, *Liang Qichao yu qingji geming*, 300.

107. Xiao Yishan, *Qingdai tongshi* [A general history of the Qing dynasty] (Shanghai: Huadong shifan daxue chubanshe, 2006), vol. 3, 1869.

108. Ibid., 1864.

109. Gao Yihan, "Xinhai geming qianhou Anhui qingnian xuesheng sixiang zhuanbian de gaikuang" [The ideological transition of Anhui's young students around the 1911 Revolution], in *Xinhai geming huiyilu* [Memoirs on the 1911 Revolution] (Beijing: Zhonghua shuju, 1961), vol. 4, 434.

110. Wang Yunzi, "Tongmenghui yu chuanxi gelaohui" [The Revolutionary Alliance and the Sworn Brothers in west Sichuan], in Sichuan sheng zhengxie wenshi ziliao weiyuanhui, ed., *Sichuan wenshi ziliao jicui*, vol. 1, 253.

111. Zhang, *Liang Qichao yu qingji geming*, 297.

112. Nazama Naoki, "Xinmin shuo lue lun" [A short study on the New Citizen discourse], in Hazama, *Liang Qichao, Mingzhi Riben, Xifang*, 78.

113. Tsuchiya, "Liang Qichao de xiyang shequ yu quanli ziyou lun," 142.

114. Liang Qichao, "Li xianfa yi" [On constitutionalism], *Qingyibao* (1901), in *Yinsbingshi heji, wenji* vol. 5, 3.

115. Ibid., 1.

116. Ibid., 1. "Every member of a country, whether he is the monarch, an official, or a member of the ordinary people, must obey [the constitution]. A constitution is the origin of all other laws in a nation. No policies, stipulations, or laws should challenge the basic principles of the constitution. . . . [In a constitutional system], the monarch has his power and there are limits on that power, the officials have their power and there are limits on that power, and the people have their power and there are limits on that power."

117. Ibid., 2.

118. Liang Qichao, "Lun lifa quan" [On legislative power], *Qingyibao* (1902), in *Yinbingshi heji, wenji* vol. 9, 105–7.

119. Liang, "Li xianfa yi," 3–4.

120. Ibid., 4–6.
121. Liang Qichao, "Jieshao xinzhu" [Introducing new works], *Xinmin congbao*, no. 6, in Hou Yijie, *Ershi shiji chu Zhongguo zhengzhi gaige fengchao: Qingmo lixian yundong shi* [The wave of political reform in early twentieth-century China: The constitutional movement of the late Qing] (Beijing: Renmin chubanshe, 1993), 34.
122. *Wang Kangnian shiyou shuzha* [Correspondence between Wang Kangnian and his friends] (Shanghai: Shanghai guji chubanshe, 1986), vol. 3, 2379–80.
123. Sun Baoxuan, *Wangshanlu riji* [Diary of Sun Baoxuan] (Shanghai: Shanghai guji chubanshe, 1983), vol. 2, 556.
124. "Lun shiju zhi kewei" [On the precarious current affairs], *Zhongwai ribao*, June 16, 1902, in Hou, *Ershi shiji chu Zhongguo zhengzhi gaige fengchao*, 38.
125. In Hou, *Ershi shiji chu Zhongguo zhengzhi gaige fengchao*, 38–39.
126. "Lun neiluan waihuan you xiangyin zhishi" [On the situation in which internal and external chaos are combining with each other], *Dagongbao*, August 18, 1903, in Hou, *Ershi shiji chu Zhongguo zhengzhi gaige fengchao*, 39.
127. Ibid.
128. According Hou Yijie, the term *lixian pai* (constitutionalists) was coined in the radical student magazine *Zhejiang chao*, no. 7, in the article "Si zhengke lun" [On four politicians] in September 1903. See Hou, *Ershi shiji chu Zhongguo zhengzhi gaige fengchao*, 39.
129. Zhang, *Liang Qichao yu qingji geming*, 112.
130. Guo Moruo, "Fanzheng qianhou" [Life around the 1911 Revolution], in *Moruo zizhuan* [Autobiography of Guo Moruo] (Xianggang: Sanlian shudian, 1978), vol. 1, 192.
131. Hu Chongshu, "Pu Dianjun yishi" [Anecdotes of Pu Dianjun], in Zhongguo renmin zhengzhi xieshang huiyi, Sichuan sheng Guang'an xian weiyuanhui wenshi ziliao bianweihui, ed., *Guang'an wenshi ziliao xuanbian* [Selected historical materials of Guang'an county] (Guang'an: 1987), vol. 4, 35.
132. Lin Dun and He Yili, "Pu Dianjun" [Pu Dianjun], in Sichuan sheng zhengxie wenshi ziliao yanjiu weiyuanhui, Sichuan sheng wenshi guan, ed., *Sichuan jinxiandai wenhua renwu* [Eminent cultural figures of modern Sichuan] (Chengdu: Sichuan Renmin chubanshe, 1989), vol. 1, 182.
133. Xiao, "Guang'an Pu Dianjun xingzhuang," 611–12. See also Lin and He, "Pu Dianjun," 182.
134. Feng Tianyu, "Fazheng daxue Zhongguo liuxuesheng yu Ezhou yuefa de zhiding" [The Hōsei University Chinese overseas students and the drafting of the Hubei constitution], *Jianghan daxue xuebao*, vol. 30, no. 5 (October 2011): 43–44. Chinese students began going to Japan in 1896, after the Qing's loss to Japan in the first Sino-Japanese War. In 1898, Japanese ambassador Yano Fumio notified the Zongli Yamen of his intent to encourage the students of the Qing empire to study in Japan. A regulation was established, and in 1898, Huguang governor-general Zhang Zhidong sent 150 students from Hubei and Hunan to study in Japan. Zhang encouraged Chinese students to study in Japan and stated that Japan was the optimum place for the Qing students owing to its proximity

to China and its similarities in language and customs to those of China. Of all the Chinese provinces, it was Hubei, Zhejiang, Jiangsu, and Sichuan that sent the most students. According to Feng Tianyu, who based his study on a great number of Japanese and Chinese records, the estimated number of Qing students sent to Japan between 1898 and 1911 was more than 45,046, with the years 1905 and 1906 being the peak, when about eight thousand students went to Japan to study in each year.

135. Feng, "Fazheng daxue Zhongguo liuxuesheng yu Ezhou yuefa de zhiding," 44.

136. Li Qicheng, ed., *Zizhengyuan yichang huiyi sujilu: Wanqing yubei guohui lunbian shilu* [Transcripts of the first National Assembly Meeting] (Shanghai: Shanghai sanlian shudian, 2011), introduction.

137. Feng, "Fazheng daxue Zhongguo liuxuesheng yu Ezhou yuefa de zhiding," 47.

138. Lecture notes of Hōsei University. Original documents in the Hōsei University Library. Fazheng daxue [Hōsei University], ed., *Fazheng suchengke jiangyilu* [Lecture notes of Hōsei University's Short-Term Program] (Tokyo: Hōsei University, 1905–1911), 57 vols. Special thanks to Wang Min for directing me to all the textbooks used by the Short-Term Program. The introduction to law, taught by Ume Kenjirō, for example, spent a great deal of energy explaining the concepts of rights and responsibility. It was the very first course that students took, and it set the tone for the rest of the program.

139. Ding Xiangshun, "Wanqing furi fazheng liuxuesheng yu Zhongguo zaoqi fazhi jindaihua" [Late Qing overseas students in Japan and the early modernization of the Chinese legal system], http://www.japanlawinfo.sdu.edu.cn/html/faxueyiban/20071201/46.html (viewed on November 14, 2013).

140. Ibid.

141. Feng, "Fazheng daxue Zhongguo liuxuesheng yu Ezhou yuefa de zhiding," 47–48.

142. Han Dayuan, "Meinongbu daji lixian zhuyi sixiang yanjiu" [A study of the constitutional thought of Minobe Tatsukichi], http://article.chinalawinfo.com/Article_Detail.asp?ArticleId=55832 (viewed on November 14, 2013).

143. Ibid.

144. Ibid.

145. Ibid.

146. Feng, "Fazheng daxue Zhongguo liuxuesheng yu Ezhou yuefa de zhiding," 48.

147. Fazheng daxue shi ziliao weiyuanhui [Committee on sources on the history of Hōsei University], ed., *Fazheng daxue Qingguo liuxuesheng fazheng suchengke teji* [Special source collection on the Hōsei Short-Term Program for the Qing overseas students], in *Hōsei Daigakushi shiryōshū* [Source collection of the history of Hōsei University] (Tokyo: Hōsei Daigaku Hyakunenshi Hensan Iinkai Shiryō Bukai, 1978–), vol. 11, 263. The total number included students who did not graduate with their own class but stayed longer and graduated later. Special thanks to Wang Min for leading me to this source.

148. Tan Yigong and Chen Xinhou, eds., *Liuri fazheng daxue xueyou lu* [Alumni list of the overseas students at Hōsei University] (Tokyo: Hōsei University, 1911), internal publication. Special thanks to Wang Min for leading me to this source.

149. Feng, "Fazheng daxue Zhongguo liuxuesheng yu Ezhou yuefa de zhiding," 47; Li, *Zizhengyuan yichang huiyi sujilu*, appendix "Short Biographies of the National Assemblymen," 740–77.

150. Pu Yaoqiong interview, in Yi Dan, *Zuoyuo yu luoxuan* [Left, right, and spiral] (Shanghai: Shanghai wenyi chubanshe, 1999), 53. Pu Yaoqiong is the daughter of Pu Dianjun.

151. Feng, "Fazheng daxue Zhongguo liuxuesheng yu Ezhou yuefa de zhiding," 48.

152. Ibid., 43.

153. Ibid., 48.

154. Zhang, *Liang Qichao yu qingji geming*, 297.

155. Benjamin Elman, *Civil Examinations and Meritocracy in Late Imperial China* (Cambridge, MA: Harvard University Press, 2013). Also see Zhang Qing, "Cewen zhong de lishi: Wanqing Zhongguo 'lishi jiyi' yanxu de yige cengmian" [One aspect of "history" in "policy questions" in the continuation of late Qing historical memory], *Fudan xuebao*, no. 5 (2005): 53–62.

156. Zhu Zhisan, *Zhu Zhisan riji* [Diary of Zhu Zhisan] (Wuhan: Huazhong shifan daxue chubanshe, 2011), January 8, 1903, 103.

157. Wang Lifu, *Wang Lifu ji* [Writings of Wang Lifu] (Shanghai: Shanghai shehui kexue chubanshe, 2006), 146.

158. Li Jieren, *Baofengyu qian* [Before the big storm], in *Li Jieren xuanji* [Collected works of Li Jieren] (Chengdu: Sichuan renmin chubanshe, 1980), vol. 1, 283.

159. Fu Chongju, *Chengdu tonglan* [Investigation of Chengdu] (Chengdu: Chengdu shidai chubanshe, 2006), 178–80.

160. Huang, "Baolu yundong zhongde Luo Lun," 165–66.

161. Li, *Baofengyu qian*, 469.

162. Ibid.

163. Ibid., 353.

164. Ibid., 450.

165. Ibid., 359.

166. Jiang and Lin, "Deng Xiaoke yu Sichuan baolu yundong," 36–37.

167. Charles Howard McIlwain, *Constitutionalism: Ancient and Modern* (Indianapolis: Liberty Fund, 2007), 21.

CHAPTER 3. THE PROJECT

1. Min Tu-Ki, *National Polity and Local Power: The Transformation of Late Imperial China* (Cambridge, MA: Harvard University Press, 1989), 208.

2. Imperial edict of the tenth day of the twelfth month of the twenty-sixth year of Guangxu, in *Guangxu chao donghua lu* [The Donghua record of the Guangxu reign], 4601–2, in Hou Yijie, *Ershi shiji chu Zhongguo zhengzhi gaige fengchao*:

Qingmo lixian yundong shi [The wave of political reform in early twentieth-century China: The constitutional movement of the late Qing] (Beijing: Renmin chubanshe, 1993), 26.

3. Ibid., 4601, in Hou, *Ershi shiji chu Zhongguo zhengzhi gaige fengchao*, 27.

4. Zhang Zhidong and Liu Kunyi, *Jiang-Chu huizou bianfa zhe* [Jointly written memorials of Zhang Zhidong and Liu Kunyi], in *Zhang Wenxiang gong quanji* [The complete works of Zhang Zhidong] (Beijing: Wenhuazhai, 1928), vol. 52, 9–29; vol. 53, 1–33; and vol. 54, 1–36.

5. "Zhuilu Li Muzhai xingshi tiaochen bianfa zhe" [Recording the memorial of Ambassador Li Shengduo on reforms], *Shibao*, November 28, 1905.

6. Zhao Binglin, "Fang luan lun" [On preventing chaos], in Hou, *Ershi shiji chu Zhongguo zhengzhi gaige fengchao*, 29.

7. Tao Mo, "Biantong zhengzhi yi wu benyuan zhe" [Memorial by Tao Mo on reforming the most essential issues], in *Tao Qinsu gong zouyi yigao* [The posthumous manuscripts and draft memorials of Tao Mo] (1924), in Hou, *Ershi shiji chu Zhongguo zhengzhi gaige fengchao*, 29.

8. *Zhengzhi guanbao*, April 22, 1903, in Mary Wright, *China in Revolution: The First Phase, 1900–1913* (New Haven, CT: Yale University Press, 1968), 28.

9. On the 1904 educational reform, see Zhu Youxian, *Jindai xuezhi shiliao* [Historical sources of educational system in modern China] (Shanghai: Huadong shifan daxue chubanshe, 1987), vol. 2, part 1. Mary Wright gives a positive appraisal of the reforms' effects: the education reform was a success—"High officials, wealthy merchants, and the prominent gentry seemed to respond to such appeals willingly. People of modest means also contributed, and patriotic suicides left notes asking that contributions in their memory be made to education. The total sum raised was inadequate, but the general public concern with modern education for a widening sector of society was manifest." Wright, *China in Revolution*, 26.

10. Mary Wright also reviews the military reforms and claims that they, like the educational reforms, were a double-edged sword: "The modern armies made possible the Chinese Empire's resistance to foreign encroachment on her frontiers, but this very role, coupled with their modern training, made them highly receptive to ideas of revolution in the name of nationalism." Ibid., 27. On the military reform, see also Zhang Haipeng and Li Xizhu, *Zhongguo jindai tongshi (5): Xinzheng, lixian yu Xinhai geming (1901–1912)* [The general history of China (5): The new policies reform, constituioanl reform, and the 1911 Revolution (1901–1912)] (Nanjing: Jiangsu renmen chubanshe, 2006), 34–37.

11. Zhou Xun, *Shuhai congtan* [Collected talks about Sichuan] (Chongqing: Chongqing Dagongbao bu, 1948), vol. 2, 12a–22b. See also Kristen Stapleton, *Civilizing Chengdu: Chinese Urban Reform, 1895–1937* (Cambridge, MA: Harvard University Press, 2000).

12. Zhang Dafu, "Weixin bianfa zai Chengdu" [The New Policies reform in Chengdu], in Sichuan sheng zhengxie wenshi ziliao weiyuanhui, ed., *Sichuan wenshi ziliao jicui* [Selected personal histories of Sichuan province] (Chengdu: Sichuan renmin chubanshe, 1996), vol. 1, 48–69.

13. Xiliang, *Xiliang yigao zougao* [Posthumous papers and memorials of Xiliang] (Beijing: Zhonghua shuju, 1959), vol. 1, 520–21.

14. In his novel *Baofengyu qian* [Before the big storm], in *Li Jieren xuanji* [Collected works of Li Jieren] (Chengdu: Sichuan renmin chubanshe, 1980), Li Jieren describes how gentry actively donated money to set up the new schools. Their motivation, according to Li, was partially to strengthen China via education, but also partially to fish for compliments from their peers. Zhang Haipeng and Li Xizhu, *Xinzheng, lixian yu Xinhai geming*, 114.

15. "Chongqing haiguan 1902–1911 shinian baogao" [Chongqing maritime custom's report of ten years (1902–1911)], n.p., in Wei Yingtao et al., *Sichuan jindaishi* [History of modern Sichuan] (Chengdu: Sichuan shehui kexue chubanshe, 1985), 290.

16. Sichuan tongxianghui [Sichuan overseas students association], "Wei Chuan-Han tielu shi jinggao quanshu fulao shu" [An open letter to all Sichuan fathers and elders on the Chuan-Han Railway matter], in Dai Zhili, ed., *Sichuan baolu yundong shiliao huizuan* [Collection of historical materials on the Sichuan Railway Protection movement] (Taipei: Zhongyang yanjiuyuan jindaishi yanjiusuo, 1994), 279–308.

17. Zhou, *Shuhai congtan*, vol. 2, 12a–22b.

18. Ralph Huenemann, *The Dragon and the Iron Horse: The Economics of Railroads in China, 1876–1937* (Cambridge, MA: Harvard University Press, 1984), 75.

19. Mi Rucheng, *Zhongguo jindai tielu shi ziliao* [Historical materials on the history of Chinese railways in the modern era] (Beijing: Zhonghua shuju, 1963), vol. 2, 423.

20. Sheng Xuanhuai, *Yuzhai cungao* [Materials preserved in Yu House] (1939; reprint; Taipei: Wenhai chubanshe, 1965), vol. 31, 31.

21. Kende, "Zhongguo tielu fazhan shi" [Development of Chinese railroads], in Wei et al., *Sichuan jindaishi*, 428.

22. Mi, *Zhongguo jindai tielu shi ziliao*, vol. 2, 466.

23. Sichuan sheng dang'an guan, ed., *Sichuan baolu yundong dang'an xuanbian* [Selected archival documents of the Sichuan Railway Protection movement] (Chengdu: Sichuan renmin chubanshe, 1981), 122.

24. Mi, *Zhongguo jindai tielu shi ziliao*, vol. 2, 426.

25. *Waijiao bao* [Newspapers of foreign affairs], Guangxu reign, the 29th year, nos. 35 and 24, in Wei et al., *Sichuan jindaishi*, 430.

26. Mi, *Zhongguo jindai tielu shi ziliao*, vol. 3, 1058.

27. Ibid., 1066.

28. "Sichuan zongdu butang Xi zouqing zishe Chuan-Han tielu gongsi zhe gao" [Memorial by Sichuan governor-general Xiliang about establishing the Chuan-Han Railway Company], in *Chuanlu yuebao* [Monthly report of the Sichuan railways] (Chengdu: 1911), vol. 1, *kaiban zouyi* [initiative memorials], 1. Original document in the Sichuan Library.

29. Ibid.

30. "Waiwu bu ju zou yifu Sichuan zongdu Xiliang zou zishe Chuan-Han tielu gongsi zhegao" [Reply by the Ministry of foreign affairs to Xiliang's memorial], in *Chuanlu yuebao*, vol. 1, *kaiban zouyi* [initiative memorials], 3.

31. "Xiliang wei zhaozhang sheli Chuan-Han tielu gongsi zouqing li'an zhe" [Memorial by Xiliang about establishing the Chuan-Han Railway Company], in Dai, ed., *Sichuan baolu yundong shiliao huizuan*, 257.

32. Ibid., 258.

33. Huenemann, *Dragon and the Iron Horse*, 65.

34. Xiliang, *Xiliang yigao zougao*, vol. 1, 455.

35. Ibid.

36. Cheng Changqi, *Jingguanzhai riji* [Diary of Jingguan hall], October 2, 1904, in Dai, ed., *Sichuan baolu yundong shiliao huizuan*, 289.

37. "Sichuan liuri xuesheng tongxianghui shang Xiliang kaiban Chuan-Han tielu gongsi yijian shu," [Sichuan overseas students association to Xiliang: Our opinions on starting the Chuan-Han Railway Company], in Dai Zhili, ed., *Sichuan baolu yundong shiliao* [Collection of historical materials on the Sichuan Railway Protection movement] (Beijing: Kexue chubanshe, 1959), 10.

38. Cheng, *Jingguanzhai riji*, October 2, 1904, in Dai, ed., 289.

39. Ibid.

40. Ibid., September 24 and 25, 1904, in Dai, ed., *Sichuan baolu yundong shiliao huizuan*, 287.

41. Ibid., October 2 and 5, 1904, in Dai, ed., *Sichuan baolu yundong shiliao huizuan*, 287.

42. Originally devised as a voluntary tax to fund the campaign to suppress the Taiping Rebellion, the *juanshu* later became a fixed surcharge.

43. Cheng, *Jingguanzhai riji*, October 8 and 22, 1904, in Dai, ed., *Sichuan baolu yundong shiliao huizuan*, 287–88.

44. Ibid., October 4, 1904, in Dai, ed., *Sichuan baolu yundong shiliao huizuan*, 288.

45. Ibid.

46. In the year 1904 the Sichuan overseas students first organized themselves formally and entered provincial politics as a group. Their reputation began to grow starting in 1904 as well.

47. Cheng, *Jingguanzhai riji*, January 20, 1905, in Dai, ed., *Sichuan baolu yundong shiliao huizuan*, 288.

48. Ibid., January 22, 1905, in Dai, ed., *Sichuan baolu yundong shiliao huizuan*, 289.

49. Ibid., January 7, 1905, in Dai, ed., *Sichuan baolu yundong shiliao huizuan*, 288.

50. There are two Hu Juns in this chapter. This Hu Jun (1869–1909) was a Chengdu gentleman who had been in contact with the Sichuanese students since 1904. He became a *jinshi* in 1895 and later served as the Chengdu branch manager of the Chuan-Han Railway Company.

51. Sichuan tongxianghui, "Shang Chuandu Xiliang kaiban Chuan-Han tielu gongsi yijian shu" [Our opinions on starting the Chuan-Han Railway Company], in Dai, ed., *Sichuan baolu yundong shiliao huizuan*, 290.

52. Ibid., 291–92.

53. Ibid., 292.

54. Ibid.

55. *Zugu* is a tax, as it was forced upon landowners in Sichuan; yet at the same time, *zugu* is a stock, as *zugu* payers became stockholders in the railway company and supposedly earned their dividends every year. I translate *zugu* as "railway tax" throughout the book, although it is not the most comprehensive translation.

56. "Chuan-Han tielu zong gongsi jigu zhangcheng" [Regulations on levying railway taxes of the Chuan-Han Railway Company], "Disanzhang" [chapter 3], "Choushou zhigu" [levied stock], in Dai, ed., *Sichuan baolu yundong shiliao huizuan*, 272.

57. Ibid.

58. An additional regulation was: "Use tenants' rent as the tax; if they pay more than 10 *dan* in rent, they should be taxed the *zugu* according to the regulated amount," in Dai, ed., *Sichuan baolu yundong shiliao huizuan*, 279.

59. "Shang-Hu-Waiwu bu huizou yifu Chuan-Han tielu zong gongsi jigu zhangcheng" [Jointly issued edict by the Ministries of Commerce, Finance, and Foreign Affairs after discussion of the chart on levying railway taxes of the Chuan-Han Railway Company], in Dai, ed., *Sichuan baolu yundong shiliao huizuan*, 267, 276–77.

60. "Chuan-Han tielu anzu chougu xiangxi zhangcheng" [Detailed regulations on railway taxation], in Dai, ed., *Sichuan baolu yundong shiliao huizuan*, 278.

61. Nishikawa Masao, "Sichuan baolu yundong qianye de shehui zhuangkuang" [The situation of society before the Railway Protection movement], trans. Wang Weiru, in Wei Yingtao and Zhao Qing, eds., *Sichuan xinhai geming shiliao* [Collected historical materials of the 1911 Revolution in Sichuan] (Chengdu: Sichuan renmin chubanshe, 1982), vol. 2, 629.

62. Ibid., 626.

63. Li Xin, *Zhonghua minguo shi* [History of Republican China] (Beijing: Zhonghua shuju, 1981), 193.

64. Sichuan tongxianghui, "Wei Chuan-Han tielu shi jinggao quanshu fulao shu," in Dai, ed., *Sichuan baolu yundong shiliao huizuan*, 297.

65. Ibid., 298.
66. Ibid.
67. Ibid., 300.
68. Ibid., 301.
69. Ibid.
70. Ibid., 303–4.
71. Ibid., 305.
72. Ibid., 306–7.
73. Ibid., 311. The size of the population here is an inaccurate number that was used only by these students at the time. The actual number was about forty-five million.
74. Ibid.

75. *Sichuan liuri xuesheng tiedao lihai xianggao* [Detailed explanation by Sichuan overseas students of the importance of railways], in Dai ed., *Sichuan baolu yundong shiliao huizuan*, 315.

76. "Gan Dazhang zou" [Gan Dazhang memorial], in *Sheng Xuanhuai dang'an ziliao xuanji* [Archival documents on Sheng Xuanhuai] (Shanghai: Shanghai renmin chubanshe, 1979), vol. 1, 80–81.

77. Sichuan tongxianghui, "Wei Chuan-Han tielu shi jinggao quanshu fulao shu," 304–5.

78. Ibid., 305.

79. Ibid.

80. Mi, *Zhongguo jindai tielu shi ziliao*, vol. 3, 1072.

81. Xiliang, *Xiliang yigao zougao*, vol. 1, 497–98.

82. This second Hu Jun (1869–1934) came from Guang'an county. He was awarded the *jinshi* in 1903 and was sent by the court to study at Hōsei University. After getting a law degree, he returned to Sichuan in 1907.

83. Chuan-Han tielu gaijinhui [Association for Improving the Chuan-Han Railway], ed., *Chuanlu gaijinhui baogao* [Report of the Association for Improving the Chuan-Han Railway Company] (Tokyo: 1904–1907), vols. 1–3, 5. Original copy in the Sichuan Provincial Library.

84. Pu Dianjun, *Gailiang Chuan-Han gongsi yi* [On improving the Chuan-Han Railway Company] (Tokyo: 1907), 4. Original pamphlet in the Sichuan Provincial Library.

85. Xiao Xiang, "Guang'an Pu Dianjun xingzhuang" [The life of Pu Dianjun of Guang'an county], in Wei and Zhao, eds., *Sichuan xinhai geming shiliao*, vol. 2, 612.

86. Pu, *Gailiang Chuan-Han gongsi yi*, 4–5.

87. Ibid., 4.

88. Ibid.

89. Ibid., 5–10.

90. Ibid., 15.

91. *Jianshe Chuan-Han tielu shangban gongsi quangaoshu* [Calling for a private Chuan-Han Railway Company], n.p. Original poster in the Sichuan Provincial Library.

92. Ibid.

93. Ibid.

94. Ibid.

95. Ibid.

96. Ibid.

97. "Tongyuanju nuoyi Chuan-Han tielu gongsi guben diaocha baogaoshu" [Report on the Copper Bureau appropriating the railway capital of the Chuan-Han Railway Company], in Chuan-Han tielu gaijinhui, *Chuanlu gaijinhui baogaoshu*, vol. 1, 10–23.

98. Ibid., 11.

99. Ibid., 17.

100. "Tongyuanju nuokuan shijian huilu" [Records on the Copper Bureau appropriating the railway capital], in Chuan-Han tielu gaijinhui, *Chuanlu gaijinhui baogaoshu*, vol. 2, 57–72.

101. "Tepaiyuan zhi baogao" [Report by the special investigator], "Yichang diaochayuan laihan" [Letter from investigator in Yichang], "Beijing diaochayuan laihan" [Letter from investigator in Beijing], in Chuan-Han tielu gaijinhui, *Chuanlu gaijinhui baogaoshu*, vol. 3, 1–21, 89–93, 95–96.

102. Xiao, "Guang'an Pu Dianjun xingzhuang," 612.

103. "Sichuan liuxuesheng gailiang Chuan-han tielu gongsi yi" [Proposal of Sichuan overseas students on improving the Chuan-han railway company], in Chuan-Han tielu gaijinhui, *Chuanlu gaijinhui baogaoshu*, vol. 4, in Dai, ed., *Sichuan baolu yundong shiliao huizuan*, 432–41.

104. Ibid.

105. Xianyu hao, "Shilun chuanlu zugu" [On the Chuan-Han railway tax], in *Lishi yanjiu* no. 2 (1982): 41–55.

106. Chuan-Han tielu gaijinhui, *Chuanlu gaijinhui baogaoshu*, vol. 5, 89–91.

107. "Gongdu" [Official documents], *Shangban Sichuan Chuan Han tielu zong gongsi baogao* [Newsletter of the private Sichuan Chuan-Han Railway Company], vol. 15, no. 19, n.p. Original newspaper in the Sichuan Provincial Library. The newsletter recorded a case from Fuzhou of the *zugu* bureau manager taking the *zugu* for his own use. Also, according to Dai Zhili, in his hometown in Wenjiang county, the *zugu* bureau's chief manager was rumored to have taken the funds. Interview with Dai Zhili in 2004.

108. Prasenjit Duara, *Culture, Power, and the State: Rural North China, 1900–1942* (Stanford, CA: Stanford University Press, 1988), 245–50. Also arguing along this line is Kristin Stapleton in *Civilizing Chengdu* and "County Administration in Late-Qing Sichuan: Conflicting Models of Rural Policing," *Late Imperial China*, vol. 18, no. 1 (1997): 100–132.

109. William Rowe, "The Public Sphere in Modern China," *Modern China*, vol. 16, no. 3 (1999): 309.

110. Mary Rankin, *Elite Activism and Political Transformation in China: Zhejiang Province, 1865–1911* (Stanford, CA: Stanford University Press, 1986).

111. Rowe, "The Public Sphere in Modern China," 309–29.

CHAPTER 4. CAN TWO SIDES WALK TOGETHER WITHOUT AGREEING TO MEET?

1. Sichuan sheng ziyiju [Sichuan provincial assembly], *Sichuan ziyiju diyici yishilu* [Transcripts of the proposals by the first Sichuan provincial assembly], in Wei Yingtao and Zhao Qing, eds., *Sichuan Xinhai geming shiliao* (Chengdu: Sichuan renmin chubanshe, 1981), vol. 1, 1.

2. Xiao Xiang, "Guang'an Pu Dianjun xingzhuang" [The life of Pu Dianjun of Guang'an county], in Wei and Zhao, eds., *Sichuan Xinhai geming shiliao*, vol. 2, 612.

3. Sichuan sheng ziyiju, *Sichuan ziyiju diyici yishilu*, in Wei and Zhao, eds., *Sichuan Xinhai geming shiliao*, vol. 1, 1.

4. Ibid., 6–7.

5. Ibid., 7.

6. Ibid., 6.

7. "Yishang yu xinren yu jiu" [Clothes, new people, and wine], *Hangzhou baihuabao*, November 25, 1901, and "Lun Zhongguo yi jiuren xing xinzheng zhi miu" [On China's mistake of using old people to conduct new politics], *Zhongwai ribao*, April 28, 1901, in Hou Yijie, *Ershi shiji chu Zhongguo zhengzhi gaige fengchao: Qingmo lixian yundong shi* [The wave of political reform in early twentieth-century China: The constitutional movement of the late Qing] (Beijing: Renmin chubanshe, 1993), 31.

8. Hou, *Ershi shiji chu Zhongguo zhengzhi gaige fengchao*, 30–39.

9. Ibid., 42–44.

10. Zhang Kaiyuan, "Lun Zhang Jian de maodun xingge" [On Zhang Jian's conflicted personality], *Lishi yanjiu*, no. 3 (1963): 87–104.

11. Yang Dongliang, "Lüelun Zhang Jian de zhengzhi zhuiqiu" [A short analysis of the political pursuits of Zhang Jian], *Qingshi yanjiu*, no. 2 (1996): 70–77.

12. Zhang Kaiyuan, *Kaituozhe de zuji: Zhang Jian zhuan'gao* [Biography of Zhang Jian] (Beijing: Zhonghua shuju, 1986). Zhu Zhisan, an ordinary late Qing literatus, used the term "great gentry" (*jushen*) to describe these people. In Zhu Zhisan, *Zhu Zhisan riji* [Diary of Zhu Zhisan] (Wuhan: Huazhong shifan daxue chubanshe, 2011), 169.

13. "Lun Ri-E zhizhan zhiyi" [On the benefits of the Russo-Japanese war], *Zhongwai ribao*, February 13, 1904, in Hou, *Ershi shiji chu Zhongguo zhengzhi gaige fengchao*, 40.

14. "Zhu huangzhong zhi jiangxing" [Celebrating the rise of the yellow race], *Zhongwai ribao*, February 19, 1904, in Hou, *Ershi shiji chu Zhongguo zhengzhi gaige fengchao*, 41.

15. Kang Jizu, ed., *Yubei lixian yijianshu* [Suggestions on preparing for constitutionalism] (Beijing: 1906), 1–2, in Hou, *Ershi shiji chu Zhongguo zhengzhi gaige fengchao*, 41.

16. "Nanyang gongxue Zhang Meiyi zhi Liangguang dushu mufu shu" [Letter from Zhang Meiyi of Nanyang public school to the staff of the governor-general of Liangguang], in Hou, *Ershi shiji chu Zhongguo zhengzhi gaige fengchao*, 46. Zhang Meiyi, alongside Zhang Yuanji and Zhao Fengchang, was a member of the Jiang-Zhe constitutionalist group, and Cen Chunxuan was the governor-general of Liangguang at this time. The letter was dated March 10, 1905, but it talked about events between February 10 and February 15, 1904.

17. Sun Baoqi, "Chushi Faguo dachen Sun shang zhengwuchu shu" [Memorial by ambassador to France, Sun Baoqi, to the Office of Governmental Affairs], in *Dongfang zazhi*, first year, no. 7, in Hou, *Ershi shiji chu Zhongguo zhengzhi gaige fengchao*, 43.

18. Hou, *Ershi shiji chu Zhongguo zhengzhi gaige fengchao*, 49–52.

19. Ibid., 53–56. See also Li Xizhu, "Difang dufu yu lixian sichao ji qingting yubei lixian zhi zuece" [Local governors and constitutional thought and the Qing court's decision to prepare for constitutionalism], in Li Xizhu, *Difang dufu yu qingmo xinzheng: Wanqing quanli geju zai yanjiu* [Local governors and the New Policies reform: A further study of the power structure of the late Qing] (Beijing: Shehui kexue wenxian chubanshe, 2012), 137–75.

20. Hou, *Ershi shiji chu Zhongguo zhengzhi gaige fengchao*, 52.
21. Ibid., 45.
22. Ibid., 57–69.
23. Ibid., 68–69.
24. Ibid., 69.
25. Xia Xiaohong, "Liang Qichao daini xianzheng zhegao kao" [An investigation of Liang Qichao's role in drafting constitutional memorials], in Xia Xiaohong, *Liang Qichao: Zai zhengzhi yu xueshu zhijian* [Liang Qichao: Between academics and politics] (Beijing: Dongfang chubanshe, 2014), 28.
26. Joseph Esherick, "Rethinking the 1911 Revolution," in Zhongguo shixuehui, ed., *Jinian xinhai geming yibai zhounian guoji xueshu yantaohui lunwenji* [Papers commemorating the hundredth anniversary of the 1911 Revolution] (Wuhan: 2011), vol. 1, 372. Such Manchu officials as Duanfang focused specifically on this problem. As Esherick notes, Duanfang, in a comprehensive memorial, proposed to end the Manchu legal privileges, promoted intermarriage of Manchus and Han, abolished Manchu posts in the bureaucracy, eliminated separation of ethnic banners in the capital guards, and put an end to the banner garrisons in the provinces.
27. Hou, *Ershi shiji chu Zhongguo zhengzhi gaige fengchao*, 68.
28. Ibid., 73.
29. "Lixian jiwen" [Chronology of the constitutional reform], in Zhongguo shixuehui, ed., *Xinhai geming* [The 1911 Revolution] (Shanghai: Shanghai renmin chubanshe, 1957), vol. 4, 14–17.
30. Hou, *Ershi shiji chu Zhongguo zhengzhi gaige fengchao*, 82–83.
31. Ibid. According to Hou Yijie, Yuan Shikai was the real power behind the scenes, even though Zaize was officially given the job of supervising the reform.
32. Edward Rhoads, *Manchus and Han: Ethnic Relations and Political Power in Late Qing and Early Republican China, 1861–1928* (Seattle: University of Washington Press, 2000), 100–101. Also in Hou, *Ershi shiji chu Zhongguo zhengzhi gaige fengchao*, 83.
33. Hou, *Ershi shiji chu Zhongguo zhengzhi gaige fengchao*, 83.
34. Reforming officials Zaize, Dai Hongci, Qu Hongji, and Xu Shichang proposed an overhaul of local administration, but Grand Councilor Sun Jia'nai and others proposed a more conservative reform. On November 5, 1906, these leaders sent a telegram outlining both proposals to all provincial officials and asked them to choose one.
35. Hou, *Ershi shiji chu Zhongguo zhengzhi gaige fengchao*, 86–91.
36. Ming-Qing dang'an bu, ed., *Qingmo choubei lixian dang'an shiliao* [Historical archival documents on preparations for constitutional government in the late Qing] (Beijing: Zhonghua shuju, 1979), vol. 1, 44.
37. For example, the reform-minded Manchu statesman Duanfang wrote to Tieliang upon this assassination: "From this moment on, there is not a single day we [Manchus] can feel at rest. Thus, given the situation, the only way we can survive is to try our best to reform and to use all methods that we can, so that all under Heaven will be benefited." In Hou, *Ershi shiji chu Zhongguo zhengzhi gaige fengchao*, 98.

38. Ibid., 99.

39. Ming-Qing dang'an bu, ed., *Qingmo choubei lixian dang'an shiliao*, vol. 1, 45–46. It was transformed from the old Institute of Political Investigation (Kaocha zhengzhi guan) established on October 19, 1906.

40. Ibid., 48.

41. Hou, *Ershi shiji chu Zhongguo zhengzhi gaige fengchao*, 100.

42. Rhoads, *Manchus and Han*, 100–101.

43. Ding Wenjiang and Zhao Fengtian, eds., *Liang Qichao nianpu changbian* [Chronicle of Liang Qichao's life] (Beijing: Zhonghua shuju, 2010), 195–96.

44. Peng Jian, *Qingji xianzheng bianchaguan yanjiu* [A study of the late-Qing Institute for Constitutional Compilation] (Beijing: Beijing daxue chubanshe, 2011), 213–30. In addition to these foreign-trained law school graduates, participants in the 1905 constitutional mission were also an important element of the institute's personnel.

45. *Zhonghua minguo yuannian diyici nongshang tongjibiao* [The first statistics on agriculture and commerce: The first year of the Republic of China] (1914), in Hou, *Ershi shiji chu Zhongguo zhengzhi gaige fengchao*, 109. See also Wang Di, *Kuachu fengbi de shijie: Changjiang shangyou quyu shehui yanjiu, 1644–1911* [Striding out of a closed world: A study of society in the upper Yangzi region, 1644–1911] (Beijing: Zhonghua shuju, 1993), 572.

46. Li Xiaoti, *Qingmo xiaceng shehui qimeng yundong 1901–1911* [The late Qing popular enlightenment movement, 1901–1911] (Taipei: Zhongyang yanjiuyuan, 1992).

47. Sanetō Keishū, *Zhongguo ren liuxue Riben shi* [History of overseas Chinese students in Japan], trans. Tan Ruqian and Li Qiyan (Beijing: Sanlian shudian, 1983), 36, 39, 81.

48. As we have seen in Chapter 2, *Xinmin congbao* had wide circulation across the Qing empire, including in Sichuan. And Zhu Zhisan, an ordinary student in a new-style school in Wuchang, frequently mentioned *Xinmin congbao* and *Zhongguohun* in his diary. He was exposed to them as early as 1902. In Zhu, *Zhu Zhisan riji*, 102, 103, 206, 225.

49. Hou, *Ershi shiji chu Zhongguo zhengzhi gaige fengchao*, 184.

50. Ding and Zhao, eds., *Liang Qichao nianpu changbian*, 189.

51. Ibid., 201.

52. Hou, *Ershi shiji chu Zhongguo zhengzhi gaige fengchao*, 184.

53. Ding and Zhao, eds., *Liang Qichao nianpu changbian*, 204.

54. Ibid., 202–4. In April 1907, Yang Du sent a private letter to Liang Qichao: "I have started propagandizing on opening a parliament in *Zhongguo xinbao*. However, this has not generated much of a reaction. In my opinion, if the two of us use *Xinmin congbao* and *Shibao* to send the message together, in the next two to three months, then the problem of the parliament would become the most important yet simple issue." Liang accepted the suggestion and replied: "This is a great idea and I will follow up on this and make sure *Shibao* responds."

55. "Lun jinnian guomin dang quanli wei guohui qingyuan yishi" [On citizens should be trying their best to petition for the opening of the parliament this year],

Shibao, February 26–27, 1908, in Hou, *Ershi shiji chu Zhongguo zhengzhi gaige fengchao*, 189.

56. *Shenbao*, November 10, 1907, in Hou, *Ershi shiji chu Zhongguo zhengzhi gaige fengchao*, 185.

57. Hou, *Ershi shiji chu Zhongguo zhengzhi gaige fengchao*, 190–98.

58. Ibid., 205–15.

59. Zhou Xun, *Shuhai congtan* [Collected talks about Sichuan] (Chongqing: Chongqing Dagongbao bu, 1948), vol. 2, 12a–22b.

60. Bradley Reed, "Gentry Activism in Nineteenth-Century Sichuan: The Three-Fees Bureau," *Late Imperial China*, vol. 10, no. 1 (1999): 100. According to Reed, "The province of Sichuan was noted by contemporaries for the large number of quasi-independent gentry bureaus (*shenju*).... Although these bureaus were established with government approval for quite limited purposes, they showed a marked ability to expand their areas of activity over time."

61. Ibid., 99.

62. Sichuan sheng ziyiju, *Sichuan sheng ziyiju diyici yishilu*, 46. The evidence here shows that before 1908, the tax on pigs was levied by the Three-Fees Bureau.

63. Reed, "Gentry Activism in Nineteenth-Century Sichuan," 119.

64. Hou, *Ershi shiji chu Zhongguo zhengzhi gaige fengchao*, 82–83.

65. Zhou, *Shuhai congtan*, vol. 2, 20a. Also according to Ba county archival documents, the New Tax Bureau started functioning very effectively from 1908.

66. Li Jieren, *Dabo* [Great wave], in *Li Jieren xuanji* [Collected works of Li Jieren] (Chengdu: Sichuan renmin chubanshe, 1980), vol. 2, 533.

67. Zhou, *Shuhai congtan*, vol. 2, 20a.

68. Ba xian dang'an [Ba county archive] quanzong 6, mulu 7 and juan 1428: "Ba xian jiehu Dingyuanxian yijie Guangxu sanshisi nian, xuantong yuannian, ernian, ji sannian tielu zugu yinqian juan" [Ba county on escorting the transferals of Dingyuan county's railway taxes for the 1908, 1909, 1910, and 1911]. Original documents in the Sichuan Archive.

69. Xiliang, *Xiliang yigao zougao* [Posthumous papers and memorials of Xiliang] (Beijing: Zhonghua shuju, 1959), vol. 1, 566.

70. *Shubao*, no. 9 (1910), "Jishi" [Chronicle]. *Shubao* was the official newspaper of the Sichuan Provincial Assembly.

71. *Fushunxianzhi* [Fushun county gazetteer], vol. 5, "Shihuo zhengque" [Economy and taxation], in Wei Yingtao et al., *Sichuan jindaishi* [History of modern Sichuan] (Chengdu: Sichuan shehui kexue chubanshe, 1985), 287.

72. *Xuantong zhengji* [Political chronicle of the Xuantong reign], vol. 4, Guangxu thirty-fourth year, twelfth month, sixth day, in Wei et al., *Sichuan jindaishi*, 287.

73. *Sichuan guanbao*, no. 1, in Wei et al., *Sichuan jindaishi*, 287–88.

74. In many of the cases in Sichuan, the negative effects of reforms seemed to outweigh any advances. The New Policies in Sichuan, especially the two bureaus that I have investigated in detail, caused a great deal of trouble for the people of Sichuan.

75. Hou, *Ershi shiji chu Zhongguo zhengzhi gaige fengchao*, 225.

76. Zhang Pengyuan, *Lixianpai yu xinhai geming* [Constitutionalists and the 1911 Revolution] (Taipei: Zhongyang yanjiuyuan jindaishi yanjiusuo, 1969), 111–20.

77. Li Xizhu, "Difang dufu yu lixianpai zai ziyiju de zhengzheng" [Political struggle in the Provincial Assembly between local governors and the constitutional group], in Li Xizhu, *Difang dufu yu qingmo xinzheng*, 291. In his diary, the conservative governor-general of Liangjiang, Zhang Renjun, wrote that Zhao Erxun "strongly propagated the new political theories," which very much worried Zhang.

78. Sichuan sheng ziyiju, *Sichuan sheng ziyiju diyici yishilu*, 3–7.

79. Ibid., 3.

80. Ibid., 4.

81. "Lun Zhongguo qiantu you kewang zhiji" [On the promising future of China], *Zhongwai ribao*, May 5, 1904, in Hou, *Ershi shiji chu Zhongguo zhengzhi gaige fengchao*, 42.

82. As we can see, there was a modern understanding of the state behind Zhao Erxun's reasoning. It is very far from the original meaning of *guo*, namely "fief." Sovereignty, though its meanings have varied across history, always has a core meaning: the supreme authority within a territory.

83. Sichuan sheng ziyiju, *Sichuan sheng ziyiju diyici yishilu*, 4.

84. Ibid.

85. Ibid.

86. Ibid., 8.

87. Ibid., 7–8.

88. Ibid., 8.

89. Ibid., 8–9.

90. Ibid.

91. Ibid., 16.

92. Ibid., 17.

93. Ibid., 25–29.

94. Ibid., 37.

95. Ibid., 82.

96. Ibid., 65–72.

97. Ibid., 82–86.

98. Ibid., 86–103.

99. Duanfang, "Qingding guoshi yi an daji zhe" [Memorial to set up the principle of the country], in *Duan minzhong gong zougao* [The draft memorials of Duanfang], vol. 6, in Hou, *Ershi shiji chu Zhongguo zhengzhi gaige fengchao*, 69.

100. Sichuan sheng ziyiju, *Sichuan sheng ziyiju diyici yishilu*, 37.

101. Ibid., 37–38.

102. *Zhengshui*, although the term sometimes still refers to the *diliang* or land tax, was more widely used after the New Policies reform. *Fujiashui* originally referred to the surcharge on the land tax. The "main tax" originally referred to the land tax (*diliang*). However, after the late Qing Taiping Rebellion, more taxes were levied by other methods yet were also called "main tax."

103. See Madeleine Zelin, *The Magistrate's Tael: Rationalizing Fiscal Reform in Eighteenth-Century Ch'ing China* (Berkeley: University of California Press, 1984), 88–115. Yongzheng hoped to rationally manage state revenue and control how local magistrates gained their income. Officials in each province could collect a fixed-percentage surcharge on all regular land and other taxes remitted to the central government. See also Ray Huang, *Fiscal Administration during the Ming Dynasty* (Cambridge: Cambridge University Press, 1969), on the rationale of the fiscal system of Ming and Qing China.

104. Sichuan sheng ziyiju, *Sichuan sheng ziyiju diyici yishilu*, 39.

105. Ibid., 39–40.

106. Ibid., 40.

107. Ibid.

108. The assemblymen did not clarify which "local" they were talking about, whether it was the local self-government organizations (*difang zizhi*) or the local government (*difang xingzheng*). This was intentional. The *difang xingzheng* was a gray area. Zhao Erxun believed it belonged to the state (*guojia*), and thus, he used the New Tax Bureau to levy taxes for the local government. However, the assemblymen decided to make the *difang xingzheng* part of their territory, by only emphasizing *difang* (i.e., local). Both had legal backing on this issue.

109. Sichuan sheng ziyiju, *Sichuan sheng ziyiju diyici yishilu*, 41. Zhao's claim was inaccurate, as explained earlier regarding the meaning of *fujiashui* and its relation to *huohao*.

110. Ibid.

111. Ibid., 42.

112. Ibid.

113. Ibid., 43.

114. Ibid., 45.

115. Ibid., 47.

116. Ibid., 10.

117. Ibid.

118. Ibid.

119. Jia Yuying, *Songdai jiancha zhidu* [The monitoring system in the Song dynasty] (Zhengzhou: Henan daxue chubanshe, 2006).

120. Sichuan sheng ziyiju, *Sichuan sheng ziyiju diyici yishilu*, 11.

121. Ibid.

122. Ibid.

CHAPTER 5. THE RHETORIC OF REVOLUTION

1. A systematic reading of *Baxian dang'an* [Ba county archival records], "Qing xuantong" [Qing period xuantong reign] (1911), *Xinjin dang'an* [Xinjin county archives], and "Minguo" [Republican period] (1911–1913), reveals that township-level assemblies were regularly convened, despite the disruption of the revolution.

2. Sichuan sheng baoye zhi bianji bu, ed., *Sichuan baoye dashiji (1897–1995)* [Chronicle of the history of the Sichuan press (1897–1995)] (Chengdu: Sichuan renmin chubanshe, 1996), 1–19.

3. Han Dayuan, "Meinongbu daji lixian zhuyi sixiang yanjiu" [A study of the constitutional thought of Minobe Tatsukichi], http://article.chinalawinfo.com/Article_Detail.asp?ArticleId=55832 (viewed on November 14, 2013).

4. Zhang Pengyuan, *Lixianpai yu xinhai geming* [Constitutionalists and the 1911 Revolution] (Taipei: Zhongyang yanjiuyuan jindaishi yanjiusuo, 1969), 58.

5. Ibid., 64.

6. Ibid.

7. The Qing court's attitude during the 1910 National Assembly further exasperated the constitutionalists. The 1910 National Assembly was a key moment in which constitutionalists came together and voiced their political objectives. In the middle of the meeting, the assembly passed a motion to impeach the Grand Council and memorialized it to the Qing court. To be sure, the assembly was careful to focus on the Grand Council rather than on the court. It even asserted that its interest was to protect the "sacred inviolability of imperial authority," which followed the spirit of all previous appeals for constitutional government. Nonetheless, Zaifeng took the impeachment as a personal insult and rejected the appeal in an imperial edict. As Assemblyman Yi Zongkui argued: "Yesterday's edict came from the Regent himself. He has thus left us no room. . . . He treated us as an enemy and considered that the assembly was opposing the monarch. In that case, how are the politics of today different from an autocracy?" The tone of the assemblymen toward the Qing court changed dramatically after Zaifeng's edict. In Li Qicheng, ed., *Zizhengyuan yichang huiyi sujilu: Wanqing yubei guohui lunbian shilu* [Transcripts of the first National Assembly meeting] (Shanghai: Shanghai sanlian shudian, 2011), transcript no. 21.

8. Zhang, *Lixianpai yu xinhai geming*, 64.

9. "Qingdi tielu ganxian shougui guoyou yu" [Imperial edict on nationalizing the trunk lines of the railway], in Dai Zhili, ed., *Sichuan baolu yundong shiliao huizuan* [Collection of historical materials on the Sichuan Railway Protection movement] (Taipei: Zhongyang yanjiuyuan jindaishi yanjiusuo, 1994), 527.

10. Su Kanshi, "Xianglu an" [The case of Hunan railways], in *Xinhai geming* [The Xinhai Revolution], vol. 4, 551, in Zhang, *Lixianpai yu xinhai geming*, 114.

11. "Shi Changxin zouqing jiding tielu ganxian wei guoyou zhe" [Memorial from Shi Changxin on nationalizing the trunk lines], in Dai, ed., *Sichuan baolu yundong shiliao huizuan*, 522–24.

12. "Hubei Hunan liangsheng jingnei Yue-Han; Hubei jingnei Chuan-Han tielu jiekuan hetong" [Huguang foreign loan agreement], in Dai, ed., *Sichuan baolu yundong shiliao huizuan*, 540–48.

13. "Youchuanbu xiuzheng Chuan-Yue-Han tielu jiekuan ji ganlu guoyou banfa bianmingshu" [Explanation of the revised plans for nationalizing the Chuan-Han and Yue-Han railways and taking out foreign loans], in Dai, ed., *Sichuan baolu yundong shiliao huizuan*, 1664.

14. Ralph Huenemann, *The Dragon and the Iron Horse: The Economics of Railroads in China, 1876–1937* (Cambridge, MA: Harvard University Press, 1984), 71.

15. Ibid., 72.

16. Ibid., 73.

17. Ma Linghe, *Qingmo minchu tielu waizhai guan yanjiu* [A study of the idea of taking out foreign loans in building railways in the late Qing and early Republican eras] (Shanghai: Fudan daxue chubanshe, 2004), chap. 4; Su Quanyou, *Qingmo youchuanbu yanjiu* [A study of the Department of Posts and Communications in the late Qing] (Beijing: Zhonghua shuju, 2005), chaps. 6 and 7.

18. *Meiguo waijiao wenjian* [Diplomatic documents of the United States], for the year 1911, in Dai, ed., *Sichuan baolu yundong shiliao huizuan*, 537.

19. The full text of the foreign loan agreement is in Dai, ed., *Sichuan baolu yundong shiliao huizuan*, 540–48.

20. Chang Peng-yuan, "The Constitutionalists," in Mary Wright, ed., *China in Revolution: The First Phase, 1900–1913* (New Haven, CT: Yale University Press, 1968), 174. In fact, seven of thirteen members of the company's board of directors were Chairman Pu's followers.

21. There were a total of eight telegrams circulated among the Chengdu headquarters, Yichang branch, Shanghai branch, and the Beijing-based official Qiao Shunan, including telegrams on May 11, 13, and 15. In *Chuanlu shouhui guoyou wanglai yaodian* [Key telegrams concerning the nationalization of the Sichuan railways]. Original document from Professor Dai Zhili. See also Dai, ed., *Sichuan baolu yundong shiliao huizuan*, 553–56.

22. *Shubao*, no. 12, 1911. This article was later republished in an independent pamphlet. In Dai, ed., *Sichuan baolu yundong shiliao huizuan*, vol. 1, 559–60.

23. Ibid., 561–62.

24. Ibid., 562.

25. "Sichuan jingguan Gan Dazhang, Song Yuren deng lianming cheng youbu qingjiang chuanlu gukuan furu guojia lugu yi zuo chuanren xiuzhu cheng-kui tielu wen" [Joint memorial by metropolitan officials Gan Dazhang, Song Yuren, and others asking to nationalize the commercial shares of the railway company as capital to build the Chengdu-Kuizhou line], in Dai, ed., *Sichuan baolu yundong shiliao huizuan*, 749–50.

26. "Chengdu zong gongsi zhi Yichang gongsi dian" [Telegrams from the Chengdu headquarters to the Yichang branch], in Dai, ed., *Sichuan baolu yundong shiliao huizuan*, 604 and 606.

27. "Sheng Xuanhuai, Duanfang zhi Wang Renwen dian" [Telegram from Sheng Xuanhuai and Duanfang to Wang Renwen], June 1, 1911, in *Chuanlu shouhui guoyou wanglai yaodian*, 10–11.

28. Ibid.

29. Zhang, *Lixianpai yu xinhai geming*, 112.

30. *Sichuan baolu tongzhihui dianwen yaolu* [Key telegrams of the Sichuan Railway Protection Association], 15–27. I thank Professor Dai Zhili for providing

me with this original document. The full text of the foreign loan agreement is also in Dai, ed., *Sichuan baolu yundong shiliao huizuan*, 540–48.

31. "Sichuan shenmin Luo Lun deng qianzhu Yue-han Chuan-han tielu jiekuan hetong" [A critique of the Huguang Foreign Loan Agreement by Luo Lun and others], in Dai, ed., *Sichuan baolu yundong shiliao huizuan*, 638–43.

32. Ibid., 643.

33. *Shubao*, special issue, June 17, 1911, in Dai, ed., *Sichuan baolu yundong shiliao huizuan*, 633.

34. This charge is particularly nonsensical because it was normal practice for interest to be saved up to pay the lenders.

35. This refers to the May 9 nationalization policy edict that pledged to protect the interests of the Sichuan people. The central government soon changed its attitude and wanted all of the money held by the Chuan-Han Railway Company for itself.

36. *Shubao*, special issue, June 17, 1911, in Dai, ed., *Sichuan baolu yundong shiliao huizuan*, 633–38.

37. *Kangxi cidian* [Kangxi dictionary], online version, http://www.kangxizidian.com/index2.php (viewed in May 2008).

38. *Shubao*, special issue, June 17, 1911, in Dai, ed., *Sichuan baolu yundong shiliao huizuan*, 633–38.

39. *Sichuan shanghui gongbao*, June 21, 1911, in Dai, ed., *Sichuan baolu yundong shiliao huizuan*, 657.

40. Ibid.

41. Ibid., 656.

42. Deng Xiaoke, "Da Bingmang" [To answer questions from Bingmang], *Baolu tongzhihui baogao* (hereafter *Baogao*), no. 21, July 21, 1911.

43. "Baolu tongzhihui xuanyan shu" [Declaration of the Railway Protection Association], *Baogao*, no. 9, July 6, 1911.

44. "Qing aiguo zhe zhuyi" [Patriots, please pay attention], *Baogao*, no. 11, July 8, 1911.

45. Ibid.

46. Deng, "Da Bingmang," *Baogao*, no. 21, July 21, 1911.

47. Ibid.

48. Luo Yishi, "Gao quanguo fulao shu" [Talk to all elders and fathers], *Baogao*, no. 18, July 18, 1911.

49. "Chuanren zhi aiguo re" [Patriotic passion of the Sichuan people], *Baogao*, no. 2, June 27, 1911.

50. "Wang Renwen zhi neige, youchuanbu, ji Duan daren dian" [Telegram from Wang Renwen to the Cabinet, the Ministry of Posts and Communications, and Duanfang], in Chen Xulu et al., eds., *Xinhai geming qianhou* [Around the time of the 1911 Revolution] (Shanghai: Shanghai renmin chubanshe, 1979), vol. 1, 102.

51. Li Jieren, *Baofengyu qian* [Before the big storm], in *Li Jieren xuanji* [Collected works of Li Jieren] (Chengdu: Sichuan renmin chubanshe, 1980), vol. 1, 36 and 41.

52. "Tielu guoyou an" [The case for nationalizing the railways], in *Manqing yeshi* [The unofficial history of the Manchu Qing dynasty], vol. 4, item 13. Original document (from Professor Dai Zhili) was first published in 1920.

53. Li Jieren, *Dabo* [Great wave], in *Li Jieren xuanji*, vol. 1, 36.

54. Ibid., 41.

55. "Tielu guoyou an."

56. Li, *Dabo*, 41; "Tielu guoyou an."

57. In Li, *Dabo*, 57, the number is seven hundred. In "Tielu guoyou an," the number is four thousand. In Wang Renwen's telegram, it is two thousand. In *Baogao*, no. 2, June 27, 1911, the number is several thousand. In "Telegram to Xiao Xiang and Li Wenxi," in *Shibao*, July 3, 1911, it is five thousand. Later, the number reached fifteen thousand copies, as is verified by the advertisement in *Baogao*, no. 21, July 21, 1911.

58. Li, *Dabo*, 33.

59. Ibid., 34.

60. Ibid., 38.

61. Ibid., 41–42.

62. "Chengdu Yin shu fansi Liang zhi Duan daren dian" [Telegram from Yinliang to Duanfang], in Sheng Xuanhuai, *Yuzhai cungao* [Materials preserved in Yu House] (1939; reprint, Taipei: Wenhai chubanshe, 1965), vol. 78, 9.

63. Peng Fen, *Xinhai xunqing zhengbian fayuan ji* [The origins of the Qing regime change in 1911] (Chengdu: Fumin gongsi, 1933), 31. Original document from Professor Dai Zhili.

64. Ibid. Peng recollected, "In general, there were about 10 people in each prefecture.... The average travel fund for these students was 10 yuan."

65. "Benhui zhi jingfei" [Budget of this association], *Baogao*, no. 12, July 11, 1911.

66. "Sichuan baolu tongzhihui jianzhang" [Regulations concerning the Sichuan Railway Protection Association], in Dai, ed., *Sichuan baolu yundong shiliao huizuan*, 674.

67. Ibid., 683. Pu Dianjun, the behind-the-scenes mastermind, did not assume any public position in the Railway Protection Association but was heavily involved in all of its activities.

68. Ibid., 674.

69. Ibid., 678–79.

70. Ibid., 676.

71. Ibid., 675.

72. Ibid., 679–81.

73. "Guanwai wenbaochu zhi aiguo re" [Patriotism in the border area], *Baogao*, no. 17, July 17, 1911.

74. "Chashe shaonian zhi aiguo re" [Teahouse young man's patriotism], *Baogao*, no. 17, July 17, 1911.

75. "Baozhi ganren" [A touching newspaper], *Xigubao*, no. 36, in Dai, ed., *Sichuan baolu yundong shiliao huizuan*, 694–95.

76. "Zhuyi, zhuyi, zhuyi: Baolu tongzhihui tebie guanggao" [Attention, attention, attention: Special advertisement of the Railway Protection Association], *Baogao*, no. 2, June 27, 1911.

77. "Baolu tongzhihui xuanyan shu" [Declaration of the Sichuan Railway Protection association], *Baogao*, no. 9, July 6, 1911.

78. Ibid.

79. Ibid.

80. Sidney Tarrow, *Power in Movement: Social Movements, Collective Action and Politics* (New York: Cambridge University Press, 1994), 4.

81. Ibid., 4–5.

82. "Yang jun juankuan zhi jueyi" [The decision of Mr. Yang's donation], *Baogao*, no. 3, June 28, 1911.

83. Li, *Dabo*, 117.

84. "Yang jun juankuan zhi jueyi" [The decision of Mr. Yang's donation], *Baogao*, no. 3, June 28, 1911.

85. "Yanglang qu you xu" [The song for Yang now has a preamble], *Baogao*, no. 4, June 29, 1911.

86. "Xiao lingguan zhi aiguo re" [Patriotism of a small actor], *Baogao*, no. 3, June 28, 1911.

87. Li, *Dabo*, 117.

88. "Jiehu! Guojun jing xian si" [The early and unexpected death of gentleman Guo], *Baogao*, no. 6, July 1, 1911.

89. Ibid.

90. As a matter of fact, Guo Huanwen's death had nothing to do with the issue of "recovering the railways and breaking the treaty." Guo died as a result of mental illness, yet to make use of his death, writers for the newsletter made it meaningful. Li, *Dabo*, 45–47.

91. "Guo lieshi xunlu xiangqing" [Details about Martyr Guo dying for the railroad], *Baogao*, no. 7, July 2, 1911.

92. Ibid.

93. *Baogao*, no. 13, July 12, 1911; no. 14, July 13, 1991; and no. 15, July 14, 1911.

94. Li, *Dabo*, 116–17.

95. "Siguo jiekuan hetong ge" [On the foreign loan treaty], *Baogao*, no. 2, June 27, 1911.

96. Ibid.

97. "Yue-Han Chuan-Han tielu jiekuang hetong cuoshang dingyi zhe" [Negotiationg on the foreign loan treaty concerning the Yuan-Han Chuan-Han railways], *Baogao*, no. 3, June 28, 1911; no. 4, June 29, 1911; no. 5, June 30, 1911; and no. 6, July 1, 1911.

98. "Tielu guoyou ge" [On nationalizing raiways], *Baogao*, no. 5, June 30, 1911.

99. "Falü baohu ge" [On legal protection], *Baogao*, no. 9, July 6, 1911.

100. "Tielu guoyou ge" [On nationalizing raiways], *Baogao*, no. 5, June 30, 1911.

101. "Chuanmin yutian ge" [Sichuan people pleading to Heaven], *Baogao*, no. 6, July 1, 1911.

102. "Qing aiguozhe zhuyi" [Patriotic fellows: please pay attention], *Baogao*, no. 11, July 8, 1911.

103. Ibid.

104. This also was related to the cultural and legal transformation in China at that time. For example, in the new Criminal Code, for the first time in Chinese history, the principle of everyone being politically equal before the law was established.

105. "Chuanmin yutian ge" [Sichuan people pleading to Heaven], *Baogao*, no. 6, July 1, 1911.

106. Mary Rankin has made a similar point: in her words, "Sichuan activists also presented a stark contrast between the dead Guangxu emperor and the new regency." Guangxu had "'boldly' prepared for a constitution and sought rapport with the people, but the new cabinet, represented by the evil Sheng Xuanhuai, had cheated the people and abandoned the goals of the former ruler." Mary Rankin, "Nationalistic Contestation and Mobilization Politics: Practice and Rhetoric of Railway-rights Recovery at the End of the Qing," *Modern China* 28, no. 3 (July 2002): 343.

107. "Chuanmin yutian ge" [Sichuan people pleading to Heaven], *Baogao*, no. 6, July 1, 1911.

108. These cultural symbols appeared in *Baogao*, no. 2, June 27, 1911; no. 6, July 1, 1911; and no. 11, July 8, 1911.

109. "Guzhe zhi aiguo re" [Blind people's patriotism], *Baogao*, no. 19, July 19, 1911.

110. "Benhui dahui zhixiang" [A detailed record of our mass assembly], *Baogao*, no. 8, July 5, 1911.

111. "Crying for seven days in the Qin courtyard" refers to a famous story from the Spring and Autumn period. As the kingdom of Chu was attacked by the kingdom of Wu, a Chu minister by the name of Shen Baoxu was dispatched to the kingdom of Qin for reinforcements. Shen cried in the Qin imperial courtyard all day and all night for seven days. After the seventh day, Qin decided to send an army to help Chu.

112. "Benhui dahui zhixiang" [A detailed record of our mass assembly], *Baogao*, no. 8, July 5, 1911.

113. Ibid.

114. Local literati took Jing Ke's famous poem and simply replaced "Yi shui" (the Yi River), which flowed in Jing Ke's hometown, with "Jin shui" (the Jin River), which flows through Chengdu, so as to evoke a similar sense of heroism to that which was so famously presented in Jing Ke's poem. *Baogao*, no. 19, July 19, 1911.

115. Guo Moruo, "Fanzheng qianhou" [Life around the 1911 Revolution], in *Moruo zizhuan* [Autobiography of Guo Moruo] (Xianggang: Sanlian shudian, 1978), vol. 1, 223–28.

116. David Kertzer, *Comrades and Christians: Religion and Political Struggles in Communist Italy* (New York: Cambridge University Press, 1988), 188, in Tarrow, *Power in Movement*, 18.

117. Charles Tilly, *From Mobilization to Revolution* (Reading, MA: Addison-Wesley, 1978), chap. 6, in Tarrow, *Power in Movement*, 19.
118. Tarrow, *Power in Movement*, 19.

CHAPTER 6. THE PRACTICE OF REVOLUTION

1. Peng Fen, *Xinhai xunqing zhengbian fayuan ji* [The origins of the Qing regime change in 1911] (Chengdu: Fumin gongsi, 1933), 31. Original document from Professor Dai Zhili. Peng Fen recollected: "In general, there were about ten people in each prefecture.... The average travel fund for these students was ten yuan."
2. Wu Yusheng, "Sichuan baolu yundong zhong de xinjin baoweizhan" [The Xinjin battle in the Sichuan Railway Protection movement], *Sichuan difangzhi tongxun*, no. 3 (1984): 44. Special thanks to Dr. Gou Deyi for providing me with this special issue.
3. Jiajin, "Rexue ning de fengbei zai: Mingshan baolu douzheng shulue" [Success achieved with blood: Railway movement in Mingshan county], ibid., 57.
4. "Yanjiangbu qishi" [Special notice from the Speech Division], *Baolu tongzhihui baogao* (hereafter *Baogao*), no. 16, July 15, 1911.
5. Ibid.
6. "Zhi ge fu ting zhou xian yousi qi" [Letter to officials in all prefecture, department, and county governments], *Baogao*. no. 5, June 30, 1911.
7. "Guanyu yanjiang zhi yaowen" [News concerning giving lectures], *Baogao*. no. 9, July 6, 1911.
8. During the very exciting month of July 1911, besides the influential *Newsletter of Sichuan Railway Protection Association*, other newspapers were used to propagandize the views of the Chengdu headquarters. On July 26, 1911, the powerful *Xigubao* was set up. Later came Jiang Sancheng's *Vernacular Newspaper* (*Baihua bao*) and *Enlightening Pictorial* (*Qizhi huabao*) in addition to the official newspaper of the Sichuan Provincial Assembly, *Shubao*, all solely focused on the topic of the railway movement. Owing to the effective propaganda work by movement leaders and the lively stories depicted in these newspapers, sales kept increasing. According to a contemporary statistic, the combined propaganda papers issued 160,000 copies. Conversation with Professor Dai Zhili in 2006.
9. "Chongqing tongzhi zhi aiguo re" [Patriotism of comrades of Chongqing], *Baogao*, no. 14, July 13, 1911.
10. Ibid.
11. "Chengkou ting tongzhi zhi aiguo re" [Patriotism of comrades of Chengkou district], *Baogao*, no. 18, July 18, 1911.
12. "Chongning tongzhi zhi aiguo re" [Patriotism of comrades of Chongning county], *Baogao*, no. 22, July 23, 1911.
13. Ibid.
14. Ibid.
15. Ibid.
16. Wei Yingtao et al., *Sichuan jindaishi* [History of modern Sichuan] (Chengdu: Sichuan shehui kexue chubanshe, 1985), 481.
17. Yang Kajia, "Chuanlu fengchao zhi yanbian" [The development of the Sichuan Railway Protection incident], in *Zhonghua minguo kaiguo wushi zhou-*

nian wenxian, 197, in Wei et al., *Sichuan jindaishi* [History of modern Sichuan] (Chengdu: Sichuan shehui kexue chubanshe, 1985), 477.

18. In Dai Zhili, ed., *Sichuan baolu yundong shiliao huizuan* [Collection of historical materials on the Sichuan Railway Protection movement] (Taipei: Zhongyang yanjiuyuan jindaishi yanjiusuo, 1994), 695–729, 1015–79.

19. "Qingzhen tongzhi zhi aiguo re" [Patriotism of Chinese Muslims], *Baogao*, no. 29, August 6, 1911.

20. "Du Maozhou longmu zhangguan tusi He Maogong yuanshu" [Reading the petition letter from He Maogong, a tribal leader from Maozhou, Longmu], *Baogao*, no. 16, July 15, 1911.

21. "Chongning fangwai ren zhi aiguo re" [Patriotism of Buddhist monks], *Baogao*, no. 23, July 25, 1911.

22. Monks also appeared in the following issues of *Baogao*: no. 3, June 28, 1911; no. 4, June 29, 1911; and no. 23, July 25, 1911.

23. "Xiaoxue sheng zhi aiguo re" [Patriotism from elementary school students], *Baogao*, no. 12, July 11, 1911.

24. "Shiling nüsheng zhi aiguo re" [Patriotism from a ten-year old girl], *Baogao*, no. 36, August 20, 1911.

25. "Xiao guomin zhi aiguo re" [Patriotism of young citizens], *Baogao*, no. 8, July 5, 1911.

26. "Sichuan nüzi baolu tongzhi hui baogaoshu" [Reports from women comrades], *Baogao*, no. 24, July 27, 1911.

27. "Baolu nütongzhi hui dahui ji" [Chronicle of the meeting of women comrades], *Baogao*, no. 10, July 7, 1911.

28. "Nütongzhi hui chengli baogao" [Report on the founding meeting of the women railway protection association], *Baogao*, no. 31, August 10, 1911. It reported that on July 14, at the founding meeting of the sub-branch in the east district of Chengdu, a blind woman who heard the news came to the meeting hall, asking others to write down her name. The Chongqing sub-branch of the Women's Branch had as many as four hundred members, many of whom donated their savings.

29. "Mawang miao laodongzhe juankuan yuanshu [Letter from laborers at the Mawang temple pledging to donate], *Baogao*, no. 33, August 14, 1911.

30. "Shangzhong yiqian zhi da aiguo re" [Merchants and their patriotism for hoping to institute the one coin donation], *Baogao*, no. 16, July 15, 1911.

31. Li Jieren, *Dabo* [Great wave], in *Li Jieren xuanji* [Collected works of Li Jieren] (Chengdu: Sichuan renmin chubanshe, 1980), vol. 2, 290.

32. Guo Moruo, "Fanzheng qianhou" [Life around the 1911 Revolution], in *Moruo zizhuan* [Autobiography of Guo Moruo] (Xianggang: Sanlian shudian, 1978), vol. 1, 223–28.

33. "Benhui aiguo re zhi yishu" [A summary of the patriotism of our association], *Baogao*, no. 7, July 2, 1911.

34. Almost all books concerning the Sichuan Railway Protection movement emphasize the link between the Tongmenghui and the Gowned Brothers. In fact, on the Chengdu Plain, where the Railway Protection movement was the most heated, the influence of the Revolutionary Alliance was both weak and scattered. After a

failed riot against the Qing in 1908, Chengdu's Tongmenghui branch went dormant. See Wei et al., *Sichuan jindaishi*, 510–16.

35. Wang Chunwu, *Paoge tanmi* [Exploring the secrets of the Gowned Brothers] (Chengdu: Bashu shushe, 1993), 139.

36. "Xiang Dizhang" [Xiang Dizhang], http://baike.baidu.com/view/2579671.htm (viewed in August 2009).

37. "Qin Zaigeng," in *Shuzhong xianlie beizhenglu* [Record of the campaigns of Sichuan martyrs] (Chongqing: Qiyu shuju, 1928), vol. 2, 12b–13b.

38. Gao Zhaolin, who made an impassioned public speech at the opening meeting of the Chongqing branch of the association, was also a famous Gowned Brothers leader. See "Gao Zhaolin," in *Shuzhong xianlie beizhenglu*, vol. 2, 40a–40b. Also in Wang Chunwu, *Paoge tanmi* [Exploring the secrets of the Gowned Brothers] (Chengdu: Bashu shushe, 1993), 120.

39. In the Qing dynasty, ten households (*hu*) were organized into one *pai*, ten *pai* into one *jia*, and ten *jia* into one *bao*. A *bao* was thus, in theory, one thousand households. See *Qingchao wenxian tongkao* [A comprehensive study of Qing institutions], vol. 19, *Hukou* 1. During his reign, Kangxi ordered officials to reinforce the *baojia* system. He emphasized that even though there might not have been enough people in any particular area to fill the ranks of a *bao*, it nonetheless needed to be established. In *Qingchao wenxian tongkao*, vol. 22, *Zhiyi* 2 [Service 2]. In Wang Di, *Kuachu fengbi de shijie: Changjiang shangyou quyu shehui yanjiu, 1644–1911* [Striding out of a closed world: A study of society in the upper Yangzi region, 1644–1911] (Beijing: Zhonghua shuju, 1993). Thus, in some places a *bao* encompassed fewer than a thousand households.

40. Liu Shiliang, *Hanliu shi* [History of the Gowned Brothers] (1938), in Wang, *Paoge tanmi*, 19.

41. See Chapter 1 for details.

42. Wang, *Paoge tanmi*, 1–8.

43. In December 1905 Luo Lun became a history and literature teacher in the local Shunqing Middle School. Luo was exposed to *Minbao*, which argued for *minquan* and anti-Manchuism.

44. "Zhao Erfeng tongchi yanshuo daibu luo lun liyou zha fu quanmin ge" [Zhao Erfeng's explanation of capturing Luo Lun and the propaganda song] (September 19, 1911), in Sichuan sheng dang'an guan, ed., *Sichuan baolu yundong dang'an xuanbian* [Selected archival documents of Sichuan Railway Protection movement] (Chengdu: Sichuan renmin chubanshe, 1981), 182–83.

45. Duanfang, "Duanfang zhi neige" [Duanfang to the cabinet], in Dai, ed., *Sichuan baolu yundong shiliao huizuan*, 1113.

46. "Chongqing haiguan daili shuiwu si shitelaoqi zhi Beijing haiguan shuiwu zongshu an'ge lian de xin" [Letters of the Chongqing customs officer Strauch to the Beijing customs officer Aglen], July 1911–November 1911, in Sichuan sheng dang'an guan, ed., *Sichuan baolu yundong dang'an xuanbian*, 310–11.

47. "Chongqing haiguan daili shuiwusi cheng Beijing haiguan zong shuiwusi de baogao" [Report from the Chongqing customs officer to the Beijing customs offi-

cer], November 11, 1911–May 1912, in Sichuan sheng dang'an guan, ed., *Sichuan baolu yundong dang'an xuanbian*, 367.

48. Huang Shou, "Baolu yundong zhong de Luo Lun" [Luo Lun in the Railway Protection movement], in Sichuan sheng zhengxie wenshi ziliao weiyuanhui, ed., *Sichuan wenshi ziliao jicui* [Selected personal histories of Sichuan province] (Chengdu: Sichuan renmin chubanshe, 1996), vol. 1, 167.

49. Hou Lishi [Wife of Hou Baozhai], "Hou Baozhai fuzi can bei mouhai yuanbai" [Petition on the brutal murder of Hou Baozhai and his son], in *Xinjin dang'an* [Xinjin county archives], "Minguo" [Republican period] 138, no. 12 (1911).

50. Ibid.

51. "Hou Bangfu" [Hou Bangfu, i.e., Hou Baozhai], in *Shuzhong xianlie beizhenglu*, vol. 2, 41a–42a.

52. Ibid.

53. Xinjin jiucheng tuanti ji gejie tongbao [The nine groups of Xinjin and other compatriots], "Dahan chuannan baolu tongzhihui zhang Hou jun Baozhai ji zi Anting yunan gongbu" [Announcement of the murders of the leader of the South Sichuan Railway Protection Association, Hou Baozhai, and his son, Hou Anting], in *Xinjin dang'an*, "Minguo" [Republican period] 138, no. 13 (1911).

54. Ibid.

55. Ibid.

56. Wang, *Paoge tanmi*, 114.

57. Huang Shou, unpublished memoir of Huang Shou, n.p., author bought in Chengdu in 2007, personal possession, section on Wu Qingxi.

58. Peng, *Xinhai xunqing zhengbian fayuan ji*. This quote is from Wei and Zhao, eds., *Sichuan Xinhai geming shiliao* [Collected historical materials of the 1911 Revolution in Sichuan] (Chengdu: Sichuan renmin chubanshe, 1982), vol. 1, 337.

59. "Wang Renwen zhi neige dian" (Telegram from Wang Renwen to the cabinet), in Chen Xulu et al., eds., *Xinhai geming qianhou* [Around the time of the 1911 Revolution] (Shanghai: Shanghai renmin chubanshe, 1979), vol. 1, 121.

60. Zhou Shanpei, *Xinhai geming zhi wo* [The 1911 Revolution and I] (1929), author bought in Chengdu in 2007, personal possession, no publication information, 9–19.

61. Ibid.

62. *Xuantong zhengji* [Political chronicle of the Xuantong reign], vol. 56, in Wei et al., *Sichuan jindaishi*, 488.

63. "Ji Chengdu Zhao zhijun Erfeng" [Letter to Governor Zhao Erfeng in Chengdu], in Sheng Xuanhuai, *Yuzhai cungao* [Materials preserved in Yu House] (1939; reprint, Taipei: Wenhai chubanshe, 1965), vol. 78, in Wei et al., *Sichuan jindaishi*, 488.

64. Chen et al., *Xinhai geming qianhou*, 102–3, in Dai, ed., *Sichuan baolu yundong shiliao huizuan*, 750.

65. *Sichuan baolu tongzhihui dianwen yaolu* [Key telegrams of the Sichuan Railway Protection Association], 9, in Dai, ed., *Sichuan baolu yundong shiliao huizuan*, 752.

66. "Tong shen gongfen" [Expressing our collective anger], *Baogao*, no. 20, July 20, 1911.

67. *Minlibao*, July 9, 1911, in Dai, ed., *Sichuan baolu yundong shiliao huizuan*, 759–61.

68. "Tongxianghui zhi aiguo re" [The patriotic enthusiasm of the hometown associations], *Baogao*, no. 4, June 29, 1911.

69. Attaches on Gan and Song appeared in *Baogao* issues no. 4, June 29, 1911; no. 9, July 6, 1911; and no. 31, August 10, 1911. Also, "Letter from Gan Dazhang to Song Yuren," in *Xinhai geming qianhou*, 113, in Dai, ed., *Sichuan baolu yundong shiliao huizuan*, 769–70.

70. At the beginning of the railway movement in early June, Li Jixun resisted the nationalization policy. On June 18, 1911, after receiving Chengdu's directive asking him "not to give up the railways" and to "continue the construction of the railways," Li accepted the order and urged Chengdu to treat the financial capital of the railway (*lukuan*) as more important than the ownership of the railway (*luquan*). Li argued that the bottom line for the struggle was to "keep the capital." In *Chuanlu shouhui guoyou wanglai yaodian* [Key telegrams concerning the nationalization of the Sichuan railways], 13–14. Li also got the people of Yichang to back him up; in *Yiju laidian* [Telegram from Yichang Bureau], original pamphlet in the Sichuan Provincial Library, n.p.; also in Dai, ed., *Sichuan baolu yundong shiliao huizuan*, 740–43. On June 27, Li sent a telegram to Chengdu, saying that he would personally go to Beijing and discuss the matter with the metropolitan officials from Sichuan. It was during this trip that Li Jixun changed his mind on the matter. Throughout this time, Chengdu kept explaining to Li Jixun that "if we cannot break the foreign loan treaty, there is no way that we can talk about the railway [and its capital]." In *Sichuan baolu tongzhihui dianwen yaolu*, 16; also in Dai, ed., *Sichuan baolu yundong shiliao huizuan*, 743–44. However, Li Jixun had a different take. Over the years, Li had felt rather constrained and somewhat unsupported by the leadership in the Chengdu headquarters. As the manager of the only branch that was actually constructing rail lines for the Chuan-Han Railway, Li understood what it was like to have little power in allocating railway capital or appointing personnel, even for his own branch. Finally, on July 5, 1911, he agreed to accept Beijing's proposal, that is, to take the seven million taels of silver in Chengdu and use it to build the section from Chengdu to Kuizhou. "Ji Wuchang Duan dachen" [Sheng Xuanhuai, Letter to Duanfang], on July 5, in Sheng, *Yuzhai cungao*, vol. 78, 11, in Dai, ed., *Sichuan baolu yundong shiliao huizuan*, 772.

71. "Duan dachen laidian" [Telegram from Duanfang] on July 13 and July 16, in Sheng, *Yuzhai cungao*, vol. 78, 18–19, 11, and 25–26, in Dai, ed., *Sichuan baolu yundong shiliao huizuan*, 773.

72. On July 8, the Yichang branch, led by Li Jixun, sent a telegram to Chengdu, asking Chengdu to give the railway to Beijing. Li urged his fellow Sichuanese to think of the option that Beijing offered. "I urge you, my fellow men, to think this: if all the stock of the Chuan-Han Railway Company is converted into national stock and every year we have a dividend of 6 percent and are allowed to share the profits (*fenhong*), and if the state takes care of everything—the money used, the money lost, and the money that remains, and even the money for sending students

abroad to study—then this [nationalization policy] is only beneficial to shareholders"; in *Yiju laidian*, n.p. Again, on July 15, being "willing to use the current *zugu* to build the section from Yichang to Zigui," Li Jixun again sent a telegram to Chengdu, urging the Chengdu elite to think about the state's offer. He wrote: "The state's policy is adamant and it seems that we have no room to maneuver. . . . The central government, besides being willing to repay us the construction money used in Yichang, is likely to give non-dividend-bearing stock for the money used in Chengdu, Chongqing, and other branch bureaus and the money spent in Yichang before the construction started. Whenever I wanted to say something [hoping to gain a better deal], they always replied, 'You started construction late, wasted a lot of capital, and lost a great deal too.'" Under these circumstances, Li told Chengdu: "Striking a better deal is the key." In "Ji Wuchang Duan dachen" [Sheng Xuanhuai, letter to Duanfang], on July 15, in *Yuzhai cungao*, vol. 78, 28.

73. Their stated reasons were as follows: First, because Sheng Xuanhuai had no respect for the cabinet or for the legislative branch (the organ that represented the people), which "directly destroys constitutional politics." Second, because the policy of nationalizing the railways betrayed the previous emperor's edict, violated the law, robbed people of their property, and thus was barbaric and presumptuous to a degree never before experienced. Third, because Beijing's method in dealing with the Sichuan people was unacceptable: Sheng Xuanhuai and his people ignored the letters sent by Governor-General Wang Renwen, ignored the petition of the Sichuan metropolitan officials, and ignored the begging of the people. In Dai, ed., *Sichuan baolu yundong shiliao huizuan*, 806–7.

74. "Gudong dahui qingwu zhanban xin, chang juanshu yi kuanchou lukuan an" [The Shareholder Meeting on stop turning in the *juanshu* to help with the railway capital], in Dai, ed., *Sichuan baolu yundong shiliao huizuan*, 845–47.

75. "Duan dachen laidian" [Telegram from Duanfang], on July 28, in Sheng, *Yuzhai cungao*, vol. 78, 37–38, in Dai, ed., *Sichuan baolu yundong shiliao huizuan*, 791–92.

76. Ibid.

77. "Qingdi chi Zhao Erfeng jiancheng furen yanjin gudong dahui feifa jihui yu" [Imperial edict ordering Zhao Erfeng to arrive in Chengdu and to ban all meetings other than the shareholder meeting], in Dai, ed., *Sichuan baolu yundong shiliao huizuan*, 794.

78. "Zhao Erfeng dui Chuan-Han tielu gongsi gudong dahui xunci" [Short speech of Zhao Erfeng at the shareholder meeting], in Dai, ed., *Sichuan baolu yundong shiliao huizuan*, 816.

79. "Qingkan Duanfang zhi mandian" [Please look at the overbearing telegram from Duanfang], *Baogao*, no. 31, August 10, 1911. See also Dai, ed., *Sichuan baolu yundong shiliao huizuan*, 824.

80. *Xigubao*, no. 21, August 16, 1911, in Dai, ed., *Sichuan baolu yundong shiliao huizuan*, 782.

81. "Chuan-Han tielu guodong zhunbei hui jishi" [Records on the preparation meeting of the shareholder meeting of the Chuan-Han Railway Company], in Dai, ed., *Sichuan baolu yundong shiliao huizuan*, 806.

82. Ibid.

83. "Duan dachen laidian" [Telegram from Duanfang], August 23, 1911, in Wei et al., *Sichuan jindaishi*, 495.

84. Shi Tiyuan, "Yi Chengdu baolu yundong" [Remembering the Railway Protection movement], in *Xinhai geming huiyilu* [Memoirs of the 1911 Revolution] (Beijing: Wenshi ziliao chubanshe, 1961), vol. 3, 57. Translation in Wang Di, *Street Culture in Chengdu: Public Space, Urban Commoners, and Local Politics, 1870–1930* (Stanford, CA: Stanford University Press, 2003), 214.

85. "Qingdi ling Zhao Erfeng yanxing tanya bashi bake yu" [Edict to Zhao Erfeng on quickly suppressing the strikes], in Dai Zhili, ed., *Sichuan baolu yundong shiliao* [Collection of historical materials on the Sichuan Railway Protection movement] (Beijing: Kexue chubanshe, 1959), 273.

86. "Zhao Erfeng zhi neige chen chuanren reng zhu lugui shangban bing jiang jiekuan xiulu jiao Zizhengyuan yijue dian" [Telegram by Zhao Erfeng to the cabinent on Sichuanese's insistence in keeping the railway commercialized and in forwarding the case to the National Assembly for discussion], in Dai, ed., *Sichuan baolu yundong shiliao*, 277.

87. Wang, *Street Culture*, 215–16.

88. "Zhao Erfeng zhi neige chen chuanren zhenglu bashi bake qingxing dian" [Telegram by Zhao Erfeng to the cabinet on Sichuan's strikes], Dai Zhili, ed., *Sichuan baolu yundong shiliao* [Collection of historical materials on the Sichuan Railway Protection movement] (Beijing: Kexue chubanshe, 1959), 276–77.

89. "Sichuan baolu tongzhihui gongqi" [Public notice of the Sichuan Railway Protection Association], in Wei et al., *Sichuan jindaishi*, 497.

90. "Xuejie huiyi huizhi" [Collected transcripts of the meetings of the learned circles], *Xigubao*, no. 40, in Wei et al., *Sichuan jindaishi*, 498–99.

91. "Yushi Fan Zhijie zouqing heping chuli chuanshi zhe" [Memorial by censor Fan Zhijie on handling the Sichuan case peacefully], in Dai, ed., *Sichuan baolu yundong shiliao*, 312. In 1908, one Chinese li equaled 0.576 kilometers.

92. Wei et al., *Sichuan jindaishi*, 498–99.

93. *Xigubao*, no. 37, September 2, 1911, in Dai, ed., *Sichuan baolu yundong shiliao huizuan*, 906.

94. "Chuan-Han tielu gongsi tebie gudong hui tingban juanshu ge" [The propaganda song on not submitting voluntary surcharge taxes by the special shareholder meeting of the Chuan-Han Railway Company], in Sichuan sheng dang'an guan, ed., *Sichuan baolu yundong dang'an xuanbian*, 168–69.

95. Ibid., 170.

96. Ibid.

97. Ibid., 171–72.

98. "Chuan-Han tielu gongsi zongjingli Zeng Pei deng yu Zhao Erfeng bianlun yi guxi koudi zhengliang deng wenti" [General manager of the Chuan-Han Railway Company Zeng Pei discussing with Zhao Erfeng on issues like using *zugu* interests to count as land tax], in Dai, ed., *Sichuan baolu yundong shiliao huizuan*, 910.

99. "Wuchang Duan dachen laidian" [Telegram from Duanfang in Wuchang], September 8, 1911, in *Yuzhai cungao*, vol. 82, 1–2, in Dai, ed., *Sichuan baolu yundong shiliao huizuan*, 918.

100. Ibid.
101. *Xigubao*, no. 37, in Dai, ed., *Sichuan baolu yundong shiliao huizuan*, 906.
102. Yukun, *Rongcheng jiashu* [Letters from Chengdu], September 7. In Dai, ed., *Sichuan baolu yundong shiliao huizuan*, 916–17.
103. In Dai, ed., *Sichuan baolu yundong shiliao huizuan*, 913.The poster read: "First, from now on, we will not pay land taxes. We will not pay *juanshu*. That which has been collected already, we will not send in. That which has not been levied yet, we will stop levying. Second, our proposal will be sent to the railway company, to the Provincial Assembly, and eventually to the National Assembly. We will also make sure all levels of officials know about it. Third, from now on, we will let the entire country know that we do not assume the burden of paying the interest on the foreign loans. Fourth, all Sichuanese (*quan chuanren*) should not sell or buy property. Fifth, after we accomplish the above four goals, we will open the market and students will go back to school."
104. *Xigubao*, no. 41, in Wei et al., *Sichuan jindaishi*, 501.
105. *Xigubao*, no. 39, in Wei et al., *Sichuan jindaishi*, 502.
106. *Xuantong zhengji*, vol. 59, in Wei et al., *Sichuan jindaishi*, 502.
107. In Dai, ed., *Sichuan baolu yundong shiliao huizuan*, 933–37.
108. Ibid., 946–47.
109. Ibid., 948–49, 955.
110. Ibid., 960.
111. Ibid., 950, 962–63, 964.
112. Ibid., 996–1002. In fact, by this point, the Qing court had made up its mind to crush the Sichuan Railway Protection movement, mostly due to Duanfang's and Sheng Xuanhuai's constant pressure. Starting on August 27, Duanfang repeatedly sent telegrams to Beijing (to Sheng Xuanhuai and Zaize), castigating Zhao Erfeng for "allying with the Sichuan bandits." Duanfang urged them to influence the court's decision to send in other ministers to replace Zhao and solve the railway matter. Duanfang, Sheng Xuanhuai, Zaize, and Ruicheng together urged the court to replace Zhao. On September 2, the court decided to send Duanfang to Sichuan to suppress the Sichuan movement. On September 3, Duanfang asked Zaize and Sheng Xuanhuai to speak for him in front of the court again, asking it to give him the power to command the Sichuan armies and to get reinforcements from Hubei. On the same day, however, Duanfang changed his mind and asked to *not* be appointed to suppress the Sichuan movement, but the court insisted on sending him to Sichuan. On September 5, Duanfang had no choice but to accept the court's wishes. The official appointment came on September 6. In the appointment letter, Duanfang was given the power to command the Sichuan armies. He started preparing the next day.
113. Ibid., 1002–3.
114. Ibid., 1106.
115. Ibid., 1107–9.
116. Ibid., 1124–25.
117. Ibid., 1125.
118. Wang, *Street Culture*, 217.

119. "Zhao Erfeng tusha Chengdu shimin zhi chubu qingdan" [List of people who died in the Chengdu massacre], in Dai, ed., *Sichuan baolu yundong shiliao huizuan*, 1133–34.

120. Wang, *Street Culture*, 218.

121. In Dai, ed., *Sichuan baolu yundong shiliao huizuan*, 1112.

122. Ibid., 1111.

123. Ibid., 1114–16.

124. Ibid., 1116.

125. Ibid., 1115.

126. Ibid., 1114–16.

127. In Dai, ed., *Sichuan baolu yundong shiliao huizuan*, 1117. Zhou Shanpei was unfairly rumored to have participated in Zhao Erfeng's plot to arrest the railway movement leaders. On the contrary, Zhou was actually on the Sichuan elite's side and later played a key role in persuading Zhao to release the movement's leaders. The reason Zhou was rumored to be the perpetrator had much to do with his strict policies in reexamining and vetting the recent graduates from Sichuan's various legal schools before giving them governmental posts.

128. Ibid., 1117–18.

129. Ibid., 1119.

130. Li, *Dabo*, 638.

CHAPTER 7. THE EXPANSION AND DIVISION OF REVOLUTION

1. In Dai Zhili, ed., *Sichuan baolu yundong shiliao huizuan* [Collection of historical materials on the Sichuan Railway Protection movement] (Taipei: Zhongyang yanjiuyuan jindaishi yanjiusuo, 1994), 1166.

2. Ibid., 1182.

3. Ibid., 1166–67.

4. Ibid., 1137.

5. Ibid., 1138.

6. "Sanxia zhong zhi zhengren lei" [The tears of soldiers up in the Three Gorges], *Minlibao*, October 3, 1911, in Dai Zhili, ed., *Sichuan baolu yundong shiliao huizuan*, 1137.

7. In Dai, ed., *Sichuan baolu yundong shiliao huizuan*, 1183.

8. Ibid.

9. Sichuan sheng dang'an guan, ed., *Sichuan baolu yundong dang'an xuanbian* [Selected archival documents of Sichuan Railway Protection movement] (Chengdu: Sichuan renmin chubanshe, 1981), 310–11.

10. In Dai, ed., *Sichuan baolu yundong shiliao huizuan*, 1167.

11. "Qin Zaigeng," in *Shuzhong xianlie beizhenglu* [Record of the campaigns of Sichuan martyrs] (Chongqing: Qiyu shuju, 1928), vol. 2, 12b–13b.

12. "Hou Bangfu" [Hou Bangfu, i.e., Hou Baozhai], in *Shuzhong xianlie beizhenglu*, vol. 2, 41b–42a.

13. Wei Yingtao et al., *Sichuan jindaishi* [History of modern Sichuan] (Chengdu: Sichuan shehui kexue chubanshe, 1985), 526.

14. In Dai, ed., *Sichuan baolu yundong shiliao huizuan*, 1143–44.

Notes to Chapter 7

15. Ibid., 1144. In Wei Yingtao et al., *Sichuan jindaishi* [History of modern Sichuan] (Chengdu: Sichuan shehui kexue chubanshe, 1985), 526, Li Xianzhou is called Li Tingzhou.
16. In Dai, ed., *Sichuan baolu yundong shiliao huizuan*, 1182–83.
17. Ibid., 1144.
18. Ibid., 1144–45. Originally from *Pi County Gazetteer*, vol. 6, "The Complete Story of the Railway Protection Association and Citizen Army." Compiled by Li Zhiqing and Dai Chaoji, published in 1948. The *Pi County Gazetteer* states that Zhang Zun from Pi, Sun Zepei from Chongqing, Wu Qingxi from Wenjiang, and Zhang Xi from Guan county were the Gowned Brothers leaders of the Sichuan Railway Protection Association of western Sichuan (Chuanxi tongzhihui).
19. Wei et al., *Sichuan jindaishi*, 527. Rushing to Chengdu in hopes of entering from the city's north gate was Hanzhou Gowned Brothers leader Hou Juyuan, who had organized a railway protection army that carried out attacks against the Qing soldiers, and other Hanzhou militia leaders.
20. Sichuan sheng dang'an guan, ed., *Sichuan baolu yundong dang'an xuanbian*, 304–5.
21. In Dai, ed., *Sichuan baolu yundong shiliao huizuan*, 1147.
22. Ibid., 1157–58.
23. Ibid., 1183.
24. Ibid., 1285.
25. Ibid., 1162.
26. Ibid., 1171.
27. Ibid., 1185.
28. Ibid., 1171.
29. Wei et al., *Sichuan jindaishi*, 528.
30. In Dai, ed., *Sichuan baolu yundong shiliao huizuan*, 1148.
31. Ibid., 1149–54.
32. Ibid., 1195–96.
33. Ibid., 1199.
34. Ibid., 1196.
35. Ibid., 1200–1202.
36. Ibid., 1197–99.
37. Ibid., 1186–88.
38. Ibid., 1203–4.
39. Ibid., 1205–6.
40. Ibid., 1206.
41. Ibid.
42. Ibid., 1207.
43. Ibid., 1214.
44. Ibid., 1166.
45. Wei et al., *Sichuan jindaishi*, 529.
46. Ibid.
47. In Dai, ed., *Sichuan baolu yundong shiliao huizuan*, 1138–39.
48. Ibid., 1139–40.

49. Ibid., 1260–62.
50. Ibid., 1262.
51. Ibid., 1264.
52. Ibid., 1189.
53. Wei et al., *Sichuan jindaishi*, 530.
54. In Sichuan sheng dang'an guan, ed., *Sichuan baolu yundong dang'an xuanbian*, 305.
55. In Dai, ed., *Sichuan baolu yundong shiliao huizuan*, 1323–50.
56. Ibid., 1351–73.
57. Ibid., 1402–27.
58. Ibid., 1373–93.
59. Xinjin jiucheng tuanti ji gejie tongbao [The nine groups of Xinjin and other compatriots], "Dahan chuannan baolu tongzhihui zhang Hou jun Baozhai ji zi Anting yunan gongbu" [Announcement of the murders of the leader of South Sichuan Railway Protection Association Hou Baozhai and his son Hou Anting], in *Xinjin dang'an* [Xinjin county archives], "Minguo" [Republican period] 138, no. 13 (1911).
60. Wei et al., *Sichuan jindaishi*, 530.
61. Ibid.
62. In Dai, ed., *Sichuan baolu yundong shiliao huizuan*, 1327.
63. Zhou did not help plan the September 7 massacre. He had always been sympathetic to the railway movement. The reason Zhou was singled out had much to do with his role in the New Policies reform in Sichuan. After Zhou became the provincial surveillance commissioner, for example, he was strict in weeding out students who were not qualified, which incurred a good deal of resentment. As explained in Chapter 6, Zhou was implicated mainly because of the rumors about him, which only demonstrates how unpopular he was, such that people were willing to believe the bad things said about him.
64. Wei et al., *Sichuan jindaishi*, 530.
65. In Dai, ed., *Sichuan baolu yundong shiliao huizuan*, 1141.
66. Ibid., 1346.
67. Wei et al., *Sichuan jindaishi*, 530.
68. In Dai, ed., *Sichuan baolu yundong shiliao huizuan*, 1355.
69. Ibid., 1352.
70. Ibid., 1299.
71. Ibid., 1285.
72. Ibid., 1290.
73. Ibid.
74. Ibid., 1300.
75. Ibid., 1302.
76. Ibid., 1304.
77. Ibid., 1306 and 1308.
78. Ibid., 1311.
79. Ibid., 1312.
80. Ibid., 1316.

81. Ibid., 1317–18.
82. Ibid., 1320.
83. Tian Zhenbang's memorial on February 2, 1912, also made this point. In ibid., 1882.
84. Xiong Kewu et al., *Shudang shigao* [Draft history of the Sichuan comrades], in Zhang Kaiyuan, Luo Fuhui, and Yan Changhong, eds. *Xinhai gemingshi ziliao xinbian* [New compilation of historical documents on the 1911 Revolution] (Wuhan: Hubei renmin chubanshe, 2011), vol. 1, 231.
85. Sichuan daxue lishixi Xinhai geming shi diaocha zu [The 1911 Revolution investigative team of Sichuan University's History Department], interview transcripts (March 1977), in Sichuan University History department archives. Thanks to Li Deying for making this document available for me.
86. Qin Zaigeng was killed in Jingyan on November 19.
87. There is a good deal of debate over when Rong county declared independence. Wu Yuzhang first wrote it was on September 25, in Wu Yuzhang, *Wu Yuzhang wenji* [Writings of Wu Yuzhang] (Chongqing: Chongqing chubanshe, 1987), vol. 2, 914. Sichuan historian He Yimin believes that the date was September 28, in He Yimin, "Xinhai geming shishi kao sanze" [Examining three historical facts concerning the 1911 Revolution], *Jindaishi yanjiu*, no. 5 (1987): 200–205. Historian Wu Dade takes the view that the date should be October 29, in Wu Dade, "Wu Yuzhang yu Sichuan Xinhai geming," *Jindaishi yanjiu*, no. 3 (1994): 281–84. Here I have taken Wu Dade's latest work on the date, which I find the most convincing. Wu's sources included the 1929 *Rong County Gazetteer* and the February 7 and February 8 issues of the newspaper *Dahan guomin bao*.
88. *Changshou xianzhi* [Gazetteer of Changshou county] (1944), vol. 16, in Dai, ed., *Sichuan baolu yundong shiliao huizuan*, 1757.
89. *Fulingxian xuxiu Fuzhou zhi* [The new gazetteer of Fuzhou, Fuling county] (1928): "Fuling xian jishi" [Main events of Fuling county], in Dai, ed., *Sichuan baolu yundong shiliao huizuan*, 1763.
90. *Jiangjinxianzhi* [Gazetteer of Jiangjin county] (1924), vol. 3, in Dai, ed., *Sichuan baolu yundong shiliao huizuan*, 1761.
91. Wei et al., *Sichuan jindaishi*, 541–43.
92. Ibid.
93. Ibid.
94. In Sichuan sheng dang'an guan, ed., *Sichuan baolu yundong dang'an xuanbian*, 311 and 333.
95. In Dai, ed., *Sichuan baolu yundong shiliao huizuan*, 1767–76.
96. Ibid., 1763.
97. *Nanchuanxianzhi* [Gazetteer of Nanchuan county], vol. 13, "Qianshi" [Previous events], in Wei et al., *Sichuan jindaishi*, 548.
98. Wei et al., *Sichuan jindaishi*, 558.
99. Ibid.
100. Author's interview with Wei Yingtao on September 10, 2004. Mao Zedong argued in his famous essay "Xin minzhu zhuyi lun" [On new democracy]:

"The 1911 Revolution was a great revolution. . . . Its failure lies in the weakness of the national bourgeoisie." In Wu Yuzhang, *Xinhai geming* [The 1911 Revolution] (Beijing: Renmin chubanshe, 1960), 3. Wu Yuzhang's book was first written in 1960 and was among the first historical works that defended the Maoist interpretation of the 1911 Revolution. In this book, Wu argues that the social context of the 1911 Revolution was the result of the development of capitalism in China: "Though the bourgeoisie appeared around the 1880s, at the beginning of the twentieth century, it became a class. . . . In the year 1906, there were 136 enterprises owned by the national bourgeoisie." This has set the tone for the study of the 1911 Revolution in mainland China. The very comprehensive and high-quality standard historical works, such as Jin Chongji and Hu Shengwu's *Xinhai geming shigao* [Draft history of the 1911 Revolution] and Li Xin's *Zhonghua minguoshi* [History of Republican China] all make great efforts to examine the situation of the cities and the newly emerging bourgeoisie of China at that time.

101. Tang Zongyao and Hu Gongxian, "Zizhou Luoquanjing Huiyi yu zuzhi Tongzhijun" [The meeting of Luoquanjing in Zizhou and the organizing of the Railway Comrade Army], in *Xinhai geming huiyilu* [Memoirs of the 1911 Revolution] (Beijing: Wenshi ziliao chubanshe, 1961), vol. 3, 142–44.

102. Wei et al., *Sichuan jindaishi*, 521.

103. Sun Zepei, for example, at this moment was still in Guan county, according to his close friend Chen Shixiong. In *Sichuan baolu fengyunlu* [Stories of the Sichuan Railway Protection movement] (Chengdu: Sichuan renmin chubanshe, 1981), 91, 147–50. Also, Zhang Dasan, another Gowned Brothers leader who allegedly attended the meeting, was actually still in Pi county, according to Wang Yunzi, who stated this in his memoir of Zhang Dasan. In *Xinhai geming huiyilu*, vol. 3, 57.

104. There is no evidence that either author, Tang Zongyao or Hu Gongxian, had attended the Luoquanjing meeting. Tang was a Tongmenghui member and later a Nationalist provincial assemblyman. Hu, born in 1899, was only twelve years old at the time. Both Tang and Hu were members of the Nationalist Party and served as local historians in the 1950s in Sichuan. In the histories they have written about the 1911 Revolution in Sichuan, they particularly emphasize the "leadership" of the Tongmenghui. See also Yang Pengcheng, "Zizhou Luoquanjing huiyi kao" [An examination of the Luoquanjing meeting in Zizhou], in *Xinhai geming yu Zhongguo xiandaihua* [The 1911 Revolution and the modernization of China] (Chengdu: Sichuan jiaoyu chubanshe, 2001), 297–305.

105. Wei Yingtao and He Yimin divide the Sichuan events of 1911 into two parts: the railway movement came first and then was followed by the 1911 Revolution. They argue that the railway movement was led by constitutionalists and was peaceful, while the armed 1911 Revolution was led by the Tongmenghui. In fact, the divide between the railway movement and the 1911 Revolution is artificial. Sichuan's 1911 Revolution as a whole was led by the constitutionalists, and political culture served as the uniting force throughout the entire movement.

106. Wei et al., *Sichuan jindaishi*, 560.

107. *Xinhai geming huiyilu*, vol. 3, 104, in Wei et al., *Sichuan jindaishi*, 561.

108. In Dai, ed., *Sichuan baolu yundong shiliao huizuan*, 1767–68. At that time, all the counties neighboring Zizhou—Longchang, Rongchang, Zizhou, Ziyang, Jianzhou, and Weiyuan—had been occupied by the East Route Railway Protection Army. The news of the Wuchang uprising had spread to the Hubei New Army soldiers. On November 18, Duanfang arrived in Zizhou and was stuck there. Chengdu was hard to get to, and Duanfang was unable to return to Chongqing, where the Tongmenghui had been planning a revolt.

109. In Dai, ed., *Sichuan baolu yundong shiliao huizuan*, 1291.

111. Ibid., 1294, 1295.

112. Ibid., 1297.

113. Dai Zhili, ed., *Sichuan baolu yundong shiliao* [Collection of historical materials on the Sichuan Railway Protection movement] (Beijing: Kexue chubanshe, 1959), 472.

114. Wei et al., *Sichuan jindaishi*, 563.

115. Ibid.

116. *Xinhai geming ziliao*, vol. 4, 429–30, in Wei et al., *Sichuan jindaishi*, 564.

117. Zhou Shanpei, *Xinhai geming zhi wo* [The 1911 Revolution and I] (1929), author bought in Chengdu in 2007, personal possession, no publication information, 47–49.

118. *Xinhai geming ziliao*, vol. 4, 429–30, in Wei et al., *Sichuan jindaishi*, 564.

119. In Dai, ed., *Sichuan baolu yundong shiliao*, 503–6.

120. Zhou, *Xinhai geming zhi wo*, 45–46.

121. In Dai, ed., *Sichuan baolu yundong shiliao*, 511–12, in Dai, ed., *Sichuan baolu yundong shiliao huizuan*, 1877.

122. Wei et al., *Sichuan jindaishi*, 563.

123. In Sichuan sheng dang'an guan, ed., *Sichuan baolu yundong dang'an xuanbian*, 311.

CHAPTER 8. THE END OF REVOLUTION

1. In Dai Zhili, ed., *Sichuan baolu yundong shiliao huizuan* [Collection of historical materials on the Sichuan Railway Protection movement] (Taipei: Zhongyang yanjiuyuan jindaishi yanjiusuo, 1994), 1872.

2. Ibid.

3. Wang Youyu, "Dahan Sichuan junzhengfu chengli qianhou jianwen" [The events around the establishment of the Great Han Sichuan Military Government], in Sichuan sheng zhengxie wenshi ziliao weiyuanhui, ed., *Sichuan wenshi ziliao jicui* [Selected personal histories of Sichuan province] (Chengdu: Sichuan renmin chubanshe, 1996), vol. 1, 247–48.

4. In Dai, ed., *Sichuan baolu yundong shiliao huizuan*, 1918.

5. Ibid.

6. Ibid., 1864.

7. Wang, "Dahan Sichuan junzhengfu chengli qianhou jianwen," 247–48.

8. There is no reliable source on Yin joining the Revoluitonary Alliance before 1911.

9. Wang, "Dahan Sichuan junzhengfu chengli qianhou jianwen," 248.

10. Peng Guanglie's letter to Li Jieren, in Dai, ed., *Sichuan baolu yundong shiliao huizuan*, 1908.

11. Zhou, *Xinhai geming zhi wo*, [The 1911 Revolution and I] (1929), author bought in Chengdu in 2007, personal possession, no publication information, 43–44.

12. Wang Di, *Street Culture in Chengdu: Public Space, Urban Commoners, and Local Politics, 1870–1930* (Stanford, CA: Stanford University Press, 2003), 221.

13. Ibid.

14. Ibid., 222.

15. Wang, "Dahan Sichuan junzhengfu chengli qianhou jianwen," 248.

16. Qin Nan, *Shuxin* [The ordeal of Sichuan] (Chengdu: 1914) Original document from Professor Dai Zhili, vol. 2., 9. Qin Nan worked as a clerk for the provincial government. In this book, he carefully recorded how contemporary people viewed the railway movement. In addition, this same number was reported in "Turmoil of Chengdu," *Minlibao*, January 2, 1912, in Dai, ed., *Sichuan baolu yundong shiliao huizuan*, 1904.

17. "Wang Youyu zai zhi Li Jieren shu Yin Changheng ren Sichuan junzhengfu dudu neimu shu" [Wang Youwu's second letter to Li Jieren on the details of Yin becoming the Sichuan military government's governor], in Dai, ed., *Sichuan baolu yundong shiliao huizuan*, 1932–33; and Wang Yunzi, "Tongmenghui yu Chuanxi Gelaohui" [The Revolutionary Alliance and the Sworn Brothers in west Sichuan], in Sichuan sheng zhengxie wenshi ziliao weiyuanhui, ed., *Sichuan wenshi ziliao jicui*, vol. 1, 255.

18. Zhou, *Xinhai geming zhi wo*, 43–44.

19. In Dai, ed., *Sichuan baolu yundong shiliao huizuan*, 1923–24.

20. Ibid., 1925.

21. Qin, *Shuxin*, vol. 2, 9.

22. In Dai, ed., *Sichuan baolu yundong shiliao huizuan*, 1911.

23. Zhao had ordered Fu Huafeng to get back to Chengdu long before December 8, but Fu was stuck in Ya'an by the Railway Protection troops there. Yin Changheng accused Zhao of ordering Fu to return to Chengdu to overthrow the regime and claimed he captured the messenger. However, no letters by Zhao to this effect seem to exist and the story about the messenger does not add up given the timing of Zhao's previous orders to Fu. As for the second piece of evidence, Zhao using the title "governor-general" in the announcements he issued can hardly be used to prove that he actually planned to overthrow the new regime.

24. Wei et al., *Sichuan jindaishi*, 578.

25. *Qianweixianzhi* [Qianwei gazateer], "Shiji" [Main events], in Wei et al., *Sichuan jindaishi*, 581.

26. *Leshanxianzhi* [Leshan gazateer], "Biannian jishi biao" [Chart of events] and Hanyuanxianzhi [Hanyuan gazateer], "Wubei zhi xia" [Military affairs, second part], in Wei et al., *Sichuan jindaishi*, 581.

27. *Deyangxianzhi* [Geyang gazateer], "Fengsu zhi" [Customs], in Wei et al., *Sichuan jindaishi*, 581.

28. "Wan xian Xiong Fei shang Sichuan gedi junzhengfu dudu jianyi tongyi hebing shu" [Petition for uniting Sichuan from Wan county's Xiong Fei], *Guangyi congbao* (year 9 no. 29), in Wei et al., *Sichuan jindaishi*, 582.

29. In Dai, ed., *Sichuan baolu yundong shiliao huizuan*, 1973.

30. Ibid., 1976–80.

31. Wei et al., *Sichuan jindaishi*, 582. Other developments that lent the issue of unification greater urgency were the imminent uprisings in Tibet, the probable invasion of those rebels into the Sichuan-Tibetan border region, and the possible movement of the Beiyang Army into Sichuan.

32. In Dai, ed., *Sichuan baolu yundong shiliao huizuan*, 2027–34.

33. "Zuzhi quanguo huiyi tuan tonggao shu" [Announcement for organizing a national United Convention], in Guojia tushuguan shanben bu, ed., *Zhao Fengchang cangzha* [A collection of Zhao Fengchang's letters] (Beijing: Guojia tushuguan chubanshe, 2009), vol. 3, 584.

34. Ibid.

35. Ibid.

36. Liao Dawei, "Gesheng dudufu daibiao lianhehui shulun" [On the United Convention of the Delegates of Provincial Governments], *Shilin*, no. 3 (1998): 61–63.

37. Ibid., 65.

38. Fan Fuchao, "Yuan Shikai dangxuan dazongtong qian de nanbei boyi" [Negotiations between the south and the north before Yuan Shikai's presidency], http://www.aisixiang.com/data/32323.html (viewed on September 7, 2014).

39. Liao, "Gesheng dudufu daibiao lianhehui shulun," 66.

40. Fan, "Yuan Shikai dangxuan dazongtong qian de nanbei boyi."

41. Ibid.

42. Liao, "Gesheng dudufu daibiao lianhehui shulun," 66–67.

43. Zhao Zunyue, "Xiyin tang xinhai geming ji" [Chronicle of Xiyin Hall's 1911 Revolution], in Jindaishi yanjiusuo jindaishi ziliao bianji bu, ed., *Jindaishi ziliao* [Sources on modern Chinese history] (Beijing: Zhongguo shehui kexue chubanshe, 2002), vol. 102, 253–54.

44. Zhao, "Xiyin tang xinhai geming ji," 254.

45. Liao, "Gesheng dudufu daibiao lianhehui shulun," 69–70. Huang Xing received one vote. Sichuan's delegates were Xiao Xiang and Zhou Daiben, and both had studied at Hōsei University.

46. Zhao, "Xiyin tang xinhai geming ji," 254–55.

47. Zhang Yaojie, "Shi shui qicao le qingdi xunwei zhaoshu?" [Who penned the Manchu Abdication Edict?], http://history.people.com.cn/GB/205396/17108477.html (viewed on December 30, 2015).

48. Qu Jun, "Xinhai geming yu Shanghai gonggong kongjian" [The 1911 Revolution and public space in Shanghai] (PhD diss., East China Normal University, 2007), 36–51.

49. Henrietta Harrison, *The Making of the Republican Citizen: Political Ceremonies and Symbols in China, 1911–1929* (New York: Oxford University Press, 2000).

50. David Strand, *An Unfinished Republic: Leading by Word and Deed in Modern China* (Berkeley: University of California Press, 2011).

51. *Luxianzhi* [Lu county gazetteer], vol. 3, "Fengsu" [Customs], in Wei et al., *Sichuan jindaishi*, 595.

52. Ibid.

53. *Anxianzhi* [An county gazetteer], vol. 55, "Lisu" [Rituals and Customs], in Wei et al., *Sichuan jindaishi*, 595.

54. *Hechuanxianzhi* [Hechuan county gazetteer], vol. 25, "Zhengfa" [Politics and laws], in Wei et al., *Sichuan jindaishi*, 595.

55. *Anxianzhi*, vol. 55, "Lisu" [Rituals and Customs], in Wei et al., *Sichuan jindaishi*, 595.

56. Zhang Yongle, *Jiubang xinzao* [The remaking of an old country] (Beijing: Beijing daxue chubanshe, 2011), 49–81.

57. Ibid., 112–15.

58. Ibid. This also caused many needless legal battles. The most serious of these was the 1917 fight between President Li Yuanhong and Prime Minister Duan Qirui, in which both cited the Provisional Constitution as evidence, with each accusing the other of "violating the law."

59. Zhang Yufa, *Minguo chunian de zhengdang* [Political parties in the early Republic] (Changsha: Yuelu shushe, 2004).

60. Xiaowei Zheng, "Building a Republic without Revolution: Pu Dianjun and His Constitutional Endeavors, 1911–1925," submitted to *Twentieth-Century China*, n.p.

61. Zhang Yongle, *Jiubang xinzao*, 49–81.

62. Ibid. See also Ernest Young, *The Presidency of Yuan Shih-k'ai: Liberalism and Dictatorship in Early Republican China* (Ann Arbor: University of Michigan Press, 1977).

63. Chen Ming, "Jiquan yu fenquan: minguo yuannian de junmin fenzhi zhi zheng" [Centralization or decentralization: The act of separating civic power and military power in the first year of the Republic], *Xueshu yanjiu*, no.9 (2011): 116–27.

64. Zhang Yong, *Minguo chunian de Jinbudang yu yihui zhengdang zhengzhi* [Early years of the Progressive Party and parliamentary party politics] (Beijing: Beijing daxue chubanshe, 2008), 193–281. The newest research on this topic has shown that neither Yuan Shikai nor Zhao Bingjun, the prime minister of Yuan's cabinet, planned or approved the assassination. According to Zhang Yong, neither Yuan Shikai nor Zhao Bingjun knew about the plan ahead of time. In addition, in 1913, only the Nationalist newspapers claimed that Yuan and Zhao were implicated; the public in China did not agree with this judgment. The death of Song Jiaoren led to the Second Revolution. In fact, by starting the revolution, the Nationalists essentially abandoned the legal solution to this problem and disrespected the Provisional Constitution that they themselves had created.

65. In Dai, ed., *Sichuan baolu yundong shiliao huizuan*, 2027–34.

66. A Chongqing native and one of Yin Changheng's teachers, Hu was a former instructor at the Sichuan Military Preparatory Academy (Sichuan lujun wubei xu-

etang) and had also served as the master of the Yunnan Army Primary School (Yunnan lujun xiaoxue) and the Yunnan Military Academy (Yunnan jiangwu xuetang).

67. Wei et al., *Sichuan jindaishi*, 583.

68. Wei et al., *Sichuan Jindaishi*, 598.

69. Tang Zongyao "Erci geming qianhou Sichuan sheng yihui de xingfei" [A short history of Sichuan's provincial assembly around the Second Revolution], Sichuan sheng zhengxie wenshi ziliao weiyuanhui, ed., *Sichuan wenshi ziliao jicui* [Selected personal histories of Sichuan province] (Chengdu: Sichuan renmin chubanshe, 1996), vol. 1, 372.

70. Wei et al., *Sichuan jindaishi*, 598.

71. Center for Chinese Research Materials, reprints, *Jinbudang xuanyan shu* [Declaration of the Progressive Party] (Washington, DC, 1969), 2, 5, 6. The new party's 1913 manifesto stated: "The party has relied on statism to construct and strengthen the government. It respects people's opinions and vindicates their legally granted freedom. It enhances China's wealth and peace, following global trends." In the following several years, the Progressive Party engaged in and experimented with parliamentary politics. It cooperated with various Beiyang warlords in the process, to no avail.

72. Zheng, "Building a Republic without Revolution."

73. Zhang Yong, *Minguo chunian de Jinbudang yu yihui zhengdang zhengzhi*, 193–281.

74. Zhang Yongle, *Jiubang xinzao*, 112–16.

75. Ibid., 114.

76. Ibid., 115.

77. Yan Quan, *Shibai de yichan: Zhonghua shoujie guohui zhixian 1913–1923* [The legacy of failure: The constitutional attempts of the first parliament, 1913–1923] (Guilin: Guangxi shifan daxue chubanshe, 2007).

78. Zhang Yongle, *Jiubang xinzao*, 115. See also Zhang Yong, *Minguo chunian de Jinbudang yu yihui zhengdang zhengzhi*, 314–22.

79. Gordon Wood, *The Creation of the American Republic, 1776–1787* (Chapel Hill: University of North Carolina Press, 1998), 344–89.

80. Zheng, "Building a Republic Without Revolution."

81. Ibid.

82. Geng Yunzhi and Cui Zhihai, *Liang Qichao* [Liang Qichao] (Guangzhou: Guangdong renmin chubanshe, 1994), 316.

83. Lin Dun and He Yili, "Pu Dianjun" [Pu Dianjun], in Sichuan sheng zhengxie wenshi ziliao yanjiu weiyuanhui, Sichuan sheng wenshi guan, ed., *Sichuan jinxiandai wenhua renwu* [Eminent cultural figures of modern Sichuan] (Chengdu: Sichuan renmin chubanshe, 1989), vol. 1, 185.

CONCLUSION

1. Xiaowei Zheng, "Building a Republic without Revolution: Pu Dianjun and His Endeavors for a Constitutional China, 1911–1925," submitted to *Twentieth-Century China*, n.p.

2. Zhang Yongle, *Jiubang xinzao* [The remaking of an old country] (Beijing: Beijing daxue chubanshe, 2011), 12.

3. Zheng, "Building a Republic without Revolution."

4. Han Dayuan, "Meinongbu daji lixian zhuyi sixiang yanjiu" [A study of the constitutional thought of Minobe Tatsukichi], http://www.calaw.cn/article/default.asp?id=5051 (viewed on November 14, 2013).

5. Ibid.

6. Feng Tianyu, "Fazheng daxue Zhongguo liuxuesheng yu Ezhou yuefa de zhiding" [The Hōsei University Chinese overseas students and the drafting of the Hubei constitution], *Jianghan daxue xuebao*, vol. 30, no. 5 (October 2011): 47.

7. Li Qicheng, ed., *Zizhengyuan yichang huiyi sujilu: Wanqing yubei guohui lunbian shilu* [Transcripts of the first National Assembly meeting] (Shanghai: Shanghai sanlian shudian, 2011), appendix, "Short Biographies of the National Assemblymen," 740–77.

8. Zhang Yong, *Minguo chunian de Jinbudang yu yihui zhengdang zhengzhi* [Early years of the Progressive Party and parliamentary party politics] (Beijing: Beijing daxue chubanshe, 2008), 319.

9. Feng Xiaocai, "Counterfeiting Legitimacy: Reflections on the Usurpation of Popular Politics and the 'Political Culture' of China, 1912–1949," *Frontiers of History in China*, vol. 8, no. 3 (2013), 202–22.

Bibliography

Adshead, S. A. M. *Province and Politics in Late Imperial China: Viceregal Government in Szechwan.* London: Curzon Press, 1984.
Balazs, Étienne. *Chinese Civilization and Bureaucracy: Variations on a Theme.* New Haven, CT: Yale University Press, 1964.
Baolu tongzhihui baogao [Newsletter of the Sichuan Railway Protection Association]. Chengdu: 1911.
Barfield, Thomas. *The Perilous Frontier: Nomadic Empires and China 220 BC to AD 1757.* Oxford: Blackwell, 1989.
Baxian dang'an [Ba county archives], Sichuan Provincial Archives, Chengdu.
Bergère, Marie-Claire. *Sun Yat-sen.* Stanford, CA: Stanford University Press, 2000.
Bol, Peter. *Neo-Confucianism in History.* Cambridge, MA: Harvard University Press, 2008.
———. "Tang Song zhuanxing de fansi: yi sixiangshi de bianhua wei zhu" [Reflecting upon the Tang-Song transition: From an intellectual history perspective]. *Zhongguo xueshu* [Chinese academics], vol. 3, no. 1 (2000): 63–87.
Center for Chinese Research Materials. *Jinbudang xuanyan shu* [Declaration of the Progressive Party]. Reprint. Washington, DC, 1969.
Chan, Hok-lam, and Wm. Theodore de Bary, eds. *Yuan Thought: Chinese Thought and Religion Under the Mongols.* New York: Columbia University Press, 1982.
Chang Chung-li. *The Chinese Gentry: Studies on their Role in Nineteenth-Century Chinese Society.* Seattle: University of Washington Press, 1967.
Chang Hao. *Liang Ch'i-ch'ao and Intellectual Transition in China, 1890–1907.* Cambridge, MA: Harvard University Press, 1971.
Chang Peng-yuan. "The Constitutionalists." Pp. 143–83 in Mary Wright, ed., *China in Revolution: The First Phase, 1900–1913.* New Haven, CT: Yale University Press, 1968.
Chen Ming. "Jiquan yu fenquan: Minguo yuannian de junmin fenzhi zhi zheng" [Centralization or decentralization: The act of separating civic power and military power in the first year of the Republic], *Xueshu yanjiu* [Academic Research], no. 9 (2011): 116–27.
Chen Xulu. *Jindai Zhongguo shehui de xinchen daixie* [The evolution of modern Chinese society]. Beijing: Zhongguo renmin daxue chubanshe, 2012.
Chen Xulu et al., eds. *Xinhai geming qianhou* [Around the time of the 1911 Revolution]. Shanghai: Shanghai renmin chubanshe, 1979.
Chen Yushen. *Wanqing baoye shi* [The history of the late Qing press]. Ji'nan: Shandong huabao chubanshe, 2003.

Chengdu shi zhengxie wenshi ziliao weiyuanhui, ed. *Sichuan xinhai fenglei* [Thunder and wind in Sichuan in the 1911 Revolution]. Chengdu: Chengdu chubanshe, 1991.
Chow Kai-wing. *The Rise of Confucian Ritualism in Late Imperial China: Ethics, Classics, and Lineage Discourse*. Stanford, CA: Stanford University Press, 1994.
Ch'ü T'ung-tsu. *Local Government in China Under the Ch'ing*. Cambridge, MA: Harvard University Press, 1962.
Chuan-Han tielu gaijinhui [Association for Improving the Chuan-Han Railway], ed. *Chuanlu gaijinhui baogaoshu* [Report of the Association for Improving the Chuan-Han Railway]. 5 vols. Tokyo: 1904–1907. Original document in the Sichuan Provincial Library.
Chuanlu shouhui guoyou wanglai yaodian [Key telegrams concerning the nationalization of Sichuan railways]. Chengdu: 1911. Original document from Professor Dai Zhili.
Chuanlu yuebao [Monthly report of the Sichuan railways]. Chengdu: 1911. Original journal in the Sichuan Provincial Library.
Chūzō Ichiko. "The Role of the Gentry: A Hypothesis." Pp. 297–318 in Mary Wright, ed., *China in Revolution: The First Phase, 1900–1913*. New Haven, CT: Yale University Press, 1968.
Cohen, Paul A. *China and Christianity: The Missionary Movement and the Growth of Chinese Antiforeignism, 1860–1870*. Cambridge, MA: Harvard University Press, 1967.
Crossley, Pamela. *A Translucent Mirror: History and Identity in Qing Imperial Ideology*. Berkeley: University of California Press, 1999.
Dai Zhili, ed. *Sichuan baolu yundong shiliao* [Historical materials on the Sichuan Railway Protection movement]. Beijing: Kexue chubanshe, 1959.
———, ed. *Sichuan baolu yundong shiliao huizuan* [Collection of historical materials on the Sichuan Railway Protection movement]. 3 vols. Taipei: Zhongyang yanjiu yuan jindaishi yanjiusuo, 1994.
Daqing jinshen quanshu [Complete directory of the gentry of the great Qing]. Beijing: Ronglu tang (1911 ed.).
Ding Wenjiang and Zhao Fengtian, eds. *Liang Qichao nianpu changbian* [Chronicle of Liang Qichao's life]. Beijing: Zhonghua shuju, 2010.
Ding Xiangshun. "Wanqing fu Ri fazheng liuxuesheng yu Zhongguo zaoqi fazhi jindaihua" [Late Qing overseas students in Japan and the early modernization of the Chinese legal system]. http://www.japanlawinfo.sdu.edu.cn/html/faxuey iban/20071201/46.html.
Duara, Prasenjit. *Culture, Power, and the State: Rural North China, 1900–1942*. Stanford, CA: Stanford University Press, 1988.
Eisenstadt, S. N. "Frederic Wakeman's Oeuvre in the Framework of World and Comparative History." Pp. xi–xix in Frederic Wakeman Jr., selected and edited by Lea Wakeman, *Telling Chinese History: A Selection of Essays*. Berkeley: University of California Press, 2009.
Elliot, Mark. *The Manchu Way: The Eight Banners and Ethnic Identity in Late Imperial China*. Stanford, CA: Stanford University Press, 2001.

Elman, Benjamin. *Civil Examinations and Meritocracy in Late Imperial China.* Cambridge, MA: Harvard University Press, 2013.

———. *Classicism, Politics, and Kinship: The Ch'ang-chou School of New Text Confucianism in Late Imperial China.* Berkeley: University of California Press, 1990.

———. *From Philosophy to Philology: Intellectual and Social Aspects of Change in Late Imperial China.* Berkeley: University of California Press, 2001.

Entenmann, Robert. "Migration and Settlement in Sichuan, 1644–1796." PhD diss., Harvard University, 1982.

Esherick Joseph. "1911: A Review." *Modern China*, vol. 2, no. 2 (1976): 141–84.

———. *Reform and Revolution: The 1911 Revolution in Hunan and Hubei.* Berkeley: University of California Press, 1976.

———. "Rethinking the 1911 Revolution." Pp. 272–80 in Zhongguo shixuehui, ed., *Jinian Xinhai geming yibai zhounian guoji xueshu yantaohui lunwenji* [Papers commemorating the hundredth anniversary of the 1911 Revolution], vol. 1. Wuhan: 2011.

Fairbank John, and Albert Feuerwerker, eds. *Cambridge History of China*, vol. 13. Cambridge: Cambridge University Press, 1986.

Fan Fuchao. "Yuan Shikai dangxuan dazongtong qian de nanbei boyi" [Negotiations between the South and the North before Yuan Shikai's presidency]. http://www.aisixiang.com/data/32323.html.

Fazheng daxue [Hōsei University], ed. *Fazheng suchengke jiangyilu* [Lecture notes of Hōsei University's Short-Term Program]. 57 vols. Tokyo: Hōsei University, 1905–1911.

Fazheng daxue shi ziliao weiyuanhui [Committee on sources on the history of Hōsei University], ed. *Fazheng daxue qingguo liuxuesheng fazheng suchengke teji* [Special source collection on the Hōsei Short-Term Program for the Qing overseas students], in *Hōsei Daigakushi shiryōshū* [Source collection of the history of Hōsei University]. Tokyo: Hōsei Daigaku Hyakunenshi Hensan Iinkai Shiryō Bukai, 1978.

Feng Feng. "Shaanxi junzhengfu yu Xinhai geming" [The Shaanxi military government and the 1911 Revolution]. Pp. 347–55 in Zhongguo shixuehui, ed., *Jinian Xinhai geming yibai zhounian guoji xueshu yantaohui lunwenji* [Papers commemorating the hundredth anniversary of the 1911 Revolution]. Wuhan: 2011.

Feng Tianyu. "Fazheng daxue Zhongguo liuxuesheng yu Ezhou yuefa de zhiding" [The Hōsei University Chinese overseas students and the drafting of the Ezhou constitution]. *Jianghan daxue xuebao* [Journal of Jianghan University], vol. 30, no. 5 (October 2011): 43–48.

Feng Xiaocai. "Counterfeiting Legitimacy: Reflections on the Usurpation of Popular Politics and the 'Political Culture' of China, 1912–1949." *Frontiers of History in China*, vol. 8, no. 3 (2013): 202–22.

Fincher, John. *Chinese Democracy: The Self-Government Movement in Local, Provincial, and National Politics (1905–1914).* Canberra: Australian National University Press, 1981.

Fogel, Joshua. *Late Qing China and Meiji Japan: Political and Cultural Aspects.* Norwalk, CT: EastBridge, 2004.
Foucault, Michel. *Foucault Live: Interviews, 1966–84.* Los Angeles: Semiotext(e), 1996.
———. *The Politics of Truth.* Los Angeles: Semiotext(e), 2007.
Fu Chongju. *Chengdu tonglan* [Investigation of Chengdu]. Chengdu: Chengdu shidai chubanshe, 2006.
Furth, Charlotte. "The Sage as Rebel: The Inner World of Chang Ping-lin." Pp. 22–53 in Charlotte Furth, ed., *The Limits of Change: Essays on Conservative Alternatives in Republican China.* Cambridge, MA: Harvard University Press, 1976.
Gao Yihan, "Xinhai geming qianhou Anhui qingnian xuesheng sixiang zhuanbian de gaikuang" [The ideological transition of Anhui's young students around the 1911 Revolution]. Pp. 431–37 in *Xinhai geming huiyilu* [Memoirs on the 1911 Revolution], vol. 4. Beijing: Zhonghua shuju, 1961.
Gasster, Michael. *Chinese Intellectuals and the Revolution of 1911: The Birth of Modern Chinese Radicalism.* Seattle: University of Washington Press, 1969.
Geng Yunzhi and Cui Zhihai. *Liang Qichao* [Liang Qichao]. Guangzhou: Guangdong renmin chubanshe, 1994.
Graham, A. C. *Disputers of the Tao: Philosophical Argument in Ancient China.* Chicago: Open Court, 1989.
Guo Moruo. "Fanzheng qianhou" [Life around the 1911 Revolution]. Pp. 153–263 in *Moruo zizhuan* [Autobiography of Guo Moruo]. Xianggang: Sanlian shudian, 1978.
Guo Songtao et al. *Lundun yu Bali riji,* in *Guo Songtao deng shixiji liuzhong* [Six diaries of the journey to the West by Guo Songtao and others]. Shanghai: Zhongxi shuju, 2012.
Guojia tushuguan shanben bu, ed. *Zhao Fengchang cangzha* [A collection of Zhao Fengchang's letters]. 10 vols. Beijing: Guojia tushuguan chubanshe, 2009.
Han Dayuan. "Meinongbu daji lixian zhuyi sixiang yanjiu" [A study of the constitutional thought of Minobe Tatsukichi]. http://article.chinalawinfo.com/Article_Detail.asp?ArticleId=55832.
Harrison, Henrietta. *Inventing the Nation: China.* New York: Oxford University Press, 2001.
———. *The Making of the Republican Citizen: Political Ceremonies and Symbols in China, 1911–1929.* New York: Oxford University Press, 2000.
Hazama Naoki, ed. *Liang Qichao, Mingzhi Riben, Xifang* [Liang Qichao, Meiji Japan, and the West: Report of the joint research of the Institute in the Humanities, Kyoto University, Japan]. Beijing: Shehui kexue wenxian chubanshe, 2012.
———. "Dongyang Lusuo Zhongjiang Zhaomin zai jindai dongya wenmingshi shang de diwei" [The role of Nakae Chōmin—Rousseau of the East—in the history of East Asian civilization]. Pp. 53–68 in Sha Peide [Peter Zarrow] and Zhang Zhejia, eds., *Jindai Zhongguo xinzhishi de jiangou* [The construction of new knowledge in modern China]. Taipei: Zhongyang yanjiu yuan, 2013.
———. "Nakae Chōmin *Minyaku yakkai* no rekishiteki igi ni tsuite" [Nakae Chōmin's translation of Rousseau's *The Social Contract*]. Pp. 1–53 in Ishikawa

Yoshihiro, Hazama Naoki, eds. *Kindai higashi ajia ni okeru hon'yaku gainen no tenkai*. Kyoto: Kyoto daigaku jinbun kagaku kenkyūjo, 2013.

He Yimin. "Xinhai geming shishi kao sanze" [Examining three historical facts concerning the 1911 Revolution]. *Jindaishi yanjiu* [Modern Chinese history studies], no. 5 (1987): 200–205.

Hou Yijie. *Ershi shiji chu Zhongguo zhengzhi gaige fengchao: Qingmo lixian yundong shi* [The wave of political reform in early twentieth-century China: The constitutional movement of the late Qing]. Beijing: Renmin chubanshe, 1993.

Hsiao Kung-chuan. *A Modern China and a New World: K'ang Yu-wei, Reformer and Utopian, 1858–1927*. Seattle: University of Washington Press, 1975.

Hsieh, Winston. *Chinese Historiography on the Revolution of 1911: A Critical Survey and a Selected Bibliography*. Stanford, CA: Hoover Institution Press, 1975.

Huang Ko-wu, ed. *Zhongguo jindai sixiangjia wenku: Yan Fu juan* [Anthology of modern Chinese thinkers: Yan Fu]. Beijing: Renmin daxue chubanshe, 2014.

Huang, Ray. *Fiscal Administration During the Ming Dynasty*. Cambridge: Cambridge University Press, 1969.

Huang Shou. "Baolu yundong zhongde Luo Lun" [Luo Lun in the Railway Protection movement], in Sichuan sheng zhengxie wenshi ziliao weiyuanhui, ed., *Sichuan wenshi ziliao jicui* [Selected personal histories of Sichuan province]. Chengdu: Sichuan renmin chubanshe, 1996, vol. 1, 165–69.

———. Unpublished memoir of Huang Shou. Bought at the flea market in Chengdu, originally stored in the Sichuan wenshiguan [Sichuan Literature and History Bureau]. 2,000 pages.

Huenemann, Ralph. *The Dragon and the Iron Horse: The Economics of Railroads in China, 1876–1937*. Cambridge, MA: Harvard University Press, 1984.

Hunt, Lynn. *Politics, Culture, and Class in the French Revolution*. Berkeley: University of California Press, 1984.

Jia Yuying. *Songdai jiancha zhidu* [The monitoring system in the Song dynasty]. Zhengzhou: Henan daxue chubanshe, 2006.

Jiang Liping and Lin Weiping. "Deng Xiaoke yu Sichuan baolu yundong" [Deng Xiaoke and the Sichuan Railway Protection Movement]. *Shucheng* [Book town] (April 2009): 1–14.

Jianshe Chuan-Han tielu shangban gongsi quangaoshu [Calling for a private Chuan-Han Railway Company]. Original poster in the Sichuan Provincial Library.

Jin Chongji and Hu Shengwu. *Xinhai geming shigao* [Draft history of the 1911 Revolution]. 4 vols. Shanghai: Shanghai renmin chubanshe, 1980–1991.

Judge, Joan. *Print and Politics: "Shibao" and the Culture of Reform in Late Qing China*. Stanford, CA: Stanford University Press, 1997.

Kangxi zidian [Kangxi dictionary]. Online version. http://www.kangxizidian.com/index2.php.

Karl, Rebecca, and Peter Zarrow, eds. *Rethinking the 1898 Reform Period: Political and Cultural Change in Late-Qing China*. Cambridge, MA: Harvard University Press, 2002.

Kirby, William, and Zhou Yan, eds. *Bu queding de yichan: Hafo Xinhai bainian luntan jiangyan lu* [The uncertain legacy: Harvard lectures on the 1911 Revolution]. Beijing: Jiuzhou chubanshe, 2012.

Kuhn, Philip. *Origins of the Modern Chinese State*. Stanford, CA: Stanford University Press, 2002.

———. *Rebellion and Its Enemies in Late Imperial China: Militarization and Social Structure, 1796–1864*. Cambridge, MA: Harvard University Press, 1970.

Levenson, Joseph. *Confucian China and Its Modern Fate*, vol. 2. Berkeley: University of California Press, 1965.

Li Danke. "Popular Culture in the Making of Anti-Imperialist and Nationalist Sentiments in Sichuan." *Modern China*, vol. 30, no. 4 (2004): 470–505.

Li Enhan. "Wanqing shouhui liquan yundong yu lixian yundong" [The sovereignty-recovery movement and the constitutional movement in the late Qing]. Pp. 84–100 in *Jindai Zhongguo shishi yanjiu lunji* [Articles on modern Chinese history], vol. 2. Taipei: Taiwan shangwu yinshuguan, 1982.

Li Jieren. [Collected works of Li Jieren], vols. 1–2. Chengdu: Sichuan renmin chubanshe, 1980.

Li Qicheng, ed. *Zizhengyuan yichang huiyi sujilu: Wanqing yubei guohui lunbian shilu* [Transcripts of the first National Assembly meeting: Preparation for constitutionalism in the late Qing era]. Shanghai: Shanghai sanlian shudian, 2011.

Li Xiaoti. *Qingmo xiaceng shehui qimeng yundong 1901–1911* [The late Qing popular enlightenment movement, 1901–1911]. Taipei: Zhongyang yanjiuyuan, 1992.

Li Xin. *Zhonghua minguo shi* [History of Republican China]. Beijing: Zhonghua shuju, 1981.

Li Xizhu. *Difang dufu yu qingmo xinzheng: Wanqing quanli geju zai yanjiu* [Local governors and the New Policies reform: A further study of the power structure of the late Qing]. Beijing: Shehui kexue wenxian chubanshe, 2012.

———. *Zhang Zhidong yu qingmo xinzheng yanjiu* [A study of Zhang Zhidong and the late Qing New Politics reform]. Shanghai: Shanghai shudian chubanshe, 2003.

Liew, K. S. *Struggle for Democracy: Sung Chiao-jen and the 1911 Chinese Revolution*. Berkeley: University of California Press, 1971.

Liang Qichao. *Yinbingshi heji* [Collected essays from an ice drinker's studio]. Beijing reprint: Zhonghua shuju, 1989.

Liao Dawei. "Gesheng dudufu daibiao lianhehui shulun" [On the United Convention of the Delegates of Provincial Governments], *Shilin* [Historical Review], no. 3 (1998): 61–70.

Lin Dun and He Yili. "Pu Dianjun" [Pu Dianjun]. Pp. 182–86 in Sichuan sheng zhengxie wenshi ziliao yanjiu weiyuanhui, Sichuan sheng wenshiguan, ed., *Sichuan jinxiandai wenhua renwu* [Eminent cultural figures of modern Sichuan], vol. 1. Chengdu: Sichuan renmin chubanshe, 1989.

Lo Jung-pang, ed. *K'ang Yu-Wei: A Biography and a Symposium*. Tucson: University of Arizona Press, 1967.

Luo Fuhui. *Xinhai geming shiqi de jingying wenhua yanjiu* [Study on the elite culture during the 1911 Revolution]. Wuhan: Huazhong shifan daxue chubanshe, 2001.

Luo Zhitian et al. *Shanyu yulai* [The coming of the storm]. Shanghai: Shanghai shudian chubanshe, 2011.

Ma Linghe. *Qingmo minchu tielu waizhai guan yanjiu* [A study of the idea of taking out foreign loans in building railways in the late Qing and early Republican eras]. Shanghai: Fudan daxue chubanshe, 2004.
Ma Min. *Shangren jingshen de shanbian: Jindai Zhongguo Shangren guannian yanjiu* [Transformation of the Chinese merchant spirit: Studies on modern Chinese merchant concepts]. Wuhan: Huazhong shifan daxue chubanshe, 2001.
Manqing yeshi [The unofficial history of the Manchu Qing dynasty]. Chengdu: Changfu gongsi. First published in 1920s. Original document from Professor Dai Zhili.
Mao Haijian. *Cong jiawu dao wuxu: Kang Youwei 'Woshi' jianzhu* [From 1895 to 1898: The textual research and annotations on Kang Youwei's autobiography (My history)]. Beijing: Sanlian shudian, 2009.
———. "Lun wuxu shiqi Liang Qichao de minzhu sixiang" [On democratic ideas of Liang Qichao around the Hundred Days' Reform era], *Xueshu yuekan* [Academic Monthly], vol. 49, no. 4 (2017): 142–43.
———. *Wuxu bianfa shishi kao chuji* [A study of historical facts of the Reform Movement of 1898, vol. 1]. Beijing: Sanlian shudian, 2005.
———. *Wuxu bianfa shishi kao erji* [A study of historical facts of the Reform Movement of 1898, vol. 2]. Beijing: Sanlian shudian, 2011.
———. *Zhang Zhidong dang'an yuedu biji: Wuxu bianfa de lingmian* [Readings of the Zhang Zhidong Archives: A study of the other sides of the Reform Movement of 1898]. Shanghai: Shanghai guji chubanshe, 2014.
Mao Zedong. *Mao Zedong xuanji* [Collected works of Mao Zedong]. Beijing: Renmin chubanshe, 1952.
McIlwain, Charles Howard. *Constitutionalism: Ancient and Modern*. Indianapolis: Liberty Fund, 2007.
Mi Rucheng. *Zhongguo jindai tielu shi ziliao* [Historical materials on the history of Chinese railways in the modern era]. 3 vols. Beijing: Zhonghua shuju, 1963.
Min Tu-Ki. *National Polity and Local Power: The Transformation of Late Imperial China*. Cambridge, MA: Harvard University Press, 1989.
Ming-Qing dang'an bu, ed. *Qingmo choubei lixian dang'an shiliao* [Historical archival documents on preparations for constitutional government in the late Qing]. 2 vols. Beijing: Zhonghua shuju, 1979.
Mittler, Barbara. *A Newspaper for China? Power, Identity, and Change in Shanghai's News Media, 1872–1912*. Cambridge, MA: Harvard University Press, 2004.
Miyazaki Ichisada. *Tōyōteki kinsei* [China's modern age]. Osaka: Kyōiku taimususha, 1950.
Nishikawa Masao. "Shisenshō Unyō-ken zakki" [Notes on Yunyang district, Sichuan province]. *Kanazawa Daigaku Bungakubu ronshū shigaku-ka hen*, no. 7 (1987): 169–224.
———. "Shisenshō kōanken bibōroku: Shinmatsu minkoku shoki no kyōshin" [Notes on Guang'an county of Sichuan province: Gentry of the late Qing and early Republican China], *Kanazawa Daigaku Bungakubu ronshū shigaku-ka hen*, no. 15 (1995): 9–92.

Peng Fen. *Xinhai xunqing zhengbian fayuan ji* [The origins of the Qing regime change in 1911]. Chengdu: Fumin gongsi, 1933. Original document from Professor Dai Zhili.

Peng Jian. *Qingji xianzheng bianchaguan yanjiu* [A study of the late Qing Institute for Constitutional Compilation]. Beijing: Beijing daxue chubanshe, 2011.

Pines, Yuri. *Envisioning Eternal Empire: Chinese Political Thought of the Warring States Era*. Honolulu: University of Hawai'i Press, 2009.

———. *The Everlasting Empire: The Political Culture of Ancient China and Its Imperial Legacy*. Princeton, NJ: Princeton University Press, 2012.

Pu Dianjun. *Gailiang Chuan-Han gongsi yi* [On improving the Chuan-Han Railway Company]. Original pamphlet in the Sichuan Provincial Library.

Pu Xiaorong. *Sichuan zhengqu yan'ge yu zhidi jinshi* [Historical and contemporary analyses of regions administered by Sichuan]. Chengdu: Sichuan renmin chubanshe, 1986.

Qin Nan. *Shu xin* [The ordeal of Sichuan] (Chengdu: 1914). Original document from Professor Dai Zhili.

Qu Jun. "Xinhai geming yu Shanghai gonggong kongjian" [The 1911 Revolution and the public space in Shanghai]. PhD diss., East China Normal University, 2007.

Rankin, Mary. *Early Chinese Revolutionaries: Radical Intellectuals in Shanghai and Chekiang, 1902–1911*. Cambridge, MA: Harvard University Press, 1971.

———. *Elite Activism and Political Transformation in China: Zhejiang Province, 1865–1911*. Stanford, CA: Stanford University Press, 1986.

———. "Nationalistic Contestation and Mobilization Politics: Practice and Rhetoric of Railway-rights Recovery at the End of the Qing." *Modern China*, vol. 28, no. 3 (2002): 315–61.

Rawski, Evelyn. *The Last Emperors: A Social History of Qing Imperial Institutions*. Berkeley: University of California Press, 1998.

Reed, Bradley. "Gentry Activism in Nineteenth-Century Sichuan: The Three-Fees Bureau." *Late Imperial China*, vol. 10, no. 1 (1999): 99–127.

———. *Talons and Teeth: County Clerks and Runners in the Qing Dynasty*. Stanford, CA: Stanford University Press, 2000.

Rhoads, Edward. *China's Republican Revolution: The Case of Kwangtung, 1895–1913*. Cambridge, MA: Harvard University Press, 1975.

———. *Manchus and Han: Ethnic Relations and Political Power in Late Qing and Early Republican China, 1861–1928*. Seattle: University of Washington Press, 2000.

Rowe, William. *China's Last Empire*. Cambridge, MA: Harvard University Press, 2012.

———. "Public Sphere in Modern China." *Modern China*, vol. 16, no. 3 (July 1999): 309–29.

Sanetō Keishō. *Zhongguo ren liuxue Riben shi* [History of overseas Chinese students in Japan]. Translated by Tan Ruqian and Lin Qiyan. Beijing: Sanlian shudian, 1983.

Schiffrin, Harold. *Sun Yat-sen and the Origins of the Chinese Revolution*. Berkeley: University of California Press, 1968.

Schoppa, Keith. *Chinese Elites and Political Change: Zhejiang Province in the Early Twentieth Century*. Cambridge, MA: Harvard University Press, 1982.
Schwartz, Benjamin. *In Search of Wealth and Power: Yen Fu and the West*. Cambridge, MA: Harvard University Press, 1964.
Shangban Sichuan Chuan-Han tielu zong gongsi baogao [Newsletter of the private Sichuan Chuan-Han Railway Company]. Original newspaper in the Sichuan Provincial Library. Chengdu: 1909.
Shen Jie. *1912 Nian: Dianpei de Gonghe* [1912: An Unstable Republic]. Shanghai: Dongfang chubanshe, 2015.
Sheng Xuanhuai. *Yuzhai cungao* [Materials preserved in Yu House]. 2 vols. 1939. Taipei: Wenhai chubanshe, 1965.
Sheng Xuanhuai dang'an ziliao xuanji [Archival documents on Sheng Xuanhuai]. 2 vols. Shanghai: Shanghai renmin chubanshe, 1979.
Shuzhong xianlie beizhenglu [Record of the campaigns of Sichuan martyrs]. 4 vols. Chongqing: Qiyu shuju, 1928.
Sichuan baolu tongzhihui dianwen yaolu [Key telegrams of the Sichuan Railway Protection Association] (1911). I thank Professor Dai Zhili for providing me with his copy of the document.
Sichuan difangzhi bianzuan weiyuanhui, ed. *Sichuan difangzhi tongxun* [Newsletter of Sichuan gazetteer studies], no. 3 (1984). Chengdu: 1984.
Sichuan sheng baoye zhi bianji bu, ed. *Sichuan baoye dashiji (1897–1995)* [Chronicle of the history of the Sichuan press (1897–1995)]. Chengdu: Sichuan renmin chubanshe, 1996.
Sichuan sheng dang'an guan, ed. *Sichuan baolu yundong dang'an xuanbian* [Selected archival documents of the Sichuan Railway Protection movement]. Chengdu: Sichuan renmin chubanshe, 1981.
———, ed. *Sichuan jiao'an yu yihequan dang'an* [Archival records on missionary cases and the Boxers in Sichuan]. Chengdu: Sichuan renmin chubanshe, 1985.
Sichuan sheng zhengxie wenshi ziliao weiyuanhui, ed. *Xinhai geming yu Zhongguo xiandaihua* [The 1911 Revolution and the modernization of China]. Chengdu: Sichuan jiaoyu chubanshe, 2001.
———, ed. *Sichuan wenshi ziliao jicui* [Selected personal histories of Sichuan province]. 6 vols. Chengdu: Sichuan renmin chubanshe, 1996.
Sichuan sheng ziyiju, ed. *Sichuan ziyiju diyici yishilu* [Transcripts of the proposals by the first Sichuan provincial assembly]. Pp. 1–151 in Wei Yingtao and Zhao Qing, eds., *Sichuan Xinhai geming shiliao* [Collected historical materials of the 1911 Revolution in Sichuan], vol. 1. Chengdu: Sichuan renmin chubanshe, 1982. Original document in the Sichuan Provincial Library.
Sichuan Xinhai fenglei [Thunder and wind in Sichuan in the 1911 Revolution]. Chengdu: Chengdu chubanshe, 1991.
Skinner, William. "Marketing and Social Structure in Rural China: Part 1." *Journal of Asian Studies*, vol. 24, no. 1 (1964): 3–43.
Skocpol, Theda. *States and Social Revolutions: A Comparative Analysis of France, Russia, and China*. Cambridge: Cambridge University Press, 1979.
Smith, Paul, and Richard von Glahn, eds. *The Song-Yuan-Ming Transition in Chinese History*. Cambridge, MA: Harvard University Press, 2004.

Stapleton, Kristin. *Civilizing Chengdu: Chinese Urban Reform, 1895–1937*. Cambridge, MA: Harvard University Press, 2000.

———. "County Administration in Late-Qing Sichuan: Conflicting Models of Rural Policing." *Late Imperial China*, vol. 18, no. 1 (1997): 100–132.

Strand, David. *An Unfinished Republic: Leading by Word and Deed in Modern China*. Berkeley: University of California Press, 2011.

Su Huilian [William Soothill]. *Litimotai zhuan* [Timothy Richard of China]. Translated by Guan Zhiyuan et al. Nanjing: Guangxi shifan daxue chubanshe, 2007.

Su Quanyou. *Qingmo youchuanbu yanjiu* [A study of the Department of Posts and Communications in the late Qing]. Beijing: Zhonghua shuju, 2005.

Sun Baoxuan. *Wangshanlu riji* [Diary of Sun Baoxuan]. Shanghai: Shanghai guji chubanshe, 1983.

Svarverud, Rune. "The Notions of 'Power' and 'Rights' in Chinese Political Discourse." Pp. 125–44 in Michael Lackner, Iwo Amelung, and Joachim Kurtz, eds., *New Terms for New Ideas: Western Knowledge and Lexical Change in Late Imperial China*. Leiden: Brill, 2001.

Tan Yigong and Chen Xinhou, eds. *Liu Ri fazheng daxue xueyou lu* [Alumni list of the overseas students at Hōsei University]. Tokyo: Hōsei University, 1911.

Tang Xiaobing. *Global Space and the Nationalist Discourse of Modernity: The Historical Thinking of Liang Qichao*. Stanford, CA: Stanford University Press, 1996.

Tang Zhijun. *Wuxu bianfa shi* [The history of the 1898 reform]. Shanghai: Shanghai shehui kexue chubanshe, 2003.

Tarrow, Sidney. *Power in Movement: Social Movements, Collective Action and Politics*. New York: Cambridge University Press, 1994.

Tocqueville, Alexis de. *The Ancien Régime and the Revolution*. Translated by Gerald Bevan. London: Penguin Classics, 2008.

Wakeman, Frederic, Jr. *The Great Enterprise: The Manchu Reconstruction of Imperial Order in Seventeenth-Century China*. Berkeley: University of California Press, 1986.

Wang Chunwu. *Paoge tanmi* [Exploring the secrets of the Gowned Brothers]. Chengdu: Bashu shushe, 1993.

Wang Di. *Kuachu fengbi de shijie: Changjiang shangyou quyu shehui yanjiu, 1644–1911* [Striding out of a closed world: A study of society in the upper Yangzi region, 1644–1911]. Beijing: Zhonghua shuju, 1993.

———. *Street Culture in Chengdu: Public Space, Urban Commoners, and Local Politics, 1870–1930*. Stanford, CA: Stanford University Press, 2003.

———. *The Teahouse: Small Business, Everyday Culture, and Public Politics in Chengdu, 1900–1950*. Stanford, CA: Stanford University Press, 2008.

Wang Jinping. "Between Family and State: Networks of Literati, Clergy, and Villagers in Shanxi, North China, 1200–1400." PhD diss., Yale University, 2011.

Wang Juan. *Merry Laughter and Angry Curses: The Shanghai Tabloid Press, 1897–1911*. Vancouver: University of British Columbia Press, 2012.

Wang Kangnian. *Wang Kangnian shiyou shuzha* [Correspondence between Wang Kangnian and his friends]. Shanghai: Shanghai guji chubanshe, 1986.

Wang Lifu. *Wang Lifu wenji* [Writings of Wang Lifu]. Shanghai: Shanghai shehui kexue chubanshe, 2006.
Wang Yao. "Lu Suo yu wanqing Zhongguo sixiang shijie (1882–1911)" [Rousseau and the intellectual world in China (1882–1911)]. PhD diss., East China Normal University, 2014.
Wei Yingtao. *Sichuan baolu yundong shi* [History of the Sichuan Railway Protection movement]. Chengdu: Sichuan renmin chubanshe, 1981.
Wei Yingtao et al. *Sichuan jindaishi* [History of modern Sichuan]. Chengdu: Sichuan shehui kexue yuan chubanshe, 1985.
Wei Yingtao and Zhao Qing, eds. *Sichuan xinhai geming shiliao* [Collected historical materials of the 1911 Revolution in Sichuan]. Chengdu: Sichuan renmin chubanshe, 1982.
Wong Young-tsu. *Search for Modern Nationalism: Zhang Binglin and Revolutionary China, 1869–1936*. Hong Kong: Oxford University Press, 1989.
Wood, Gordon. *The Creation of the American Republic, 1776–1787*. Chapel Hill: University of North Carolina Press, 1998.
Wright, Mary, ed. *China in Revolution: The First Phase, 1900–1913*. New Haven, CT: Yale University Press, 1968.
Wu Dade. "Wu Yuzhang yu Sichuan Xinhai geming," *Jindaishi yanjiu* [Modern Chinese History Studies], no. 3 (1994): 281–84.
Wu Gou. "Cong minjian zifa dao guanfu jieru: xiangyue zizhi qiannian liubian" [From local spontaneity to governmental intervention: The changing history of the xiangyue and self-governance in the past one thousand years]. http://history.sina.com.cn/bk/gds/2015-09-11/1053125459.shtml.
Wu Huan. *Minguo zhuge Zhao Fengchang yu Changzhou yingjie* [Zhao Fengchang and eminent leaders from Changzhou]. Wuhan: Changjiang wenyi chubanshe, 2010.
Wu Yuzhang. *Xinhai geming* [The 1911 Revolution]. Beijing: Renmin chubanshe, 1960.
———. *Wu Yuzhang wenji* [Writings of Wu Yuzhang]. Chongqing: Chongqing chubanshe, 1987.
Wyman, Judith. "The Ambiguities of Chinese Anti-foreignism: Chongqing, 1870–1900." *Late Imperial China*, vol. 18, no. 2 (1998), 86–122.
Xia Xiaohong. *Liang Qichao: Zai zhengzhi yu xueshu zhijian* [Liang Qichao: Between academics and politics]. Beijing: Dongfang chubanshe, 2014.
Xianyu Hao. "Shilun Chuanlu zugu" [On the Chuan-Han railway zugu], *Lishi yanjiu* [Historical Research], no. 2 (1982): 41–55.
Xiao Xiang. "Guang'an Pu Dianjun Xingzhuang" [The life of Pu Dianjun of Guang'an county]. Pp. 611–20 in Wei Yingtao and Zhao Qing, eds. *Sichuan Xinhai geming shiliao* [Collected historical materials of the 1911 Revolution in Sichuan], vol. 2. Chengdu: Sichuan renmin chubanshe, 1982.
Xiao Yishan. *Qingdai tongshi* [A general history of the Qing dynasty]. Shanghai: Huadong shifan daxue chubanshe, 2006.
Xiao-Planes, Xiaohong. "Of Constitutions and Constitutionalism: Trying to Build a New Political Order in China, 1908–1949." Pp. 37–58 in Stéphanie Balme

and Michael W. Dowdle, eds., *Building Constitutionalism in China*. New York: Palgrave Macmillan, 2009.

Xie Zengshou. *Zhang Lan nianpu xinbian* [A new chronology of Zhang Lan]. Beijing: Qunyan chubanshe, 2011.

Xiliang. *Xiliang yigao zougao* [Posthumous papers and memorials of Xiliang]. Beijing: Zhonghua shuju, 1959.

Xiong Yuezhi. *Xixue dongjian yu wanqing shehui* [Western learning and late Qing society]. Beijing: Renmin daxue chubanshe, 2011.

Xinjin dang'an [Xinjin county archive], Xinjin County Archive, Xinjin county.

Xu Xiaoqing. "Liuri xuesheng kanwu de chuanbo wangluo" [Circulation network of the magazines by the Chinese students in Japan]. *Zhongzhou xuekan* [Zhongzhou academic journal], no. 6 (2001): 92–96.

Yan Buke. *Shidafu zhengzhi yansheng shigao* [A history of the development of scholar-officials]. Beijing: Beijing daxue chubanshe, 1996.

Yan Changhong and Xu Xiaoqing. *Guimao nian wansui: 1903 nian de geming sichao yu geming yundong* [Long live the year of Guimao: Revolutionary thought and movement in the year 1903]. Wuhan: Huazhong shifan daxue chubanshe, 2001.

Yan Quan. *Shibai de yichan: Zhonghua shoujie guohui zhixian 1913–1923* [The legacy of failure: The constitutional attempts of the first parliament between 1913 and 1923]. Guilin: Guangxi shifan daxue chubanshe, 2007.

Yan Zhongping. *Zhongguo jindai jingjishi tongji ziliao xuanji* [Selected statistical materials in modern Chinese economic history]. Beijing: Kexue chubanshe, 1955.

Yang Guoqiang, "Yang Guoqiang tan wanqing de shenshi yu shenquan" [Yang Guoqiang on the gentry and the power of the gentry in late Qing China]. http://book.sohu.com/20090327/n263043062.shtml.

Yangwu zongju [Bureau of foreign affairs], ed., "Sichuan tongsheng waiguo guanyuan shangmin tongji biao" [Statistics on all Sichuan foreign officials, merchants, and citizens]. Chengdu: 1909.

Yi Dan. *Zuoyou yu luoxuan* [Left, right, and spiral]. Shanghai: Shanghai wenyi chubanshe, 1999.

Yiju laidian [Telegram from Yichang Bureau]. Original pamphlet in the Sichuan Provincial Library.

Young, Ernest. *The Presidency of Yuan Shih-k'ai: Liberalism and Dictatorship in Early Republican China*. Ann Arbor: University of Michigan Press, 1977.

Yunnan sheng zhengxie, ed. *Wenshi ziliao xuanji* [Selected personal histories of Yunnan province], vol. 4. Kunming: Yunnan renmin chubanshe, 1982.

Zarrow, Peter. "Anti-Despotism and 'Rights Talk': The Intellectual Origins of Modern Human Rights Thinking in the Late Qing," *Modern China*, vol. 34, no. 2 (2008): 179–209.

———. *After Empire: The Conceptual Transformation of the Chinese State, 1885–1924*. Stanford, CA: Stanford University Press, 2012.

———. *Educating China: Knowledge, Society and Textbooks in a Modernizing World, 1902–1937*. Cambridge: Cambridge University Press, 2015.

Zelin, Madeleine. *The Magistrate's Tael: Rationalizing Fiscal Reform in Eighteenth-Century Ch'ing China*. Berkeley: University of California, 1984.

Zhang Dafu. "Weixin bianfa zai Chengdu" [The New Policies reform in Chengdu]. Pp. 48–69 in Sichuan sheng zhengxie wenshi ziliao weiyuanhui, ed., *Sichuan wenshi ziliao jicui* [Selected personal histories of Sichuan province], vol. 1. Chengdu: Sichuan renmin chubanshe, 1996.

Zhang Haipeng and Li Xizhu, *Zhongguo jindai tongshi (5): Xinzheng, lixian yu Xinhai geming (1901–1912)* [The general history of China (5): The New Policies reform, constitutional reform, and the 1911 Revolution (1901–1912)]. Nanjing: Jiangsu renmen chubanshe, 2006.

Zhang Hairong, "Gongche shangshu ji zuozhe 'Hushang aishi laoren weihuanshi' jiujing shishui?" [Who is the author for the *Account of the Petition of Metropolitan Candidates?*], *Qingshi yanjiu* [The Qing history journal], no. 2 (2011): 138–44.

Zhang Kaiyuan. *Kaituozhe de zuji: Zhang Jian zhuan'gao* [Biography of Zhang Jian]. Beijing: Zhonghua shuju, 1986.

———. "Lun Zhang Jian de maodun xingge" [On Zhang Jian's conflicted personality]. *Lishi yanjiu* [Historical research], no. 3 (1963): 87–104.

Zhang Kaiyuan and Tian Tong. "Xin shiji zhi chu de Xinhai geming shi yanjiu (2000–2009)" [Review of studies on the history of the 1911 revolution from 2000 to 2009]. *Zhejiang shehui kexue* [Zhejiang Social Sciences], no. 9 (2010): 89–93.

———. *Zhang Jian yu jindai shehui* [Zhang Jian and modern society]. Wuhan: Huazhong shifan daxue chubanshe, 2001.

Zhang Kaiyuan, Luo Fuhui, and Yan Changhong, eds. *Xinhai gemingshi ziliao xinbian* [New compilation of historical documents on the 1911 Revolution]. 8 vols. Wuhan: Hubei renmin chubanshe, 2011.

Zhang Nan and Wang Renzhi, eds. *Xinhai geming qian shinian jian shilun xuanji* [Anthology of editorial articles from the decade before the 1911 Revolution], vol. 2. Beijing: Sanlian shudian, 1963.

Zhang Pengyuan. *Liang Qichao yu minguo zhengzhi* [Liang Qichao and republican politics]. Taipei: Shihuo chubanshe, 1978.

———. *Liang Qichao yu qingji geming* [Liang Qichao and the late Qing revolution]. Taipei: Zhongyang yanjiu yuan jindaishi yanjiusuo, 1982.

———. *Lixianpai yu Xinhai geming* [Constitutionalists and the 1911 Revolution]. Taipei: Zhongyang yanjiuyuan jindaishi yanjiusuo, 1969.

Zhang Qing. "Cewen zhong de lishi: Wanqing Zhongguo 'lishi jiyi' yanxu de yige cengmian" [One aspect of "history" in "policy questions" in the continuation of late Qing historical memory]. *Fudan xuebao* [Journal of Fudan University], no. 5 (2005): 53–62.

Zhang Ronghua, ed. *Zhongguo jindai sixiangjia wenku: Kang Youwei juan* [Anthology of modern Chinese thinkers: Kang Youwei]. Beijing: Zhongguo renmin daxue chubanshe, 2015.

Zhang Yaojie, "Shi shui qicao le qingdi xunwei zhaoshu?" [Who penned the Manchu Abdication Edict?]. http://history.people.com.cn/GB/205396/17108477.html.

Zhang Yong. *Minguo chunian de Jinbudang yu yihui zhengdang zhengzhi* [Early years of the Progressive Party and parliamentary party politics]. Beijing: Beijing daxue chubanshe, 2008.

Zhang Yongle. *Jiubang xinzao* [The remaking of an old country]. Beijing: Beijing daxue chubanshe, 2011.

Zhang Yufa. *Minguo chunian de zhengdang* [Political parties in the early Republic]. Changsha: Yuelu shushe, 2004.

———. *Qingji de geming tuanti* [Revolutionaries of the late Qing period: An analysis of groups in the revolutionary movement, 1894–1911]. Taipei: Zhongyang yanjiuyuan jindaishi yanjiusuo, 1982.

Zhang Zengyi. "Jiangnan zhizaoju de yishu huodong" [Translation activities by the Jiangnan Arsenal]. *Jindaishi yanjiu* [Modern Chinese History Studies], no. 3 (1994): 212–23.

Zhao Dingxin. *The Confucian-Legalist State: A New Theory of Chinese History*. Oxford: Oxford University, 2015.

Zhao Erxun, ed., *Qingshigao* [Draft history of the Qing dynasty]. Beijing: Zhonghua shuju, 1998.

Zhao Yuezun. "Xiyin tang Xinhai geming ji" [Chronicle of Xiyin Hall's 1911 Revolution]. Pp. 246–57 in Jindaishi yanjiusuo jindaishi ziliao bianji bu, ed., *Jindaishi ziliao* [Sources on modern Chinese history], vol. 102. Beijing: Zhongguo shehui kexue chubanshe, 2002.

Zheng, Xiaowei. "Building a Republic without Revolution: Pu Dianjun and His Constitutional Endeavors, 1911–1925." Submitted to *Twentieth-Century China*.

Zhongguo renmin zhengzhi xieshanghuiyi quanguo weiyuanhui, ed. *Xinhai geming huiyi lu* [Memoirs of the 1911 Revolution]. Beijing: Wenshi ziliao chubanshe, 1981.

Zhongguo shixuehui, ed. *Jinian xinhai geming yibai zhounian guoji xueshu yantaohui lunwenji* [Papers commemorating the hundredth anniversary of the 1911 Revolution]. 4 vols. Wuhan: 2011.

———. *Xinhai geming* [The 1911 Revolution]. 8 vols. Shanghai: Shanghai renmin chubanshe, 1957.

Zhongguohun [The Chinese spirit]. Shanghai: Guangzhi shuju, 1902, 1903, 1905, and 1907 editions.

Zhou Shanpei. *Xinhai geming zhi wo* [The 1911 Revolution and me]. 1929. Author bought in Chengdu in 2007, personal possession.

Zhou Xun. *Shuhai congtan* [Collected talks about Sichuan]. 3 vols. Chongqing: Chongqing dagongbao bu, 1948.

Zhu Weizheng, ed. *Wanguo gongbao wenxuan* [Collected essays from *Wanguo gongbao*]. Beijing: Sanlian shudian, 1998.

Zhu Ying. *Jindai Zhongguo shangren yu shehui* [Merchants and society in modern China]. Wuhan: Huazhong shifan daxue chubanshe, 2001.

Zhu Youxian. *Jindai xuezhi shiliao* [Historical sources of the educational system in modern China], vol. 2, part 1. Shanghai: Huadong shifan daxue chubanshe, 1987.

Zhu Zhisan. *Zhu Zhisan riji* [Diary of Zhu Zhisan]. Wuhan: Huazhong shifan daxue chubanshe, 2011.

Index

Page numbers followed by "f" indicate material in figures.

abdication of Manchu Qing court, 5, 237–40
Adshead, S. A. M., 15, 21, 34, 39
ages, doctrine of three, 60
Allen, John Young, 54–56
American Revolution, 266n1
Anfu clique, 246, 255
Anhui province, 5, 118, 121
announcements/proclamations, 225f; attempting to restrain masses via, 185; in Chengdu, 213; on constitutional reform (1906), 116; by Duanfeng, 221; Hou Baozhai's lie about, 177; by Liang Qichao, 81–82; opposing taxes, 188; popularizing of slogans via, 212, 218; posted rebuttals, vandalism of, 193, 206–7, 221; by Pu and Luo, 225; of Qing nationalization of railway company, 2, 141; of railway tax decision, 180; by Sichuan Railway Association, 156; slogans, concepts introduced through, 156, 197, 218; speed of travel of, 19; by Sun Zepei, 212; by Yin Changheng, 231–32; by Yu Dongchen (1897), 43–44; by Zhao Erfeng, 192–93, 203, 205–6, 232, 322n23; by Zhou Hongxun, 211
anti-Manchu revolutionaries, 266n6; intellectuals among, 66–67; *Minbao* newspaper of, 47, 80; in New Army, 3–5; Qing response to, 87; scholarship on, 218–20; Society of Heaven and Earth (Tiandihui), 175; in Tongmenghui, 6, 201, 209, 215–16, 220; as United Convention delegates, 236–37
artisans (traditional class), 12, 152, 206, 239
Association for Constitutional Government (Xianzheng gonghui), 120–21
autocracy, criticisms of, 5, 57, 62, 76, 186, 207, 211
Axioms of Humanity (*Renlei gongli*) (Kang), 58–59

ballads supporting activism, 158–61, 177, 186–88, 205
bandits: after rise of Yin, 234; attackers of Chengdu called, 201, 204, 209; *guolu* of Sichuan, 36, 277n104; Luo Lun and, 176, 201–2; and Railway Protection armies, 214; rebel bandits (*panzei*), 47; secret bandits and the Gowned Brothers, 37–39, 278n114; as separate from militias, 206, 209; Wu Qingxi and, 190, 193; Yukun and, 213; Zhao Erfeng and, 190, 193, 213, 315n112
bannermen and garrisons, 26–28, 37, 297n26
Bao Fengyang, 64
baojia system, 30, 33, 86, 95, 124–25, 169, 310n39
Baoning garrison, 27
Beijing: allied sacking of (1900), 84; attempt to centralize authority in, 117; Board of Punishment, 27, 31; as capital of republic, 239, 242–43; Li Jixun in, 183, 312n70; Liu Shengyuan's trip to, 163–64; metropolitan officials in, 104; Ministry of Posts and Communications, 151; missionary cases (*jiao'an*) in, 16, 40–45, 252; "national elite" in, 281n8; shop and vehicle taxes in, 130–31; Sichuanese officials serving in, 144; tax revenue from Sichuan, 36. *See also* imperial court
Beijing Treaty (1860), 39
Beiyang Army, 5, 7, 237, 323n31
Beiyang clique, 241–42, 244, 325n71
Bergère, Marie-Claire, 268n27
Bi Yongnian, 63
Blackburn mission, 17
Bluntschli, Johann Kaspar, 69, 72
Boissonade de Fontarable, Gustave Émile[ok], 77, 79
Book of Odes, 51
Book of Rites, 59
Boss Fu, 173–74

Boxer Protocol, 88, 111, 133
Boxer Uprising, 80, 84
Boyang Lake, 111
Britain: competing with France in China, 88–89, 91–92, 111; constitutional visit to (1905), 114; and Huguang Foreign Loan Agreement, 142; investment in Chinese railways, 89, 97; loans to China, 142, 163; as model for law, government, 119; Sheng Xuanhuai and, 163; Wang Tao in, 57. *See also* Huguang Foreign Loan Agreement; missionaries, foreign; Western influences

Canton-Hankow railroad line, 88, 141
Cao Rulin, 119
Catholicism, 39–44, 53
celebrities and revolutionary propaganda, 157–59
Cen Chunxuan, 86, 89, 113, 296n16
Chambers, William, 56
chambers of commerce, 119–20, 148–49
Chang Chung-li, 31
Changshou revolt, 216
Chen Baozhen, 61
Chen Chongji, 78, 79, 106, 222
Cheng Changqi, 91
Cheng Dequan, 5, 236–38, 241
Cheng Deyin, 216
Chengdu, 2, 312n70; bannermen stationed in, 28–29; riot against foreigners, 40, 42, 44; New Policies reform in, 80; and Chuan-Han Railway Company, 145–46; and Railway Protection movement, 93, 178–80; Special Shareholder Meeting, 180–84, 186, 189; market and school strikes, 184–86; September 7 massacre, martial law, 190–93 (192f); militia, populace uprising, 197–204 (199f), 214; outside forces around, 197, 213–14; Zhao Erfeng propaganda campaign, 204–7; Zhao requests for reinforcements, 221; Duanfang ordered to take command, 222; Zhao agreement with rebels, 222; Sichuan Military Government, 231; staged mutiny, response, 230–32; Zhao ambushed, executed, 232–33; battles around (1911), 208–13 (208f). *See also* Chongqing; Chuan-Han (Chengdu-Hankow) Railway; Li Jixun; Sichuan province
Chengdu Daily newspaper, 206
Cheng Yingdu, 154

Chen Qimei, 237–38
Chen Shixiong, 320n103
Chen Shutong, 78
Chen Wenqing, 168
Chen Yinke, 61
Chen Zhenfan, 221
Chiang Kai-shek, 268n27
"China" as national entity, 65
China Discussion newspaper, 65–68, 70
China Monthly Magazine, 53
Chinese Book and Tract Society (Tongwen shuhui), 54–55
Chinese Gentry (Chang), 31
Chinese imperial system: formal government, 25–31; informal modes of control, 31–34; political culture, 22–25
Chinese Progress newspaper, 62
Chinese Soul, The (pamphlet), 70–71
Chongqing, 214–18; anti-Christian riot, 40–43; Chongqing Division, 235, 242; Chongqing Military Government, 228; declaration of independence, 217–18; Duanfang in, 220–21; expanding revolts in, 208; financing New Army, 221; garrison in, 27, 28f; New Policies reform in, 80; Railway Protection branch in, 170–71; relations with Chengdu, 170, 235, 189, 198, 228, 234–35; response to Huang's death, 235; Tongmenghui uprisings in, 216–19, 233, 321n108; Women's Branch of, 309n28
Christians: Chinese, 172; missionary cases, 16, 39–45, 252, 279n130; missionary publications, 53–55; praying for Sichuan, 172
Chuan-Han (Chengdu-Hankow) Railway, 83; arrest of leaders and Chengdu Massacre, 191; changes in ownership structure, 99–107; Chuan-Han Railway Improvement Society, 100–101, 106; creation and management of, 48, 79, 87–90; funding efforts by overseas students, 90–94, 97–98, 168; funding for Railway Protection Association, 153–54, 168; *gongkuan/zugu* tax, 94–96, 101–6; investigation of accounts, 180; nationalization of, 2, 47, 141, 143–45, 304n35, 312nn70, 72; preserving national sovereignty, 89–90, 97; Sichuan elite and, 253; stocks, 95–96 (96f); Yichang branch of, 180. *See also* Huguang Foreign Loan Agreement

chuanmin/chuanren (citizens of Sichuan), 161–62
Chuannan Army (Railway Protection Army of Southern Sichuan), 210, 212
Ch'ü T'ung-tsu, 29, 273n26
circuit (*dao*)/circuit intendant (*daotai*), 29
citizens: call for army of, 152; as owners/stakeholders, 93, 103, 136, 147, 252–53; vocabulary describing, 148–49
civility (*li*), 23–24
civil service examinations: abolition of (1905), 84, 86; management of, 27; *New People's Journal* and, 79; *shenshi* and, 3, 31; *Wanguo gongbao* newspaper and, 55
Cixi, Empress Dowager, 84–85, 113, 114, 119, 121, 140
Cohen, Paul A., 279n130
Collection of Historical Materials on the Sichuan Railway Protection Movement (Dai), 12
collective action, 165; strikes, 194; tax resistance, 194
Commercial Code, 85, 97, 99, 101, 103, 105, 149
commoners, views toward, 52, 204
Communists, 7, 218, 268n27
company, state compared to a, 252
Company Code (Gongsilü), 101, 149
Compilations of Recent Developments in the West (*Xiguo jinshi huibian*), 56
Complete Book of True Principles and Public Laws (*Shili gongfa quanshu*) (Kang), 58, 60
"complete nation-state" (*wanquan guojia*), 67
Confucian China and Its Modern Fate (Levenson), 8
Confucianism, 22–23, 26, 50, 58–60, 63–64
Confucius as Reformer (*Kongzi gaizhi kao*) (Kang), 60
constitutionalism (*lixian*), 1–2; acceleration of (1907), 118; advent of, 72–75; boundaries of power, 111, 236; calls for a parliament, 120–21, 140–41; conflicts between elites and statesmen, 126–27; constitutional associations, 120; "constitutionalists," 267n6; as crucial for Revolution, 250; fact-finding missions (1905–1906), 114; failure of, 240–46; formal launch of (1906), 115; influence of Hōsei University on, 75–79; Kang's promotion of, 61–62; key principles for, 115, 118; Liang on, 72–75, 115–16, 119, 137–38, 241, 246; Minobe on, 77–78; need for checks and balances, 247; physical clashes within committees, 246; popular support for, 3, 5, 74, 81; promoted in Provincial Assembly (1909), 109–10; proposals for constitutional monarchy, 74, 85; public debate on, 65–72, 85; rhetoric of, 139; and rights of the people, 149–50, 245; Russo-Japanese War and, 111–13; statement by Chengdu rebels, 206–7; state policies implementing, 116–19; as state policy (1905), 113–14; as strengthening center, 114–16; ultimate failure of, 254; and United Convention delegates, 236–37; vocabulary of, 139; Western publications on, 54–56. *See also* New Policies reform
"Constitutional Outline" (Xianfa dagang), 122
Constitution Draft Committee, 243, 245
Constitution Research Group, 245–46
coolies, 3, 164, 165, 173
copper: coin bureaus funds, 91, 104; coins during silver shortage, 85; elementary students donating coins, 172; one-cash tax of, 183; silver conversion rate of, 33, 35–36
cosmic harmony, 23
councils, local and county, 118
county militia members (*lian*), 37
court. *See* imperial court (*daquan tongyu chaoting*)
cultural symbols, use of, 194, 254

Dai Hongci, 114–16, 119, 297n34
Dai Zhili, 12, 218, 295n107, 303–4n30
Daoguang emperor, 53
Daoism/Daoists, 23, 131, 172
datong ("great unity"), 59–60
decapitation, 221
declaration of independence (Sichuan), 222–26
Defense Army (*fangjun*) reorganization, 28
Democratic Party (Minzhudang), 241, 243
democratic principles: and democratic impulse, 255; Kang's petition based on, 61; publications introducing, 54–58; in rebel group publications, 212–13; and republicanism, 266n1
Deng Rong, 100, 106
Deng Xiaoke: arrested, 191; in Democratic Party, 243; educational background, 47;

Deng Xiaoke (*continued*)
  at founding of Railway Protection Association, 152–53; heading Documents Division, 154–55; influence of Hōsei University on, 79, 108; in Ministry of Finance, 47; petitions and open letters, 92–93, 113, 143–44, 149–50; presenting petition to government, 153, 178; use of funds, 154
Deyang, 234
Ding Baozhen, 36
Ding Xiangshun, 77
doctrine of three ages, 60
Dong Zhongshu, 23
Duanfang: Sun Baoqi letter to, 112; supporting constitutionalism, 113; on constitutional mission, 114–15; meaning of constitutionalism to, 116; reform proposals by, 297n26, 37; investigating Chuan-Han branch, 144; and nationalization campaign, 145–46; denouncements against, 152, 158; and Luo Lun, 152, 176; support from Sichuanese officials, 179; alliance with Li Jixun, 180, 182, 184; opposing Railway Protection movement, 181–82, 190; commanding armies in Sichuan, 190, 315n112; feud with Zhao Erfung, 192, 222–23, 315n112; public denouncements of, 193; pacification strategy of, 220–21, 321n108; killed by insurrectionists, 221
Duanjin, 221
Duan Qirui, 246, 255, 324n58
Duara, Prasenjit, 107

East Route in Sichuan, 20f
East Route Railway Protection Army, 201, 208f, 209, 212, 215–16, 219, 321n108
education: modern-style schools, 120; reforms under New Policies, 86. *See also* overseas students
Eight-Nation Expeditionary Force, 111
Eisenstadt, S. N., 23
Elder Brothers Society (*Gelaohui*), 4, 278n114
elites: collapse of union of (1914), 244; "established literati," 8, 10–11, 281n8; failure to govern, 246; local government a threat to, 122; walking with commoners to present petition, 153. *See also* gentry; Gowned Brothers (*Paoge*); local elites; *shenliang* (gentry and landowners)
Elman, Benjamin, 50
embezzlement of railway funds, 102, 104, 106
emperor and right to rule, 23, 57, 252
emperor organ theory, 78
Enlightening Pictorials, 191
Enming, 118
Entenmann, Robert, 35
equality (*pingdeng*), 81; between classes, 240; Kang Youwei on, 57–59; before the law, 161; "misunderstood" by people, 216, 239; political discourse on, 63–64, 79, 139, 211; Western influences, 54–57, 255. *See also* popular sovereignty
Esherick, Joseph, 10, 297n26
Essays of Protest (Feng), 51–52
"established literati," 8, 10–11, 281n8. *See also* literati
ethnicities in Chinese republic, 240
eventalization, 271n41
"exhortation song" (*quanmin ge*), 205

"fake republic," 246
Fan Yuanlian, 76
Fan Zhui, 63
federalism as revolutionary model, 5, 224, 235
Federalist Papers (Madison), 52
Fei Daochun, 106
Feng Guifen, 51–52, 57
Feng Tianyu, 288n134
flag of Great Han Sichuan Military Government, 223
folk songs, 159–61
foreign loans in railway building, 142–43, 146–52, 154–56
Foucault, Michel, 10, 173, 271n41
Four Books (*Great Learning, Doctrine of the Mean, Analects, Mencius*), 24
France, 245, 256; Boissonade and Tokyo School of Law, 77, 79; Chinese interest in Montesquieu, 73; Chinese interest in Rousseau, 66–69; competing with Britain in China, 88–89, 91–92, 111; constitutional visit to (1905), 114; influence on Hōsei University, 241, 255; loans to China, 142, 163; missionary cases in China, 39, 41–42, 44; Republic compared to China's, 245, 256, 266n1; Sheng

Xuanhuai and, 163; Zhou Hongxun and, 210. *See also* Huguang Foreign Loan Agreement; missionaries, foreign; Western influences
Fryer, John, 56
Fu, Boss, 173
Fu Chongju, 34, 37, 80
Fu Huafeng, 209, 232, 322n23
Fujian province, 4, 55
Fuzhou uprising, 216

Gan Dazhang, 144, 179
Gao Yaheng, 216
Gao Yihan, 71
Gao Zhaolin, 175, 310n38
garrison rule, 26–29 (28f)
"General Arguments for Reform," (Liang), 56, 62
gentry (*shenshi*), 3, 9, 250, 253; bureaus (*shenju*) run by, 299n60; and Chengdu unrest, massacre, 188, 190–93, 204; and Christianity, 41–43; and civil service examinations, 31; and constitutional reform, 111; Duanfang and, 182; and funding of railway, 92, 99; and *juanshu* tax, 183, 194; and Liang Qichao's essay, 252; Li Jieren on, 291n14; managing *zugu* tax, 95, 106–7; and neighborhood administrative system (*baojia*), 124–25; as part of rebellion, 3–6, 9, 38, 47; place of in society, 12, 31–34, 49–50, 81, 87, 239; and Provincial Assembly (Sichuan), 125–26; as railway company managers, 100, 102, 104–5; as Railway Protection Association leaders, 2, 106, 168–69, 171, 173, 220; replaced by New Tax Bureau, 123, 133; self-interest versus public will, 101; Shi Changxin on, 142; Shi Wenlong's statement on, 205–6; studying in Japan, 47; supporting Railway Protection Army, 213–14; during Taiping Rebellion, 5–6; as traditional class, 12, 152, 206, 239; Wang Renwen and, 178; Yin Changheng and, 230, 234; Yuan Tingjiao rebellion against, 36; Zhao Erfeng and, 222–23; Zhao Erxun and, 110, 122, 125, 127–29, 131–33
gentry and landowners. *See shenliang*
Germany: Duan Qirui declaring war against, 246; and Jiangxi province, 111; loans to China, 142, 163; as model for law, government, 77, 85, 112, 119, 128, 141–42, 229; Shandong railroad line, 88; Sheng Xuanhuai and, 163. *See also* Huguang Foreign Loan Agreement; Western influences
"*Ge* Telegram," 145–46
Globe, The (*Xunhuan ribao*), 57
Globe Magazine (*Wanguo gongbao*), 53–56
"Golden Age," 22
gongkuan tax. See *zugu* tax
governor-general position, 26–27, 31, 123
Gowned Brothers (*Paoge*), 278n114; after Taiping Rebellion, 37; attacking Chengdu, 177, 201; and Chengdu Plain battles, 208–10, 212; forming alliance with elites, 44–45, 71, 146; and Gao Zhaolin, 310n38; and Hou Juyuan, 317n19; and missionary cases, 42–44; "Nine Groups" of, 177, 201; origins and growth of, 38–39; planning mutiny (December 1911), 230; policing tax collectors, 36; and Railway Protection Association, 174–78, 209; response to Chengdu massacre, 197, 200–203; in Sichuan, 175; as third in power, 31; and Tongmenghui, 174, 214–16, 219–20, 229–30, 309–10n34; Yin Changheng and, 230, 233, 234; and Yu Dongchen Rebellion, 43–44, 251; and Zhang Dasan, 320n103. *See also* Hou Baozhai; Luo Lun
Gramscian hegemony, 25
Grand Council (Junjichu), 117, 141
Grand Secretariat (Neige), 117
Great Han Sichuan Military Government, 223–26 (224f, 225f), 228
"great unity" (*datong*), 59
Green Standard Army (Governing Battalions, *zhiying*), 27–28
Guangdong province: constitutional association in, 120; in contrast to Sichuan, 11; essay competition in, 55; independence declaration in, 5; publications in, 53, 55; railway rights movement in, 100; railway stockholders in, 95, 145. *See also* Yue-Han railway
Guangxi, 5
Guangxu Emperor: calling for public discussion, 128, 139; convicting Luo Yuanyi, 42; death of, 140; demonstrators using memorials to, 185, 191, 307n106; and Empress Dowager Cixi, 84, 113; and Hundred Days' Reform, 52, 64; Kang's "ten-thousand-word letter" to, 56;

Guangxu Emperor (*continued*)
  L'Impartial (*Dagongbao*) "birthday greeting" to, 74–75; refusals to kneel to, 81; and Sheng Xuanhuai, 163; on ultimate power, 128
Gu Bie, 93
"guest armies," 228
Guizhou province, 4, 120–21, 228
guo, shifting meanings of, 147–50, 160–62, 165
Guo Huanwen, 157–59, 306n90
Guo Moruo, 75, 164, 165, 173
guoquan (rights of the nation), 2, 49, 66, 72, 139, 162, 165, 250
Guo Songtao, 57, 61–62, 265n1
Guo Xianghan, 216

Han dynasty, 23
Han ethnic group, 26, 240
Hanyuan, 234
Harrison, Henrietta, 8, 239
Hazama Naoki, 72
He Laibao, 63
Henan province, 121
He Xiegong, 172
He Yimin, 320n105
He Zuyi, 202
hierarchical relationships obscured, 240
homeland, love for, 162
Homely Words to Aid Governance (Chambers), 56
Hooge, Prince Aisin Gioro, 22
Hōsei University: French influence on, 241, 255; Law Department at, 77; notable graduates of, 47, 76, 108, 109, 323n45; provincial assemblymen at, 78; short-term program at, 76–77, 81; teaching parliamentarianism, 140, 241. *See also* overseas students
Hosie, Alexander, 21
Hou Baozhai, 39, 168, 176–77, 199f, 200–202, 209–11
Hou Juyuan, 317n19
Hou Yijie, 75, 84, 117, 267n6, 297n31
HSBC Bank, 146
Hsieh, Winston, 268n26
Huang Bin, 172
Huang Fang, 235
Huang Jiqing, 71
Huang Maoxun, 202
Huang Shou, 80, 176, 231
Huang Xuedian, 172

Huang Zhongkai, 78
Huayang, 201
Hubei province: and Chuan-Han nationalization, 145; Hubei Military Government, 237; Hubei New Army, 192, 197, 221, 228, 237; impact of Sichuan on, 11; *likin* tax in, 142, 146; October 10 mutiny, 3; railway rights movement in, 100; railway stockholders in, 95; students sent to Japan, 287–88n134; and United Convention, 237–38; and White Lotus Rebellion, 37; and Wuchang uprising, 215–16, 321n108; Yue-Han railway, 142. *See also* Huguang Foreign Loan Agreement
Huenemann, Ralph, 88, 142
Hu Gongxian, 320n104
Huguang Foreign Loan Agreement, 142–43, 146–52, 154–56
Hui ethnic group, 240
Hu Jingyi, 242
Hu Jintao, 268n27
Hu Jun (Chengdu elite), 93, 105–6, 179, 292n50
Hu Jun (overseas student), 100, 294n82
"Humbly Telling Our Brothers of Sichuan," 225
Hu Menghui, 217
Hunan Army, 221
Hunan province: army of, 28; and Chuan-Han nationalization, 145; constitutional association, 120–21; impact of Sichuan on, 11; Jinmen–Hanyang railway, 143; *likin* tax in, 142, 146; New Army uprising in, 3–4; railway rights movement in, 100; Shiwu Academy in, 60, 63–64; students sent to Japan, 287n134; Yue-Han railway, 142. *See also* Duanfang; Huguang Foreign Loan Agreement; Yue-Han railway
Hundred Days' Reform (1898), 52, 61, 64
Hunt, Lynn, 10
Hu Tan (Hu Chongyi), 210
Hu Ying, 237

imperial court (*daquan tongyu chaoting*): on abusiveness of police, 124; citizen petitions to, 140–41; government under, 25–34; Kang's proposal for "court gentlemen," 61; public differences with Wang, 178–79; satire about, 151f; Zhao Erxun and, 25–34

inalienable rights of the people, 54, 63, 68–69, 128
individual, moral authority of the, 24
Inquiry into the Classics Forged During the Xin Period, An (*Xinxue weijing kao*) (Kang), 59
Institute for Constitutional Compilation, 118–19, 121, 133
intellectual/cultural history, 8
"Items of Preparation" (Zhunian choubei shiyi qingdan), 122
Itō Hirobumi, 136

Japan: constitutional visit to (1905), 114; gentry studying in, 47–48; government leading railway construction, 142; Kang Youwei in exile in, 64; Liang Qichao in exiled in, 64–69, 76; as model for law, government, 85, 141–42; overseas students in, 74–76, 87, 103, 120, 125–26, 256, 287–88n134; petitions against peace treaty with, 61; political ideas from, 65; Russo-Japanese War, 111–13; Sheng Xuanhuai legal codes, 85; Zhang Jian in, 111
Jiangbei missionary case, 40–41
Jiang Guanyun, 120
Jiangjin uprising, 216–17
Jiangnan Arsenal translations on Western thought, 56
Jiang Sancheng, 135–36, 154, 172, 191
Jiangsu province: constitutionalists in, 4–5, 111–13, 121, 140, 235, 237–38; essay competition in, 55; railway rights movement in, 100; students sent to Japan, 287–88n134; supporting federalism, 5
Jiangxi province, 4, 111, 121
Jiang Zanchen, 41
Jiang-Zhe constitutionalists, 112–14, 120–21, 238, 241, 296n16
Jilin province, 120–21
Jing Ke, 164, 307n114
Jordan, Sir John, 83, 213–14
juanshu tax, 92, 124, 181, 183, 186–90, 194, 207
junquan, meaning of, 265n1
junzhu, meaning of, 265n1
Ju Zheng, 76, 78, 255

Kangxi reign, 35, 277n104, 310n39
Kang Youwei: advocating for constitution, 61–62; on Chinese imperial culture, 58; Cixi on, 84; comparing China and West, 59; criticisms of, 64, 69; on *datong*, 60; dissemination of ideas, 81; on equality, 59; essay competition award, 55; exile to Japan, 64; family background, 58; and *minquan*, 265n1; Old Text forgery charges, 59; Pu Dianjun influenced by, 75; reforming Confucianism, 60, 61, 63–64; students of, 47–48; "ten-thousand-word letter," 56, 61; Western influences on, 53, 56–58
Kertzer, David, 164
kneeling, end of, 239–40
Kuhn, Philip, 8, 50–52, 61, 281n8

landowners (*lianghu*), 31, 32–33
land tax (*tianfu*), 34–35
land tax surcharge, 94
language of revolution, 234
Learned Circles Association, 185
lectures, public, 155, 173–74, 204–6, 250
Legalism, 22, 23
Lei Fen, 76
Leshan, 234
letterwriting campaigns, 169, 174
Levenson, Joseph, 8, 26
Lhasa, 111
Liang Qichao, 8, 252; exiled to Japan, 64–69, 75; trip to United States, 72; as a fugitive, 115; return to China, 243; *Chinese Progress* newspaper, 62; *Chinese Soul, The* (pamphlet), 70–71; concerns about New Policies reforms, 111; on constitutionalism, 72–75, 115–16, 137–38, 241, 246; on *datong*, 60; dissemination of ideas of, 80, 81, 108, 121; "General Arguments for Reform," 56, 62; guidelines for reform, 116, 119; influential followers of, 47–48; lost essays of, 115; Mao Haijian on, 284n68; memorials written by, 115; on *minquan*, 62–64, 66, 68–69, 72, 265n1; as "Mr. New People," 79, 148, 252; on nation-state, 70; *New People's Journal* newspaper, 65, 70–71, 73–74, 79; opposing Duan and Anfu clique, 246; Political Information Institute (Zhengwenshe), 120–21; and Progressive Party, 243; as a propagandist, 69–70; on Rousseau, 67–68, 72; shop-state analogy, 69–70, 161; sovereignty of the people, 187, 255; on statism, 68; Western influences on, 56, 62, 66–67; and Yang Du, 298n54

Liao Ping, 59–60
Liao Shuxun, 216
liberalism versus republicanism, 266n1
liberty (*ziyou*), 139
liberty bell symbol, 212
Li Dajun, 100
Li Dazhao, 255
Li Jieren, 34, 80–81, 152, 159, 173
Li Jixun, 194; as overseas graduate, 119; nationalists recruiting attempts, 144, 145, 180, 312n70; shareholders' attempt to fire, 182–84; assassination threats, 183; shareholders overruled, 184; appeal to cabinet, 189; rioters denouncing, 193; advocating Beijing takeover of railway, 312n72
Li Lelun, 168
Linzhuang Primary School training, 216
Li Shaoyi, 217
Li Shengduo, 85, 114
literati, established, 8, 10–11, 281n8
Liu Fenglu, 50
Liu Guangdi, 75
Liu Kunyi, 84, 85
Liu Shengyuan, 154, 163–64
Liu Xin, 59
Liu Yiming, 104
Li Weiru, 216
Li Wuchu, 210
lixian (constitutionalism), 2, 139, 149
Li Xianzhou, 202
Li Yongzhong, 209
Li Yuanhong, 228, 237–38, 241, 324n58
local elites: activism of, 137; as avid newspaper readers, 80; and bureaus, 125, 131–33; crumbling of alliance with state, 45; duties and status of, 33–34; and "Proposal for the Reform of Local Administration," 117–18, 122; relationship with old regime, 251; supporting Railway Protection movement, 146, 170–71, 205; and Taiping Rebellion, 7, 16, 37, 107–8; and Tongmenhui, 214, 220; and Yu Dongchen Rebellion, 44. *See also* gentry; *shenliang*
Local Government in China Under the Ch'ing (Ch'ü), 29
local government versus local self-government, 133
local leaders (*lizheng* or *jiazheng*), 123, 169–71
local militia (*tuanlian*), 37

London and Paris Diaries (*Lundun yu Bali riji*) (Guo), 57, 265n1
Long Mingjian, 201, 209, 215, 219–20
Louis XVI, 266n1
Luo Bingzhang, 28
Luo Jie, 76
Luo Lun: family background, 47, 175; as radical teacher, 47, 310n43; promoting ideas from *Minbao*, 80; ties to the Gowned Brothers, 175–77, 202, 231; Pu Dianjun and, 75, 146; in Sichuan Provincial Assembly, 42, 146; critique of Huguang loan agreement, 146–47, 152; at founding of Sichuan Railway Protection Association, 152, 155–56, 176; at petition march, 153, 178; speeches on behalf of Railway Protection Association, 155–56, 160, 168; crying onstage, 164; *Shubao* publication of speeches, 174–75; Wang Renwen support for, 178; Wu Qingxi support for, 175; chairing Special Shareholder Meeting, 181; march to Zhao Erfeng's office, 183; tax boycott idea, 187; arrested for rebellion, 176, 191, 193, 197, 205; demonstrations for, 201–2, 213, 221; Zhao's denouncement of, 203; propaganda campaign against, 205–6; Railway Protection Association statements on, 206–7; release of, 222; Chongqing leaders denouncing, 228; disagreements with Pu Dianjun, 229; argument over official seal, 229; supporting Yin over Pu, 231–32, 234; as vice-governor of Chengdu, 231; as Military Council chair, 235; and Democratic Party, 243
Luo Rizeng (Luo Zizhou), 209–10, 212
Luo Yishi, 150
Luo Yuanyi, 40–42
Lu Yuqing, 7
Luzhou prefecture, 12, 79–80, 86, 217, 239
Lu Zongyu, 119

Madison, James, 52
magistrates, 29–30
Manchu Abdication Edict, 5, 237–40
Manchu ethnic group, 26–29, 240
Manchuria, 111
Mandate of Heaven, 23, 25–26, 252
Mao Haijian, 61, 284
Mao Zedong, 218, 269n29, 319–20n100
Marie Antoinette, 163

market strikes (1911), 184–86
Martin, W. A. P., 54
Martyrs of the Railway Protection Movement monument, 257f
Marxist and non-Marxist interpretations, 7
Ma Ying-jeou, 268n27
McIlwain, Charles, 81
"Memorial to Reorganize the System of Administration," (Duanfang and Dai), 115, 116
"Memorial to Set Up the Principle of the Country" (Duanfang), 115, 131
Mencius, 49, 68–69
Meng Gongfu, 152–53, 178
Meng Maihuai, 70
merchants (traditional class), 12, 152, 119–20, 206, 239
Miline, William, 53
militias (*lianfei, tuanlian, mintuan*): and Changshou revolt, 216; distinguishing from bandits, 209; funding of, 124, 130; and the Gowned Brothers, 38–39, 176–77, 201; public statements on Chengdu, 207; responding to Chengdu massacre, 197–203, 209–10, 213–15, 217, 220; traditional duties of, 37; and Yin's seizure of power, 234; Zhao's attempt to recruit, 204–6
minben (people as the base), 26, 49, 68
Ming dynasty, 24, 26, 34–35, 175
Ministry of Commerce, 85, 90
Minobe Tatsukichi, 76–78, 140, 255
minquan (rights/power of the people), 2, 139; Chengdu's embrace of, 206; and constitutionalism, 72–73, 76, 149, 162, 165; elite enlightenment and, 80; and *guaquan*, 72; and Japanese *minken*, 66; versus *junquan*, 57; Liang Qichao on, 62–64, 66, 69, 72; meanings of, 265–66n1; versus *minben*, 68; versus *minzhu*, 265–66n1; as a motto/slogan, 65, 211; objections to, 63–64; Zhou Hongxun on, 211
minzhu. *See* popular sovereignty
missionaries, foreign, 16, 39–45, 53, 252
Mitsukuri Rinshō, 77
Miyazaki Ichisada, 274n44
modernization theory, 8
monarchy: attacks on, 62–63; and constitutionalism, 255; end of, 237; and republicanism, 266n1. *See also* democratic principles

Mongols, 24, 240
Montesquieu, 73
Morrison, Robert, 53
Moye, Jean-Martin, 39
"Mr. New People." *See* Liang Qichao
Muslims of China (*huimin*), 172

Naitō Konan, 274n44
National Assembly (Zizhengyuan), 117, 119; Cixi edict on, 119; and constitutionalism, 302n7; convening of, 149; explaining to populace, 161–62; and Huguang Foreign Loan Agreement, 149–50, 187, 189; powers of, 144, 149, 156; preparations for, 117; "three heroes" at, 76
nationalism: Liang on, 67–68; Mao on, 269n29; and military reforms, 290n10; and the railway, 90, 143, 158, 170, 173; schools and, 120. *See also* Sun Yatsen
Nationalist Party, 7, 218, 241–45, 255, 268n27, 320n104, 324n64
nationalization of Chuan-Han Railway, 47, 85, 141, 143–46, 158, 304n35, 312nn70, 72
natural rights, 54, 63
neighborhood system (*baojia*), 30, 33, 86, 95, 124–25, 169, 310n39
Neo-Confucianism, 24–25
New Army: blamed for revolution, 6–7; conflicts within (Nov. 1911), 228–29; formation of, 86; November 1911 uprisings within, 217; October 1911 uprisings within, 3–4
"new learning," 3, 62, 75, 86–87, 126
New Policies reform, 114; Cixi's edicts prompting, 84; criticisms of, 111–12, 203; Defense Army reorganization, 28; governor-general position, 26–27, 31, 123, 130; new-style schools during, 79–80; and overseas students, 83; scholarship on, 107–8; stages of, 84–87, 113–14. *See also* Chuan-Han (Chengdu-Hankow) Railway; New Tax Bureau
Newsletter of the Sichuan Railway Protection Association, 2, 174, 191; banned by Zhao Erfeng, 191; circulation to outer counties, 155; commemorating Guo Huanwen's suicide, 158–59; coverage of Yang Sulan, 157–58; elites' allegiance to emperor in, 170; foreign loan treaty in, 160; on impact of anti-treaty movement,

Newsletter of the Sichuan . . . (continued)
174; movement manifesto in, 156; on nation, people, and government, 148, 150; on National and Provincial Assemblies, 149; Speech Division on, 169

newsletters/newspapers: banning of, 191; *Chengdu Daily*, 206; countering rebellion, 206; Deng Xiaoke on, 154; Documents Division, 155; letters from readers, 164, 174; *New People's Journal (Xinmin congbao)*, 65, 70–71, 73–74, 79, 120–21, 298n54; *Newsletter of the Private Sichuan Chuan-Han Railway Company*, 106; *Newsletter of the Sichuan Chamber of Commerce*, 148, 149; *People's Independent Daily (Minlibao)*, 207; *Pi County Gazetteer*, 118; plays on words/neologisms in, 161–62; *Political Gazette*, 118; *Shibao* newspaper, 75, 80, 92, 121, 146, 298n54; *Shubao* newspaper, 143–44, 147–48, 152, 174–75, 299n70; in Sichuan early 1900s, 80; *Sichuan Gazette*, 38, 124; as source material for speeches, 155; statements by officials in, 170; *Xigubao*, 155, 183, 186, 188, 191, 308n8. See also *Newsletter of the Sichuan Railway Protection Association*; propaganda

New Tax Bureau (Jingzhengju), 123–24, 131–34

New Text Confucianism, 50, 59–60

Ningyuan garrison, 27

Nishikawa Masao, 95

North Route in Sichuan, 20f

"No taxation without supervision," 110, 135–37, 187, 253

Old Text versus New Text, 50, 59–60

"One Cash Association" (Yiqianhui), 173

"one-cash tax" (*yiwen juan*), 181, 183, 205

On Improving the Chuan-Han Railway Company (Pu), 101–2

"On Legal Protection" folk song, 161

On the New Text and Ancient Text Learning (Jin gu xue kao) (Liao), 59

Opium War, 53

Ou Qujia, 63

"Our Opinions on Returning the Power" (Deng), 113

"Outline of Election Regulations" (Xuanjufa yaoling), 122

"Outline of Parliamentary Regulations" (Yiyuanfa yaoling), 122

overseas students: allied with metropolitan officials, 104; becoming political elite, 108; competing with provincial officials, 99; debating monarchy, 74, 103, 125–26; investigative reports by, 104, 106; as part of New Policies reform, 83, 87; petition letters, advertisements by, 97–98; promoting commercialization of railways, 99–101, 103; promoting shareholder associations, 105–6; Qing Overseas Students, 76–77; raising money for railways, 90–99. See also Hōsei University; Sichuan Overseas Students Association

ownership, private versus national, 253

pamphlets, 70, 98, 101, 107, 190–92

parliamentary system, 120–21, 140–41, 241, 243–44

partnership with state, 251

Patrol and Defense Forces (*xunfang*), 28; "mutiny" by (Dec. 8), 230–32

peasants (traditional class), 12, 152, 206, 239

Peng Fen, 153–54, 191, 308n1

Peng Guanglie, 230

Peng Jian, 119

"the people": learning public discourse, 249; legacy of the Revolution for, 256; power of "public opinion," 227, 250–51; and tyranny of the majority, 245; vocabulary describing, 148–49; Yin Changheng and, 231, 233

"people as the base" (*minben*), 49, 68, 225

People's Independent Daily (Minlibao), 207

Perkins, Dwight, 21

petitions: to Cheng Dequan, 5; and Chengdu Massacre, 191; for constitution, 48; on Copper Bureau, 104; to form a parliament, 121, 140–41; to form Chuan-Han Railway Company, 89–90; by Gan and Song, 179; on official misdeeds, 104; to parliament, 73; against peace treaty with Japan, 61; on railway tax, 179; against railway treaty, 153, 163–64; received by Wang Renwen, 178, 313n73; by students on fundraising, 92–94, 97–98; value of, 107–8, 184

pingdeng ("equality"), 2; and *datong*, 60; discourse of, 49; *renlei pingdeng* ("Equality among humanity"), 58; as key word for revolution, 139, 211, 250; *quanquan pingdeng* ("all powers are equal"), 63

pingquan ("equal rights"), 67
policing, 33; clearing path for marchers, 153; Police Bureau (Jingchaju), 123–25
political culture, 2; democratic, 197; forming a modern Chinese, 9, 50, 195, 225, 227, 240; importance of constitutionalism, 250, 320n105; irrevocable changes in, 257; of old regime, 22–25, 50; primary sources for, 11–12; revolutionary, 234; scholarship on, 8, 10, 239; unresolved issues of, 247, 250; valorizing "the people," 244–46, 254
Political Information Institute (Zhengwenshe), 120–21
political systems, constitutional and autocratic, 72–73
"politics of public opinion," 255
poll tax (*dingyin*), 30
popular sovereignty, 2, 255–58; access to knowledge about, 120; and constitutionalism, 225, 245, 250; debating, 65; educating the public on, 2, 81, 194, 197; Hōsei University shaping ideas of, 49, 77–79, 255–56; and Liang Qichao, 65, 68–70, 72, 74, 76, 116, 252; *minzhu/minquan*, 139, 265–66n1; in political culture, 246; in post-revolution China, 257–58; and Pu Dianjun, 76; and railway issue, 103, 160; and republicanism, 266n1; and rhetoric of *guo*, 150; and rule of law, 187; Sichuan elite and, 137–38; and taxation issue, 253; and US constitution, 245; and Yin Changheng, 228–34; and Zhao Erxun, 135
posters, 102–3, 107, 205, 315n103
power, boundaries of, 127–29, 132, 135–37, 149
prefectures (*fu*)/subprefectures (*zhilizhou*), 29
presidentialism versus parliamentarism, 241, 244
"prince cabinet," 141
principles of political legitimacy, 207
privatization under New Policies, 85
Progressive Party, 243–45
propaganda, 163–65, 171; coverage of Yang Sulan, 157–58; Duanfang announcement, 221; editorial graffiti/paint on announcements, 193, 206–7, 221; folk songs explaining abstract concepts, 159–61; formal denunciations by elites, 206–7; Hou Baozhai announcement, 211; Luo Rizeng announcement, 212; posters, 102–3, 107, 205, 315n103; promoting collective action, 165, 174; public lectures, 155, 173, 204–6; Qin Zaigeng announcement, 212; repurposing old symbols/tropes, 162–65; against Sheng Xuanhuai, 163; slogans, 147, 150, 156–57; songs, 167; speeches by students, 168; Sun Zepei announcement, 212; Zhao Erfeng campaign, 204–7; Zhao Erfeng's ban on, 191; Zhou Hongxun proclamation, 211. *See also* newsletters/newspapers; rhetoric; slogans
"Proposal for the Reform of Local Administration," (Yikuang and Sun), 117–18, 122
"Proposing a Private Chuan-Han Railway Company" poster, 102
Protestantism, 39–40, 53. *See also* missionaries, foreign
Provincial Assemblies: Hōsei University students in, 78, 108; petitioning for parliament, 140; provincial level reform, 117–18, 122; provincial officials, 5, 76, 117, 127–28; and railway issue, 189; and rights of the people, 161, 187; United Convention of the Delegates of Provincial Governments, 236–38
Provincial Assembly (Anhui), 5
Provincial Assembly (Fujian), 4
Provincial Assembly (Guangdong), 5
Provincial Assembly (Guangxi), 5
Provincial Assembly (Guizhou), 4
Provincial Assembly (Hubei), 3
Provincial Assembly (Jiangsu), 140
Provincial Assembly (Shanxi), 4
Provincial Assembly (Sichuan), 137–38; after constitutional reform, 109–11, 129–30; arrests of leaders, 191, 207; declaring independence, 5; disagreement over boundaries of power, 127–29, 132, 135–37, 149; elections of 1913, 243; first year of, 109–11, 127–37, 139, 206; gentry (*shenshi*) and, 125–26; petitioning for a parliament, 120–21, 140–41; procession to provincial government, 153; profile of assemblymen, 125–26; rhetoric of rights in, 79, 253; taxation debates, 131–37, 253. *See also* constitutionalism; Deng Xiaoke; Long Mingjian; Luo Lun; Pu Dianjun
Provincial Assembly (Yunan), 4

Provincial Assembly (Zhejiang), 4
Provincial Assembly (Zhili), 140
Provisional Constitution, 78, 237–38, 241, 243–44, 256, 324n64
public lectures/meetings, 155, 173–74, 204–6, 250
public local mobilization, 168–74
public schools, statutes on, 86
Pu Dianjun, 5, 49f; family and early education, 48 (48f), 259–64; education at Hōsei, 48–49, 75–76, 108, 119, 255; as chair of Sichuan Provincial Assembly, 109–10, 128–30; government positions, 48; insisting on supervision by the people, 136; and Kang-Liang reform ideas, 75–76; and Luo Lun, 75; and Zhang Lan, 75; and Chuan-Han Railway Improvement Society, 100–106; investigating Copper Bureau, 104; member of constitutionalist party, 141; petitioning for a parliament, 141; as co-leader of Railway Protection movement, 145–47, 189, 305n67; accused of rebellion, 176, 193; arrested by Zhao Erfeng, 191–92, 207; popular uprising in support of, 198, 201, 207, 212; Duanfang demanding release of, 221; released, made governor-general, 222, 223 (223f), 228; attempting to stop unrest, 225–26, 230; disagreement with Luo over government, 229; fleeing from staged mutiny, 230; break with Luo, 231; as member of Democratic Party, 243; on "fake republic," 246; "no taxation without supervision" credo, 79; predicting revolution, 141
Pulan, Prince, 119
Puyi, 246

Qianjiang missionary case, 40
Qiao Shunan, 100, 105–6
Qin dynasty, 23
Qing, Prince, 154
Qing/Manchu dynasty, 7–8, 24–34, 37, 50, 236–38. *See also* Cixi, Empress Dowager; Guangxu Emperor; New Policies reform
Qin Hui, 163–64
Qin Nan, 322n16
Qin Zaigeng, 175, 177, 199f, 201, 209, 212, 215, 219
Qiongzhou, 208
Qishan, 163
Qu Hongji, 112–13, 297n34

railroads: Jinmen–Hanyang railway, 143; Yue-Han (Canton-Hankow) railway, 88, 141–44. *See also* Chuan-Han (Chengdu-Hankow) Railway
Railway Protection Armies, 201, 208–10 (208f), 212, 215
Railway Protection Association (Sichuan): founding of, 2, 150–53; arrest of leaders, 191; attacks on Chengdu, 198, 201–2, 213; battles on Chengdu Plain, 208–9 (208f); Beijing's attempts to disrupt, 181; branches in outer counties, 156, 168; cause of insurgency, 204; celebrity support for, 157–59; in Changshou, 216; Children's Branch, 171–72; Chongqing supporting Chengdu, 170; denouncing Gan and Song, 179; Documents Division, 154–55; expansion of, 170; funding sources, 153–54; gaining support of Wang Renwen, 178–79; and the Gowned Brothers, 174–78, 317n18; and Hou Baozhai, 211; local mobilization and mutual support, 162, 168–74; manifesto of, 156–57; newsletter for, 2, 155, 160, 191; in novel *Great Wave*, 173; open to non-Sichuanese, 155; opposing foreign loan treaty, 156–57; opposing nationalization, 2; organization and structure of, 153–56, 168–71; Qin Zaigeng on, 212; resisting taxes, 188; rhetoric of, 139–40; slogan of, 156–57; Speech Division, 154–56, 168–69; subordinate to national loyalty, 162; supporting strikes, 186; Women's Branch, 171–73, 309n28; Zhao denouncing, 203, 205–8; Zhou's proclamations regarding, 211
railway tax (*gongkuan/zugu*): bureaus for overseeing, 95; calls for resistance to, 188; and calls for shareholder control, 99–101, 103; county bureaus of shareholders, 105–6; court's cancellation of, 180; embezzlement of, 102–4, 106, 295n107; expansion to all taxpayers, 95–96; Gan and Song petitions against, 179; a hardship for peasants, 98, 102; land tax as replacement for, 184; Lou Lun on, 187; overseas students championing, 97–99; portrayed as investment, 96; proposed as payment for local line, 179, 313; as rationale for nationalization, 142; shareholder associations, 106; as stock in Chuan-Han Railway, 95, 103–4, 293n55; support for central government manage-

ment of, 144; as surcharge to land tax, 94, 173
railway transportation: in 1800s, 87–88; first provincial railroads chartered, 90; international competition over, 88–89, 91–92; national sovereignty concerns, 89; privatization under New Policies, 85; Rights Recovery movement, 100, 120–21; support for in Sichuan, 22
Rankin, Mary, 7, 107, 307n106
Reed, Bradley, 299n60
Reform and Revolution (Esherick), 10
Reid, Gilbert, 54
Report on Improving the Chuan-Han Railway Company, 100–101, 104, 106
republicanism, 9, 266n1; citizenship under, 239; and failure of constitutionalism, 1; inability to govern, 244–45; Qing abdication and birth of, 238–39; Sichuan defense of, 12; as slogan, 218; United States as model for, 235–36 (236f); Zhang Jian's promotion of, 235
Republican Party (Gonghedang), 241, 243
"responsible cabinet" (*zeren neige*), 141
"revolutionaries," meaning of, 266–67n6
Revolutionary Alliance. *See* Tongmenghui
revolutionary process, source of unity in, 251
revolutionary scholarship, 6–12
rhetoric, 139–40; on constitutionalism and rights, 156, 189; emperor calling for public discussion, 128, 139; failing in practice, 1; including action items, 181, 250; linking *guo* with *min*, 150, 165; manipulation by, 257–58; mobilizing masses through, 10, 211, 251; parliamentarianism learned at Hōsei, 140, 241; people of Sichuan (*chuanmin/chuanren*), 161–62; as performative act, 139; public critique of treaty, 146–47; as resource for propaganda, 147; of rights, 2, 79, 146–50, 227, 253, 256; on rule of law, equality before the law, 161; of self-rule, 234; shaped by political concepts, 1–2, 10; Sun's use of *minquan*, 265n1; valorizing "the people," 244. *See also* newsletters/newspapers; propaganda
Richard, Timothy, 55–56
Richthofen, Ferdinand von, 17, 21, 39
righteousness, 101, 157, 162–63, 193, 254
"rights" (*quan, quanli, minquan*, and *guoquan*), 2, 257; both political and economic, 252–53; as conferred by state, 128; vocabulary and rhetoric of, 2, 146–50, 227, 253, 256. *See also* popular sovereignty
Rights Recovery movement, 100, 120–21
right to rule, 23, 57, 252
rivers of Sichuan, 18–19 (18f, 19f)
"river telegraph," 198–201 (200f)
Rong County rebellion, 209, 215–16
Rousseau, Jean-Jacques, 66–69
Rowe, William, 107–8
Ruicheng, 184, 204, 315n112
rule of law, 161, 187
Russo-Japanese War (1904–1905), 111–13

satire, 151f
Schiffrin, Harold, 268n28
scholar-officials (*shidafu*), 24–25
scholarship: on 1911 Revolution, 6–9, 11–12; on Qing reform efforts, 107–8
schools: new-style, 87, 120; strikes in (1911), 184–86. *See also* overseas students
Second Revolution, 243
self-governance: accusation of tyranny, 234; boundaries for, 115; and common goals, 212; elites as self-governing tyrants, 127, 171, 183, 234, 251; funding for, 131; local government versus local self-government, 133–34, 301n108; Minobe on, 77; schools of, 120; *shenliang* not participants in, 33; and Sichuan Declaration of Independence, 224; and taxes, 131, 133; via petitions, 121; Yin Changheng and, 231–32; Zhao Erxun on, 135
Self-Strengthening movement, 84, 87, 114–15
separation of powers, 9, 117
Seventeenth Regiment (Sichuan), 86
Shaanxi province, 4, 11, 37, 84, 121, 221
Shandong province, 88, 121
Shang Qiheng, 114
Shanxi province, 4, 121
Shao Cong'en, 78, 79, 106, 222, 243
shareholder associations, 105–6, 180–84, 186, 189
Shen Baoxu, 307n111
Shen Bingkun, 100
Sheng Xuanhuai: alliance with Duanfang, 181, 190, 315n112; alliance with Li Juxun, 179–80, 182–84; denounced

Sheng Xuanhuai (continued)
  by Luo Lun, 152; denounced in Shubao, 148–49; "Ge Telegram," 145–46; and Guo Huanwen suicide, 158–59; investigating Chuan-Han Railway Company, 144, 145; New Army refusing orders from, 204; opposing Zhao Erfeng, 315n112; popular opposition to, 158, 163–64, 169–70, 178–79, 193, 307n106, 313n73; praising German, Japanese legal codes, 85; promoting nationalization, 85, 144, 145, 158
Shen Junru, 4, 76, 255
shenliang (gentry and landowners), 31; duties of, 32–33; and the Gowned Brothers, 38, 252; militias organized by, 37; and missionary cases, 40–41, 43–44; protests over fees by, 35–36; relation of to emperor, 251–52
Shen Shandeng, 56
Shibao newspaper, 75, 80, 92, 121, 146, 298n54
Shi Changxin, 142
Shi Dianzhang, 100
Shi Wenlong, 205
Shiwu Academy, 63–64
shop-state analogy, 69–70
Shubao newspaper, 143–44, 147–48, 152, 174–75, 299n70
Sichuan baolu yundong shi (Wei), 269n29
Sichuan Gazette, 38, 124
Sichuan Military Government (Shujun zhengfu), 217
Sichuan Military Government (Sichuan junzhengfu), 231, 233, 234
Sichuan Military Government, Great Han (Dahan Sichuan junzhengfu), 223–24, 224f, 225f, 228
Sichuan New Army, 204, 217, 222, 228, 230, 235
Sichuan Overseas Students Association, 90–92, 98. See also overseas students
Sichuan province, 11-12, 16f, 80; agriculture and trade in, 17; as "best" province, 15; energy resources of, 21; family structure in, 17–18; geography, transportation in, 16–22 (16f, 18f–20f); independence declaration in, 5; isolation of, 22; keeping order in, 36–37; Liang and enlightenment in, 79–81; local government, 29–31; Manchu subjugation of, 22; money and taxes, 34–36; New Policies reform, 86–87; overpopulation in, 35; provincial government, 26–29 (28f); under Qing government, 22–31, 35–36; railway nationalization, 145; rebellion in, 37, 203–4, 222–26, 229; republican government of, 242–43; urbanization of, 21. See also Chengdu; Gowned Brothers; overseas students; Provincial Assembly (Sichuan); Railway Protection Association (Sichuan)
silver prices and tax rates, 35
Sino-Japanese War (1894–1895), 36, 42, 61, 287n134
slogans, 254; emphasizing common purpose, 212; escalating to actions, 187, 194, 212; key railway slogan, 156–57; "No taxation without supervision," 110, 135–37, 253; publication of, 147; "republicanism," 218; by Zhou Hongxun, 211. See also propaganda
social contract (minyue) theory, 67, 69
social networks, use of, 194
Society for National Preservation (Baoguohui), 75
Society for the Diffusion of Christian and General Knowledge among the Chinese (Guangxuehui), 54–55
Society of Heaven and Earth (Tiandihui), 175
Song Jiaoren: at Hōsei University, 76, 78, 255; on Sichuan people, 11, 207; endorsing federalist proposal, 236; advocating parliamentarianism, 241; opposing Yuan, 242; assassination of, 242–43, 324n64
Songpan garrison, 27–29
songs/ballads supporting activism, 158–61, 177, 186–88, 205
Song Yuren, 144, 179
Southern Song period, 24, 163
South Route in Sichuan, 20f
South Route Railway Protection Army, 208f, 209–10, 235
sovereignty of the people. See popular sovereignty
Special Shareholder Meeting (July–August 1911), 180–84, 186, 189, 190
"spectacle," 10, 173
"standard tax" (zhengliang), 30
statism, 68, 127–28, 325n71
stock, railway, 93–96 (96f), 145
Strand, David, 8, 239
Street Culture in Chengdu (Wang), 184

Striding out of a Closed World (Wang), 29
strikes in market and schools, 184–86, 189, 194, 213
structure and ideas, interaction of, 251–54
students. *See* overseas students
Suggestions to the Sichuan People pamphlet, 190–91
suicides, 6, 158, 159, 290n9
Sun Baoqi, 112
Sun Baoxuan, 112
Sun Hongyi, 140–41
Sun Jia'nai, 117, 297n34
Sun Jia'nan, 119
Sun Yat-sen, 5–7; advocating presidentialism, 241; and Chongqing Military Government, 228; elite support for, 5; historical/political portrayals of, 107, 268nn26–28; and Liang Qichao, 66, 74; as provisional president of Republic, 237–39; severing ties with Beiyang clique, 242; use of term *minquan* by, 265n1. *See also* Tongmenghui
Sun Zepei, 176, 199f, 202–3, 209, 212, 320n103
Sun Zhaoluan, 230

Taiping Rebellion: and Defense Army, 28; effects of on governance, 7, 16, 34; funding of, 44, 132, 186, 292n42; and local elite activism, 107; loyalties during, 5–6; use of militias during, 37
Tang Caichang, 63
Tang Hualong, 3, 76, 78–79, 141, 241, 255
Tang Shaoyi, 237
Tang Shijun, 172
Tang Shiqing, 172
Tang Shouqian, 111, 112, 121, 236–38
Tang Zhiping, 217
Tang Zongyao, 320n104
Tan Sitong, 56
Tan Yankai, 3–4
Tao Mo, 85
Tarrow, Sidney, 157
taxation: call for local control of, 190; land taxes, 32–33; need for supervision of, 110; New Tax Bureau, 123–24, 131; "No taxation without supervision," 110, 135–37, 187, 253; for railway bonds, 92–94; resistance to, 35–36, 184–89; in Sichuan, 34–36, 91, 130–37; state versus local, 131; surcharge (*huohao/fujiashui*), 132–33; traditional method of, 123. *See also zugu* tax

Temple Draft Constitution (1913), 243–44, 256
"Theory of Political Expert Bluntschli, The" (Liang), 72
"The Patriotism of a Little Performer" (Yang), 157–58
"Thirty Regulations on Sichuan's Independence," 222
three ages doctrine, 60
Tianjin Treaty (1858), 39
Tian Zhenbang, 211
Tian Zhengkui, 193
Tibet, 27–29; ethnic group, 240; proposed rail linkages to, 89, 144; troops on border with, 89–90, 179, 209, 214, 222, 242, 323n31
Tilly, Charles, 164
Tocqueville, Alexis de, 8, 225
Tongmenghui (Revolutionary Alliance), 6–7, 201; after revolution, 240–43; anti-Manchu revolutionaries in, 6, 201, 209, 215–16, 220; and the Gowned Brothers, 174, 214–16, 219–20, 229–30, 309–10n34; led by Sun Yat-sen, 228; memoirs of, 218–19; October–November battles, 214–18; role of, 7, 218–20; slaughter of Huang Fang, 235; Song Jiaoren on Sichuanese rebels, 11, 207; uprisings in Chongqing, 216–19, 233, 321n108; Yin Changheng joining, 229–30; Zhang Dasan joining, 71. *See also* Sun Yat-sen
Toratarō, Miyama, 66
traitor (*hanjian*), 162–63
transportation in Sichuan, 17–21 (18f–20f)
treacherousness (*jian*), 162–63
tribal leaders, 172
Tsuchiya Hideo, 69, 72
Tu Defeng, 216

Ume Kenjirō, 76–77, 288n138
Unification Party, 243
United Convention of the Delegates of Provincial Governments, 236–38
United States: American Revolution, 266n1; anti-American violence, 42; antimajoritarian constitution of, 245; Chinese reading books, newspapers from, 56; Chinese travel to, 57; constitutional visit to (1905), 114; Constitution and tyranny of the majority, 245; direct election of representatives, 54; federalism of as model, 5, 224, 235; and Huguang Foreign Loan

United States (continued)
  Agreement, 142; investment in Chinese railways, 89, 97; James Madison on civic nature, 52; Liang Qichao's visit to, 72; loans to China, 142, 163; as model for law, government, 5, 119, 229, 235–36, 241, 245; railway profitability in, 97; Sheng Xuanhuai and, 163; and Sun Yat-sen, 107, 241; united convention based on, 236f. *See also* Huguang Foreign Loan Agreement; missionaries, foreign
"universal" principles, 224

viable states, 254
"Victory of the Masses, The" (Li), 255
von Falkenhausen, Lothar, 21
von Strauch, E., 176, 204, 214

Wang Chonghui, 237
Wang Chunwu, 175
Wang Di, 18, 29, 33, 40, 184, 191–92, 230
Wang Jingwei, 67, 76, 237, 255
Wang Jubo, 217
Wang Lifu, 79
Wang Mang, 59
Wang Mingxin, 191
Wang Renwen, 145, 151, 178–79, 181, 305n57, 313n73
Wang Tao, 57
Wang Tianjie, 199f, 209, 215
Wanguo gongbao (Globe Magazine), 53–56
Wang Yao, 66–67
Wang Youyu, 231
Wang Zhengting, 237
Warring States cosmology, 23
Wei Guangtao, 112
Wei Yingtao, 218, 269n29, 320n105
Wei Yuan, 49–52
Wei Zhongxian, 163
Western Concerns Newspaper (*Xigubao*), 155, 183, 186, 188, 191, 308n8
Western influences, 51–60, 65
West Route in Sichuan, 20f
West Route Railway Protection Army, 208f, 209, 212
"white face" for treachery, 163
White Lotus Rebellion, 37
Wilkinson, William, 198, 214, 229, 232
Williamson, Alexander, 50, 54–55
women, status of, 58–59
Women's Branch, Railway Protection Association, 171–73, 309n28

Wright, Mary, 290nn9, 10
Wu Bihua, 222
Wuchang uprising, 3–6, 78, 197, 215–16, 222, 321n108
Wu Daquan, 91
Wu Qingxi, 175–76, 178, 199f, 202–3, 209
Wu Songsheng, 153, 178
Wu Tingfang, 237
Wu Yuzhang, 215–16, 218, 220, 269n29, 320n100
Wu Zhisan (Wu Congying), 202–3
Wyman, Judith, 40

Xia Fengxun, 216
Xianfeng reign (1850–1861), 36
Xiang Dizhang, 175, 199f, 201–2
Xianyouhui (Association of the Friends of the Constitution), 141
Xiaowei Zheng, 266n1
Xiao Xiang, 79, 100, 106, 108, 109, 141, 154
Xiao Yishan, 71
Xia Xiaohong, 115
Xia Zhishi, 217, 235
Xigubao newspaper, 155, 183, 186, 188, 191, 308n8
Xiguo jinshi huibian (Compilations of Recent Developments in the West), 56
Xiliang: establishing Chuan-Han Railway Company, 89–90, 273n25; funding Chuan-Han Railway Company, 91–95; shared management in railway company, 100; Copper Bureau incident, 104; announcing railway privatization, 105; funding for new police system, 124; reforming schools, 86–87; on Sichuan as rich in resources, 17; on Sichuan people as impetuous, 90; use of overseas fact-finding missions, 113
Xindu, 185–86
Xinhai geming (Wu), 269n29
Xinjin county: Railway Protection Association in, 168, 177; July 11 meeting in, 201, 210; attack on Chengdu, 198, 199f, 208, 210; as rebel stronghold, 210; Battle of, 211–12. *See also* Chen Wenqing; Hou Baozhai; South Route Railway Protection Army
Xinmin congbao newspaper, 65, 70–71, 73–74, 79, 120–21, 298n54
Xiong Xiling, 120, 241
Xuantong reign, 18, 29, 154, 189

Xu Fosu, 120
Xunhuan ribao (*The Globe*), 57
Xu Shichang, 297n34
Xu Xilin, 118

yamen runners and clerks, 117, 176
Yan Fu, 62, 67, 119, 265n1
Yang Du, 74, 120–21, 255, 298n54
Yang Hongzhong, 36
Yang Rui, 75
Yang Ruirao, 170
Yang Shu, 76
Yang Sulan, 157–59
Yangzi River, 18–20 (18f, 19f), 90, 242
Yan Jigu, 48
Yan Kai, 47–48, 181, 184, 191, 229–30
Yano Fumio, 287n134
Yan Quan, 244
Yan Song, 163
Yantai Treaty (1874), 39–40
Yan Xishan, 4
Ye Bingcheng, 191
Yikuang, Prince, 117–18
Yin Changheng, 86, 228–35, 242, 322n23
Ying Lianzhi, 117
Yinliang, 145, 153
Yi Zongkui, 76, 302n7
Yongzheng reign, 35, 41, 132, 277n104, 301n103
Yuan Shikai, 297n31; and Jiang-Zhe constitutionalists, 112–14, 121; supporting constitutional reform, 85, 112–14; negotiations on opening parliament, 121; role in revolution, 6–7; at South-North peace talks, 5, 237; negotiating for presidency, 237–43; negotiating Qing abdication, 237–38; negotiating power of presidency, 239–42; backing Hu Jingyi, 242; ordering Zhang Peijue to Beijing, 242; and Song Jiaoren assassination, 242, 324n64; elected president, 243; constitution limiting powers of, 243–44; dismissing parliament, 244; attempt to become emperor defeated, 12; death of, 245
Yuan Tingjiao, 36, 251
Yu Dongchen, 40, 43–44, 251–52
Yue-Han (Canton-Hankow) railway, 88, 141–44
Yukun, 188, 203, 213
Yunnan province: and Chengdu mutiny, 228, 234–35; French and British railroad plans, 88–89; Hu deal with army, 242; impact of Sichuan on, 11; influence of Sichuan on, 11; October 30 New Army attack, 4; Zhou Hongxun in, 210
Yu Youren, 236

Zaifeng, 140, 302n7
Zaize, Imperial Prince, 114, 116, 181, 190, 297nn31, 34
Zeng Du (Zeng Shengzhai), 217
Zeng Jian, 119
Zhang Baixi, 86
Zhang Binlin, 241
Zhang Dasan, 71, 199f, 320n103
Zhang Dinghua, 58
Zhang Guorong, 78
Zhang Jian: visit to Japan, 111; advocating constitutionalism, 112–13; initiating parliamentary petitions, 121, 140–41; as member of defecting elites, 5, 235–36; endorsing federalist proposal, 236, 241; statement on Qing collapse, 6
Zhang Jiexian Army, 199f
Zhang Kaiyuan, 7
Zhang Lan, 48, 75, 113, 181, 191, 243
Zhang Luocheng, 100
Zhang Meiyi, 296n16
Zhang Peijue, 235, 242
Zhang Pengyuan, 8, 125
Zhang Renjun, 300n77
Zhang Taiyan, 56, 67
Zhang Xi, 202, 209
Zhang Xianzhong Rebellion, 35
Zhang Xun, 246
Zhang Yong, 256, 324n64
Zhang Yongle, 243, 254–55
Zhang Yuanji, 296n16
Zhang Zhiben, 78
Zhang Zhidong, 64, 84–86, 88, 112–13, 121, 142–43, 287n134
Zhang Zhiyuan, 100
Zhang Zongxiang, 119
Zhang Zun, 202–3, 209
Zhao Bingjun, 324n64
Zhao Binglin, 85
Zhao Dingxin, 23
Zhao Erfeng, 182f; arrest of Luo, 176, 197; announcement mischaracterized by Hou, 177; ordered back to Chengdu, 179, 181; initial support of railway leaders, 182; requested to impeach Sheng, Li, 183, 184; on strike's use of emperor's tablets, 185; initial support of elites, citizens,

Zhao Erfeng (*continued*)
189–90; mass arrests of strike leaders, 191, 212; Chengdu massacre, martial law, 191–92 (192f), 197; rationale for actions, 192–93, 198; Duanfang and, 220–23, 315n112; closing of city gates, 200; statements on attackers, 201–3; statements on "stupid commoners," 204; attempting to raise own militia, 204; unsuccessful propaganda campaign by, 204–8; forces arrayed against, 47, 209; counterattacking Xinjin, 210–11; on rebels versus robbers, 213; forces losing ground to rebels, 221–22; releasing movement leaders, 5, 222; requesting reinforcements, 221; releasing nine railway leaders, 222; accepting Sichuan independence, 222–23, 228; framed for mutiny, executed, 232–33

Zhao Erxun: reorganizing Defense Army, 28, 109–10; reforming Three-Fees Bureau, 122–23; steamships proposal, 273n25; creating New Tax Bureau, 123–25, 301n108; creating Police Bureau with Zhou Shanpei, 123–25; advocating constitutionalism, 109–10, 126; addressing Sichuan Provincial Assembly, 109–10, 127–29, 134–37, 206; tax reallocation debates, 130–35, 137; as governor-general of Manchuria, 178; meaning of state to, 300n82

Zhao Fengchang, 5, 235–36, 238, 241, 296n16

Zhao Xi, 179

Zhao Xi'en, 98

Zhejiang province: constitutionalists in, 4–5, 112–13, 121, 235; endorsing constitutional convention, 237–38; essay competition in, 55; overseas student in Japan, 288n134; Rights Recovery movement in, 100, 121; and Zhang Jian, 111–12

zhengfu (government), 148, 150, 163

zhengliang ("standard tax"), 30

Zhengsu baihua bao newspaper, 206

Zheng Xiaoxu, 111, 121

Zhili province, 55, 86–87, 112–13, 121, 140–41

zhong (loyalty), 162, 165, 254

Zhongguo guomindang shigao (Zou), 268n26

Zhou dynasty, 22–24

Zhou Fu, 113

Zhou Hongxun, 208–11, 235

Zhou Jun, 242

Zhou Shanpei: accused of aiding Zhao Erfeng, 316n217, 318n63; aligning with Chengdu elite, 181, 189, 222; blamed for rebellion, 193, 211; on Governor-General Zhao, 223; on Luo Lun, 231; new police system under, 86, 124; supporting independence, 222–23; weeding out unqualified students, 316n217, 318n63

Zhou Xun, 27, 123–24

Zhou Ziting, 92–93

Zhuang Cunyu, 50

Zhuang Yunkuan, 5, 235

Zhu Li, 172

Zhu Qinglan, 211, 222, 223f, 228, 230

Zhu Shan, 152–53, 168, 172, 178

Zhu Xi, 24–25

Zhu Youji, 203–4

Zhu Zhihong, 219

Zhu Zhisan, 79, 296n12, 298n48

Zhu Ziqi, 58

Zongli Yamen, 41–42, 287n134

Zou Lu, 268n26

zugu tax, 293n55; bureaus to levy, 95, 105–6; embezzlement, waste of, 102, 104, 106, 142, 295n107; formerly *gongkuan*, 94; Gan and Song denouncing, 179; Li Jixun on, 313n73; promoted by overseas students, 96, 98, 99–100; Pu on shareholder rights, 101, 103; and Shareholder Meeting, 187–88; Shi Changxin denouncing, 142; who should pay, 94–95

The authorized representative in the EU for product safety and compliance is:
Mare Nostrum Group
B.V Doelen 72
4831 GR Breda
The Netherlands

www.ingramcontent.com/pod-product-compliance
Lightning Source LLC
Chambersburg PA
CBHW031752220426
43662CB00007B/373

9 781503 601086